ANALYTICAL MARXISM

CONTEMPORARY SOCIAL THEORY

Series Editor:
Mark Gottdiener
University of California, Riverside

CONTEMPORARY SOCIAL THEORY books are brief, introductory texts designed to make current trends in social theory accessible to undergraduate students in the social sciences.

VOLUMES IN THIS SERIES

SERIES EDITORIAL BOARD

ANALYTICAL MARXISM

TOM MAYER

CONTEMPORARY SOCIAL THEORY

VOLUME 1

SAGE Publications
International Educational and Professional Publisher
Thousand Oaks   London   New Delhi

For information address:

SAGE Publications, Inc.
2455 Teller Road
Thousand Oaks, California 91320

SAGE Publications Ltd.
6 Bonhill Street
London EC2A 4PU
United Kingdom

SAGE Publications India Pvt. Ltd.
M-32 Market
Greater Kailash I
New Delhi 110048 India

Printed in the United States of America

Library of Congress Cataloging-in-Publication Data

Mayer, Thomas. F., 1937-
    Analytical Marxism/Thomas F. Mayer.
    p. cm—(Contemporary social theory)
    Includes bibliographical references and index.
    ISBN 0-8039-4680-5.—ISBN 0-8039-4681-3 (pbk.)
    1. Communism. 2. Marxist school of sociology. 3. Marxian
economics. I. Title. II. Series: Contemporary social theory, v. 1.
HX73.M42   1994
335.4—dc20   94-4601

94 95 96 97 10 9 8 7 6 5 4 3 2 1

Sage Production Editor: Diane S. Foster

CONTENTS

PREFACE

The reader is entitled to a few warnings about this book. The first warning concerns my interpretation of Analytical Marxism. I choose to interpret this subject in a broad rather than a narrow way. That is, I include some writers who came before the establishment of anything like Analytical Marxism and others who know of the field but do not consider themselves Analytical Marxists. I always try to explain why such a writer is included. While recognizing the diversity of Analytical Marxism, I do try to identify some principles of unity. Some of these principles might not be acknowledged by the mainstays of the field.

The second warning concerns the background required to read this book. Parts of Analytical Marxism are highly technical. I have struggled to produce a book that is accessible to many people yet remains scrupulously faithful to the intellectual content of the subject. Against my own predilections, this book does not contain a single equation. I sometimes take a lot of trouble to explain the meaning of an equation and to provide an understandable illustration. Whether this procedure creates sufficient comprehension, the reader must decide. I can truthfully say that no formal mathematical or statistical background is required to read this book. I can also truthfully say that the advice to authors proffered by Strunk and White in *The Elements of Style* was taken very seriously: be clear, be brief, be bold.

The third warning to readers concerns my political orientation. This book is written by a partisan of Analytical Marxism. I try to keep my partisanship under wraps enough to achieve a measure of objectivity. I try to be truthful. I present criticisms fully and as plainly as I can. I do not gerrymander the topics to make Analytical Marxism look good. Nevertheless, the attentive reader will easily perceive where my sympathies lie.

It is a pleasure to acknowledge the assistance I have received in preparing for and writing this book. The idea of writing a book about Analytical Marxism was suggested by my friend and subsequent editor Mark Gottdiener. Mark gave me penetrating feedback and tolerated delays with more good humor than I had any right to expect. John Roemer did not see any part of this manuscript in advance of publication, but the inspiration provided by his work bears much responsibility for its writing. I have discussed with John, both in person and via correspondence, some of the ideas contained herein. I have also benefited from many discussions over many years with my friends Ken Boulding, Jim Downton, Martha Gimenez, Ed Greenberg, Bill Livant, and Tracy Mott and with my brother Bernie Mayer.

The colleagueship and technical support provided by the Institute of Behavioral Science at the University of Colorado, under the directorship of Dick Jessor, surely made the task of writing easier and hopefully made the result better. I want to single out Jean Umbreit, who has given steady secretarial support to the program on Political and Economic Change of the Institute for almost two decades, and Lindy Shultz, who provides superb library assistance with a cheerful and unassuming manner.

Most of this book was written while I was on sabbatical leave from the University of Colorado. I thank Gary Marx, Chair of the Department of Sociology, and Chuck Middleton, Dean of the College of Arts and Sciences, for making this sabbatical possible. I thank Carol Lynch, Dean of the Graduate School, for making available funds to cover permission fees.

I must also acknowledge the help given by people at Sage Publications. Mitch Allen removed the last barriers to publication. Frances Borghi and Tricia Howell helped me get through the administrative aspects of the publication process. Diane Foster and Elisabeth Magnus improved the style and consistency of the manuscript.

The deepest and most valuable assistance I received in writing this book was from my wife and partner of over three decades, Sara Mayer. Sara supported me financially during the process of writing, listened to my ideas during breakfast and supper and a lot of other times as well, occasionally badgered me into getting things done, and sustained my good humor with frequent mountain biking and ski touring trips. Thanks Sara.

TOM MAYER
Boulder, Colorado

1

FOUNDATIONS OF ANALYTICAL MARXISM

What Is Analytical Marxism?

Often a school of thought defines itself initially by what it opposes; only later does it acquire a positive identity. This is true for the theoretical tendency known as Analytical Marxism. The people whom I consider to be Analytical Marxists initially carved out their positions through what they opposed in the Marxist tradition, and their intellectual unity derived largely from this common opposition. Finding positive theoretical or methodological principles that all, or even most, Analytical Marxists could accept has been a slow and difficult process.

One thing to which Analytical Marxists object is the absence of clarity in much Marxist writing. A disturbing number of Marxist texts are memorable chiefly for their lack of lucidity, but virtually every important Analytical Marxist stresses the overriding importance of clarity in her own intellectual endeavors. Given this emphasis on intelligibility, it is hardly surprising that the first systematic statements of Analytical Marxism came from the field of analytical philosophy, which defines itself largely in terms of lucid argumentation.

A related aspect of the Marxist tradition, unanimously rejected by the Analytical Marxists, is Hegelian logic. The idea that *dialectics* constitutes a sound way of reasoning, superior to formal logic for purposes of elaborating social theory, is regarded as both false and pernicious. The use of contradiction as an explanatory category obscures the distinction between valid and invalid

1

modes of inference and thereby undermines orderly thinking. The Hegelian influence has reduced the intelligibility of Marxist analysis, allowed invalid arguments to creep into theoretical discussions, fostered a lot of sophisticated-sounding confusion, and generally inhibited the emergence of competent scientific practice among Marxists.

Analytical Marxists also reject the claim that Marxists should practice a unique methodology different from the methodologies used by other social scientists.[1] What is distinctive about Marxism is not its method but its substantive ideas about how the world works. Efforts to practice a unique methodology isolate Marxists from useful methods developed by other social scientists, encourage defective forms of empirical inquiry, and obstruct revision of faulty theoretical assertions. In place of the fruitless effort to define a unique Marxist methodology, Analytical Marxists recommend bold use of the sophisticated techniques developed by modern social science: game theory, linear programming, structural equation modeling, modal logic, and so on.

Classical Marxist economic analysis was based upon the *labor theory of value,* from which were derived the concept of *exploitation*, the theory of a tendency toward a *falling rate of profit*, and the theory of *capitalist economic crises*. Analytical Marxists, however, abandon the labor theory of value, which they regard as conceptually flawed, empirically refuted, and inconsistent with other parts of Marxist theory (especially the vital relationship between class and exploitation). This abandonment saddles them with the formidable task of reconstructing Marxist economics on logically sound foundations without sacrificing either its theoretical power or its critical thrust. During scarcely more than a decade of existence, Analytical Marxism has already made great strides in this direction.

Almost all Analytical Marxists are inspired by the vision of creating a theory of society that is genuinely scientific and genuinely useful for purposes of human emancipation. In pursuit of this vision, they assail those elements of the Marxist tradition that seem to hinder the emergence of a scientific and emancipatory theory. At its present stage, Analytical Marxism is best understood as a movement in Marxist theory rather than a unified theoretical doctrine. The family of theories currently within its domain are not even mutually consistent, but Analytical Marxists hope to foster a scientific process that converges upon a unified theory of society. In an essay entitled "What Is Analytical Marxism?" one of the founders, Erik Wright, says, "I believe that the Marxism which will emerge from the present period of theoretical transformation will not only be more powerful theoretically than the Marxism of the heyday of the New Left, but also of more political relevance as well" (Wright 1989, p. 36).

Analytical Marxists emphasize careful elaboration of basic theoretical concepts. In the literature of Analytical Marxism one encounters painstaking—but not necessarily orthodox—discussions of concepts like productive forces, economic structure, exploitation, class structure, fetishism, base and superstructure, and the state. This conceptual exegesis may strike the casual reader as abstract and nitpicking, but Analytical Marxists hold that theoretical development cannot progress unless the underlying concepts are thoroughly understood.

The meticulous elaboration of concepts parallels an insistence on systematic and rigorous articulation of the theoretical logic connecting concepts. Loose reasoning can utterly derail otherwise promising theoretical investigations. This insight underlies the predilection for formal logic and mathematical modeling characteristic of Analytical Marxism. It also explains the frequent use of hypothetical examples (sometimes called thought experiments) expressly concocted to illustrate the meaning and check the validity of theoretical arguments.

Analytical Marxists treat the individual person as a vital unit of analysis, an assumption that has major theoretical and ethical consequences. Theoretically, it means that a satisfactory explanation of any social event must explain why the individual persons involved acted as they did. Explaining an event exclusively at the macrosocial level through the logic of corporations, states, classes, productive forces, or the like is not sufficient. Some Analytical Marxists, taking a more radical stance, insist that any satisfactory explanation must derive a social phenomenon entirely from properties of individual people, a principle known as *methodological individualism*. Methodological individualism does not require abandoning class analysis, but it does suggest that the theoretical centrality of class should be deduced from more elementary principles about individuals rather than adopted as an axiomatic assumption.

The value accorded to individual persons renders certain courses of action ethically intolerable. For example, policies that destroy particular individuals in hopes of benefiting some larger group are rarely justifiable. Nor is it permissible to subordinate the real interests of living people to the hypothetical interests of future generations. The ethical principles suggested by Analytical Marxism require rethinking the morality of revolutionary action.

Who Are the Analytical Marxists?

The emergence of Analytical Marxism is sometimes connected with the publication of Gerald Cohen's important book, *Karl Marx's Theory of History: A Defence*, in 1978. I trace the origins of Analytical Marxism 18 years earlier to the appearance of Piero Sraffa's pathbreaking critique of marginalist economic theory, *Production of Commodities by Means of Commodities* (1960). Sraffa was not concerned with founding a new type of Marxism, and his book never even mentions the subject. But the style and substance of *Production of Commodities by Means of Commodities* are entirely congenial with the spirit of Analytical Marxism, and Sraffa's example encouraged the kind of relationship between Marxism and mainstream social science later advocated by self-conscious Analytical Marxists.

Using elementary algebra and careful reasoning, Sraffa shows how the concept of *capital*, as formulated within marginalist economic theory, generates theoretical paradoxes that undermine the plausibility of the mainstream approach. The British economist Ian Steedman applied Sraffa's ideas to formulate a broad critique of Marxist economics. He insisted upon the need for a *materialist* analysis of capitalist society but denied any general tendency toward a falling profit rate and urged abandoning the labor theory of value as both illogical and irrelevant (Steedman 1977).

A parallel route toward Analytical Marxism appears in the work of Michio Morishima (1973), who tries to reformulate the economics of Karl Marx with the tools of modern mathematics. According to Morishima, Marx should be regarded as a cofounder of *general equilibrium theory* (along with Leon Walras), and the

Marxist conception of economic reproduction closely resembles the input-output analysis of Nobel prizewinning economist Wassily Leontief. Furthermore, many of John von Neumann's pathbreaking ideas about economic growth (Neumann 1945) are stated quite clearly in *Capital* (Marx [1867] 1977, [1884] 1981, [1891] 1989).

Marxist economic theory claims that capitalist profit is founded upon exploitation. Morishima proves mathematically that the equilibrium rate of profit is positive if and only if the rate of exploitation is also positive. This result has become known as the *Fundamental Marxian Theorem*. It establishes that profit and exploitation are logically equivalent under conditions of economic equilibrium and greatly increases the credibility of Marxist economic analysis.

The forerunners of Analytical Marxism appeared in the field of economics, which has greater theoretical coherence than other social sciences and in which sharp tension exists between the loose reasoning of Marx and Engels and the formal logic of modern mathematical models. Self-conscious Analytical Marxism arrives with the publication of G. A. Cohen's *Karl Marx's Theory of History: A Defence*. This work dealt with the conceptual core of Marxist theory, showing it was possible to use the methods of analytical philosophy without forsaking either Marxism or radical politics. Cohen defended a traditional version of *historical materialism,* in which the motive force of history is development of productive capacity and in which functionalist reasoning explains the connection between productive capacity and the institutions of society.

The importance of this book derived less from its theoretical propositions, which were not new, and more from its way of supporting these propositions. Cohen avoided using a specialized vocabulary, crafted his sentences with great care, strove for simplicity of expression, and insisted upon high standards of clarity. He chose definitions not on grounds of textual authority but for purposes of constructing theory. He introduced many subtle distinctions, used logically precise arguments, and deemphasized certain parts of classical Marxism in the interest of giving a generally coherent account. Although many Analytical Marxists have criticized the positions taken by Cohen, *Karl Marx's Theory of History* remains the most broadly accepted model of what Analytical Marxist work should be like.

In a subsequent volume published 10 years later, Cohen assembles various replies to critics and presents a more restricted interpretation of historical materialism confined largely to the explanation of material development (Cohen 1988).

The person most responsible for giving Analytical Marxism creative vigor and making it controversial is the mathematical economist John Roemer. Whereas Cohen seeks to defend the main ideas of Karl Marx using the tools of analytical philosophy, Roemer thrives on revision. He holds sacred no part of the received canon and eagerly embraces provocative hypotheses with the aim of reforging Marxist theory as a logically consistent but still revolutionary doctrine. The spirit of Roemer's approach is aptly expressed in the last few paragraphs of his first book, *Analytical Foundations of Marxian Economic Theory*:

> Marxian theory is in a Ptolemaic crisis. At present Marxism does not provide a compelling theory for explaining the developments of late twentieth-century society. I think this is due, in large part, to the epicycle approach its practitioners often take: the hope that small perturbation of the categories of a century old theory can explain developments today. Of all methodologies, Marxism should be the last to fall into this trap. . . . It is by separating the historical-materialist kernel from its specific application as Marxism, the theory of nineteenth-century capitalism, that progress will be made. (Roemer 1981, pp. 209-10)

The extent of Roemer's originality only became apparent with the publication of his second book, *A General Theory of Exploitation and Class* (1982), which is both a devastating assault upon classical Marxist economic theory and a work of consummate theoretical imagination. Twelve years after its publication, it remains the most impressive monument of Analytical Marxism and the chief focus of critical assault.

A General Theory of Exploitation and Class does the following things: (a) argues that differential ownership of productive resources rather than the nature of the labor process is the crucial determinant of economic exploitation; (b) generalizes the notion of exploitation, using concepts from game theory; (c) reinterprets historical materialism as a theory of how forms of exploitation are sequentially eliminated; (d) shows how both class and exploitation result from differential ownership of productive assets; (e) establishes an analytical relationship between class position and exploitation status (the *Class Exploitation Correspondence Principle*); (f) uses this principle to develop a profound critique of the labor theory of value; (g) proves that capitalism with only a labor market has exactly the same class structure as capitalism with only a credit market; and (h) explores what forms of exploitation exist within societies of the Soviet type.

The most comprehensive application of the Analytical Marxist approach to the ideas of Karl Marx is the book *Making Sense of Marx* (1985) by the Norwegian political scientist Jon Elster. This volume criticizes the philosophy, economics, theory of history, and interpretation of revolution implicit within the work of Karl Marx and attempts to reconstruct Marxist theory using rational choice concepts. In contrast to Cohen, Elster reproaches Marx for using functional explanation because it invites such unscientific practices as teleological reasoning and radical holism. Functional explanation is legitimate only if it provides an adequate account of individual action and only if it does not endow collective units (such as classes or states) with the same action capacities as individual people.

To guard against these unscientific practices, Elster thinks Marxists should adopt the principle of *methodological individualism* mentioned earlier. This doctrine is founded on the idea that only individual people can act and requires that all social scientific explanations be reducible (at least in principle) to plausible accounts of individual action. Methodological individualism does not require an assumption of *individual rationality*, but the former is certainly congenial to the latter. The connection between the two is effectively illustrated by the advice Elster gives about explaining collective action.

> To explain the collective action simply in terms of the benefits for the group is to beg all sorts of questions, and in particular the question why collective action so often fails to take place even when it would greatly benefit the agents. The individual-level explanations should be constructed according to the following heuristic principle: first assume that behavior is both rational and self-interested; if that does not work, assume at least rationality; only if this is unsuccessful too should one assume that individual participation in collective action is irrational. Finally the danger of

premature reductionism should be constantly kept in mind. Collective action may simply be too complex for individual-level
explanations to be feasible at the current stage. (Elster 1985,
p. 359)

The principle of methodological individualism is controversial
among Analytical Marxists and among other social scientists.
Though most Analytical Marxists do want to provide microfoundations for social theory, some believe that methodological
individualism is not a sensible way of doing this (Levine, Sober,
and Wright 1987). I will say more about the pros and cons of
methodological individualism in subsequent chapters.

Also controversial is Elster's advocacy of *game theory* as a
general tool of Marxist analysis (Elster 1982, 1986). Game theory
is the branch of rational choice theory that studies strategic
interaction. It examines processes of social interaction where
the outcome depends upon choices made by actors with divergent interests. Game theory specifies what strategies rational
actors should use to achieve favorable results and what outcomes
will occur from using these strategies (Başar and Olsder 1982;
Fudenberg and Tirole 1991).

The need for game theory arises, according to Elster, because
(a) social outcomes depend upon the actions chosen by individuals, (b) social structure does not fully determine individual
action, (c) individuals choose the actions that they think will
yield the best results, and (d) individuals regard other individuals
as rational actors like themselves. Game theory is relevant to
Marxism because "classes crystallize into collective actors that
confront each other over the distribution of income and power, as
well as over the nature of property relations" (Elster 1982, p. 464).

Jon Elster stands on the conservative end of Analytical Marxism. He is even more critical of classical Marxist theory than
Roemer. Scarcely a sentence written by Marx or Engels gains his
unqualified approval. Moreover, he seems exceedingly dubious
about both the possibility and the desirability of radical social
change. Elster doubts that capitalism will ever generate the
conditions needed for its own transformation and also doubts
that anything resembling the Marxist idea of communism is
feasible or even agreeable. Social revolution is unlikely to happen
in advanced capitalist societies, but if it did, the outcome would
probably be disastrous. He clearly rejects Marxism as a theory

of revolution and accepts it only as a critique, but as a critique of a society it is powerless to transform (Elster 1985, pp. 513-31).

The Analytical Marxist who has worked hardest to bridge the gap between theory and research is Erik Olin Wright. Wright's research focuses upon the *class structure* of modern capitalist societies, and he regards proper conceptualization of the *middle class* as key to understanding the entire capitalist class structure. Since completing his doctoral degree in 1976, Wright has advanced two major interpretations of capitalist class structure. His first conceptualization, developed as an alternative to the Althusserian class analysis of Nicos Poulantzas, centered on the notion of *contradictory class locations* (Wright 1978, 1979). His second major interpretation of capitalist class structure emerged partly as a critique of the first and partly from his encounter with John Roemer's theory of exploitation (Wright 1985; Wright, Howe, and Cho 1989). This second conceptualization places Wright squarely within the Analytical Marxism camp.

Wright has made extensive use of survey research and causal modeling to test propositions derived from Marxist theory. He has organized an ambitious series of cross-national surveys about capitalist class structure, two of which are discussed in his book *Classes* (1985). This widely discussed work presents Wright's second framework for analyzing class structure, centered on the concept of exploitation, and applies it to survey data from Sweden and the United States.

The conception of capitalist class structure presented in *Classes* postulates three kinds of exploitation that intersect in complex ways: exploitation based upon ownership of capital, exploitation based upon control of organizations, and exploitation based upon possession of productive skills. Wright interprets a middle-class location as a position that is exploiting in some ways but subject to exploitation in others. The results of both the Swedish and the U.S. surveys indicate that Wright's exploitation-centered concept of class has more explanatory power than do alternative Marxist interpretations. It is particularly effective in explaining the patterns of income inequality and class consciousness existing in these two rather dissimilar societies. Wright's framework also illuminates the structural differences between Swedish and American capitalism.

Erik Wright's publications are distinguished by broad theoretical range, clarity of exposition, critical acuteness in analyzing the work of other social scientists, willingness to engage in searching self-criticism, and ability to extract political implications from both abstract theoretical propositions and empirical findings. An example of Wright's theoretical fertility is his use of the exploitation-based concept of class structure to suggest a far-reaching reinterpretation of historical materialism (Wright 1985, pp. 114-18). In contrast to Elster, Wright seems relatively optimistic about the prospects for a socialist future.

If Wright has taken the lead in devising empirical tests of Analytical Marxism, Adam Przeworski has pioneered the systematic investigation of its political implications. Przeworski concentrates on the problem of why socialist movements are so weak in advanced capitalist societies (Przeworski 1985a; Przeworski and Sprague 1986). His research combines a comparative historical approach with extensive use of rational choice models. Perhaps the most striking conclusion reached by Przeworski is that purely economic considerations will not induce workers or any other class in capitalist society to struggle for socialism. This is not due to false consciousness, betrayal by leaders, or political repression. Capitalism, whatever its faults, does not prevent subordinate classes from improving their material condition, and historical experience painfully demonstrates that the costs of transforming capitalist society can be extremely high.

Socialist parties that participate in bourgeois politics face a painful dilemma, according to Przeworski. If they remain strictly working-class parties, they have no chance of electoral success because economic structure prevents the working class (defined as the industrial proletariat) from becoming a majority in advanced capitalist societies. On the other hand, if socialist parties opt to acquire a mass constituency, they lose ideological vitality, weaken their connection with exploited classes, and become parties of reform rather than revolution. Faced with this alternative, most socialist parties have chosen the latter strategy, which explains why social democracy has become the main form of working-class politics in advanced capitalist societies.

Przeworski and his coworkers use game theory to model class conflict under capitalism. Michael Wallerstein and he have adapted

Lancaster's differential game model of capitalism to study the three-way strategic interaction between owners, workers, and state managers (Przeworski and Wallerstein 1982, 1988). This game theoretic analysis suggests that by adopting appropriate taxation policies, a state sympathetic to the working class can redistribute income toward wage earners without abolishing capitalist control of investment and without inviting economic disaster.

Przeworski's most recent work involves the use of game theory to analyze political and economic reform in Eastern Europe and Latin America (Przeworski 1991b). He argues that mechanisms of allocation are more important than forms of property in determining the future of these societies, and he favors an economic system in which regulated markets allocate resources and the state guarantees a certain level of welfare. Such a system would not require a revolutionary transformation of existing social organization. It could arise as either a social democratic reform of capitalism or a market reform of state socialism. The fall of Communism convinces Przeworski that no radical departures from existing economic systems are feasible:

> What died in Eastern Europe is the very idea of rationally administering things to satisfy human needs—the feasibility of implementing public ownership of productive resources through centralized command; the very project of basing a society on disinterested cooperation—the possibility of dissociating social contributions from individual rewards. . . . The socialist project—the project that was forged in Western Europe between 1848 and 1891 and that had animated social movements all over the world since then—failed, in the East and in the West. (Przeworski 1991b, p. 7)

The list of scholars discussed above by no means exhausts the ranks of Analytical Marxism. Other writers whom I consider to be Analytical Marxists include Michael Albert, Pranab Bardham, Sam Bowles, Robert Brenner, Alan Carling, Joshua Cohen, Robin Hahnel, Andrew Levine, Stephen Marglin, David Miller, Richard Miller, Elliott Sober, G. E. M. de Sainte Croix, Philippe Van Parijs, Michael Wallerstein, and Allen Wood. Although I shall not ignore the work of these people, this book will concentrate upon G. A. Cohen, Roemer, Elster, Wright, and Przeworski—the authors who give Analytical Marxism its distinctive identity.

The Use of Examples in Analytical Marxism

As mentioned earlier, one of the characteristic features of Analytical Marxism is extensive use of examples. Examples become important because Analytical Marxists assume that scientific theories should be logically consistent and preferably organized as axiomatic systems. Examples can be used to investigate the logical properties of scientific theories. The existence of an example satisfying all the axioms of the system proves that these axioms are indeed logically consistent. A well-chosen example can establish that an entity of a certain type is not excluded by the axiom system under consideration. The empirical frequency of the example is not relevant here because the issue at stake is that of logical possibility.

Consider a simplified version of an example proposed by John Roemer (Roemer 1982a, p. 39). The example is intended to show that exploitation can exist without a labor market and without accumulation of capital. To demonstrate such a possibility, imagine an economy with only two people: Norma and Murray. In this economy each person requires one unit of corn and one unit of berries per week, but nothing more. Suppose that one unit of corn exchanges for one unit of berries. Norma owns land containing berry bushes and can produce one unit of berries (net) with 1 day's labor. Murray owns land suitable for producing corn and can produce one unit of corn (net) with 2 days' labor.

Norma and Murray agree to exchange one unit of corn for one unit of berries per week. To make this possible, Norma works 2 days and produces two units of berries. She consumes one unit of berries and exchanges the other with Murray for a unit of corn. Murray, on the other hand, works 4 days to produce two units of corn. He consumes one unit of corn himself and exchanges the other with Norma for a unit of berries. Thus each person ends up with a unit of corn and a unit of berries, but Murray works 4 days per week while Norma only works 2.

The socially necessary amount of labor needed to produce one unit of corn plus one unit of berries in our example is 3 days because if a person possessed all the required resources and knew all the available technologies, she would need to work 3 days to produce these goods. Because Murray must work more than is socially necessary while Norma can work less, Roemer claims Murray is exploited and Norma is an exploiter. This exploitation happens because Norma and Murray own different kinds of land and because one unit of corn exchanges for one unit of berries.[2]

To make these claims a little more plausible, think about the following possibilities. Suppose Norma kills Murray and takes his berry-producing land. She now possess more land, but without Murray to exchange with she needs to work 3 days (the socially necessary amount) instead of only 2. Thus Norma is worse off without Murray even though she has seized his possessions. Now suppose the reverse: Murray kills Norma and takes her land. Because he now possesses the berry-producing resources, Murray need only work 3 days instead of 4; with Norma gone his lot has improved.

The asymmetric consequences of these two murders strengthen Roemer's claim that the relationship between Norma and Murray involves exploitation even though each is an independent producer. Roemer develops this example in a more abstract and general way, but the theoretical point is the same: exploitation does not require the existence of a labor market or the accumulation of capital. We elaborate this point further in Chapter 4 when discussing exploitation in subsistence economies.

The Norma and Murray case is of course a drastic oversimplification: no real economy could be so limited. But simplicity is also the example's strength. If exploitation between independent producers can happen under such elementary circumstances, how much more readily could it occur with more realistic conditions? We shall return to this simple but telling example several times in subsequent chapters.

Next consider how G. A. Cohen uses examples to explore why the proletarian class lacks freedom (Cohen 1988, pp. 261-63). Cohen wants to show that the proletarian class is compelled to sell its labor power and is therefore unfree even though some opportunity to move out of the working class and into the petty bourgeoisie does exist. To make this point he distinguishes between individual freedom and collective freedom and gives the following example.

A group of 10 people are locked in a room with a single door. In the middle of the room is a key that any one of the 10 people can use to unlock the door and leave the room. However, only one person can leave the room in this way; the nine others must remain. It so happens that none of the 10 people in the locked room actually chooses to leave. Perhaps each person feels solidarity with the others so that, without a general liberation, her own individual escape would not be satisfying.

Each person in the room, maintains Cohen, is individually free to leave because each person can take the key and unlock the door. But each individual's freedom requires that no one else exercise her own freedom. The moment one person takes the key, the freedom of everyone else disappears. The group as a whole is collectively unfree because there is no way all members can escape.

Cohen compares this example to the situation of the British proletariat:

> There are more exits from the British proletariat than there are workers trying to leave it. Therefore, British workers are individually free to leave the proletariat.
> There are very few exits from the British proletariat and there are very many workers in it. Therefore, British workers are collectively unfree to leave the proletariat. (Cohen 1988, p. 266)

Jon Elster and Karl Ove Moene use an example to demonstrate that inferior economic systems can be stable and superior systems unstable (Elster and Moene 1989, p. 9). Suppose all workers prefer an economic system where every firm is controlled by its workers (market socialism) over a system where all firms are owned and controlled by capitalists (pure capitalism). In terms of preferences, therefore, market socialism is superior to pure capitalism; but leaving pure capitalism may be very difficult. Suppose severe economic hardships await any band of workers who abandon pure capitalism and organize a worker-controlled firm. These pioneers actually become worse off than they were under pure capitalism. Recognizing this, rational workers will have no incentive to leave pure capitalism, which, though clearly inferior to market socialism, is nevertheless stable.

Conversely, although market socialism is universally preferred over pure capitalism, it could still be undermined by defections. To see this, suppose market socialism exists. Suppose further that workers in any particular firm can improve their individual welfare if they alone liquidate workers' control and restructure

their organization on a capitalist basis while everyone else retains socialist work relations. This does not contradict the assumption of a universal preference for market socialism over
pure capitalism. The defection, while benefiting the defectors,
harms everyone else. Hence market socialism, the universally
favored system, is vulnerable to defection and cannot maintain
itself in face of rational egoistic behavior.

This is a Prisoner's Dilemma type of situation and shows that
individually rational behavior can lead to Pareto-inferior outcomes. According to Elster and Moene, if actions taken by
individuals pursuing their own objectives have significant consequences for the welfare of others (i.e., if "externalities" exist),
then individual preferences may not be a suitable guide for social
choice.

Is Analytical Marxism Marxist?

A number of writers, including Ronald Kieve (1986), Michael
Lebowitz (1988), David Ruccio (1988), and Ellen Wood (1989),
question whether Analytical Marxism is really Marxist. These
people say Analytical Marxists make so many concessions to
bourgeois social science and so drastically revise the ideas of
Marx and Engels that they abandon Marxism. Though discussion
about the truth of ideas is generally more fruitful than controversy on how the ideas should be labeled, this issue deserves
some attention. In addition to being a social theory, Marxism is
also a collective endeavor to transform society, and the issue of
labeling involves who can legitimately participate in the transformation project.

Analytical Marxists tend to use a very broad definition of
Marxism, often treating it as a tradition rather than a specific
doctrine. The major works of Analytical Marxism are presented
as reconstructions of what Karl Marx meant (or should have
meant), or as particular developments within Marxist theory, or
as empirical applications of Marxist concepts, but never as
canonical expositions of the true Marxism. Analytical Marxists
often emphasize distinctions between (a) the questions Marx
poses, (b) his strategies for answering these questions, and (c)
the substance of the answers he gives. Indicative of this focus

on questions and strategies rather than answers are the intellectual guidelines offered by G. A. Cohen:

> I think that three questions should command the attention of those of us who work within the Marxist tradition today. They are the questions of design, justification, and strategy, in relation to the project of opposing and overcoming capitalism. The first question is, What do we want? What, in general, and even not so general terms, is the form of the socialist society that we seek? The second question is, Why do we want it? What exactly is wrong with capitalism, and what is right about socialism? And the third question is, How can we achieve it? What are the implications for practice of the fact that the working class in advanced capitalist society is not now what it was, or what it was once thought to be? (Cohen 1988, p. xii)

According to Jon Elster, the Analytical Marxists have subjected virtually every tenet of classical Marxism to "insistent criticism," but the foregoing quotation (as well the previous quotation from Roemer) should clarify why most of these critics still identify themselves as Marxist. Much of the scholarship produced by Analytical Marxists addresses one or more of the three questions posed by Cohen and explores the possibilities of transcending capitalism. "Perhaps the greatest task of Marxism today," suggests Roemer (1986a, p. 25), "is to construct a modern theory of socialism." The emphasis on using the full methodological armory of modern social science stems from the desire to give better answers to questions about the longevity of capitalism and the viability of socialism.

These explanations do not satisfy the critics of Analytical Marxism. Commitment to the project of transcending capitalism, plus interest in questions posed by Marx, plus identification with some vague thing called the Marxist tradition, does not, according to them, make a Marxist.

But theoretical perspectives that can remain relevant in face of massive and sometimes unanticipated historical change must possess both a stable intellectual core and ample conceptual flexibility. If the stable intellectual core of Marxism involves using science to find practical possibilities for revolutionizing society, do more specific criteria of what constitutes a Marxist make sense? In a highly dynamic world deeply resistant to prophecy and poorly comprehended by any existing social theory, unwavering devotion to the concepts of classical Marxism can only obstruct the growth of rational revolutionary thought.

The Methodology of Analytical Marxism

Most Analytical Marxists admire the formal methodology used within bourgeois social science and think that techniques like mathematical modeling, statistical inference, and computer simulation should be adopted by Marxists. Analytical Marxists differ among themselves, however, about which techniques hold the greatest promise for Marxist social science. For example, Elster, Roemer, and Przeworski wax enthusiastic about using game theory to model class conflict, but other Analytical Marxists remain doubtful.

Marxists have traditionally regarded bourgeois social science as ideologically contaminated and have systematically rejected both its theories and its methods. Analytical Marxists strenuously oppose this approach. The relationship between *bourgeois social science* and bourgeois society is far more complicated than such an across-the-board rejection suggests. The results of bourgeois social science do not always support the capitalist system or indicate that alternative economic systems are unworkable. Some Analytical Marxists discard the very concept of "bourgeois" social science because it sabotages the effort to build a scientific Marxism and derives from a defective theory of ideology.

An important example of how Analytical Marxists relate to mainstream social science is John Roemer's use of *general equilibrium* models to elaborate modern Marxist economic theory. Roemer regards the theory of general economic equilibrium as an outstanding intellectual achievement that can be of great value to Marxists. Nor is he the first Marxist to reach this conclusion. The famous Polish economist Oskar Lange had general equilibrium theory in mind when claiming that Marxist economics is the economics of capitalism and bourgeois economics is the economics of socialism. The rejection of equilibrium analysis by most Marxists, says Roemer, indicates a faulty understanding of the equilibrium concept, a concept that actually means consistency between the actions of individual units and the logical properties of the system rather than stability and the absence of change.

Methodological discussion among Analytical Marxists has centered on two related issues: *functional explanation* and *methodological individualism*. In a sense these are not different issues at all but different interpretations about how Marxist explanation should proceed.

The important questions about *functional explanation* are whether it is a legitimate form of scientific reasoning and whether Marxists should use it. G. A. Cohen, the foremost Marxist exponent of functional explanation, answers affirmatively to both questions: he regards it as scientifically unimpeachable and as indispensable for giving a coherent account of historical materialism. Cohen sometimes refers to functional explanation as *consequence explanation* because it explains an event by means of its consequences or, more precisely, its propensity to have consequences of a certain sort.[3] The kind of relationship that Marxists postulate between the economic base and the political superstructure of society requires functional explanation. Marxists claim that the base explains the superstructure, but they also say that the superstructure stabilizes and integrates the base. These two assertions can only be reconciled, argues Cohen, by a functional type of explanation.

Although Cohen's ideas have considerable authority among Analytical Marxists, many of the latter oppose functional explanation as untestable, inherently incomplete, and generally unsatisfactory for scientific purposes. They do not regard the mere propensity of an event to have a certain consequence as sufficient to explain the event's occurrence. Proper scientific explanation requires specification of a process by which this propensity is parlayed into occurrence of the event: "[It] is generally not the case that functional outcomes can result without any conscious intervention whatsoever. Functional explanations unconnected to intentional explanations are usually unsatisfactory precisely because no plausible mechanism for achieving functional outcomes can be found" (Wright, Levine, and Sober 1992, p. 67). Cohen responds to this criticism by arguing that one need not identify the exact process by which propensity is translated into occurrence, provided the existence of some such process can be established.

According to *methodological individualism,* all social phenomena must ultimately be explained through the properties of individual people, such as motivations, values, feelings, capacities, perceptions, and information. The most developed form of explanation deduces collective realities from assumptions about individuals, but the immaturity of social science often renders that temporarily infeasible.

A related but not quite identical idea is that of providing *microfoundations* for social theory. Providing microfoundations means explaining how individual people act. According to this perspective, an adequate theory of any social phenomena must explain why the individual people involved act as they do, but it need not deduce these phenomena from assumptions about individuals. The microfoundations approach thus recognizes the unique theoretical status of the individual human being but avoids the psychological reductionism implicit within methodological individualism.

Within the domain of Analytical Marxism, the foremost advocate of methodological individualism is Jon Elster. He views methodological individualism as vital protection against antiscientific practices such as radical holism that attribute characteristics of individuals to collective entities of various sorts and thereby give the latter explanatory priority over their constituent persons. Due to the biological separation of persons and the location of thought in the individual mind, action is a capacity of individuals and only individuals. The explanation of social action is the essential task of social science, from which it follows that individuals are the logical starting point of social theory, Marxist or otherwise.

John Roemer, who also favors methodological individualism, associates it with the effort to create genuinely deductive forms of Marxist theory. Not only are assumptions about individuals the most parsimonious and plausible foundations for social theory, but by starting in this way Marxists can sometimes derive as theorems propositions formerly used as assumptions. Such achievements greatly enhance the elegance and credibility of Marxist theory. Roemer thinks the whole of Marxist class theory can be derived from assumptions about the material endowments of individuals and the exchanges between them. The most impressive example of this is Roemer's own Class Exploitation

Correspondence Principle, which deduces the previously axiomatic relationship between class and exploitation from assumptions about individual endowments (Roemer 1982a, pp. 113-46).

But not all Analytical Marxists favor methodological individualism. Levine, Sober, and Wright (1987) question the scientific value of methodological individualism because macrosocial phenomena cannot always be explained in terms of assumptions about individuals. Sometimes quite different distributions of individual characteristics can generate the same macrosocial phenomenon, which precludes establishing any simple correspondence between macro- and micro-level events. Though rejecting methodological individualism as a general explanatory principle, Levine, Sober, and Wright—who call their philosophy of explanation antireductionist—affirm the importance of providing microfoundations for macrosocial theory and endorse the effort to explain macrosocial occurrences through assumptions about individuals whenever this is possible.[4]

Ethics and Analytical Marxism

The status of ethical principles within classical Marxism is ambiguous. On the one hand, Marx and Engels appear to denounce exploitation and economic systems practicing exploitation on ethical grounds. On the other hand, they deny that ethical judgments can have any universal validity, and they also deny that their critique of capitalism is based upon ethics.

By contrast, most Analytical Marxists think ethical judgments are an essential part of coherent social criticism. They strive to formulate a consistent and appealing system of ethics and to integrate this with a scientific analysis of human society. The tenor of the Analytical Marxist approach to ethics is aptly expressed in the preface to Roemer's *Free to Lose*:

> In the century since Marx wrote, his ideas have been important in large part because they provide an argument for the immorality of the capitalist system; and my theme is, similarly, to trace the connections between the economic concepts of Marxism and the ethical ideas to which they relate. Whereas contemporary neoclassical economics advertises its moral neutrality, the task of Marxist

economics is to challenge the defensibility, from a moral view-point, of an economic system based on private ownership of the means of production. (Roemer 1988a, p. vii)

Careful analysis of the role of ethics within classical Marxism has generally been the first step toward formulating a coherent Analytical Marxist ethical system. An important article by Norman Geras (1985) examines the controversy over whether Marx condemned capitalism as unjust. After studying pertinent writings of Marx and modern interpretations of these texts, Geras hypothesizes that "Marx did think capitalism was unjust but he did not think he thought so" (p. 70). He favors elaborating a Marxist concept of justice, observing that the absence of such a concept has had terrible consequences: "Within the complex of historical causes of the crimes and tragedies which have disgraced socialism, is the moral cynicism that has sometimes dressed itself in the authority of traditional 'anti-ethical' pronouncements" (Geras 1985, p. 85).

Analytical Marxists do not accept most of the arguments traditionally used by Marxists against ethical judgments. They do not think the integration of normative thinking with Marxist theory will compromise the scientific value of the latter. They do not think a clearly articulated Marxist ethics will foster utopian illusions about the possibilities for human liberation. Nor do they think it denies the causal priority Marxists attribute to material conditions in the development of human history. On the contrary, acknowledgment of appropriate moral principles facilitates theoretical clarity, provides valuable guidance to political action, and may render the positive assertions of Marxist theory more testable.

Of course, acknowledging the importance of ethics and elaborating a viable ethical system are quite different things, the latter being considerably harder than the former. The initial impulse was to place the concept of exploitation at the heart of Marxist ethics. Exploitation seemed to provide the crucial link between the positive and normative elements of Marxist theory, and was something that all Analytical Marxists could recognize as morally obnoxious. Upon closer examination, however, exploitation revealed greater moral ambiguity than anticipated. As we shall see in a later chapter, Analytical Marxists produced examples in which exploitation did not seem immoral.

Concern about exploitation remains strong, but another ethical theme voiced by Analytical Marxists revolves around the development of social equality. Equality is seen as an important ethical value, but the level of equality attainable at any time depends upon the degree of economic development. Efforts to push the level of equality beyond that warranted by the existing forces of production can have truly disastrous results. Nevertheless, the ethical meaning of history is the growth of equality, or rather the growth of material conditions that can sustain progressively higher levels of social equality. According to this conception, inequality based upon limited development of productive capabilities is not grounds for moral condemnation. However, inequality exceeding that mandated by the existing maturity of material conditions does indeed justify moral censure.

Neither resistance to exploitation nor development of social equality is generally accepted as the core of Marxist ethics. Adam Przeworski, for example, emphasizes that freedom has moral priority over equality, at least for purposes of building socialism (Przeworski 1985a, p. 244). Other Analytical Marxists propose self-development as the key concept in formulating viable ethical principles. The main point is not the specific moral precepts advanced by the Analytical Marxists, but rather their idea that moral philosophy is a legitimate, indeed an essential, part of Marxist theory.

Conclusion

Analytical Marxism arises from a desire to combine the methods of modern social science with the substantive ideas of classical Marxist thought. It is based upon the premise that such a combination is feasible and that Marxist ideas will not be distorted through exploration by methods developed for non-Marxist purposes. Analytical Marxists believe that many propositions of classical Marxism are wrong and require drastic revision or outright abandonment. Such an impious orientation is considered essential for making Marxist theory both radical and relevant in the modern world.

The theoretical agenda of Analytical Marxism includes producing a coherent theory of history that neither treats the evolution of human society as highly predictable nor relegates it to the winds of sheer chance. It also includes developing systematic methods of class analysis applicable to and informative about a variety of historical contexts. Analytical Marxists think segregation of ethics and science is neither feasible nor desirable. As we shall see, they have revitalized and greatly expanded the theory of exploitation as a systematic means of bridging the gap between these domains.

People first learning about Analytical Marxism often experience it as frustrating and obscure. Much of the obscurity results from adherence to high standards of logical rigor, but some could be eliminated without sacrificing accuracy. I shall try to make this book both correct and entirely nonobscure by writing in a manner accessible to all educated people willing to give a serious effort.

The sense of frustration is harder to cope with. Many people approach Marxist theory hoping to find an integrated outlook upon human society with clear prescriptions for shaping a decent future. Analytical Marxism, in its present condition, is not very integrated and offers few if any tactical prescriptions. It contains some brilliant results, but it also includes a sometimes bewildering diversity of outlook. These characteristics are fairly typical of emerging scientific domains, and Analytical Marxists do hope to make Marxism less ideological and more scientific. The indispensable requirement for such a change is uncompromising intellectual honesty.

Some critics regard the idea of transforming Marxism from ideology to science as evidence of arrogance rather than honesty. Other critics view such a transformation as either impossible or undesirable. The critics may be right. The "truth" of Analytical Marxism may lie more in the theoretical movement it has launched than in any scientific doctrine it produces. Its practitioners do have a certain intellectual hubris; yet they can also exude infectious enthusiasm, a spirit of intellectual comradeship, and unfashionable but irrepressible hopefulness about the future.

Notes

1. Jon Elster says, "There is a specifically Marxist method for studying phenomena," but acknowledges the method is so widely practiced that few would regard it as distinctively Marxist (Elster 1985, p. 3).

2. In order to make this example as simple as possible, I have not tried to justify the exchange rate of one unit of berries for one unit of corn. This could be done by making the scenario just a little more complicated. Suppose Murray owns no land and is compelled to work on public land where the production of one corn unit or one berry unit each requires 2 days of labor. Because public land is available to everyone, and because berry and corn production require equal labor on this land, it is reasonable that one unit of berries should exchange for one unit of corn.

If no exchange between Norma and Murray happens, then Murray works 4 days per week on public land to produce a unit of berries and a unit of corn for his own consumption, whereas Norma works 1 day on her own land to produce a unit of berries and 1 day on public land to produce a unit of corn. Norma is no longer an exploiter because she now works 3 days, the socially necessary labor time. Murray, however, is still exploited because he works more than is socially necessary.

To test her understanding of this example, the reader might analyze what happens if the exchange rate is one unit of corn for two units of berries.

3. Anthony Giddens makes a very similar point in his influential critique of historical materialism (Giddens 1981, 1985). Giddens rejects functional explanation but often uses the tendency of an institution to have certain consequences in explaining why the institution exists. For example, Giddens uses the tendency of nationalism to unify nation-states as a part of his explanation of why nationalism occurs. The unifying consequences of nationalism, however, are not sufficient to explain its occurrence. According to Giddens, political leaders observe that nationalism tends to unify a nation and therefore encourage its spread. Wright, Levine, and Sober give a thoughtful appraisal of Giddens's views on historical materialism from an Analytical Marxist perspective (1992, pp. 61-88).

4. Criticisms of methodological individualism from outside of Analytical Marxism will be considered in the concluding chapter (Burawoy 1989; Cullenberg 1991; Weldes 1989; Wood 1989).

2

THEORY OF HISTORY

A General View of History

Analytical Marxism has rejuvenated the effort to build a general theory of history. The attempt to construct such a theory sets Analytical Marxism apart from the mainstream of contemporary social science, which emphasizes the particularistic and contextual nature of all historical situations and disparages efforts to formulate universal principles of historical development.

The interest in a general theory of history by Analytical Marxists has four sources. The first source is the work of Marx and Engels, which steadfastly struggles to carve out a general theory designated as *historical materialism*. This theory has received stern criticism, including some criticism by Analytical Marxists, but the unflagging endeavor of Marx and Engels to identify valid principles for comprehending history remains deeply impressive and succeeds in convincing even many critics that a general theory is possible. The second source of interest is the historical record itself. When a sufficient length of time is considered, history reveals some clear tendencies that suggest the operation of consistent forces.

The third source is the concept of explanation favored by Analytical Marxists. Genuine explanation requires reference to general principles. Interpretations of history that do not invoke general principles may be informative and even illuminating, but they are not really scientific. Hence the effort to formulate a general theory of history is firmly linked with the aspiration to have a scientific understanding of history.

The fourth and final source of interest in a general theory of history is the desire to revolutionize society. A general theory would indicate when revolutionary transformations are possible and how they should be conducted. But if no general theory exists, then revolution must be a perilous enterprise indeed, without solid intellectual foundations or reasonable prospects of success.

For Analytical Marxists, the theory of history formulated by G. A. Cohen has acquired a certain canonical status (Cohen 1978, 1988). This is not because everyone agrees with Cohen's version of historical materialism. However, his ideas are expressed with such clarity and have such broad relevance that all theoretically inclined Marxists must wrestle with them when writing about virtually any historical topic. As mentioned in the first chapter, Cohen tries to defend a traditional form of historical materialism. His entire theoretical project relies heavily upon 15 sentences from the 1859 "Preface" to *A Contribution to the Critique of Political Economy,* which he regards as Marx's most systematic and coherent presentation of historical materialism. Through Cohen's influence, the following passage has become the most important in the entire Marxist literature for Analytical Marxists:

> The mode of production of material life conditions the social, political and intellectual life process in general. It is not the consciousness of men that determines their being, but, on the contrary, their social being that determines their consciousness. At a certain stage of their development, the material productive forces of society come in conflict with the existing relations of production, or—what is but a legal expression for the same thing— with the property relations within which they have been at work hitherto. From forms of development of the productive forces these relations turn into their fetters. Then begins an epoch of social revolution. With the change of the economic foundation the entire immense superstructure is more or less rapidly transformed. (Marx [1859] 1987, p. 263)

This passage contains, in a highly condensed form, most of the principles central to the traditional version of historical materialism.

Through a painstaking reconstruction of the "Preface" and a few other Marxist texts, Cohen expounds a view of history as the growth of human freedom. The major deficiencies of human society ultimately derive from insufficient human control over nature, and the central dynamic of history is growth of the power to produce, which extends human control over nature and thereby extends the possibilities for (though perhaps not the realities of) human freedom. This vision is eloquently expressed in the very first paragraph of *History, Labour, and Freedom*:

> Marxism sees history as a protracted process of liberation—from the scarcity imposed on humanity by nature, and from the oppression imposed by some people on others. Members of ruling and subject classes share the cost of natural scarcity unequally, and Marxism predicts, and fights for, the disappearance of society's perennial class division. . . . Unfreedom, exploitation, and indignity are the price which the mass of humanity must pay for the part they play in creating the material wherewithal of human liberation. (Cohen 1988, p. vii)

A complex relationship exists between the *economic structure* of society and the growth of productive power. For most of its duration, an economic structure stimulates the growth of productive power, but eventually more productive power accumulates than the structure can safely contain. When this happens, the economic structure experiences increasingly severe difficulties and is ultimately replaced by a different economic structure better able to develop the *forces of production* at the level they have now attained.

Capitalism has a special place in the evolution of economic structures. Under capitalism human beings collectively achieve a high degree of control over nature that makes possible an entirely new relationship between nature and society. Capitalism is the last and highest form of class-divided society, but capitalist economic structure cannot implement the new relationship between nature and society made possible under its auspices. This will require a further revolution in the economic organization of humanity.

Materialism

Cohen considers himself a materialist, but the version of materialism he presents rests upon a distinction between the material and the social, not upon the difference between matter and consciousness. *Material properties* refer to those elements of the interaction with nature that confront humanity as given, the exogenous constraints to which society must adjust, the physically imposed requirements of individual and social reproduction. *Social properties*, on the other hand, designate rights and powers that some people have with respect to others.

Cohen argues that material properties underlie social properties and that material development is the main content of human history. Moreover, his treatment of scientific knowledge illustrates how much Cohen deemphasizes the matter-consciousness distinction. Scientific knowledge clearly falls within the realm of consciousness, but Cohen treats usable scientific knowledge as a productive force (i.e., a material property of society) rather than as part of the superstructure.

The distinction between the material and the social is also fundamental to Cohen's understanding of productive forces and economic structures. A *productive force* is anything that can be used to accomplish economic production; instruments of production, raw materials, and labor power are all listed as productive forces. *Productive relations* are relations of power over productive forces and over people who control productive forces. The economic structure of society consists of the whole set of productive relations.

Productive forces, Cohen stresses, are not part of the economic structure, but they determine the character of this structure. Productive forces may be seen as the material content of the economic system or perhaps even of society as a whole. The economic structure, on the other hand, is the social form of the production process. The distinction between forces and relations of production expresses Cohen's particular version of materialism: it is essentially a contrast between nature and society. This same contrast appears in the traditional Marxist differentiation between *use value* and *exchange value,* with the former representing a natural relationship between things and people and the latter a social relationship.

The separation between the material and the social is said to have a deep revolutionary meaning. It establishes the possibility of revolutionary criticism because the same material content can be served by different social forms, and existing social forms may actually constrain the material relationship between nature and humanity. Revolution occurs when the material relationship with nature outgrows the social forms that contain it, and may be conceived as a process of liberating material content from social form.

Principles of Historical Development

The *technological version of historical materialism* defended by Cohen gives causal primacy to the productive forces. It has three main principles of historical development:

Development Thesis: The productive forces tend to develop throughout history.

Primacy Thesis: The level of development of the productive forces explains the nature of the productive relations.

Superstructure Thesis: The nature of the economic structure explains the noneconomic institutions contained in the superstructure.

Why are the Primacy Thesis and the Superstructure Thesis considered principles of historical *development*? The Primacy Thesis implies that productive relations adjust to the level of the productive forces, which (according to the Development Thesis) develop throughout history. Hence productive relations should change in a manner explicable through the dynamics of productive forces. The same reasoning applies to the Superstructure Thesis, which asserts that the superstructure adjusts to the economic base. Because the latter develops more or less in coordination with the productive forces, the superstructure can be expected to undergo transformations correlated to those of the base.

How does Cohen justify these three theses? The Development Thesis is explained as a consequence of human rationality operating in the face of economic scarcity. Development of productive forces reduces economic scarcity, and human beings are rational creatures strongly motivated to overcome scarcity. Hence the productive forces of society tend to develop.

Justification of the Primacy Thesis is more complicated. Productive relations, Cohen asserts, affect the development of productive forces. In fact, it is the disposition of productive relations to develop the current forces of production that explains the existence of these relations. Cohen makes an even stronger claim: existing productive relations are those optimal for developing the forces of production (given the current level of the latter). This is clearly functional or consequence explanation, and Cohen thinks such explanation is needed to reconcile the influence exerted by productive relations on productive forces with the thesis that the latter explains the former.

Functional explanation is also involved in justifying the Superstructure Thesis. An economic structure requires a suitable superstructure to maintain stability, and it is the propensity of superstructural institutions to stabilize the economic structure that explains their existence. Cohen actually defines the superstructure of society in a way that makes the Superstructure Thesis a tautology: the superstructure consists of those noneconomic institutions whose character is explained by the economic structure. However, he also contends that most noneconomic institutions are included in the superstructure.

How good are these justifications? Several critics, though sympathetic to Analytical Marxism and impressed with Cohen's overall theoretical achievement, find them seriously deficient (Levine and Wright 1980; J. Cohen 1982; Miller 1984; Elster 1985; Brenner 1985a, 1986; Wright et al. 1992).

Consider the rationality argument used to justify the Development Thesis. Human beings may have a capacity for rationality, but is it plausible to assume the invariant ahistoric kind of rationality required by Cohen's argument? Would the elimination of scarcity—that is, the satisfaction of material need—be a purpose of individual rational action throughout history, and when it is, would the actor be inclined to advance the productive forces rather than seizing other means of satisfying material need? The inclination to advance productive forces may spur rational action under capitalism, but would it be a focus of individual rationality under drastically different forms of economic organization?

Rationality might even cut against the Development Thesis. Consider a class-divided society in which the ruling class is able to control development of the productive forces. Suppose the ruling class, being rational, recognizes that development of the productive forces will eventually undermine its dominance. As a defensive strategy, a rational ruling class might systematically block further growth of the productive forces. The greater the rationality of the ruling class, the less the productive forces would develop. Nor is this possibility entirely fanciful, as the regression in agricultural productivity associated with the so-called "second serfdom" of Eastern Europe (1500-1800) and the stagnation of agriculture in southern France during the same period both indicate[1] (J. Cohen 1982; Brenner 1985a, 1985b).

The collective outcome of actions by a group of persons all of whom are motivated to advance the forces of production need not be development of the productive forces. The Prisoner's Dilemma interaction gives a simple example of how such a perverse result can happen. How individual motivation is translated into collective outcome depends almost entirely upon the social structure within which the interaction takes place. But Cohen tries to endow development of productive forces with an autonomous suprasocial momentum and to use this momentum to explain the nature of social institutions. Recognition that the dynamism of productive forces is not autonomous but depends for its very existence upon the character of social structure undermines this theoretical strategy.

In response to criticisms of this sort, Cohen has modified his argument slightly (Cohen 1988, pp. 25-29). He qualifies the Development Thesis to mean that productive forces tend to develop over the broad course of human history, but not in each particular society. This happens because production techniques can only be replaced by superior techniques and because technical progress will sooner or later occur someplace. Societies that make technical progress will tend to dominate ones that do not, and the innovations will spread from the former to the latter. But if this Darwinian selection process is how productive forces develop, why should we expect any particular connection between productive forces and economic structure?

Erik Wright and his coauthors offer a somewhat different defense of the Development Thesis (Wright et al. 1992, p. 81). Rather than emphasizing growth of productive forces, they stress constraints against the reduction of productive capacity. They give four reasons why productive forces rarely contract: (a) no group in society has an interest in reducing the productivity of labor, (b) knowledge about productive technology rarely disappears, (c) human "needs" evolve in response to existing technology and come to require it for their satisfaction, and (d) groups motivated to increase the productivity of labor always exist (e.g., direct producers want to eliminate unpleasant work). Even if successful, arguments of this sort can only sustain a weak version of the Development Thesis: productive forces tend not to regress.

Now consider the functional arguments Cohen uses to sustain both the Primacy Thesis and the Superstructure Thesis. The disposition of a social institution to have functional consequences can legitimately be used as part of the explanation of why it exists. Here there is no serious dispute. Controversy arises, however, about whether such a consequence argument can be a sufficient explanation. Is it necessary to show exactly how an institution's disposition to have functional consequences expedites its existence? Cohen argues it is not always necessary to give such an account, provided one can be certain that a satisfactory account exists. The critics say that a consequence argument alone cannot be a sufficient explanation of why a social institution exists. If that were permissible, the mere presence of an institution would be sufficient to explain all the social conditions necessary for its existence.

Cohen tries to explain how functional relationships come into being. He does not give anything like a systematic account and admits to not knowing how productive forces acquire economic structures that promote their development, but he does identify three general ways a functional relationship can occur: purposive, Darwinian, and Lamarckian. The purposive way rests upon the rationality of people with power. Decision makers recognize that an institution would have functional consequences and act to implement it. The Darwinian way of establishing a functional relationship derives from a process of historical selection. A variety of institutional structures arise, and, through the trial of history, the most successful variant is selected. In the Lamarckian method, social conflict causes an institution to undergo adaptive change, ultimately resulting in a functional relationship between the institution and society. Cohen's discussion of these three methods does not answer the objections to functional explanations, but it does suggest ways of elaborating the latter to make them more satisfactory.

How does *class struggle* fit into these principles of historical development? Cohen does not dispute the classical Marxist dictum that history is the history of class struggle, which he interprets to mean that class struggle is the *immediate* driving force of history and the *immediate* explanation of social transformations. He even regards class struggle as the dominant factor in political affairs. But he considers neither politics nor class struggle to be the fundamental explanation of historical development. Class struggle happens all the time. In order to explain when class struggle succeeds in transforming society, one must examine the relationship between economic structure and forces of production.

When the economic structure is optimal for developing the forces of production, the ruling class is also the class best suited to superintend the growth of productive forces. Because everyone has a stake in thriving production, such a ruling class attracts allies and has little difficulty resisting challenges from exploited classes. If, on the other hand, economic structure hinders development of the productive forces, then the ruling class constitutes an economic burden to society, experiences difficulty attracting class allies, and proves vulnerable to challenges by insurgent movements based upon the exploited classes.

Levine and Wright (1980) criticize Cohen's version of historical materialism for disregarding the *capacity* of classes to accomplish social change. Cohen seems to think class interests determine class capacities, but this is clearly false because a class may have a strong interest in changing society but no corresponding capacity to bring the change about. Capitalism, Levine and Wright point out, gives workers a keen interest in attaining socialism, but it does not automatically develop their collective capacity to make a socialist transformation.

More generally, class capacity is vital to how an incompatibility between forces and relations of production will evolve. Unless a new potential ruling class with the capacity to organize development of the productive forces arises, the incompatibility will evolve into a condition of permanent stagnation (as happened in the Ming and Ch'ing dynasties of China) rather than spur any kind of social revolution.

Levine and Wright emphatically deny that class capacity can be explained entirely through the dynamics of productive forces. Productive forces are relevant, but class capacity also depends upon relations of production as well as superstructural considerations. If this is so, and if class capacity is indeed crucial to the rise and fall of economic structures, then Cohen's attribution of causal primacy to forces of production does not make much sense. Nor would it be sensible to relegate class struggle to a secondary rank of explanatory importance.

Stages of Historical Development

In the "Preface" to *A Contribution to the Critique of Political Economy* Marx writes: "No social formation ever perishes before all the productive forces for which there is room in it have developed; and new, higher relations of production never appear before the material conditions of their existence have matured in the womb of the old society itself" (Marx [1859] 1987, p. 263). Productive forces, this passage suggests, develop in a somewhat continuous fashion, but economic structures occur in discrete stages with definite ruptures between them. What are the major stages of historical development, and how do they correspond to the development of the productive forces? In the "Preface" Marx mentions "Asiatic, ancient, feudal, and modern bourgeois modes of production" as "progressive epochs in the economic formation of society" ([1859] 1987, p. 263). Elsewhere he or Engels sometimes identifies the principal stages of history slightly differently. The issue of *periodization*—and particularly the expected periodization of history after capitalism—has been rather difficult for modern Marxists to resolve.

In his technological interpretation of historical materialism Cohen (1978) makes *surplus production*—production beyond what is needed to reproduce the laboring class—the crucial measure of how developed the productive forces are. Productive capacity cannot advance rapidly unless surplus, which can be used to create new means of production, is reasonably large. Cohen identifies four successive levels of productive development: no surplus, some surplus, moderately high surplus, and massive surplus. A definite type of economic structure corresponds to each of these productive levels:

Level of Productive Development	*Corresponding Type of Economic Structure*
1. no surplus	1. preclass society
2. some surplus	2. precapitalist class society
3. moderately high surplus	3. capitalist society
4. massive surplus	4. postclass society

What is the logic behind this correspondence? Consider the first level of development: production without a surplus. If no economic surplus exists, then no group of people can avoid work by taking the excess production of others; there is no excess production to take. The absence of surplus thus prevents enduring relations of economic inequality, thereby inducing a nonclass society.

But without classes the development of productive forces cannot get very far. Classes are needed because advancement of the productive forces requires large amounts of labor, and productive labor is extremely onerous (at least until the forces of production become highly developed and a huge surplus is available). Human beings would not voluntarily impose such burdens upon themselves; therefore the productive forces can advance only if a class of nonworkers emerges that is able to impose arduous labor upon other people and able to appropriate their surplus production.

This argument might explain why classes emerge in Development Levels 2 and 3, but it does not explain why low and moderate amounts of surplus should engender different class structures. Capitalism, claims Cohen, cannot endure in a low-surplus environment, and precapitalist class structures such as slavery and serfdom are difficult to reconcile with advanced productive forces. Capitalism is based upon competition between productive units, which requires continual accumulation of capital. Continual accumulation requires large and continuing investment, which cannot occur unless surplus exists in substantial and regularly available amounts.

Precapitalist class structures rely upon noneconomic means of extracting surplus from the direct producers: sometimes naked coercion. This devalues human labor and reduces the motivation of servile workers to acquire the skills needed in advanced production methods. The use of coercive means for extracting surplus labor also increases the likelihood that complex production equipment—if any such equipment exists—will depreciate rapidly. Moreover, the intense coordination of labor demanded by advanced production methods encourages political organization of the subordinate class and induces frequent rebellion against a condition of blatant servility. For all these reasons, economic structures based upon serfdom and slavery are not suitable for developing forces of production beyond a very rudimentary level.

The extraction of surplus by noneconomic means is a characteristic shared by precapitalist class societies of various kinds (e.g., slave, feudal, bureaucratic empire). The Primacy Thesis implies that the differences between these precapitalist societies can be explained through variations in productive power, but Cohen questions whether this is really feasible. Inability to provide standard explanations for the differences between slave, feudal, and bureaucratic societies is a minor embarrassment to historical materialism, but Cohen does not want to make insupportable theoretical claims.[2]

Note that many of the arguments discussed in this section are based upon functional reasoning but have a counterfunctional form. They explain why a particular economic structure would not develop productive forces if these forces stood at a particular level, or why the structure could not reproduce itself given such productive forces. The conclusion is that this economic structure and these productive forces could not coexist for long. Such reasoning is highly vulnerable to the "class capacity" criticism leveled by Levine and Wright (1980). For example, it is not enough to establish that productive forces cannot develop in the absence of class structure. To explain the emergence of class inequality, one must also demonstrate the existence of a group with both the capacity and the motivation to create a class structure.

This functional and structuralist reasoning also fails the test of methodological individualism. Arguments couched exclusively in terms of social aggregates can be theoretically suggestive but are never conclusive. To establish the desired correspondence between level of development and economic structure, one must show how *individual people* are systematically induced to sustain economic structures when they enhance productivity, but to transform them when they hinder the growth of productivity.

There remains the question of why the most developed productive forces, which generate surplus in massive amounts, should beget a postclass society (i.e., socialism). Why doesn't capitalism accommodate indefinite development of the productive forces? We postpone full discussion of this issue until the next section, but a few remarks are needed here.

Throughout its history the capitalist system experiences economic crises of various kinds. Although the forces of production remain underdeveloped, these crises are eventually overcome because no real alternative to capitalism exists: a class society is mandatory to advance the productive forces, and no other class society advances these forces nearly so energetically as capitalism. But the situation changes when economic productivity approaches a level rendering socialism feasible: class division is no longer imperative because labor need not be severely burdensome. Now the crises of capitalism encounter a working class increasingly aware that an alternative system with qualitatively greater freedom for working people is possible. The survival of capitalism is no longer assured. Eventually the working class will acquire sufficient consciousness and organization to abolish the capitalist economic system.

> Marx was not a breakdown theorist, but he did hold that, once capitalism is fully formed, then each crisis it undergoes is worse than its predecessor. . . . It follows that the more severe a crisis is, the more developed are the forces whose progress it arrests. Therefore socialism grows more and more feasible as crises get worse and worse. . . . There is no economically legislated final breakdown, but what is *de facto* the last depression occurs when there is a downturn in the cycle *and* the forces are ready to accept a socialist structure *and* the proletariat is sufficiently class conscious and organized. (Cohen 1978, pp. 203-4)

This analysis does not derive the demise of capitalism from inability to develop the forces of production. Developmental liabilities appear only to the extent that capitalism experiences continuing crises. Capitalism falls because an economic structure more appealing to the working class appears on the horizon. The argument contains four critical assumptions, which are considered in various parts of this book: (a) capitalism will experience economic crises (and they may become more severe as the capitalist system matures); (b) a nonclass society (i.e., socialism) becomes feasible due to the growth of productivity accomplished by capitalism; (c) workers increasingly comprehend the feasibility of socialism and increasingly desire its realization; and (d) the working class has the ability to implement socialism.

Contradictions of Capitalism

> A *contradiction* obtains when a society's economic organization frustrates the optimal use and development of its accumulated productive power, when prospects opened by its productive forces are closed by its production relations. . . . No connection is intended between our use of it and the meaning it has in logic. (Cohen 1978, p. 297)

All Marxists are keenly interested in the contradictions of capitalism because the prospects for socialism hinge upon the crises experienced by capitalist society. Analytical Marxists have studied the contradictions of capitalism, but they do not present a unified theory on this subject. Their contributions have been (a) lucid reformulation of classical Marxist ideas about capitalist contradictions, adjusting for the special features of contemporary capitalism; (b) investigation of the logical validity of Marxist claims about capitalist crises; and (c) explication of the conditions under which specific crises occur. We shall discuss examples of Analytical Marxist work from each of these three domains.

Output Expansion Bias

Gerald Cohen's contribution to the analysis of capitalist contradictions fits in category (a). Capitalists initiate production with the object of turning a profit, whereas workers participate in order to earn a wage. Making useful things is the main purpose of neither capitalists nor workers. Thus exchange value supplants use value as the regulator of production and the main object of human desire under capitalism. What Cohen sees as the distinctive contradiction of advanced capitalism arises from the tension between use value and exchange value.

The highly developed production forces available under advanced capitalism make possible either the expansion of output or the reduction of toil. Due to relentless competition and the struggle for profit, capitalism can only promote the expansion of output, even though toil reduction would definitely contribute more to individual satisfaction and collective welfare. A balanced human existence and a genuine experience of abundance requires reduction of toil, but this capitalism—incorrigibly lured by the carrot of profit and driven by the stick of competition—cannot accomplish.

The need to stimulate effective demand compels capitalism to promote irrational consumption—irrational in the double sense of failing to give appropriate satisfaction and exhausting nonrenewable resources. Moreover, the output expansion bias of capitalism has disastrous ecological consequences, the full extent of which is difficult to evaluate. Bias toward output expansion is not a contingent characteristic of capitalist society but an integral part of its basic nature. It cannot be eliminated by reforms that preserve the capitalist economic structure. Abolishing the output expansion bias of capitalism requires abolishing capitalism itself.

Suppose advanced capitalism is indeed biased toward output expansion when toil reduction would yield more social welfare. Is this a contradiction in the sense indicated above? Granted, advanced capitalism's use of accumulated productive power does not maximize collective welfare, but is it optimal for developing the forces of production? Surely output expansion does not inherently hinder the growth of productivity. On the contrary, it is quite likely to stimulate such growth. The only part of Cohen's argument that suggests less than maximum productivity growth is his brief comments about the ecological consequences of advanced capitalism. These remarks do not depict any constraints upon development of productive forces; they merely point toward the unfortunate results that such development would have.

Nor does Cohen's output expansion contradiction establish a plausible basis for the elimination of capitalism. Uncontrolled output expansion is not a structural barrier to the reproduction of capitalist institutions. Although strenuous protests by limited groups may burst out sporadically, the alleged contradiction fails to engender systematic opposition from any well-defined class of capitalist society. The proconsumption consciousness induced by capitalist social relations would seem to make the perpetual output expansion a thoroughly popular situation. It is not evident how the output expansion contradiction can exercise the transformative role required of it by Cohen's technological interpretation of historical materialism. It is not evident that it would cause a crisis of any sort.

The Falling Rate of Profit

Now consider a different sort of contribution that Analytical Marxism has made toward our understanding of contradictions: exploring the logical validity of various theories about capitalist crises.

Perhaps the most important crisis theory in classical Marxism is that based on the idea of a *falling rate of profit*. Profit is the main incentive to the owners of capital, and also the main regulator of the capitalist economic system. If the rate of profit has a irrepressible tendency to decline, then the capitalist economy will frequently malfunction and ultimately collapse. Marx and Engels, basing their reasoning on the labor theory of value, concluded that the rate of profit did have a tendency to decline. This tendency came from technical changes imposed on capitalists by competition. Profits, reasoned the founders of Marxism, came from the exploitation of living labor. Competition, however, forced capitalists to replace living labor with machines, thus expunging the real source of profits and establishing a tendency toward a falling profit rate.

John Roemer devotes three chapters of *Analytical Foundations of Marxist Economic Theory* to mathematical exploration of the falling rate of profit theory (Roemer 1981, pp. 87-145). This book greatly extends a result originally proved by the Japanese economist Okishio (1961). Roemer starts with the simplest possible model of economic production, which posits a linear relationship between inputs and outputs and no fixed capital.[3] He assumes that the real wages received by workers are fixed and that capitalists introduce new technologies only if they reduce production costs. Using the famous Frobenius-Perron

theorem on positive matrices, Roemer then compares the equilibrium profit rates that pertain before and after capitalists have
made cost-reducing changes in technology.

The mathematical results of this comparison are unequivocal:
there is no tendency toward a falling rate of profit. On the
contrary, under the assumptions made by Roemer, competitively
viable technical change (i.e., technical change that reduces
production costs) will always *raise* the rate of profit.

Roemer also gets several other pertinent results. He defines a
technical change to be socially desirable if the new technology
reduces the total amounts of labor needed to produce each and
every good in the economy. Using this definition, he shows that
there are technical changes that are socially desirable but that
capitalists will not introduce because they do not lower production costs. And it is possible to be even more specific about the
effect of technical change on the rate of profit. Suppose that a
new production technology uses more capital but less direct
labor than the existing technology. If this new technology is
competitively viable and thus introduced by capitalists, then it
will also be socially desirable in the sense specified above. On
the other hand, if the opposite situation holds—if the new production technology uses less capital but more direct labor than
the existing technology—then the new technology can be cost
saving (i.e., competitively viable) but not socially desirable.

While investigating the falling rate of profit theory for capitalist economies, Roemer arrives at some results pertaining to
partially planned economic systems (Roemer calls these systems
market socialism). Consider an economy in which central
planners choose the technology, but which otherwise is identical to the capitalist system we have discussed. Suppose the
central planners adopt only socially desirable technical changes.
In such a partially planned economy the rate of profit may indeed
fall.

Having obtained an impressive set of results under the assumption of a simple linear technology with no fixed capital, Roemer
proceeds to show that all the results discussed above remain true
in a more complex technological environment that allows fixed
capital and production of several different goods with the same
process.[4] A falling rate of profit theory, he concludes, is always

false in a competitive equilibrium environment with a constant real wage. If there is to be a falling rate of profit in such an economic environment, it must result from an increase in real wages or imposition of some other cost not included in these purely production models.

Elaborating on this last idea, Roemer suggests three ways in which the stringent assumptions of the models he has been using could be relaxed to allow a falling rate of profit: (a) models with changing real wages, (b) models with rising state expenditures, and (c) models with deteriorating terms of trade. Although models of these kinds can give rise to a falling rate of profit, Roemer does not think a theory of capitalist crisis should be premised upon the falling rate of profit concept:

> It would be a great fallacy to make a theory of the eventual demise of capitalism rest on *any* theory of the falling rate of profit. It is hoped that one effect of the argument presented here will be to rectify the "economist" position of many Marxists that socialism necessarily follows from capitalist crisis, which necessarily follows from the decline in the rate of profit. Social revolution depends on processes much more political and intricate than enter into the usual discussions of the falling rate of profit. (Roemer 1981, p. 109)

Roemer's analysis and the previous theoretical work from which it springs effectively demolish the claim that the profit rate falls as a routine consequence of the expansion of capital. However, the analysis also highlights a troublesome aspect of the model-building approach, a difficulty that Roemer alludes to when explaining the difference between theory and model. A theory, says Roemer, is a rather vague thing that lives mostly in the domain of intuition. Due to its inherent vagueness, one cannot generally determine whether a theory is true. Evaluating the theory requires constructing models that represent the theory schematically and allow rigorous derivations to be made. Unfortunately, a single theory can have many different models that point toward quite different conclusions. Therefore the results of model building often seem indecisive. The existence of contradictory models will, Roemer hopes, compel refinement of the underlying theory; but it could equally well induce long episodes of unproductive controversy.

Three Capitalist Crises

Having raised some doubts about the model-building enterprise, we now come to its defense by discussing some of the brilliant results model building can yield. Our purpose is to show how Analytical Marxism has explicated the conditions under which various kinds of capitalist crises can occur. Once again we turn to the work of John Roemer, who is the first Marxist to show that capitalist crises of three different kinds can be represented by a single model (Roemer 1981, pp. 177-98).

In addition to crises based upon the falling rate of profit, Marxists have considered several other varieties of capitalist economic crises. Three of the most frequently discussed are profit squeeze crises, realization crises (also called *underconsumption crises*), and fiscal crises. A *profit squeeze crisis* occurs because workers consume so much of the economic product that capitalists, who control investment, have insufficient incentive to accumulate. A *realization crisis* happens when the volume of production exceeds existing demand and inventories of unsold goods accumulate. It happens because the working class has limited buying power, whereas capitalists are not inclined to purchase all that they could. A *fiscal crisis* develops when taxation snatches so much capitalist profit that the incentive to accumulate collapses.

Within the Marxist literature these crises were usually treated as entirely separate phenomena, and arguments raged about which crisis would be the death angel of capitalism. John Roemer is able to show that all three crises can result from the very same economic process. I will not present all the elements of Roemer's ingenious model, only those that seem most relevant for a nontechnical understanding of its basic structure.

The crucial variable in Roemer's crisis model is the number of workers employed, or rather the employment rate. The key assumption is what Roemer calls the "class struggle equation," which asserts that the bargaining power of workers increases as the employment rate goes up. This assumption reflects the classical Marxist idea that the reserve army of the unemployed restrains working-class wages. But unemployed people do not simply disappear from society; the model assumes they are supported by the state at a minimal level through a tax upon profits. This places the capitalist class in a dilemma: if employment is very high, it will drive up wages and thus diminish profits; but if employment is very low, production will also be low, and profits will be heavily taxed to pay for unemployment benefits. Roemer also assumes that the desire of capitalists for economic growth varies directly with the after-tax rate of profit.

A capitalist economic crisis exists if the economy is not in equilibrium and if employment is decreasing. There prove to be three regions of capitalist economic crisis, each one defined in terms of the employment rate. At the very highest rates of employment, we have a profit squeeze crisis. At the very lowest rates of employment, there is a fiscal crisis. Somewhere in the middle is a region where a realization crisis occurs. These three regions of crisis do not touch each other; they are separated by intervening regions in which employment increases.

Unless they generate class-based political movements, the profit squeeze and realization crises will not of themselves overturn capitalism. Within Roemer's model each of these crises is self-correcting. The profit squeeze crisis corrects itself by decreasing employment, thereby increasing profits until an equilibrium is attained. The realization crisis corrects itself in a rather more surprising way. Employment decreases, reducing production, and taxes on profits increase to pay for welfare to the increasing pool of unemployed. Thus workers' consumption does not fall off as rapidly as production, and eventually the unwanted inventory of goods characteristic of the realization crisis is eliminated and equilibrium restored, though at a reduced profit rate.

The fiscal crisis is not self-correcting within Roemer's model. If taken literally, this formulation implies that employment goes to zero once a fiscal crisis takes hold. The model also leads us to expect two basic kinds of capitalist economy: a high-employment and relatively low-profit economy subject to profit squeeze crises, and a relatively low-employment and high-profit economy subject to crises of the realization variety.

This model of capitalist crises, critics will object, involves a tremendous simplification of an enormously complicated process, besides containing assumptions highly open to challenge. Fair enough; but Roemer's model also provides striking insights about the economic dynamics underlying various capitalist crises, and equally striking insights about the relationships between these crises. Anyone who struggles through the formidable mathematics is transported beyond the realm of easy intuition and emerges with a clearer image of the pathologies to which capitalist production is subject. To my way of thinking, this is no mean achievement.

Exploitation and History

No other Analytical Marxist has proposed a theory of history nearly as coherent and carefully elaborated as Gerald Cohen's. There are, however, other Analytical Marxist views on historical development that deserve attention. Some of these do not conflict with Cohen's interpretation but give the process of history a different emphasis. John Roemer, for example, accepts the main concepts of Cohen's technological rendition of historical materialism but focuses upon the evolution of exploitation (Roemer 1982a, pp. 194-237; 1988a, pp. 108-47). We shall discuss Roemer's ideas about exploitation at some length in the next two chapters, but it is useful to outline his general vision of history here.

As we shall see, Roemer defines exploitation in terms of *property relations*, and says that different forms of exploitation correspond to different property relations. For example, feudal property relations consist in rights over the labor power of other people, and *feudal exploitation* exists because these rights are unequally distributed. Capitalist property, on the other hand, includes only those means of production that are separable from the individual person (e.g., land, machines, patents), and *capitalist exploitation* arises when such alienable means of production are distributed unequally. Socialism abolishes capitalist property, but not all forms of property. Socialist property consists of ownership over one's individual productive skills, and *socialist exploitation* exists because such skills are unequally distributed and individuals can secure differential earnings from them.

Over the last two millennia, Roemer observes, the forms of productive property considered socially tolerable have steadily diminished. A feudal society tolerates feudal property, capitalist property, and socialist property (although feudal property is economically most important). A capitalist society tolerates both capitalist and socialist property. A socialist society allows only productive property of the socialist form. Roemer, like Cohen, attributes the steady elimination of property forms to the primacy of productive forces: in the last analysis, types of ownership disappear because they hinder development of economic productivity. But exploitation has an important hand in this process.

Because forms of exploitation correspond to forms of productive property, the elimination of a property type implies the elimination of the associated exploitation. Thus the broad sweep of history can be seen as the progressive elimination of exploitation in its various forms. Moreover, the reaction against a specific form of exploitation is often the dynamic factor in class struggles leading to the elimination of the associated property type.

Unfortunately, the elimination of exploitation categories may not signify a net reduction in exploitation. New property relations often drastically intensify forms of exploitation that existed previously but were not energetically practiced. Roemer also acknowledges that property and exploitation may exist in shapes that do not enter the abstract conception of an economic system. In principle, socialism has only socialist exploitation, but in practice all state socialist societies also exhibit what Roemer calls *status exploitation* based upon differential prestige and organizational position. The underlying theme of history may be the elimination of exploitation, but it is certainly not a linear parable of increasing betterment.

Nor should exploitation be conceived as an unmitigated evil. Roemer considers a form of exploitation as socially necessary if it is needed to develop the forces of production. For example, a specific form of exploitation might be needed to create effective economic incentives or stimulate technical change. Any form of exploitation, hypothesizes Roemer, can only have a temporary historical justification, but attempts to eliminate it prematurely can have disastrous consequences, as shown by the Chinese Cultural Revolution.

Erik Wright has elaborated the concept of history as the evolution of exploitation (Wright 1983, 1985). Wright accepts Roemer's definition of exploitation and, also like Roemer, specifies four kinds of property on which exploitation can be based: labor power, means of production, organizational assets, and skills. In addition to feudalism, capitalism, and socialism—the three societies that Roemer analyzes—Wright considers *statist* (i.e., state bureaucratic socialist) and *communist* social formations. Each of these five social formations can be characterized by the forms of property it allows and hence the types of exploitation that can occur within it. This establishes an orderly sequence of social formations, each one differing from the one before by allowing one less form of property. Statism falls between capitalism and socialism in this sequence, and communism comes after socialism. Table 2.1 depicts the relationship between exploitation and social formation postulated by Wright.

Movement from one type of social formation to another involves a revolutionary transformation abolishing a particular kind of exploitation. Development of the productive forces renders such a transformation feasible but not inevitable. As the productive forces mature within a particular social formation, the classes within it are thus faced by an achievable historic task that may or may not be accomplished, but whose increasing feasibility shapes the political content of class relations.

Given this conception, the natural course of historical development would seem to be from feudalism to capitalism to statism to socialism to communism. Wright takes pains to emphasize that this pattern of development is not an iron law and that stages can be skipped. For example, he thinks it possible to move directly from capitalism to socialism without an intervening statist period.

The collapse of Communist societies in recent years raises the possibility of reverse movement along this postulated historical sequence. This is something that Wright does not discuss, nor is it evident from the bare outlines of his scheme why it should happen. Two possibilities present themselves. Perhaps the forces of production were not sufficiently developed in the Communist societies to warrant abolition of private property in the means of production. If so, then capitalist exploitation was always socially necessary (in Roemer's terms), and the attempt to eliminate it must be regarded as ill conceived from the very start. Alternatively, state socialism might not be a stable social formation, as Wright's scheme implies, but a temporary expedient needed to accomplish the transition from feudalism to capitalism. This suggests that the evolution of exploitation is far more complicated than either Roemer or Wright recognizes. A form of exploitation might be temporarily abolished only to lay the basis for its subsequent reimposition with far greater intensity.

Table 2.1   Exploitation and Social Formation

Type of Social Formation	Exploitation-Generating Asset Inequality				Historic Task of Revolutionary Transformation
	Labor Power	Means of Production	Organization	Skill	
Feudalism	yes	yes	yes	yes	individual liberty
Capitalism	no	yes	yes	yes	socializing means of production
Statism	no	no	yes	yes	democratization of organizational control
Socialism	no	no	no	yes	substantive quality
Communism	no	no	no	no	self-actualization

SOURCE: Wright (1985), Table 4.1, p. 115

Wright has also proposed a fascinating reinterpretation of the role of class struggle in historical development. The essential class struggle in any mode of production is between the basic exploiting class and the basic class victimized by exploitation (e.g., between lords and serfs in the feudal mode of production). Classes exist, however, that occupy a contradictory or middle position because in some ways they are exploiters and in other ways they are victims of exploitation (e.g., the bourgeoisie under feudalism or managers under capitalism). The outcome of any revolutionary transformation resulting from class struggle between the exploiting and exploited classes is unlikely to be the triumph of the latter. It is far more probable, says Wright, that a class occupying a contradictory position in the former production mode will become the dominant exploiting class under the new economic system.

Under capitalism, managers and bureaucrats have a contradictory class location, being exploiters with respect to organizational assets but being exploited with respect to means of production. Wright thinks that state socialism (rather than real socialism) is likely to succeed capitalism precisely because managers and bureaucrats are well situated to become a new ruling class should capitalism fall. The elements of Wright's interpretation of class succession are presented in Table 2.2.

Table 2.2   Contending Classes and Contradictory Classes

Mode of Production	Basic Contending Classes	Principal Contradictory Classes
Feudalism	Lords and serfs	Bourgeoisie
Capitalism	Bourgeoisie and proletariat	Managers/bureaucrats
State socialism	Bureaucrats and workers	Intelligentsia/experts

SOURCE: Wright (1985), Table 3.4, p. 89

Another Version of Historical Development

Analytical Marxists often reconstruct concepts or theories found in the texts of classical Marxism. Jon Elster thinks modern interpretations of historical materialism draw excessively upon the "Preface" and neglect other writings of Marx and Engels. On the basis of a close reading of the *Grundrisse* (Marx 1973) and volume 3 of *Capital* (Marx [1894] 1981), Elster reconstructs an alternative cyclical periodization of history that he regards equally important in the work of Marx taken as a whole.

> In addition to the linear theory of modes of production, Marx offered a cyclical periodization of world history in terms of the changing purposes of productive activity. Production for immediate persistence turns into production for exchange, which in turn becomes production for surplus-value. After one run of this sequence, ending with slavery, serfdom marks the beginning of the second. Broadly speaking, the first run corresponds to the Asiatic and ancient modes of production, the second to feudalism and capitalism. This provides a rationale for the frequent comparisons in Marx's work between slavery and capitalism. . . . The dynamic element of this process is external and internal trade, neither class struggle nor the development of the productive forces. . . . Yet . . . it is no less central [to the work of Marx] than the better-known theory of the rise and fall of property right structures in accordance with their ability to promote the productive forces. (Elster 1985, pp. 316-17)

Elster criticizes Marx for not reconciling this cyclical periodization of history with his famous linear conception of production modes. The cyclical periodization, if we take it seriously, casts severe doubt on both the Development Thesis and the Primacy Thesis. How can productive forces have a monotonic tendency to develop if the basic pattern of history is cyclical and if enormous productive retrogressions, like that intervening between the end of one cycle and the beginning of the next, can occur? How can the level of the productive forces explain the economic structure if productive forces of similar maturity correspond to drastically different economic structures? For example, the production of surplus value gave rise to commercial slavery in the ancient world but to capitalism at the end of the feudal epoch.

How to cope with these difficulties is not entirely clear. One might question Elster's reconstruction of the cyclical periodization of history. He derives this mainly by examining Marx's historical discussion of the ancient world rather than from explicit theoretical statements. It is not evident that Marx wanted to postulate a definite theoretical pattern rather than merely comment upon some surprising but not causally relevant similarities between ancient and modern history. Alternatively, one might think that the cyclical periodization detected by Elster unfolds within the linear sequence and that the latter should be regarded as the dominant pattern. Then the second appearance of the cycle would not be a true repetition of the first but something like a faint reprise carried out at a substantially higher level of social development.

On the basis of the evidence Elster presents, it seems unwarranted to exclude class struggle from being a dynamic element of the historical process. Differences in the nature of class struggle appear closely associated with the different economic structures that emerged in ancient and feudal societies. If Marx intended to give trade equal status with class struggle as a dynamic of historical change, he surely would have said so. Instead he wrote numerous passages leading us to think otherwise. It is not evident, moreover, that any general theory of history can be constructed from Elster's cyclical reinterpretation of Marx.

Class Struggle as the Basis of Historical Development

An approach to the theory of history very different from that of either Cohen or Elster is taken by the Marxist economic historian Robert Brenner (1977, 1985a, 1985b, 1986). Brenner regards class struggle—not development of productive forces, or trade, or demographic change—as the prime mover of economic development: "[It] is the structure of class relations, of class power, which will determine the manner and degree to which particular demographic and commercial changes will affect long-term trends in the distribution of income and economic growth—and not vice versa" (Brenner 1985a, p. 11).

The basic causal sequence in economic life is the following: the form of property relations (i.e, the class structure of society) shapes the rules by which individual economic actors reproduce themselves, and these rules determine the long-term pattern of economic development (or nondevelopment). The economic institutions of society embody this causal sequence and, once established, are not easily altered. Disruptions of existing property relations may come from several quarters, but the most potent disrupting force is class struggle.

Brenner (1977, 1985a) thinks most theories of economic development, whether Marxist or non-Marxist, ascribe to the economic logic outlined by Adam Smith over two centuries ago. According to this logic, economic development is a direct consequence of individual rationality. Rational economic producers are characterized by the actions they reject as well as the actions they choose. Rational producers, in Brenner's interpretation of Smith, will (a) maximize the exchange value of what they produce (rather than producing all their own subsistence needs); (b) market their entire output (rather than marketing only their surplus production); (c) steadily improve their production capacity (rather than improving their capacity to get things by force); and (d) implement their rational choices and reap the resulting economic rewards (rather than capitulating to noneconomic constraints). But these actions, argues Brenner, do not reflect any general economic rationality; they only reflect the very specific economic rationality of capitalism. Adam Smith's economic logic assumes the existence of capitalist property relations and thus cannot explain why capitalist relations arise in the first place.

Economic agents do tend to be rational actors, Brenner believes, but the nature of economic rationality depends upon what property relations exist. Rational actors in precapitalist societies must behave very differently from rational actors under capitalism. Brenner's approach to economic development rests upon six fundamental theses (Brenner 1986, pp. 25-26):

1. Only under specific property relations is it rational for economic agents to act in ways that generate economic growth.
2. During most of history, property relations motivated people to act in ways subverting economic growth.
3. Transitions from precapitalist to capitalist property relations rarely occur as a result of economically rational actions.
4. Rational class action in precapitalist economies usually maintains precapitalist property relations.
5. Modern economic growth requires a transition to capitalist property relations.
6. Transition to capitalist property relations is an unintended consequence. It usually results from conflict between precapitalist classes.

The distinctive features of economic rationality in precapitalist societies arise mainly because producers have direct access to their means of subsistence. Hence exploiters can appropriate a share of the economic product only by using extraeconomic coercion, which induces them to develop the means of coercion rather than the means of production. Nor are the producing classes in precapitalist societies, being subject to coercive expropriation, inclined to improve their productive facilities. Thus no systematic tendency to develop the forces of production exists prior to capitalism.

The continual expansion of productivity under capitalism results not from any particular technology or method of organization but from the systematic compulsion to reduce costs stemming from capitalist competition. Brenner uses this analysis to attack the technological interpretation of Marxism advocated by Cohen:

> [If] one believes . . . that the unprecedented productiveness of capitalism derives not from any particular productive force or technique, but is a consequence of the property relations themselves, it becomes just about impossible to see how the sort of argument Cohen makes for the primacy of the productive forces can be sustained. . . . [On] this premise, no particular advance in technique—no increase in the productive forces—is necessary to bring about either capitalist property relations or the tremendous

increases in productiveness associated with them. Thus, capitalism could appear at a point when no new techniques beyond those already available to the economic actors under feudalism had yet come into existence; in this case it would still yield a tremendous increase in productiveness. (Brenner 1986, p. 47n.)

To illustrate that class struggle and not the development of productive forces is the basic cause of economic change, Brenner presents a detailed account of how European capitalism emerged from feudal society (Brenner 1985a, 1985b). The gist of his argument is that European societies with similar economic structures developed in very different ways depending upon the outcome of class struggles within them.

Consider the disparate patterns of economic development found in England, France, and Europe east of the Elbe River. When the Black Plague struck Europe in 1349, the class structures and productive forces in these three regions were still quite similar. The plague reduced the population of Europe by a third, and intense class struggles between peasants and lords followed in many parts of the continent. Peasants in England and France were able to weaken and then eliminate serfdom. In Eastern Europe, however, the landed class successfully imposed an expanded and intensified form of serfdom on the peasant population, with drastic consequences for economic development: "[The] newly emergent structure of class relations in the east had as its outcome the 'development of underdevelopment,' the preclusion of increased productivity in general, and of industrialization in particular. . . . [The] possibility of balanced economic growth was destroyed and eastern Europe consigned to backwardness for centuries" (Brenner 1985a, p. 45).

Yet the elimination of serfdom in England and France did not guarantee the growth of capitalism in these countries. The possibility of capitalism depended upon the outcome of further class struggles. The English monarchy allied itself with the landlords, enabling them to overcome peasant opposition and gain possession of most arable land. This was leased in large chunks to capitalist farmers and ultimately led to successful capitalist development in England.

The French monarchy, however, sought to exploit the emancipated peasantry directly (through taxation) and therefore helped the peasant class resist the French nobility's attempts to

appropriate land. Thus small-scale technologically stagnant peasant property was preserved in France, and agrarian capitalism
could not emerge. This generated what Brenner describes as a
"dismal pattern of economic development": "Not only was there
a long-term failure of agricultural productivity, but a corresponding inability to develop the home market. Thus, ironically, the
most complete freedom and property rights for the rural population meant poverty and a self-perpetuating cycle of backwardness" (Brenner 1985a, p. 62).

Robert Brenner's class struggle interpretation of history presents a powerful challenge both to mainstream historians and to
the version of historical materialism offered by Cohen. I place
Brenner within the realm of Analytical Marxism because he en-
gages in careful theory construction and tries to interpret historical action as rationally motivated. His class struggle conception
of history raises many questions. I shall mention only two.

Brenner's reasons for denying the relevance of Adam Smith's
economic logic to precapitalist societies are not entirely cogent.
As mentioned above, the principal reason why this logic seems
faulty is that precapitalist producers supposedly have direct access
to their means of subsistence. But if exploiters possess potent
means of coercion, what prevents them from expropriating the
producers, making them a propertyless labor force, and reaping
the gains of improved productivity? Something systematically prevents the exploiters from doing this in precapitalist societies. Could
it be that insufficient development of productive forces renders
exploiters unable or unmotivated to expropriate the producers?

This leads directly to my second point. The difference between the technological and class struggle interpretations of
historical materialism may not be as great as Brenner thinks.
Class struggle between lords and peasants about the continuation of serfdom could have been placed on the historical agenda
by the level of productive capacity attained. This itself might
sustain the Primacy Thesis even if productive forces did not
influence the outcome of the class struggle.

It turns out, however, that productive forces are not irrelevant
to the outcome of class struggle. In Brenner's detailed accounts
of how particular class struggles unfold, he makes extensive use
of arguments founded on productive forces.

Conclusion

Discussions of the theory of history by Analytical Marxists continue to revolve around *Karl Marx's Theory of History* by G. A. Cohen (1978). It is well known that Cohen's argument has serious flaws, and Cohen himself has expressed doubts about veracity of the position he so lucidly supported (Cohen 1988, pp. 132-79). But in its totality, Cohen's defense of a technological version of historical materialism remains impressive even to people who reject his major theoretical propositions. Nor is Cohen's credibility weakened by the recent collapse of Communist societies, for he repeatedly emphasizes the possibility of premature anticapitalist revolution: "No socialist revolution will succeed until 'capitalist production has already developed the productive forces of labor in general to a sufficiently high level.' Premature attempts at revolution, whatever their immediate outcome, will eventuate in a restoration of capitalist society" (Cohen 1978, p. 206).

Even sharp critics of *Karl Marx's Theory of History* sometimes make remarkable concessions to its theses. It is clear, for example, that the theory of history recently adumbrated by Erik Wright owes a great deal to Cohen's interpretation of historical materialism (Wright 1985, pp. 114-18). Given a little flexibility about the meaning of causation, Robert Brenner's class struggle conception of history may prove compatible with Cohen's account. Whatever its shortcomings, *Karl Marx's Theory of History* will remain the Marxist standard until someone produces an even more tightly reasoned theory of human history or until Marxists decide that general theories of history are useless endeavors.

Despite a number of valid criticisms, the Development Thesis has definite merit if one considers historical intervals of sufficient duration. Of course, it is not an iron law, and glaring exceptions exist. Nevertheless, historical evidence shows at least some development of productive forces in every major region of the world even prior to the advent of capitalism. The social and psychological mechanisms underlying the tendency of productive forces to develop—economic scarcity, disutility of labor, human rationality, the competitive advantage of more developed societies, and so forth—are often potent and unlikely to remain dormant indefinitely.

The Primacy Thesis is quite another matter. The functionalist reasoning used by Cohen to support the Primacy Thesis is simply not compelling. All claims about causal primacy, suggest Wright et al. (1992), should be reformulated as quantitative assertions of causal asymmetry. They recommend recasting the Primacy Thesis as three separate propositions:

1. Forces of production tend to destabilize relations of production.
2. Superstructure tends to reproduce existing relations of production.
3. Forces of production affect relations of production more power-fully than does the superstructure. (Wright et al. 1992, p. 159)

Although the meaning of causal primacy is often obscure, and although this reformulation may clarify the Primacy Thesis, the reformulation does not make the thesis any more plausible. We must now justify three separate propositions, none of which is self-evident. As matters now stand, there is little theoretical or empirical reason to think the Primacy Thesis is true.

Surely the most important part of the Marxist theory of history is the contention that capitalism is doomed and must, sooner or later, be replaced by another mode of production. This has been the heart of Marxist theory since 1848. Analytical Marxists have identified some fundamental and seemingly ineradicable pa-thologies in how capitalist societies function and have given much greater logical rigor to classical Marxist theories of capi-talist crisis. The work of Analytical Marxists has shown that the demise of capitalism is possible, but few if any think it is inevitable or even very likely within our own lifespan.

Proving that any mode of production is doomed may be an impossible task, but Analytical Marxism has made notable pro-gress toward building a viable Marxist theory of postcapitalist society. It has (a) challenged the utopian complacency that formerly paralyzed Marxist theorizing about postcapitalist socie-ties, (b) demonstrated that socialism is not the only conceivable future for capitalist social formations, and (c) provided rational explanations of why capitalism will not be the last exploitative form of social organization. The next chapter examines Analyti-cal Marxist theories of exploitation.

Notes

1. See the section "Class Struggle as the Basis of Historical Development" in this chapter for further discussion of these issues.

2. For further discussion of how Analytical Marxists conceptualize differences between precapitalist societies, see the sections on theoretical and historical subsistence economies in Chapter 3.

3. A model of this kind is called a *Leontief production system* or a *Leontief technology* after the Nobel-prizewinning economist Wassily Leontief.

4. This is called a *von Neumann technology* after the famous mathematician and founder of game theory John von Neumann.

3

EXPLOITATION

Conceptual Issues

The Concept of Exploitation

Exploitation is the concept most characteristic of Marxist social theory. It is also a concept that has been extensively discussed and reinterpreted by Analytical Marxists. Exploitation provides a means of describing and also of criticizing social relations. Thus it links Marxism as a positive theory of historical development with Marxism as a moral critique of society.

Exploitation signifies a particular kind of asymmetric relationship. Exploitation exists if one group of people (the *exploiters*) gains advantages from the activities of another group (the *exploited*), but the advantages gained are not reciprocal. The second group is in someway harmed, weakened, or deprived by the relationship. The crux of exploitation is the causal connection between the advantages of the exploiters and the disadvantages of the exploited.

Although exploitation can be considered a form of oppression, it differs from other forms of oppression because it occurs through the routine performance of useful activities when the benefits of these activities are distributed asymmetrically. Exploiters are not intrinsically hostile to the people they exploit. They do not want to injure, depress, or destroy the exploited because such actions disrupt the very relationship from which the exploiters benefit.

Classical Marxist theory traces exploitation to the appropria-tion of *surplus labor*, that is, labor over and above what is needed to reproduce the laborer plus the tools and materials used up in production. People from whom surplus labor is extracted are exploited, and people who commandeer surplus labor are exploiters.

Classical Marxist theory saw a deep connection between class and exploitation. Enduring class inequality rests upon exploita-tion, but the nature of that exploitation differs sharply from one economic system to another. One important difference lies in the means by which surplus labor is extracted from the laborer. In slave systems surplus labor is extracted through direct coer-cion of the slave, in feudal economies by a combination of coercion and ideology, and in capitalist economies by means of the labor market. Capitalist exploitation is so thoroughly con-cealed that most people living under capitalism, even the victims of exploitation, do not recognize it exists.

Another difference between types of exploitation lies in the economic form through which surplus labor is appropriated. Under slavery surplus labor is appropriated as a quantity of labor: the slave is compelled to perform a certain amount of labor for the master's benefit. Under feudalism surplus labor is appropriated as a useful product (e.g., grain or vegetables): the lord takes a certain share of what the serf has produced. Under capitalism surplus labor is appropriated through the sale of *labor power*: the capitalist buys labor power for less than she can produce using that labor power.

Understanding capitalist exploitation poses special problems. Because labor power under capitalism is distributed through a market and not by means of coercion, how can one group appropriate surplus labor from another? To answer this ques-tion, Marx used the *labor theory of value*. According to this theory, one unit of labor power should exchange for the money equivalent of the total labor required to produce it. But Marx showed that one unit of labor power can be produced by less than one unit of labor. Thus wages (the value of labor power) are less than the value of what labor power can produce, and this difference belongs to the capitalist who buys the labor power. Marx interpreted the difference between wages and the value of what labor power produces as the hidden key to capitalist exploitation.

Unfortunately, however, the labor theory of value is seriously flawed as an explanation of exchange in a capitalist economy (Robinson 1942; Sweezy 1942; Sraffa 1960; Meek 1973; Steedman 1977; Roemer 1981). This raises serious doubts about the adequacy of classical Marxist analysis of capitalist exploitation. Other problems with this analysis have also been noted. For example: How can we define exploitation if human beings have tremendously varying capacities to work, or if completely different kinds of labor power exist? Does exploitation have any meaning under complex production technologies where one process yields several different products, or where the efficiency of a production process depends heavily upon its scale of operation?

But the most troublesome questions concern the existence of exploitation in modern noncapitalist societies. Does exploitation exist in state socialist societies of the Soviet type? Does it exist in a genuinely socialist society? In a communist society? How should exploitation be defined in societies without private ownership of the means of production? Is it a political aberration or a necessary social development?

By far the most penetrating analysis of exploitation in many decades appears in three books by John Roemer: *A General Theory of Exploitation and Class* (1982a), *Value, Exploitation and Class* (1986b), and *Free to Lose* (1988a). Roemer applies the basic concepts of historical materialism to modern social and economic conditions in highly original ways. Like G. A. Cohen, he favors economic or materialist explanations over ones resting upon sociological or political premises. He tries to construct a general theory of exploitation, of which the traditional Marxist concept of exploitation and exploitation in state socialist societies are both special cases.

Roemer's ideas about exploitation have stirred up considerable controversy among Marxists. Most of this chapter and the next deal with his formulations. This chapter addresses basic conceptual issues such as what causes exploitation, how it should be modeled, and how exploitation functions in both subsistence and capitalist economies. Chapter 4 deals with relations between exploitation and other social concepts such as class, technology, and public ownership of productive facilities.

What Causes Exploitation?

In the first Chapter I discussed a simple two-person economy involving exchange of corn and berries between Norma and Murray. Following Roemer, I showed that Norma was an exploiter because she could work less than was socially necessary, and that Murray was exploited because he had to work more than was socially necessary. To dramatize this point, I showed that Norma would work more if she killed Murray and seized his resources, but Murray would labor less if he murdered Norma and confiscated her possessions.

This simple example illustrates two important points. Exploitation—at least exploitation measured in terms of the compulsion to work—is a social phenomenon. Some people (e.g., Norma) are able to work less precisely because other people (e.g., Murray) must work more. The production technology, together with the social relations between Norma and Murray, determines how long each one must labor. The example also shows that exploitation can occur in very simple economic situations with no labor market, no surplus production, and no accumulation of wealth. Norma is able to exploit Murray entirely through the exchange of consumer goods and merely because she owns more valuable resources than he does.

Exploitation is of interest primarily to Marxists. Other social scientists think exploitation does not exist, or is not very important, or is not a suitable subject for scholarly inquiry. Hence almost all discussion about the theory of exploitation takes place between Marxists. We currently have two broad explanations of why exploitation exists: the *point-of-production* interpretation and the *property relations* interpretation.

The point-of-production interpretation—which is also the classical Marxist view—locates the occurrence of exploitation at the physical site of production and roots its existence in the coercive social relations that permeate the production process. Capitalist exploitation concerns the extraction of labor from labor power: the primitive logic of capitalism is to pay workers little and make them work long and hard. According to the point-of-production interpretation, market exchange is peripheral to exploitation. The marketplace is a realm of illusion where a false equality between buyer and seller seems to prevail. Marketplace mirages must be shattered to reveal the underlying reality of exploitation.

The property relations interpretation of exploitation was first proposed by John Roemer and has subsequently been adopted by most Analytical Marxists. It attributes exploitation to differential ownership of productive property. Exploitation does indeed rest upon coercion, but the coercion it rests upon is that maintaining differential property ownership, not that occurring within the process of production itself. The Norma and Murray example favors the property relations interpretation because it shows how exploitation can arise from unequal possession of productive resources even without a coercive production process. Different kinds of productive property give rise to different kinds of exploitation: for example, unequal ownership of labor power creates *feudal exploitation*, unequal ownership of capital begets *capitalist exploitation*, and unequal ownership of productive skills establishes *socialist exploitation*.

Market exchange assumes enormous importance for the property relations outlook on exploitation. Setting aside slavery, serfdom, and other nonvoluntary means of extracting labor, market processes determine whether a person can convert ownership of productive property into an exploitative advantage. For example, if a commodity market exists, a person can often convert ownership of capital (defined here as alienable productive property) into exploitative advantage. The existence of a market enabled Norma to exploit Murray. Exploitation could not have occurred in this situation without the exchange of corn and berries.

But markets and differential ownership of capital do not guarantee the existence of exploitation. Suppose there is more capital but less available labor power than society needs. Under these conditions, ownership of capital will not enable a person to become an exploiter. The owners of capital will bid up the price of labor until wages absorb all surplus and no exploitation can happen.

An example may clarify the difference between the point-of-production and the property relations interpretations of exploitation. Consider a society of 300 corn producers who own equal amounts of productive property and want to work only the minimum necessary to feed themselves and reproduce their society. Each person must consume 2 bushels of corn per month, and each person owns 1 bushel of corn to be used for seed. Our hypothetical society has two available technologies for producing corn:

capital-intensive technology

> 1 bushel of corn + 5 days labor → 2 bushels of corn
> (i.e., 1 bushel of corn net)

labor-intensive technology

> 10 days labor → 1 bushel of corn

How can this society reproduce itself? Social reproduction can be accomplished in several different ways. Perhaps the simplest method has each producer working entirely independently. She works 5 days per month on the capital-intensive technology, using her 1 bushel of corn as seed and producing 2 bushels of corn as the gross output. One of these replaces the bushel used as seed, and the other is consumed. Because she owns just 1 bushel of corn, our producer cannot operate the capital-intensive technology more than 5 days per month. To get the remaining bushel of corn needed for consumption, she must work 10 days with the labor-intensive technology, which requires no initial corn input. Thus our self-sufficient producer works a total of 15 days per month, during which she produces 2 bushels of corn for consumption and 1 bushel to replace the seed corn. All 300 producers follow the same production schedule, and 15 days is clearly the socially necessary amount of time each person must work. We call this the *self-sufficient method of social reproduction.*

Consider a slightly more complicated way this society can reproduce itself. In this method, which is based upon wage labor, the society divides into a class of 200 employers and a class of 100 wage workers. Each wage worker labors 5 days on the capital-intensive technology using her own seed corn. During these 5 days, she replaces her seed corn and produces 1 bushel of corn for her own consumption. She is then hired for 5 days by each of two employers at a wage of 0.1 bushel per day. Our wage worker uses the capital-intensive technology plus the seed corn owned by her two employers. As a result of her labors she is able to replace all the seed corn used up, provide 0.5 bushel of corn for each employer's consumption, and earn a bushel of corn for herself. Thus each of the 100 wage workers secures her 2-bushel consumption requirement by laboring a total of 15 days: 5 days for herself and 10 days for her two employers.

Meanwhile each employer works 15 days on the labor-intensive technology, producing 1.5 bushels of corn for her own consumption. This, together with the 0.5 bushel the employer receives through the efforts of her employee, satisfies the 2-bushel consumption requirement. The employer, like the wage worker, labors a total of 15 days. In this two-class system featuring wage labor production, all consumption requirements are satisfied and initial seed stocks are replaced. Call this the *wage labor method of social reproduction.*

Does exploitation occur under either of these methods of social reproduction? According to the point-of-production interpretation, no exploitation occurs under the self-sufficient reproduction method because the individual producers are entirely autonomous: they do not endure coercive social relations while working, and their surplus labor is not appropriated by anyone else. The wage labor reproduction method, however, is quite a different story. Here the point-of-production outlook does find exploitation. The wage laborers suffer the authority of their employers, who appropriate their surplus labor.

The property relations approach sees things quite differently. The two methods of social reproduction are regarded as entirely equivalent, and exploitation occurs in neither one of them. Under both methods everyone works exactly the same amount, and all productive property is reproduced. The wage labor reproduction method does not enable one part of society to extract labor from another; it merely rearranges the aegis under which work is performed. If, as we have assumed, producers only care about feeding themselves and reproducing society with the minimum labor possible, they should be indifferent among functioning as wage laborers, employers, and independent producers within the two scenarios outlined above.

Models of Exploitation

Having discussed two explanations of why exploitation occurs and having clarified the differences between them, I now outline two attempts by John Roemer (1982a, 1988a) to model exploitation more precisely. I shall call these models *labor exploitation* and *comparative exploitation* respectively.

Labor exploitation is an attempt to generalize the idea that exploiters appropriate the surplus labor of the people they exploit. This idea is hard to use because often we cannot distinguish necessary from surplus labor or identify who appropriates labor from whom. To avoid these difficulties without totally abandoning the idea of labor appropriation, Roemer compares the amount of labor a person gives to society with the amount she receives in return. If a person, acting in the most rational way possible, unambiguously gives more labor to society than she receives in return, that person is exploited. Conversely, if a person clearly receives more labor than she gets, that person is an exploiter. And finally, if a person gives just as much labor as she gets, she is considered *exploitation neutral*.

Roemer sometimes refers to labor exploitation as *Marxist exploitation*. I resist this terminology because both models of exploitation proposed by Roemer have roots in the work of Marx and Engels. The labor exploitation model does not require specifying who is exploited by whom. Exploitation status derives from a person's position within the economy as a whole, not from her relationship to any particular others.

In order to use the labor exploitation model it is necessary to determine how much labor a person receives from society. This is taken to mean the amount of *labor embodied* in the goods a person is able to consume. Defining embodied labor can be difficult or impossible with complicated technologies but is relatively straightforward under many feasible methods of production.

The amount of labor embodied in a good is the sum of all the labor directly or indirectly expended on producing it. Consider the capital-intensive corn-producing technology discussed in the previous section. In that technology, 2.5 days of labor plus 0.5 bushels of corn are needed to produce 1 bushel of corn. Thus 2.5 days are directly expended in producing 1 bushel of corn.

But the production process also uses 0.5 bushels of corn as input, and (with the same technology) 1.25 days of labor plus 0.25 bushels of corn are required to produce this corn input. Continuing in this fashion, we are led to the following series of direct and indirect labor expenditures:

$$5/2 + 5/4 + 5/8 + \ldots = 5(1/2 + 1/4 + 1/8 + \ldots) = 5$$

Thus 5 days of labor are embodied in 1 bushel of corn under the capital-intensive technology.

Another way of thinking about the amount of labor embodied in a good is in terms of *net* production. The amount of labor embodied in a good equals the quantity of labor needed to produce it as a net product. To see how this works, recall our description of the capital-intensive technology for producing corn:

1 bushel of corn + 5 days labor → 2 bushels of corn
(i.e., 1 bushel of corn net)

Five days of labor plus 1 bushel of corn suffice to produce 2 bushels of corn. One of these bushels replaces the corn input, leaving 1 bushel of corn as the net product. We conclude that 5 days is the amount of labor embodied in 1 bushel of corn, which agrees with the computation made in the previous paragraph.

It is also possible to write equations for the labor embodied in various goods. These equations are based on the idea that the amount of labor embodied in a good equals the quantity of labor embodied in goods used to produce it plus the amount of labor expended directly in its production. As a simple example, consider the following technology for producing coal and iron:

3 tons coal + 1 ton iron + 5 days labor → 3 tons iron
1 ton coal + 1 ton iron + 7 days labor → 12 tons coal

The embodied labor equations for this technology are:

$$3c + i + 5 = 3i$$
$$c + i + 7 = 12c$$

where c is the labor embodied in a ton of coal and i is the labor embodied in a ton of iron. Solving these two simultaneous linear equations, we find that a ton of coal embodies 1 day of labor ($c = 1$) and a ton of iron embodies 4 days of labor ($i = 4$).

With more elaborate technology of this same general sort (i.e., Leontief technology), embodied labor is calculated by means of matrix algebra, but the underlying idea is exactly the same as in our coal and iron example.

We now turn to Roemer's second way of modeling exploitation, which I call *comparative exploitation*. This method is closely connected with the property relations interpretation of exploitation discussed in the previous section. It defines exploitation by comparing the distribution of income occurring under existing property relations with the distribution expected if a certain form of property were abolished. It identifies several different kinds of exploitation depending on the form of property abolished. A person who gains income through the abolition of a particular property form is exploited (in the manner corresponding to that property form), and a person losing income is an exploiter.

The comparative model of exploitation recognizes that several kinds of exploitation can exist simultaneously and are easily confounded with each other. Roemer considers three main forms of exploitation: feudal, capitalist, and socialist. According to classical versions of historical materialism, these forms of exploitation will be sequentially eliminated: first feudal exploitation, then capitalist exploitation, and finally socialist exploitation.

To determine the extent of *feudal exploitation,* we compare the existing income distribution with the distribution expected if feudal property were abolished: if everyone owned his or her own labor power or, more exactly, were entitled to the full earnings of all production factors actually in his or her possession. To measure *capitalist exploitation,* we compare the existing income distribution with the distribution expected if private ownership of capital were abolished. To measure *socialist exploitation,* we contrast the existing income distribution with the income distribution expected if socialist property were abolished: that is, if everyone had the same productive skills.

The tricky thing about the comparative exploitation model is determining the income distribution expected when a particular property form disappears. Roemer attacks this problem by considering a hypothetical coalition formation process. By this conception, any coalition of individuals can withdraw from the economy with its per capita share of the property in question and set up production on its own. If the coalition's joint income increases after withdrawing while the joint income of everyone else diminishes, then the members of the coalition are exploited under existing property relations.

The coalition crucial for analyzing a particular kind of exploitation is that consisting of all people who own less than the per capita share of the corresponding property. The income distribution resulting when this coalition withdraws with its proportional share of the property is also the distribution expected when the property form is abolished entirely.

The main advantages of this conceptualization are (a) emphasis on property relations as the heart of exploitation, (b) specification of the alternative to which a situation is compared when an exploitation claim is made, and (c) allowance for different types of exploitation, including ones not yet anticipated. When developed further, the comparative model leads to an analysis of exploitation based on game theory, which we discuss in the next chapter. Roemer's method of defining expected income distributions works reasonably well with constant return technologies but encounters nontrivial difficulties when confronting either increasing or decreasing return production technologies.

Exploitation in Subsistence Economies

The analysis of *subsistence economies* is valuable for its own sake but also because it clarifies the relationships between property, exploitation, and class. The relative simplicity of subsistence economies deepens our understanding of how property ownership induces exploitation and class division. It is by no means accidental that many illuminating theoretical examples concern subsistence economies.

The distinguishing characteristic of subsistence economies, as modeled by Roemer, is that producers try to minimize their labor rather than to maximize their income.[1] Because producers minimize their labor, no accumulation happens within subsistence economies, but both exploitation and class divisions can occur. A bundle of goods is specified as necessary for subsistence, and each person tries to work the least amount sufficient to acquire this subsistence bundle. If the length of time a person must work to get the subsistence bundle is less than she is physically able to work, then the subsistence economy has the capacity to produce a surplus.

Roemer's models of subsistence economies assume a Leontief technology. This is a relatively simple production technology that ignores fixed capital. It specifies only one process for producing a good and allows only one kind of good to result from each production process. A Leontief technology is a linear or constant return production method, which means that doubling all the inputs also doubles the output, halving all the inputs halves the output, and so on. A Leontief technology enables us to calculate the amount of labor embodied in each good, using methods like those outlined in the previous section. This defines the amount of labor embodied in the subsistence bundle, which turns out to be an important quantity. A society can reproduce itself economically only if a single producer can actually perform the amount of labor embodied in the subsistence bundle.

All the subsistence economies modeled by Roemer include a market in consumer goods. We shall examine three of Roemer's subsistence economies: *simple commodity production with communal ownership of production inputs* (SE1), *simple commodity production with private ownership of production inputs* (SE2), and *commodity production with private ownership of stocks and a labor market* (SE3). These three subsistence economies form a fascinating social progression: SE1 has neither exploitation nor class division, SE2 has exploitation but no class division, and SE3 has both exploitation and class division.

Each producer within each subsistence economy acts rationally. Each producer, that is, finds a way of acquiring the subsistence bundle with the least labor possible, given the material resources at her disposal and the available technology. Under SE1, with communal ownership of all production inputs, the main constraints are a person's capacity to work and her obligation to repay the community for the inputs used in production. Under SE2, with private ownership of stocks, an additional constraint appears: a producer must start with sufficient wealth to obtain the necessary production inputs. Under SE3, which adds a labor market, the constraints of SE2 still hold, but the decision problem becomes more complicated because a producer must decide not only what to produce but how much labor power to hire and sell.

How does society combine these individual decisions into a workable system enabling individuals to survive and also enabling the economy as a whole to perpetuate itself over time? Assuming that property relations and technology are not subject to change, the instruments used to forge a workable system are the prices of the commodities produced and the price of labor (if there is a labor market). To describe how this happens, Roemer introduces the concept of a reproducible solution, which means about the same thing as a price equilibrium. A *reproducible solution* is a set of market prices that (a) allow each person in the economy to solve her individual decision problem (i.e., to act rationally and survive), (b) enable society as a whole to reproduce its production stocks, (c) call forth economic activity requiring no more production inputs than society actually has available, and (if a labor market exists) (d) balance the labor power bought and sold.

Exploitation in a Subsistence Economy With Communal Ownership of Production Inputs

Consider SE1: a subsistence economy in which the community owns the material inputs needed to start production. In this economy each person borrows production inputs from the common stock. She uses these inputs to produce certain commodities, relying entirely upon her own labor and technologies available to everyone. The producer then sells the commodities she has produced, using the income to purchase the goods needed for subsistence and to repay—with no interest—the materials she borrowed from the common stock. All production decisions are guided by a wish to minimize the amount of work.

SE1 is important because it reveals the social consequences of the simplest possible market. The crucial feature of SE1 is that production inputs are obtained from the community. Thus a producer needs no private property to start production, and all technologies are available to everyone.

A reproducible solution in SE1 insures that the total economic product covers the subsistence needs of all producers and re-places all inputs used in production. Aggregate inputs borrowed at the outset of production cannot exceed what is available in the common stock.

Although SE1 is an extremely simple economy, it generates some interesting results. All prices in any reproducible solution must be proportional to the amount of labor embodied in a commodity. The much-criticized labor theory of value thus holds true in this elementary economy. Moreover, each producer works exactly the socially necessary labor time, that is, the labor time embodied in the subsistence bundle. Because everyone works the same amount, no exploitation occurs under this economic system.

Without more extensive private property, there is no basis for class differentiation. With communal ownership of production stocks and a work-minimizing consciousness, no producer gains an enduring advantage over the others. SE1 shows that a market can exist without creating social inequality. Despite the extreme simplicity of the SE1 economy, this idea is relevant to modern debates on the feasibility of market socialism (Bardham and Roemer 1993).

Exploitation in a Subsistence Economy With Private Ownership of Production Inputs

Things get much more complicated under SE2, where com-mon ownership is replaced by private ownership of production inputs. Whereas people in SE1 are functionally identical, pro-ducers in SE2 are sharply differentiated because they own differ-ent amounts of production inputs. There is, however, no labor market, and thus each person must work the production re-sources she owns with her individual labor. Before starting production, a person must obtain the necessary inputs. She does this by selling resources she owns but does not need and buying resources she needs but does not own. The value of the produc-tion inputs she ends up using cannot exceed the value of the inputs she already owns (i.e., her wealth).

Because producers in SE2 try to minimize the amount they work, they seek production activities requiring the least labor.

But not everyone can afford the inputs required by these production processes. Wealthy producers have a large range of production activities to choose from and choose capital-intensive activities. Poor people have little latitude of choice and are compelled to select labor-intensive activities. Even without a labor market, exploitation can occur in SE2 and correlates strongly with wealth when it does. Rich producers work less and poor producers work more than is socially necessary to produce subsistence. Because there is no labor market, even rich producers must do some work. The dynamics of exploitation in SE2 are illustrated by the Norma and Murray example given in Chapter 1.

In contrast to SE1, a range of different reproducible solutions are possible in SE2. Under certain circumstances, prices can be proportional to embodied labor times, as predicted by the labor theory of value. There proves to be a strong connection between such labor value pricing and exploitation. Labor value pricing occurs if and only if all producers work exactly the amount of time socially necessary, which is a necessary and sufficient condition for the absence of exploitation. Its association with equal work times suggests that labor value pricing is in some way fair pricing.

Different reproducible solutions can have divergent consequences for the organization of society. Roemer constructs a two-person SE2 economy with two different reproducible solutions. Under one of these solutions, Person A exploits Person B. Under the other solution, Person B exploits Person A.

This is an extremely important result deserving more attention than it has received. Roemer uses the example to argue that intrinsic capacity cannot explain why one person is able to exploit another. It also shows that property alone does not determine the nature of social hierarchy. The basis for radically different social hierarchies can slumber within a single property structure. Because social conflict often concerns the nature of social hierarchy, this has profound consequences for structural theories of social conflict. Social conflict deriving from the economic structure of society, the result suggests, can focus on which of several possible social hierarchies emerges rather than on changing the existence or distribution of property.

Exploitation exists in SE2 due to differential ownership of productive property and competitive markets. Its occurrence requires neither surplus production nor accumulation of wealth nor the sale of labor power. These findings clarify the social foundations of exploitation.

Because SE2 contains no labor market, everyone must work, even though some people must work less than others. Survival requires possession of some productive property; the society has no place for people who own nothing. All producers in SE2 relate to the means of production in the same way: they work for themselves. Thus a private ownership subsistence economy without a labor market lacks class division. Exploiters and exploited are certainly not equal, but they do have the same class location.

Exploitation in a Subsistence Economy
With a Labor Market

SE3 is SE2 with a labor market. It becomes possible to buy and sell labor power, and the introduction of a labor market changes many things. There are now three different ways of relating to the means of production: working for oneself (as in SE1 and SE2), working for someone else (i.e., selling labor power), or hiring other people to operate one's own production facilities (i.e., buying labor power). Each of these relationships defines a class position in the Marxist sense. Thus the introduction of a labor market induces a class structure in the subsistence economy. The motivation of producers is still working as little as possible, which is why SE3 remains a subsistence economy.

Why would a person in SE3 want to buy labor power? Only because it might reduce the amount the buyer must work. Because buyers of labor power are assumed to be rational, the wage rate cannot exceed the productivity of labor (the rate at which labor creates net value). If it did, the employer would gain nothing by hiring anyone. Because the wage rate cannot exceed the productivity of labor (and is usually less), why would a person want to sell labor power? Only because the seller lacks the wherewithal to initiate production on her own. Under most circumstances, a person with sufficient means could work less by operating her own production facilities or, better yet, by hiring other people to do so.

If a labor market penetrated an economy where everyone had enough wealth to produce his or her own subsistence, it would have no effect. No one would sell his or her labor power. This shows the importance of capital scarcity—or, more exactly, unequal distribution of capital—in maintaining the institution of wage labor.

Because everyone tries to minimize the amount he or she works, no surplus is produced in SE3. The net economic product exactly equals the total subsistence requirements of producers. The total quantity of labor performed exactly equals the quantity socially necessary to produce these subsistence requirements; but of course the amount of labor individuals perform is seldom equally distributed. A person who earns a living entirely by selling labor power—a pure proletarian—can never work less than the socially necessary labor time (and must usually work more). On the other hand, the wage rate in any reproducible solution must suffice to purchase the subsistence necessities.

Exploitation occurs in SE3 under all but a few special circumstances, and it has a remarkable connection with both wealth and class. Roemer (1982a) proves that the more wealth a person has, the less she must work. If the aggregate stocks available to society exceed the bare minimum required for reproduction, then the very existence of exploitation implies the existence of people who do not work at all: a class of pure capitalists. When the economy is at equilibrium (i.e., at a reproducible solution), each person in SE3 who buys labor power is an exploiter, and each person who sells labor power is exploited. Roemer calls this the *Class Exploitation Correspondence Principle* (CECP), and we say more about it later. This principle is regarded as a self-evident truth in classical Marxist theory, but it occurs as a theorem in Roemer's analysis of exploitation.

The *Fundamental Marxian Theorem*, mentioned in Chapter 1, also makes its first appearance under SE3. This theorem, first proved by Morishima (1973), states that the existence of exploitation and the possibility of positive profits are equivalent to each other: without exploitation positive profits cannot exist, and, conversely, if positive profits are possible then there must be exploitation. Although the theoretical significance of this theorem has been questioned, it remains a highly robust result true in accumulating economies and with sophisticated production technologies (Bowles and Gintis 1981).

The profit rate on capital also reveals some interesting differences between SE2 and SE3. When a labor market exists, as in SE3, the equilibrium profit rate is identical in all production sectors, and hence equilibrium prices prove to be the traditional Marxist prices of production. No rational producer will operate an industry yielding less than the maximum rate of profit. Finding herself within such an industry, a producer would immediately reinvest her capital into a maximum profit sector. Even if her wealth is not sufficient to provide subsistence through self employment and/or hiring others, a rational producer in SE3 will invest what capital she does have only in maximum profit industries while securing the rest of her subsistence through wage labor.

Without a labor market, the last option is not available in SE2. A person cannot invest her capital at the maximum profit rate and get her remaining subsistence requirements by selling labor power. She must find a production process she can operate and survive upon within the scope of her limited means, and this may require accepting a lower profit rate. Thus the rate of profit within SE2 need not be uniform over all industries.

Due to unequal profit rates, the self-employed producers of SE2 can be exploiters or they can be exploited. This raises questions about the exploitation status of self-employed producers in SE3. Are they exploiters? Are they exploited? Are they exploitation neutral? Exploring these issues will lead us to the more subtle aspects of the Class Exploitation Correspondence Principle.

The most important theoretical insight obtained from SE3 is the connection between class division and the appropriation of labor. The appropriation of labor can occur without the emergence of class division, as it did in SE2. However, class division cannot occur unless one group appropriates the labor of another. The absence of a labor market or any other means for transferring labor on a large scale means that labor appropriation remains quite limited in SE2. Even though the people of SE3 are still labor minimizers and not wealth accumulators, the appearance of a labor market allows both large-scale transfers of labor and the emergence of class structure.

Exploitation in Early Human
Subsistence Economies

Although Roemer studies exploitation in subsistence econo-mies almost entirely for the sake of conceptual clarification, it is useful to compare his models with evidence about real subsis-tence economies. Anthropologists identify four general types of subsistence economies in early human history: hunting and gathering, pastoral, horticultural (often partitioned into simple and intensive horticultural economies), and agrarian.[2] Property in early subsistence economies evolves slowly from communi-tarian toward private ownership. Technological advance, when it occurs, is more often induced by population pressure than by hopes of improving living standards.

Several major differences between Roemer's abstract models and real subsistence economies are immediately evident. In real subsistence economies almost all production is for use rather than exchange, and markets, when they do exist, encompass only a small share of total production. Exploitation, where it occurs, involves coercive extraction of surplus rather than any form of unequal exchange. Despite these dissimilarities, Roemer's models provide useful insights and suggestive comparisons.

Ninety-nine percent of the human species' time on earth has been spent in hunting and gathering societies. Many of these societies could produce an economic surplus but did not do so, probably because people saw no advantage in accumulating objects. Hunters and gatherers, like the actors in Roemer's subsistence models, choose to minimize labor rather than maxi-mize production.[3] Almost all property is owned by the commu-nity, and distribution of goods occurs without expectation of immediate or equivalent reciprocity. Males, who usually special-ize in hunting, tend to have higher status than females, who specialize in gathering, but there is no evidence of economic exploitation as understood by Roemer.

About 10,000 years ago a slow transition to agriculture began, first in the Middle East and then in East Asia and Central America. The earliest form of agricultural society was based upon slash and burn cultivation, extremely long fallow periods, and abun-dant land. Agricultural production required more labor than hunting and gathering, and social inequality also increased. But simple horticultural societies still lacked sytematic exploitation or anything resembling class division. The informal budget constraints to which members were subject derived from a rough equality of labor time, and thus simple horticultural economies—notwithstanding the absence of a market and price system—show affinities with Roemer's SE1.

Unambiguous economic exploitation arrives with the adoption of more advanced agricultural methods, including use of the hoe, soil fertilization, and shorter fallow periods. Such societies, of which Inca Peru and Aztec Mexico are examples, often spawn a hereditary division between chiefs and commoners, with chiefs supported by some form of economic tribute from commoners. This relationship is obviously exploitative in that chiefs exercise coercive political power while performing little or no mandatory labor. Yet chiefs and commoners remain connected by important kinship ties that constrain development of a full-blown class structure. Intensive horticultural societies resemble Roemer's SE2 in generating exploitation without clear-cut class distinctions.

Ancient Greece and Rome, Chou China, Mughal India, Ottoman Turkey, and medieval Europe are all examples of what anthropologists call agrarian economies. Agricultural technology has advanced over the horticultural level, and farming is conducted with plows, draft animals, extensive fertilization, elaborate irrigation systems, and continuous use of land. Agrarian society is sharply divided into a dominant class based upon control of land and a subordinate class of agricultural producers. The subordinate class must work much harder than did producers in earlier subsistence economies, and members are subject to various forms of coercion by their overlords. Markets exist in agrarian societies but do not touch all production. These societies can be compared with Roemer's SE3 because they generate both exploitation and class without having methodical accumulation.

Exploitation in a Capitalist Economy

In the models of subsistence economies, people are labor minimizers. Subsistence has no place in Roemer's models of capitalist economies; all producers are treated as income maximizers. Reproducing a capitalist economy—at least in theory—does not require that all producers get a subsistence minimum; it is only necessary that the outputs of production equal or exceed the necessary inputs.

Many of Roemer's models of capitalist economies retain the assumption of a Leontief production technology. Some of them, however, incorporate more complicated technologies such as von Neumann activity analysis technology, cone technology, or general convex technology. We examine the social consequences of more complex technologies in an appendix to Chapter 4, but here we continue to assume a Leontief technology.

Because there is no subsistence concept in a capitalist economy, we cannot define exploitation through the amount of labor socially necessary to produce a subsistence bundle. Capitalist economies require a revised definition of exploitation. Although different in its specific content, the definition Roemer uses continues to compare the labor a producer gives to society with the labor equivalent that person receives in return. A producer in a capitalist economy is exploited if she works longer than the amount of labor embodied in any bundle of goods she can afford to purchase. By the same token, a person is an exploiter if her income always commands more embodied labor than she worked. Exploitation under capitalism means an unambiguous imbalance in the amount of labor given and received.

By this definition there can be people who are neither exploited nor exploiters: people who can buy some bundles of goods embodying more labor and other bundles of goods embodying less labor than they give to society. For the same reason, there can also be capitalist economies with exploiters but no people who are exploited or, vice versa, economies with victims of exploitation but no exploiters.

Already in subsistence economies, the identification of exploiters and exploited depends upon the particular economic equilibrium that prevails.[4] Under Roemer's definition of capitalist exploitation, exploitation depends even more heavily on which reproducible solution is in effect. Every set of equilibrium prices induces a somewhat different exploitation structure because it alters the value of a person's possessions and the extent to which she must sell her labor power, and also because it changes the collections of goods obtainable with any given income level.

The association between exploitation and economic equilibrium raises several theoretical questions. Is there a plausible definition of exploitation that depends only on production technology and the distribution of real property among producers and that does not rely upon the reproducible solution? If more than one reproducible solution is feasible, how is a particular solution determined? Is it possible that determination of a reproducible solution occurs through a process of class struggle and that producers whose exploitation status rests upon the specific solution implemented have an important role in this class struggle?

In a capitalist economy, as in a subsistence economy with a labor market (SE3), prices at any reproducible solution must equalize the rate of profit over all sectors of the economy. Any sector with a less than maximum profit rate will not be operated by rational income-maximizing capitalists. With a zero profit rate there are neither exploiters nor exploited, but if the profit rate is greater than zero a close connection exists between wealth and exploitation in a capitalist economy. For any reproducible solution it is possible to specify two wealth levels, W_1 and W_2, such that a person is exploited if and only if her wealth is less than W_1, and a person is an exploiter if and only if her wealth exceeds W_2.

The Class Exploitation Correspondence Principle is true in capitalist societies. Every person in a labor-hiring class is an exploiter, and every person in a labor-selling class is exploited. The relationship between class and exploitation in capitalist economies does not hinge on the particular goods a person prefers, implying that subjective consumption preferences are irrelevant to the class-exploitation nexus. As we shall see, the principle holds not only for relatively simple Leontief technologies but also for highly sophisticated production technologies (provided they have constant returns).

According to Roemer's analysis, there exist three kinds of reproducible solutions in capitalist economies: solutions with positive profit and positive wage rates, solutions with zero wage and maximum profit rates, and solutions with zero profit and positive wage rates. Which of these three solution types arises depends upon the balance between the available capital stock and the available labor supply.

If there is an excess supply of labor—that is, if more labor is available than can be employed on existing capital stock—then the only reproducible solution combines a zero wage rate with maximum profits. On the other hand, if the supply of labor is insufficient—if less labor is available than can be employed on existing capital stock—then the only reproducible solution features a zero profit rate. If and only if available labor exactly equals what is required by existing capital, the reproducible solution will have both positive wage and positive profit rates. Yet the positive wage and positive profit solution is the only reasonable one. If this can only happen on the knife edge of exactly balanced labor and capital supplies, then something is wrong with Roemer's models.

Roemer's definition of a reproducible solution seems overly restrictive. Can this definition be relaxed without sacrificing the remarkable theorems Roemer is able to prove? Although Roemer has successfully relaunched the theory of exploitation, he has—perhaps fortunately—not solved every problem within it. This is one of the questions future theorists of exploitation must address.

Is Exploitation a Useful Concept?

Revitalizing and reinterpreting the concept of exploitation is surely one of the most notable achievements of Analytical Marxism. This being so, it behooves us to ask whether exploitation is a sufficiently useful concept to justify the revitalization effort and the complexity of the models used for its reinterpretation. In the next chapter we shall consider the merits of exploitation as a moral concept. Here we ponder its utility for acquiring positive knowledge.

The Marxist approach to social science involves a candid identification with the victims of social organization. This does not diminish the commitment of Marxists to scientific veracity, but it does compel them to specify the victims, the victimizers, and the extent of victimization. The theory of exploitation is an effort to address these issues; however, it is much more as well.

Exploitation, as indicated at the beginning of this chapter, is not the same as oppression, and it is not the same as victimization either. Victimization indicates who suffers. Exploitation suggests how a social order might be changed, and who the agents of change might be. This is why a deep connection between class and exploitation exists. Exploitation is a useless or even pernicious concept for social scientists who do not identify with victims and have little desire to change society. But exploitation, or some concept very much like it, is almost mandatory for a Marxist scholar.

Some critics claim that *exploitation* is merely a term of abuse adding nothing to our understanding of social situations (Dalton 1974). Use of the term, say the critics, is a matter of arbitrary definition, commanding no general agreement among scholars or anyone else.

The use of any theoretical concept is, in a certain sense, a matter of arbitrary definition. Yet the idea of exploitation is not a figment of the Marxist imagination. Most people recognize certain manifestations of exploitation. They would probably agree that the relationship between a toiling slave and a sedentary master is exploitative. There would be far less agreement about whether a propertyless worker in a capitalist industry experiences exploitation. Such agreement is not necessary to make exploitation a useful concept. To be a useful concept, exploitation should (a) be defined in a way that permits consistent usage, (b) correctly classify cases about which general agreement exists, and (c) suggest interesting and testable propositions. The Analytical Marxist concept of exploitation satisfies all these conditions.

As we have seen, Analytical Marxists define exploitation in terms of property. In fact one Analytical Marxist defines all of Marxism as "the consequences of forms of property for historical processes" (Przeworski 1985b, p. 380). Property exists in many different forms, and exploitation arises from unequal property distributions. *Exploitation* in the Analytical Marxist sense signifies the economic advantages and disadvantages to individuals resulting from an unequal property distribution.

The measurement of exploitation requires acceptance of a model specifying the consequences of an unequal property distribution. Constructing a reasonable model may present certain practical difficulties, but nothing about the inherent nature of the exploitation concept as understood by Analytical Marxists prevents empirical measurement. Computation of class exploitation statistics is no less feasible than computation of national income statistics.

Even without quantitative measures of exploitation, it is still possible to test propositions derived from exploitation theory. Consider the proposition that social evolution abolishes exploitation one form at a time. This proposition excludes certain social transformations such as direct transitions from feudalism to socialism or from capitalism to communism. By examining what transitions have actually occurred in history, the assertion can be tested without any quantitative measurements of exploitation.

Whatever else it may be, exploitation is a highly suggestive concept. The intellectual tension resulting from the concept's location on the boundary between positive science and moral critique is probably the source of its suggestiveness. By liberating the concept of exploitation from its integument within the labor theory of value and by proliferating concepts of forms of exploitation, Analytical Marxists have instigated a resurgence of exploitation theory some fruits of which are explored in the next chapter.

To illustrate the empirical fertility of the exploitation concept, I list below three testable propositions about exploitation culled from the Analytical Marxist literature:

- *Proposition A* (exploitation and opposition): Movements opposing a form of property are based upon the exploitation that property generates. People exploited from the distribution of that property are more likely to join an opposition movement. However, such movements may not include the poorest or most oppressed members of society.
- *Proposition B* (exploitation and political stability): Consider any form of exploitation prevalent within a society. Divide the members of society into three groups based on that exploitation: exploiting, exploited, and exploitation neutral (neither exploiting nor exploited). People in the exploitation-neutral group will show greater variability in their political beliefs and less stability over time in their political behavior than people in the exploited or exploiting groups.
- *Proposition C* (exploitation and the ruling class): Consider a transition from one form of social organization to another. The ruling class in the new social organization is not the class most fully exploited in the previous form of society. It is a class that formerly had a contradictory exploitation status: exploited on one dimension of exploitation but exploiting on another.

These propositions may or may not be true; yet their very existence emphasizes the subtlety, the flexibility, and therefore the utility of the exploitation concept.

Conclusion

Classical Marxist theory derived capitalist exploitation from the nature of the wage bargain: the capitalist pays the full value of labor power and gets the full value that labor can produce, the latter being considerably larger than the former. The validity of this argument depends upon the highly doubtful claim that value is created in proportion to the amount of labor expended. If this claim is rejected, the classical Marxist analysis of exploitation falls with it.

A major achievement of Analytical Marxism is showing that the existence of capitalist exploitation does not depend upon the labor theory of value. Exploitation occurs in any profit-oriented system of production whenever (a) ownership of capital is unequally distributed, (b) the use of capital for productive purposes requires that its owners receive a reward (i.e., profit exists), and (c) the price structure enables reproduction of the economy.

Nor is the Analytical Marxist concept of exploitation merely an arbitrary formulation. The logical properties of the concept closely match what classical Marxist theory (and intuition) leads us to expect from exploitation. For example, the existence of profit proves equivalent to the existence of exploitation, and exploitation status corresponds closely to class location. By connecting exploitation with inequality in the distribution of property, Analytical Marxists demystify the concept and render it suitable for fine-grained empirical investigation. It is scarcely possible to deny the existence of exploitation in the Analytical Marxist sense, although one might conclude it is not an important or a morally reprehensible phenomenon.

As we have seen, some kinks remain in the Analytical Marxist theory of exploitation, but these more or less inevitable flaws should not obscure the enormous theoretical advance that has been made. The kinks are not being ignored. Theoretical efforts to remove the defects and streamline the exploitation concept continue. Having discussed its conceptual foundations, we now explore connections between exploitation and other Marxist ideas.

Notes

1. Much of this section is based upon Chapters 1 and 2 in *A General Theory of Exploitation and Class* (Roemer 1982a).

2. This section is based upon Mark Cohen, *The Food Crisis in Prehistory* (1977); G. E. M. de Sainte Croix, *The Class Struggle in the Ancient Greek World* (1981); Gerhard Lenski, *Power and Privilege* (1966); Marshal Sahlins, *Stone Age Economics* (1972); and Stephen Sanderson, *Macrosociology* (1988).

3. Marshal Sahlins refers to hunting and gathering as the "original affluent society" (Sahlins 1972).

4. As I mentioned in the earlier section "Exploitation in a Subsistence Economy With Private Ownership of Production Inputs," Roemer constructs an example of a two-person SE2 economy in which Person A exploits Person B under one price equilibrium, but Person B exploits Person A under another. The generality of such radical turnabouts is not entirely certain (Roemer 1982a, pp. 44-47).

4

EXPLOITATION

Applications and Elaborations

Using the Concept of Exploitation

Exploitation, I have said, is the concept most characteristic of Marxist social theory, and one of the landmark achievements of Analytical Marxism is revitalizing the theory of exploitation. This revitalization has improved the logical rigor of exploitation theory but has also made the concept more subtle and perhaps more difficult to use. Understanding the meaning and power of modern exploitation theory requires doing some abstract thinking but is well worth the mental effort necessary.

I do not present a truly systematic exposition of the modern theory of exploitation. Such an exposition requires elaborate mathematical symbolism, and the interested reader should consult John Roemer's classic treatise *A General Theory of Exploitation and Class* (1982a).[1] Instead I offer a wide-ranging series of theoretical and historical examples of how exploitation theory can be used. I hope these examples will communicate the main ideas of modern exploitation theory as well as the main controversies surrounding it. I think they illustrate the intellectual breadth of the exploitation concept and its capacity to connect positive and normative domains of analysis.

This is a long and occasionally difficult chapter touching upon some of the most original contributions of Analytical Marxism. I have placed two sections—"Exploitation and Technology" and "Exploitation as a Conflict of Interests"—as appendices to the main body of the chapter. This is not because the topics covered in these sections are less important or more mathematical than others. But some of the concepts discussed therein are fairly abstract, and some of the examples used are rather intricate. Though subsequent chapters do not require familiarity with the two appendices, readers seeking a thorough understanding of the methods used by Analytical Marxists may want to study the material they contain.

Exploitation and the Collapse of the Roman Empire

A historical example may be a good place to start. Let us consider the role of exploitation in the collapse of the Roman Empire. This section is based upon Geoffrey de Sainte Croix's monumental work *The Class Struggle in the Ancient Greek World* (1981), which might be characterized as an analysis of exploitation in the Mediterranean basin over the 1,300 years between 700 B.C. and 650 A.D. This is surely the most sustained and detailed attempt ever made to understand the process of exploitation over a long historical period. In fact, the book could well have been called *Exploitation in the Ancient Greek World*.

Exploitation, as understood by de Sainte Croix, is closely connected with class and class struggle:

> *Class* (essentially a relationship) is the collective social expression of the fact of exploitation, the way in which exploitation is embodied in the social structure. By *exploitation* I mean the appropriation of part of the product of the labor of others. . . . I use the expression *class struggle* for the fundamental relationship between classes (and their respective individual members), involving essentially exploitation or resistance to it. (de Sainte Croix 1981, pp. 43-44)

Exploitation for de Sainte Croix (as for John Roemer) is based upon property relations. The most important form of property in the ancient Mediterranean world was land and control over unfree labor. The dominant class over the entire 13-century period surveyed was the class of large landowners. Unfree labor existed in three main forms: chattel slavery, serfdom, and debt bondage. Of these three forms, slavery was much the most significant because it yielded the largest surplus to the dominant class of landowners.

De Sainte Croix classifies Greece and Rome as slave societies not because most people were slaves—at least until the end of the third century most people were free peasants—but because the dominant class extracted surplus from direct producers mainly by means of slavery. He theorizes that "the most significant distinguishing feature of each 'mode of production' . . . is not so much *how the bulk of the labor of production is done*, as *how the dominant propertied classes*, controlling the conditions of production, *ensure the extraction of surplus* which makes their own leisured existence possible" [author's italics] (de Sainte Croix 1981, p. 52).

The explanation for the collapse of the Roman empire lies in the evolution of slavery and the increasing exploitation of the formerly free peasant population. While the Roman Empire was expanding, captured "barbarians" provided a plentiful and cheap supply of slaves. When the expansion slowed down and then stopped entirely, the external supply of slaves dried up and slaves had to be bred within the empire. The breeding of slaves was more costly to the landowning class and diminished the surplus it obtained from slave labor. This caused the propertied class to increase its exploitation of the free population.

During the first few centuries of the Christian era, land became increasingly concentrated in the possession of a few owners. This led to increasing impoverishment of the peasantry and its gradual reduction to a condition of serfdom or debt bondage. From the third century onward, pressure on the frontiers of the Roman Empire tended to increase, and the costs of defending the empire increased even more dramatically. These costs fell primarily upon the peasantry.

The outcome of these processes was a merciless exploitation of the great majority of people for the benefit of a few. Peasants suffering from this exploitation became increasingly indifferent to maintaining the imperial system and may even have welcomed the "barbarian" conquests.

[The] Roman political system (especially when Greek democracy had been wiped out) . . . facilitated a most intense and ultimately destructive economic exploitation of the great mass of the people, whether slave or free, and it made radical reform impossible. The

result was that the propertied class, the men of real wealth, who
had deliberately created this system for their own benefit, drained
the life-blood from their world and thus destroyed Graeco-Roman
civilization over a large part of the empire. . . . [The] causes of the
decline were above all economic and social. . . . [It] was precisely
the propertied class as such which in the long run monopolized
political power, with the definite purpose of maintaining and
increasing its share of the comparatively small surplus which could
be extracted from the primary producers. . . . The burden of
maintaining the imperial military and bureaucratic machine, and
the Church, in addition to a leisured class consisting mainly of
absentee landowners, fell primarily upon the peasantry, who formed
the great bulk of the population. . . . [The] merciless exploitation
of the peasants made many of them receive, if not with enthusiasm
at least with indifference, the barbarian invaders who might at
least be expected—vainly, as it turned out—to shatter the oppressive
imperial financial machine. (de Sainte Croix 1981, pp. 502-03)

Because Geoffrey de Sainte Croix has not defined himself as an
Analytical Marxist, why is his work emphasized in a book on that
subject? As already indicated, I interpret Analytical Marxism not
as an intellectual sect but as a broad and coherent tendency in
Marxist thought. Within Analytical Marxism I include not only
those who embrace the name but also scholars whose work
embodies the Analytical Marxist approach. De Sainte Croix's
research does exactly this in several different ways.

We have already discussed the centrality of exploitation within
de Sainte Croix's conceptual framework and the fundamental connection he makes between class and exploitation. Like John Roemer
and other Analytical Marxists, he links property with exploitation:
"In Marx's scheme of things, the *nature* and *quantity* of exploitation—*how*, and how *much*, one exploits and is exploited—are among
the decisive elements in fixing a man's position in the whole system
of property relations" [author's italics] (de Sainte Croix 1981, p. 58).

The connection with Analytical Marxism is even more direct.
De Sainte Croix knows the work of Gerald Cohen and seems to prefer
it over virtually any other recent Marxist scholarship (de Sainte
Croix 1981, pp. xi, 543, n. 13). Working independently and with
quite different objectives, he and Cohen stress some of the same
passages from the writings of Marx.

De Sainte Croix's general approach to historical explanation links
him with Analytical Marxism. He not only uses similar Marxist

categories like exploitation and class struggle but also strives for conceptual precision and tries to provide general explanations for historical events. De Sainte Croix has a remarkable command of modern sociological theory and defines himself as "a historian who tries also to be a sociologist" and whose "interest in my own society is a primary one" (p. 32). Though recognizing the inevitability of ideological bias, he still stresses the importance of objectivity and truthfulness:

> In reality each of us has an ideological approach to history, resulting in a particular historical methodology and set of general concepts, whether conscious or unconscious. . . . I feel much happier, in dealing with the history of the ancient Greek world, if I can legitimately make use of categories of social analysis which are not only *precise*, in the sense that I can define them, but also *general*, in the sense that they can be applied to the analysis of other human societies. Class, in my sense, is eminently such a category [author's italics]. (de Sainte Croix 1981, pp. 34-35)

One of the many affinities between de Sainte Croix and Analytical Marxism is joint recognition of a connection between imperialism and exploitation. The next section explores this connection.

Exploitation and Imperialism

Imperialism as a relation between nations bears much resemblance to exploitation as a relation between individual producers. Imperialism can be conceived as a form of domination enabling one nation to extract wealth from another. Whatever the origins of imperialist domination, routine imperialist extraction need not rely upon force. It can rest upon various social or economic characteristics that give one country structural advantages over another.

The idea that capitalist imperialism is an exploitative relationship founded upon a structural advantage a dominant country has over the country it imperializes has been elaborated by the Greek Marxist Arghiri Emmanuel (1972). Emmanuel's theory of unequal exchange explains how economic surplus can be systematically transferred from one country to another through ordinary trade.

Emmanuel's theory rests upon the premise that capital moves easily over national boundaries, but labor power does not. Due to the relative immobility of workers, equally productive labor can receive much higher wages in rich capitalist countries than in poor countries of the capitalist world. Hence much more surplus is generated in poor countries than in rich countries and, in the absence of international trade, would remain there.

The international mobility of capital, however, equalizes the rate of profit throughout the capitalist world. This happens mainly through the process of price formation. Equalizing the profit rate makes commodities produced in poor countries cheaper and commodities produced in rich countries more expensive than they otherwise would be. International trade occurs at these equal profit rate prices, and Emmanuel claims it constitutes a subtle but massive transfer of surplus from poor to rich countries. Thus international trade is both unequal exchange and exploitation.

Emmanuel thinks all social classes in rich capitalist countries benefit from unequal exchange and all classes in poor capitalist countries are harmed by it. He believes this undermines any material basis for international working-class solidarity.

Several writers have challenged the empirical adequacy of unequal exchange as a theory of imperialism (Gibson 1980). Emmanuel's analysis of exploitation through international trade uses the value categories of classical Marxism and therefore contains significant errors in logic (Schweickart 1991). The analogy between imperialism and exploitation has persisted, however, and has been explored in a logically consistent way by Analytical Marxists.

John Roemer bases his own analysis of unequal exchange not upon unequal wages but upon differences in per capita wealth across countries (Roemer 1982a, pp. 55-60; 1983). Roemer has proposed several models of imperialism through trade. The simplest of these uses SE2, a subsistence economy with private ownership of stocks, to represent unequal exchange. The actors in this model are countries rather than individual people. These countries are assumed to have differential wealth but access to the same production technology. There is international trade in commodities but no international markets for labor or capital. Roemer also assumes—not very realistically, he acknowledges—

that each country needs to obtain a common bundle of goods and functions as a labor minimizer.

Poor countries, it follows from these assumptions, work more than rich countries because they are compelled to use more labor-intensive technologies. This lopsided transfer of labor from poor to rich is the heart of unequal exchange and closely parallels exploitation as it occurs within a single country. Within the international division of labor, a country operates only a small number of production sectors, all of which are similar in capital intensity. Despite the absence of labor and capital markets, it is possible to calculate shadow wage and profit rates for each country participating in the international economy. Rich countries turn out to have lower profit rates but higher wages than poor countries. This finding—which matches the assumptions of Emmanuel's unequal exchange theory—happens because rich countries have relatively more capital and less labor than poor countries.

The SE2 model shows that imperialist extractions—like exploitation between classes—can result from optimizing behavior in market contexts without imposition of extraeconomic coercion. Roemer has also used models of accumulating economies to examine how economic imperialism can operate through labor and capital markets (Roemer 1983, 1988a, pp. 103-06). He establishes an imperialist equivalent of the Class Exploitation Correspondence Principle, demonstrating that per capita wealth, not total wealth, determines a country's position in the international exploitation hierarchy.

David Schweickart (1991) attempts to synthesize the models of unequal exchange proposed by Emmanuel and Roemer. Though recognizing the logical superiority of Roemer's formulation, Schweickart considers it less tractable than Emmanuel's model and incapable of addressing some important questions about imperialism such as the consequences of structurally enforced unequal wages. His synthesis, which is actually much closer to Emmanuel than Roemer, suggests "that First World workers do not exploit Third World workers" (p. 32). First World workers, it also suggests, contribute far less surplus than Third World workers but benefit from this surplus at least as much, a situation Schweickart regards as highly unfair.

Schweickart's synthesis eliminates some but not all the logical inconsistencies in Emmanuel's model. His exposition unfolds by way of example and does not prove general theorems about either exploitation or imperialism. This makes it hard to discern the necessary implications of the synthesis. Contrary to Schweickart's claim, it is quite possible to build a general equilibrium model that could analyze the unequal wage situation of central concern to Emmanuel and himself.

Class and Exploitation

One of the remarkable features of the models used by Roemer is that they make no assumptions about either class or exploitation. Both class position and exploitation status emerge endogenously through the rational action of economic agents. This happens because the individual agents are differentially equipped with productive resources, operate a commonly understood technology, and function within a specified institutional environment that provides differential economic rewards. In view of the endogenous appearance of both class and exploitation, it is surprising that such strong analytic connections exist between them.

As we have seen, Roemer defines class in the traditional Marxist way as relationship to the means of production. In commodity-producing economies with private ownership of productive resources and a labor market, a person can relate to the means of production in three distinct ways: she can use her own productive resources (relationship x), she can hire other people to operate her productive facilities (relationship y), or she can sell her labor power to someone else (relationship z). These three relationships are not mutually exclusive; combinations often occur. Using the above notation, a person's overall connection with the means of production—and hence her class position—can be represented by the vector (x,y,z), where each component indicates the time expended within the corresponding relationship. For example, the vector (10 hours, 0 hours, 30 hours) indicates the class position of a person who works 10 hours per week for herself and 30 hours per week as an employed worker (and does not hire anyone else to work for her).

In practice, however, Roemer adopts a simplified way of representing class position indicating only whether a producer has established a particular productive relationship. Thus x, y, or z is + if a producer has established that specific relationship and 0 if she has not. The vector (0,+,0) designates a person who hires others to operate her means of production exclusively, that is a pure capitalist. The vector (+,0,+) signifies a person who operates her own means of production and also sells her labor power, a semiproletarian.

It is vital to grasp the theoretical meaning of these class positions. The (x,y,z) vectors represent optimal solutions to the economic decision problems faced by producers who possess specific resources; they do not necessarily indicate what real people with these resources would actually do. For example, a very rich person with no need to sell her labor power may decide to work in a factory. Her class position does *not* thereby become (0,+,+) because this is not an optimal solution to her economic decision problem.

It turns out that a rational producer need never both buy the labor power of others and sell her own labor power in order to make optimal use of her economic resources. Thus some conceivable class positions are excluded by the logic of the model. Although eight possible combinations of pluses and zeros exist, if a person must do some productive activity (eliminating [0,0,0]) and if a rational producer never both buys and sells labor power (eliminating [+,+,+] and [0,+,+]), then only five logically consistent class positions can occur.

Consider a subsistence economy with a labor market (SE3), and recall that the producers here are labor minimizers. The class positions possible in this society are given in Table 4.1, along with two sets of class names appropriate for agricultural and industrial versions of SE3 respectively.

The order in which these five classes have been listed is by no means arbitrary. They are listed in order of ascending wealth: every member of a higher class earns more than every member of a lower class. And if the rate of profit is greater than zero, every member of a higher class works less than every member of a lower class.

The Class Exploitation Correspondence Principle (CECP) asserts that every member of a class that buys labor power is an exploiter, and every member of a class that sells labor power is exploited. Thus every pure capitalist (0,+,0) and every small

Table 4.1   Class Positions in a Subsistence Economy With a Labor
Market—Agricultural and Industrial Variations

Class Position (x,y,z)	Class Name in an Agricultural Society	Class Name in an Industrial Society
(0,+,0)	landlord	pure capitalist
(+,+,0)	rich peasant	small capitalist
(+,0,0)	middle peasant	petty bourgeois
(+,0,+)	poor peasant	semiproletarian
(0,0,+)	landless laborer	proletarian

SOURCE: Roemer (1988), Table 6.1, p. 76

capitalist (+,+,0) is an exploiter because these classes buy labor power, whereas every proletarian (0,0,+) and semiproletarian (+,0,+) is exploited because these classes sell labor power.[2] The exploitation status of the petty bourgeoisie (+,0,0) proves to be a little more complicated and is linked to the organic composition of capital, a concept used by Marx ([1987] 1977, [1884] 1981) in *Capital.*

With a Leontief technology,[3] the organic composition of capital is defined for every sector of production. It is simply the ratio of dead to living labor in that sector of production. More specifically, it is the ratio of (a) the labor embodied in the material inputs used in producing a particular good (dead labor) to (b) the direct labor used in the production of this good (living labor). The organic composition of capital in a production sector is determined by technology and does not depend on the particular economic equilibrium (or in Roemer's terms, the particular reproducible solution) in effect.

If the organic composition of capital is the same in all industries, then all members of the petty bourgeoisie have the same wealth and are neither exploiters nor exploited (i.e., they are exploitation neutral). However, if the organic composition of capital is unequal across industries, then members of the petty bourgeoisie can have a range of wealth and may be either exploiters, exploited, or exploitation neutral (Roemer 1982a, p. 79).

The CECP continues to hold in capitalist economies, where producers are income maximizers rather than labor minimizers and where the meaning of exploitation shifts accordingly. We should note, however, some significant changes. Because producers maximize income, the distinction between pure capitalists (0,+,0) and small capitalists (+,+,0) loses its meaning. Both groups merge into a single capitalist class represented as (+,+,0). Class membership in a capitalist economy is still determined by wealth, and the class hierarchy depicted in Table 4.1—truncated to accommodate a single capitalist class—continues to be a hierarchy of wealth. Now, however, there is no difference in how long members of different classes work. The income maximizers of theoretical capitalism all work to the limit of their capacity.

The CECP is highly robust. Even radical changes in our model of capitalism will not disrupt it. We have steadily assumed that every producer has the same capacity to work. Suppose not: suppose some people can work longer than others. The principle remains true under conditions of differential laboring capacity: people who buy labor power are exploiters and people who sell it are exploited (even when generously endowed with ability to work).

But differential laboring capacity does disrupt the relationships between wealth on the one hand and class and exploitation on the other: a person can have considerable wealth without being either a capitalist or an exploiter. With differential working capacity, no clear connection exists between wealth and exploitation.

The CECP plays a vital part in Roemer's theoretical thinking. Roemer accepts the validity of this principle and uses it as a guide for building appropriate theoretical models. Definitions or assumptions that allow derivation of the CECP are validated; definitions or assumptions that do not are found wanting. The fact that the CECP continues to hold in capitalist economies vindicates the revised definition of exploitation used when producers maximize income. As we discuss in Appendix 4.1, the CECP helps identify a plausible way of defining embodied labor for cone technologies.[4] Roemer fully recognizes the privileged place of the CECP in his thinking: "Although the formal version of the Class Exploitation Correspondence Principle emerges as a *theorem* of the model, in fact its epistemological role in our understanding is as a *postulate*. We seek a model which will make our postulated belief true" [author's italics] (Roemer 1982a, p. 152).

Does the privileged epistemological role of the CECP discredit Roemer's analysis of the relationship between class and exploitation? In no way. The distinctive characteristic of Marxist class analysis lies in the connection it establishes between exploitation and class position. A theory of class or exploitation that makes no such linkage should not be considered Marxist. But this does not mean a relationship between class and exploitation should be stipulated as an axiom. On the contrary, a theory that derives this relationship from plausible and elementary premises will be more enlightening, more general, and also more persuasive. Roemer's method helps construct models genuinely informative to those already inclined toward Marxism but also persuasive to people who simply seek enlightenment about class or exploitation.

Exploitation in Credit Economies

What is the source of exploitation in capitalist economies? In recent years this question has caused sharp debate among Marxist theorists. For many decades, the dominant view—indeed, virtually the only view among Marxists—was that capitalist exploitation originated in the sale and purchase of labor power. Since about 1980, however, Analytical Marxists, led by John Roemer, have vigorously challenged this position.

Class and exploitation, claims Roemer, derive from private ownership of productive resources and competitive markets. They do not require a labor market. To establish this vital point, he shows that both class and exploitation can arise in an economy with a credit market but no market for labor. To make the point even more emphatic, he shows that credit markets and labor markets are functionally equivalent in terms of their impact on class and exploitation (Roemer 1982a, p. 90).

Consider the nature of a purely credit economy. People owning capital in such an economy lend it for interest (rather than hiring labor), whereas people lacking access to productive facilities borrow capital (rather than working for wages). Three kinds of productive activity exist in a purely credit economy: producing with one's own resources, producing with borrowed resources, and lending resources for interest. As we shall see, borrowing resources in a credit economy is equivalent to selling labor power in a wage economy, whereas lending resources is equivalent to buying labor power.

To understand the functional equivalence of labor and credit markets, consider once again the corn-producing example discussed in Chapter 3 in the section "What Causes Exploitation?" That society contained 300 producers, each of whom consumed 2 bushels of corn per month and owned 1 bushel to be used as corn seed. As the reader may remember, the economy contained a capital-intensive and a labor-intensive technology with these characteristics:

capital-intensive technology

> 1 bushel of corn + 5 days labor → 2 bushels of corn
> (i.e., 1 bushel of corn net)

labor-intensive technology

> 10 days labor → 1 bushel of corn

Each person in this corn-producing economy owned 1 bushel of corn, and hence the socially necessary labor time was 15 days per month. To explore the relationship between labor markets and credit markets, we retain most features of this hypothetical economy, but we change the egalitarian property distribution so that ownership of property becomes highly concentrated. Specifically, we assume that 10 producers own 30 bushels of corn as capital stock and 290 producers own only their labor power.

Suppose a labor market exists. What patterns of class and exploitation emerge? The equilibrium wage will be exactly 1 bushel of corn for 10 days work. Any higher wage will be reduced by competition because capital is in short supply, and any lower wage will be refused because producers can always grow corn with the labor-intensive technology (yielding 1 bushel of corn for 10 days labor).

Using her 30 bushels of corn stock, each member of the capital-owning class can hire 15 workers for 10 days each. In that time each worker, using the capital-intensive technology and 2 bushels of corn seed provided by the owner, can produce 4 bushels of corn. Two of these bushels will replace the corn seed input, 1 bushel constitutes the worker's wage, and the remaining bushel goes to the owner as profit. Summing over the 15 workers she has hired, the owner gets 15 bushels profit on an investment of 30 bushels: a profit rate of 50% per month.

The 150 workers who sell their labor power (15 workers for each of 10 owners) must each work 10 more days with the labor-intensive technology to secure the 2 bushels per month subsistence requirement. Because they work independently for half the month, we label these people *semiproletarians* rather than pure proletarians. They work a total of 20 days per month, exactly the amount worked by the 140 propertyless people who rely entirely upon the labor-intensive technology and never enter the labor market (we label the latter *petty bourgeois*). The process of economic reproduction in this labor market economy is summarized in Table 4.2.

The pattern of exploitation in this labor market economy is entirely evident. The 290 producers without property—irrespective of whether they sell their labor power—are clearly exploited in that they work 20 days per month when only 15 days are socially necessary. The 10 members of the property-owning class are evidently exploiters in that they each receive a surplus of 15 bushels without working at all.

Now consider the same situation with a credit market instead of a labor market. In this credit economy, the owners of capital lend corn seed rather than hire labor. People without property, on the other hand, can either work with the labor-intensive technology or borrow corn seed from the capitalists—paying them the interest rate required—and work with the capitalintensive technology. Borrowing corn seed is the economic equivalent of selling labor power.

The equilibrium interest rate is easily seen to be 50% per month on loans of corn seed. Any lower rate of interest will be bid up by competition for scarce seed, and any higher rate will be refused due to the availability of the labor-intensive technology requiring no corn seed input. Suppose each of the 10 corn stock owners loans 2 bushels to each of 15 propertyless producers. With that loan, each of the 15 borrowers will be able to produce 4 bushels of corn (gross) with 10 days labor using the capital-intensive technology. Two of these 4 bushels replace the principal of the loan, 1 bushel pays the interest, and the remaining bushel belongs to the borrower. The latter must work an additional 10 days with the labor-intensive technology to secure

Table 4.2   Economic Reproduction in a Labor Market Subsistence
Economy

A. *Pure capitalist class*—owners of capital (10 people owning 30 bushels of corn
each)

 1. Each owner offers wages of 1 bushel of corn for 10 days labor.
 2. Each owner buys 150 days of labor power.

    a. Hires 15 workers for 10 days each.

 3. Each owner uses 30 bushels of corn and 150 days of labor to operate the
    capital-intensive technology.
 4. Each owner produces 60 bushels of corn (gross).

    a. 30 bushels replace the corn used up in operating the capital-intensive
       technology.

    b. 15 bushels pay the workers.

    c. 15 bushels are surplus or capitalist profit.

 5. Each owner ends production period owning 45 bushels of corn (minus
    whatever she chooses to consume).

B. *Semiproletarian class*—part-time wage workers (150 people, each owning no
corn)

 1. Each worker sells 10 days of labor power to an owner for a wage of 1/10
    bushel per day.

    a. Each worker works 10 days on the capital-intensive technology, for
       which she receives a total of 1 bushel of corn.

 2. Each worker also labors independently for 10 days on the labor-intensive
    technology, producing 1 bushel of corn (net).
 3. Each semiproletarian labors a total of 20 days during the production period
    (10 as a wage worker and 10 as an independent producer). During that
    time she satisfies her consumption requirements but owns no corn at the
    end of the period.

C. *Petty bourgeois class*—independent producers (140 people, each owning no
corn)

 1. Each independent producer works 20 days on the labor-intensive technol-
    ogy, producing 2 bushels of corn (net).
 2. Each independent producer labors a total of 20 days during the production
    period. During that time she satisfies her consumption requirements but
    owns no corn at the end of the period.

---

the required 2 bushels of consumption. From the interest payments of the 15 borrowers, each property owner gains a total of
15 bushels in addition to replenishing her capital stock.

The remaining 140 propertyless people work 20 days using
the labor-intensive technology to produce the 2 bushels of corn

Table 4.3   Economic Reproduction in a Credit Market Subsistence
Economy

A. *Pure capitalist class*–owners of capital (10 people owning 30 bushels of corn each)

   1. Each owner offers to loan corn at an interest rate of 50% per production period.
   2. Each owner loans 30 bushels of corn.
      a. 2 bushels are loaned to each of 15 borrowers.
   3. At harvest time the owner receives payments totaling 45 bushels of corn (3 bushels from each of the 15 borrowers).
      a. 30 bushels replace the corn originally loaned.
      b. 15 bushels constitute interest.
   4. Each owner ends production period owning 45 bushels of corn (minus whatever she chooses to consume).

B. *Mixed borrowing class*–producers using borrowed capital part of the time (150 people, each owning no corn)

   1. Each producer borrows 2 bushels of corn at a 50% interest rate.
   2. Each producer uses the 2 bushels she has borrowed to operate the capital-intensive technology. She works 10 days with this technology, producing 4 bushels of corn (gross).
      a. 2 bushels replace the corn she has borrowed.
      b. 1 bushel pays interest on the loan.
      c. 1 bushel belongs to the producer.
   3. Each producer also works for 10 days with the labor-intensive technology, producing 1 bushel of corn (net).
   4. Each mixed borrower labors a total of 20 days during the production period (10 with borrowed capital on the capital-intensive technology, and 10 using only her own labor power on the labor-intensive technology). During that time she satisfies her consumption requirements but owns no corn at the end of the period.

C. *Petty bourgeois class*–nonborrowers (140 people, each owning no corn)

   1. Each nonborrower works 20 days on the labor-intensive technology, producing 2 bushels of corn (net).
   2. Each nonborrower labors a total of 20 days during the production period. During that time she satisfies her consumption requirements but owns no corn at the end of the period.

---

needed for consumption. Table 4.3 summarizes economic reproduction in this credit market economy.

Compare Table 4.3 with Table 4.2. The class structure in the credit economy exactly parallels the class structure in the corresponding labor market economy. The 10 credit givers, like the 10 labor power buyers, earn 15 bushels of corn and do not work at all. The 150 propertyless credit takers, like the 150 semiprole-tarians, earn 2 bushels for 20 days work. The 140 members of the petty bourgeois class are identical in income and productive activity in both economies. Thus each person in the credit market economy works precisely as long and earns precisely as much as her counterpart in the labor market economy.

Clearly, the structure of exploitation is identical in these two variations of the corn-producing economy. Capitalist exploita-tion, it follows, does not require the purchase of labor power.

To make this analysis a little more general, suppose we replace the labor market in SE3 with a credit market and label the resulting subsistence economy SE4. When producers in SE4 use their economic resources rationally to acquire a subsistence income while minimizing their labor, five classes emerge. The names of the five classes in SE4 appear in Table 4.4 along with the corresponding class names from SE3.[5]

All results proved in SE3 have direct analogs in SE4. Members of a higher class are wealthier and work less than members of lower class in the credit economy. The CECP asserts that all members of capital-loaning classes are exploiters and all mem-bers of capital-borrowing classes are exploited. A strong isomor-phism exists between the credit and labor market economies. For every reproducible solution in the labor market economy there is a corresponding reproducible solution in the credit economy such that all class and exploitation properties are pre-served: each producer works the same amount of time and belongs to the corresponding class in both economies (Roemer 1982a, p. 90).

Labor and credit markets are redundant within the models proposed by Roemer; if one exists the other is unnecessary. In terms of the abstract theory of class and exploitation, it does not matter whether labor hires capital or capital hires labor. Either way the rich exploit the poor.

If labor and credit markets are equivalent, why do some econo-mies hire labor whereas others extend credit? Credit markets historically emerge before labor markets and tend to represent an earlier phase of capitalist development. Credit markets are used, Roemer suggests, when producers know each other well

Table 4.4   Class Positions in Subsistence Economies With a Credit
Market (SE4) and With a Labor Market (SE3) Respectively

Class Position (x,y,z)	Class Name With Credit Market (SE4)	Class Name With Labor Market (SE3)
(0,+,0)	pure lender	pure capitalist
(+,+,0)	mixed lender	small capitalist
(+,0,0)	petty bourgeois	petty bourgeois
(+,0,+)	mixed borrower	semiproletarian
(0,0,+)	pure borrower	proletarian

SOURCE: Roemer (1982a), p. 88

and rely upon reputation to assure performance. Labor markets occur when this is not the case. Labor markets are especially suitable with pronounced economies of scale and when cooperation between producers greatly enhances efficiency.

Although the equivalence of labor and credit markets establishes that capitalist exploitation does not require wage labor (as classical Marxist theory had claimed), ignoring the difference between these markets obscures the dynamics of advanced capitalism. Hiring labor power and advancing credit are not dynamically equivalent. Changes in the profit and interest rates affect capitalist economies quite differently. Capitalists relying on profit income pursue very different strategies than capitalists depending on income derived from interest. The famous Polish economist Michał Kalecki, an important forerunner of Analytical Marxism, weaves the relationship between profit and interest into his influential theory of the business cycle under advanced capitalism (Kalecki 1971, chap. 9). The next section outlines Kalecki's theory of the business cycle and its implications regarding exploitation.

Exploitation and the Capitalist Business Cycle

Michał Kalecki (1971) identifies two components in normal capitalist economic development: a long-term *trend* and a *cycle* around this trend. His main theoretical concern, however, is with the cyclic component of capitalist development, also known as the capitalist business cycle. The most obvious symptoms of the capitalist business cycle are fluctuations in the amount of employment and fluctuations in the share of available capital equipment actually being used.

Why does a business cycle occur in a capitalist economy? Several different answers have been given to this question, but the driving force in Kalecki's theory of the business cycle is capitalist investment or, more exactly, decisions made by capitalist entrepreneurs to invest in productive assets like buildings or equipment (i.e., fixed capital) (Kalecki 1971, pp. 110-37). The business cycle arises from the dynamic relationship between (a) the amount of investment in productive assets within the capitalist economy as a whole, (b) the overall stock of fixed capital, and (c) the rate of profit.

When the amount of investment is high, the stock of fixed capital increases (because investment consists of additions to fixed capital), and the rate of profit also increases (because investment spending by some capitalists creates profit opportunities for other capitalists). When the amount of investment is low, on the other hand, the stock of fixed capital decreases (because additions to fixed capital are less than depreciation of the existing capital stock), and the rate of profit also decreases (because the dearth of investment spending diminishes opportunities to make profit). Naturally a high rate of profit encourages capitalist investment, whereas a low profit rate has the opposite effect.

Now consider how the existing stock of fixed capital influences the volume of investment and the rate of profit. When the stock of fixed capital is relatively low, many opportunities for profitable investment exist because the capacity of industry to meet demand is also relatively low. The existence of such profit-making opportunities encourages investment and boosts the rate of profit. When the stock of fixed capital is relatively high, lucrative investment opportunities are sparse because industry is now well equipped and has the capacity to meet whatever effective demand exists. The absence of profit-making opportunity diminishes both the amount of capitalist investment and the rate of profit.

Investment, according to Kalecki's theory, has a positive impact upon changes in the stock of capital and the rate of profit, but capital stock has a negative consequence for changes in investment and the profit rate. The combination of these effects, operating over time, generates a capitalist business cycle.[6] It works something like this:

> *Phase 1* (Depression): Investment and the profit rate are both low, and the value of the existing stock of capital lies well beneath what is normal for a capitalist economy. Yet the depressed condition of the economy has a silver lining. When the capital stock sinks sufficiently low, it can no longer satisfy existing demand, and new demand for investment arises. This demand is felt first in industries that make production equipment.

> *Phase 2* (Recovery): Seizing upon the opportunities for investment created by the less than normal capital stock, investment increases sharply, as does the rate of profit. Employment increases, and the stock of capital gradually builds up from the additions brought about by investment activity.[7]

> *Phase 3* (Boom): Employment is now high, and the value of the stock of capital is well above normal. The volume of investment and the rate of profit are also high. In the midst of the boom, however, the opulence of capital stock and the high level of productivity weakens demand for further investment: existing facilities are more than adequate for meeting effective demand. Naturally, the curtailment of investment demand affects the investment goods industries first.

> *Phase 4* (Recession): Responding to the decline in opportunities for lucrative expenditures, investment declines and, shortly thereafter, the profit rate does also. Employment decreases, as does the use of capital equipment. The dip in investment generates a gradual reduction in capital stock, which continues until deficiency of capital generates new investment demand.

Under normal conditions the length of the capitalist business cycle would be about 10 years, but conditions are never normal. Real business cycles, as Kalecki fully appreciates, are far more complicated than this simplified model allows; yet he still regards the relations between investment, capital stock, and profit rate described above as the analytical heart of the process.

How do exploitation and the interest rate (as opposed to the profit rate) fit into Kalecki's theory of the business cycle? Changes in the interest rate have exactly the opposite effect on the economy from changes in the profit rate. For example, an increase in the profit rate tends to increase investment, whereas an increase in the interest rate tends to diminish the latter. During the recovery phase of the business cycle, there is always a chance that interest rate escalation will prevent a full economic rejuvenation. Kalecki usually argues that the interest rate will change more slowly than the profit rate. He also regards the interest rate as a weak instrument for regulating the capitalist business cycle.

Although he seldom discusses exploitation, Kalecki has much to say about the share of wages in national income. Given his analysis of the business cycle, the wage share of national income may be taken as a rough proxy for the degree of capitalist exploitation. One of Kalecki's main concerns regarding exploitation involves correcting conventional ideas about the relationship between wages and profits. He repeatedly denies that an increase in wages causes an equivalent fall in profits.

If excess productive capacity exists, then an increase in wages will cause an increase in employment but not a redistribution of income from profits to wages. Under these circumstances, a decrease in exploitation will increase the volume of surplus produced. If excess productive capacity does not exist, then Kalecki argues an increase in wages will induce price changes without necessarily shifting the distribution of income between workers and capitalists. It follows from these arguments that the wage share of national income (and hence exploitation) is not subject to strong cyclical fluctuations.

Nevertheless, Kalecki does find some connection between exploitation and the capitalist business cycle. The connection arises primarily from two sources: trade union power and the degree of monopoly in capitalist industry. Both of these sources cause a slight increase in exploitation during the depression phase of the business cycle and a slight decrease in exploitation during the boom phase.

An increase in trade union power causes a limited redistribution of income in favor of the working class, and trade union power tends to rise and fall with employment. Within the capitalist business cycle, the organized power of the working class is greater during booms and less during depressions.

The degree of monopoly, on the other hand, is inversely related to the wage share of national income: rises in the degree of monopoly coincide with declines in the wage share and vice versa. Kalecki attributes this to the fact that large corporations can control prices and set them in a manner unfavorable to the working class.[8]

The distinction between trend and cycle is particularly evident in the evolution of capitalist concentration. Degree of monopoly shows a strong and persistent tendency to increase as capitalism matures. Kalecki also detects a much weaker cyclical process by which degree of monopoly falls during the upturn of the business cycle and rises during the downturn. Thus the main effect of concentration in a capitalist economy is long-term reduction in the wage share of national income and increasing exploitation. A subsidiary (and far more tentative) effect is a mild exploitation cycle running in tandem with the normal capitalist business cycle.

There are several reasons why Michał Kalecki can be considered a precursor of Analytical Marxism. He does not separate Marxism from other approaches to social science and indicates, by his practice, belief in a common methodology of social science. He states his theoretical assumptions carefully, uses difference equation models to study business cycles, and treats capitalist entrepreneurs—the main focus of his theoretical attentions—as rational actors of sorts. Kalecki is sometimes considered a Keynesian rather than a Marxist, but he actually integrates the two perspectives, as do theorists like Paul Sweezy (Sweezy 1942; Baran and Sweezy 1966), Josef Steindl (1952), and Stephen Marglin (1984). Treating Kalecki as a precursor registers my conviction that Analytical Marxism embraces, but does not require, a synthesis between Marxist and neoclassical economics.

Kalecki's theory of the capitalist business cycle implies an inverse relationship between trade union power and degree of monopoly. Such a relationship arises partly because trade union power presumably constrains the monopolistic tendencies of capital. Yet it is also plausible that unionization encounters less resistance in highly concentrated industries that can readily transfer wage increases to their customers.

The empirical evidence on this question is mixed. Industrial unions do tend to arise in more concentrated industries characterized by oligopolistic structure (American Social History Project 1992, chaps. 8 and 9). On the other hand, recent studies suggest that organized opposition by the capitalist class has had a vital part in reducing the power of United States labor unions from the zenith attained shortly after World War II. Moreover, industrial concentration seems to increase the ability of employers to resist labor union demands (Goldfield 1987; Kimeldorf 1988).

A Game Theoretic Approach to Exploitation[9]

Initiating the use of game theory to analyze exploitation is one of John Roemer's important theoretical contributions. Chapter 3's section "Models of Exploitation" outlined two general models of exploitation proposed by Roemer: *labor exploitation* and *comparative exploitation*. Game theory enters the picture through the comparative model of exploitation. This model analyzes exploitation by comparing an existing situation to some hypothetical alternative. The nature of the alternative defines the particular kind of exploitation being considered. The comparative model, as we shall see, invites application of game theory methods, and these methods in turn facilitate a more general definition of exploitation.

A fundamental concept in the theory of multiperson games is the idea of a *coalition*.[10] Roemer considers a coalition of people exploited within an economic system if and only if three conditions hold: (a) there exists a feasible alternative system in which members of the coalition are better off, (b) people not in the coalition fare more poorly in the alternative economic system, and (c) coalition members are currently dominated by people not in the coalition (Roemer 1982a, pp. 194-95).[11] The complement of an exploited coalition is an exploiting coalition. This approach makes exploitation a characteristic of coalitions rather than individuals. As we shall see, the focus on coalitions is vital in formulating a plausible definition of exploitation under complex production technologies.

For purposes of analyzing exploitation, Roemer (1982a) conceives of society as a game in which coalitions of producers can withdraw from the economy, taking certain resources with them, if their members find it beneficial to do so. A departing coalition sets up its own production system using existing technology and the resources it has appropriated. The nature of the resulting production process and the economic rewards received by coalition members determine the benefits of withdrawing. The nature of the resources a departing coalition can take defines the character of the *withdrawal game* and thereby the kind of exploitation at issue.

Roemer concentrates upon three different withdrawal games—feudal, capitalist, and socialist—using each game to define a corresponding form of exploitation. If the welfare of all coalition members improves after setting up production independently, then the coalition is exploited in the way defined by the withdrawal game.

A *feudal withdrawal game* allows a coalition to withdraw from an economy taking only those resources coalition members actually own. For example, individuals in an agrarian society might own their own labor power plus a certain amount of land. The feudal withdrawal game corresponding to this society allows members of a coalition to leave taking just their own labor power and the land they possess. A coalition is considered *feudally exploited* if the welfare of its members improves when the coalition sets up shop independently using only those resources actually owned by its members.

This definition reflects the idea that feudal exploitation occurs when producers do not have full control over their own resources but must relinquish part of their labor power or part of what they produce to someone else. If the producers could gain full control over the resources they actually owned, their welfare would presumably improve.

A *capitalist withdrawal game* has different rules. It allows a coalition of people to withdraw with its *per capita share* of all alienable economic resources (e.g., land, equipment, buildings, inventory). The coalition experiences *capitalist exploitation* if, after withdrawing and setting up production with these resources, the welfare of its members improves. This definition is based on the hypothesis that capitalist exploitation derives from differential ownership of capital (conceived as alienable economic resources). People burdened by capitalist exploitation would fare better if they owned their proportional share of alienable economic resources, that is, of capital.

A *socialist withdrawal game* assumes public ownership of alienable resources and allows a coalition to leave with its per capita share of inalienable resources (i.e., personal abilities like talent and capacity to work). A coalition suffers *socialist exploitation* if the economic welfare of its members would improve after withdrawing in this way. The idea of dividing up talent and capacity to work is certainly far-fetched, but Roemer intends it only as a thought experiment for purposes of identifying who endures socialist exploitation.[12] The notion that the exploitation characteristic of a genuine socialist society derives from differential ability explains how the socialist withdrawal game is defined.

Given a well-defined economic system, these three withdrawal games enable us to determine whether feudal exploitation, capitalist exploitation, and/or socialist exploitation exist. Although many complex structures of exploitation are feasible, some patterns are more common than others. In a feudal society Roemer expects to find feudal, capitalist, and socialist exploitation. In a capitalist society he expects capitalist and socialist exploitation but not feudal exploitation. In a socialist society he anticipates socialist exploitation but neither feudal nor capitalist exploitation.

To carry the analysis of exploitation further, Roemer introduces another idea taken from game theory: the concept of the *core*. The image underlying this concept is an allocation of rewards that no coalition can improve upon. More specifically, an allocation of rewards is said to be in the core of a withdrawal game if no coalition can improve the welfare of all its members by withdrawing from the economy in the way permitted by the rules of the game.[13]

It turns out that exploitation can be defined by means of the core concept. Exploitation of a particular kind occurs if and only if the existing allocation of rewards is *not* in the core of the corresponding withdrawal game. When an allocation is not in the core, there exists at least one coalition that can improve the welfare of all its members by leaving the economy. Such an alliance is called a *blocking coalition* because its departure would prevent implementation of the proposed allocation.

As an example, consider the core of the socialist withdrawal game. To make things as simple as possible, let us assume a constant return technology.[14] An allocation of rewards is in the core of the socialist withdrawal game only if everyone who participates in production gets exactly the same amount. Otherwise the economy would be vulnerable to defection. Any coalition of producers receiving less than the average allotment could help its members by withdrawing from the economy with its per capita share of alienable and inalienable resources.

Equal division, it turns out, is the only allocation in the core of the socialist withdrawal game. All other allocations lie outside the core and thus entail socialist exploitation. Hence Roemer names the one nonexploitative allocation of the socialist withdrawal game, the *equal division core*.

Consider a somewhat more complicated application of the core concept. We discussed SE2, the subsistence economy with private ownership of production inputs, in Chapter 3 in the section "Exploitation in a Subsistence Economy With Private Ownership of Production Inputs." The participants in this economy must produce their own subsistence requirements and want to work as little as possible while doing it. Their strategies of work minimization are constrained by the absence of a labor market. Define a withdrawal game for SE2 allowing producers to depart with their own labor power and their own alienable resources. When a coalition withdraws, it sets up production in the communal fashion of SE1. Under these withdrawal rules not all coalitions are economically viable. A coalition is economically viable only if it has enough resources to produce the subsistence requirements of all its members.

But not all economically viable coalitions will want to leave the SE2 economy. Because people in SE2 are assumed to be labor minimizers, members of a viable coalition will want to secede only if the new economy enables them to subsist with less work. Less work is only possible if the coalition as a whole currently works more than is socially necessary. Thus an economically viable coalition will not be motivated to secede from SE2 unless its members, taken together, currently work more than is socially necessary.

Using these results, we can define the core of the SE2 withdrawal game. A reproducible solution (i.e., an allocation of work to individuals) will be in the core of this game—named by Roemer the *private ownership core*—if and only if no viable coalition must work more than is socially necessary.

Suppose a reproducible solution is in the private enterprise core. Although some individual producers may work more than is socially necessary under this equilibrium, viable coalitions, taken collectively, cannot do so. Not all reproducible solutions for SE2 are in the private enterprise core, and in these cases a blocking coalition must exist. But no coalition consisting entirely of exploited people is economically viable, and hence no such group can function as a blocking coalition (Roemer 1982a, pp. 47-52). If exploited people respect the rules of private property, this result suggests, they have very limited capacity to disrupt economic systems based upon private ownership of production facilities.

One of the virtues of a game theoretic approach lies in defining exploitation under more complex production technologies.[15] Consider the use of game theory for identifying exploitation in economies with increasing returns to scale.[16] The reader must first understand the concepts of vulnerability and culpability: Roemer's efforts to generalize being exploited and being an exploiter.

An exploited coalition that stops being exploited when losing any single member is a *minimal exploited coalition*. Every person in a minimal exploited coalition is absolutely essential to the exploited condition of the coalition as a whole. By the same token, an exploiting coalition that is no longer exploiting when any member departs is a *minimal exploiting coalition*. Every person in a minimal exploiting coalition is absolutely essential to the exploiting status of the whole coalition.

A person is *vulnerable* if she belongs to any minimal exploited coalition and *culpable* if she belongs to a minimal exploiting coalition. If a person is neither vulnerable nor culpable, she is called *strongly neutral*. If a person is vulnerable, her presence is required to make at least one coalition exploited. This is why Roemer considers vulnerability an appropriate generalization of being exploited. Conversely, if a person is culpable, she is needed to make at least one coalition exploiting. Hence culpability seems a logical generalization of being an exploiter. Quite appropriately, the set of all vulnerable agents is an exploited coalition, and the set of all culpable agents constitutes an exploiting coalition.

The value of these concepts becomes evident when we consider exploitation under different production technologies. With constant returns to scale, the minimal exploited coalitions are all single people, and hence there is no difference between who is vulnerable and who is exploited. But this is not true with increasing returns to scale. Here we typically find individual exploiters, but no one who is individually exploited; and here the concept of vulnerability becomes useful. The appropriate question to ask in an increasing return economy is not whether a person is exploited or exploiting, but whether she is vulnerable, culpable, or strongly neutral.

To further study exploitation under increasing returns to scale, Roemer uses the theory of convex games (Shapley 1971). A *convex game* is defined through the payoffs received by various possible coalitions. Without getting too technical, the fundamental idea is that every coalition is more powerful than the sum of its parts. That is, every coalition in a convex game, acting collectively, can obtain rewards greater than the sum of the rewards available to its subgroups acting independently.[17] A little reflection shows that this characteristic is analogous to an increasing return economy where larger units are more efficient than smaller units of production.

In an economy represented by a convex game, no person can be both vulnerable and culpable: the exploiting and exploited groups are entirely separate. But this combination can occur in certain economies represented by a nonconvex game (Roemer 1982a, pp. 222-24).

The use of game theory to characterize structures and processes of exploitation is only beginning, but it has already made possible a much more sophisticated understanding of exploitation and related concepts. These lines of inquiry seem quite promising, which is why readers should wrestle with the elusive and abstract ideas presented in this section.

Socialist Exploitation

According to Marxist theory, the evolution of human society entails successive elimination of inequalities considered to be exploitative. Early in the evolution of modern economic systems, feudal, capitalist, and socialist forms of exploitation existed simultaneously. The historic task of capitalist revolution is to eliminate feudal exploitation. The historic task of socialist revolution is to eliminate capitalist exploitation. Socialist revolution does not, however, eliminate socialist exploitation: exploitation based upon the differential productive ability of producers. Socialist exploitation remains necessary under socialism. If a socialist society does not reward differential ability, then valuable skills will not be developed, and production as a whole will suffer, as it did during the Chinese Cultural Revolution. The historic task of communist revolution is to eliminate socialist exploitation, but this can only happen at a far higher level of economic and cultural development than currently exists anywhere.

What makes a form of exploitation socially necessary? Exploitation is *socially necessary*, claims Roemer, if attempts to eliminate it harm exploited people rather than helping them. It can be socially necessary in two rather different ways. It is socially necessary in a static sense if suppressing the exploitation plays havoc with the economic incentive system, rendering producers worse off in the short run. It is socially necessary in a dynamic sense if technology or other forces of production fail to develop when the exploitation is eradicated. A significant weakness in Roemer's analysis is his failure to elucidate why a given property form is suitable for developing forces of production at a certain level, and when specific types of exploitation become ripe for abolition.

The concept of socially necessary exploitation emphasizes that eliminating exploitation is not a simple matter of determination and morality. As long as human beings remain rational creatures deeply concerned with their own material well-being, good intentions and political mobilization will not suffice to abolish inequality or exploitation. But recognizing a form of exploitation as socially necessary does not mean approving it or adopting a passive attitude toward the transformation of society. Even if a socialist revolution cannot abrogate capitalist exploitation in one fell swoop, it may still be the quickest and least painful route toward eliminating this relationship.

As indicated in the previous section, a coalition is subject to socialist exploitation if the welfare of its members improves when the coalition leaves the economy with its per capital share of all productive resources (alienable and inalienable) and if the complementary coalition becomes worse off. To analyze how socialist exploitation functions, Roemer studies a variation of the subsistence economy with communal ownership of production resources (SE1).

In the original version of SE1, each producer could operate all the production processes. In the variation studied by Roemer—labeled a socialist subsistence economy (SSE)—each producer only knows how to operate a subset of all production processes. Under SSE, society as a whole works exactly the amount of time necessary to produce the subsistence requirements of all participants, and a person experiences socialist exploitation if and only if she works more than is socially necessary. Socialist exploitation happens precisely because some people, due to lack of knowledge or ability, are compelled to operate production processes requiring more than the average amount of labor. An allocation in SSE is free of socialist exploitation if and only if all producers earn strictly the same amount.

Status exploitation—economic inequality based upon possession of organizational or bureaucratic position—is distinct from, but often confused with, socialist exploitation. Whereas socialist exploitation is a natural and inevitable characteristic of socialist societies, this is not true for status exploitation. Although fully developed within most capitalist societies, the main theoretical importance of status exploitation derives from attempts to understand societies of the Soviet type. These societies exhibit both status exploitation and socialist exploitation, but distinguishing the two can be extremely difficult.

An even more difficult question concerns whether status exploitation is socially necessary within Soviet-type societies. People who think it is socially necessary argue that bureaucrats must get special economic rewards in order to perform their functions properly and that eliminating status exploitation requires introducing markets, thus regenerating capitalist social relations. In his earlier work Roemer appeared to accept these arguments, but more recently he contends that the greater efficiency resulting from markets would more than compensate for whatever inequalities they generate (Roemer 1988a, p. 146).

The collapse of Communism occurred after Roemer's main theoretical works were published. The policies adopted throughout Eastern Europe and the former Soviet Union suggest that many people regard capitalist exploitation as both preferable to and curative of status exploitation. They apparently consider capitalist exploitation as socially necessary in the current era but view status exploitation as a parasitic excrescence.

Socialist exploitation ends when every producer gets exactly the same income, and this, one might think, means the final abolition of all exploitation. Roemer thinks otherwise. Needs are not equally distributed. Under a completely egalitarian distribution of income, people with fewer needs exploit people with greater needs. After all, a coalition of needy people would prosper by withdrawing from the economy with their per capita share of aggregate human needs. Only by compensating people in proportion to the needs they have can *needs exploitation* be eliminated. This entire conception is strongly reminiscent of the famous slogan from Marx's *Critique of the Gotha Program* ([1891] 1989) about the higher phase of communist society: "from each according to his ability, to each according to his needs."

Is Exploitation Wrong?

In view of John Roemer's numerous and penetrating contributions to the theory of exploitation, it is rather surprising that his more recent work questions the value of exploitation as a moral concept. In his book *Free to Lose* (1988a), Roemer writes:

> When exploitation is an injustice, it is not because it is exploitation as such, but because the distribution of labor expended and income received in an exploitative situation are consequences of an initial distribution of assets that is unjust. The injustice of an exploitative allocation depends upon the injustice of the initial endowment. (p. 57)

And again, "The Marxist definition of exploitation is not the best tool for either positive or normative purposes. It is conceptually simpler, and more robust, to represent one's concerns with the consequences of an unequal distribution of property directly instead of taking the circuitous route through surplus labor" (p. 175).

To justify his critique of exploitation as a moral concept, Roemer provides a number of examples showing how moral conclusions based upon exploitation can be misleading. The most telling example shows that a person with less wealth but a strong preference for leisure can sometimes exploit a person with more wealth and a keen interest in acquisition. Consider a variation of Roemer's example based upon the capital-intensive and labor-intensive corn-producing technologies discussed in Chapter 1.

Joy is a leisure-loving person who owns 2 bushels of corn stock and uses them while working 10 days per month on the capital-intensive technology, producing 2 bushels of corn net. The foremost concern of Prudence, on the other hand, is economic security and acquiring ample stocks of corn. She owns 4 bushels of corn stock and works 20 days per month, also on the capital-intensive technology, producing 4 bushels of corn net. Joy would prefer to stop working and reduce her consumption to the subsistence minimum of 1 bushel per month. Prudence would prefer getting 5 bushels even if that meant working 30 days per month.

In view of these preferences, Joy agrees to lend Prudence her two bushels of corn at a 50% interest rate per month. Prudence works ten extra days using these two bushels and producing four bushels of corn gross. Two of these bushels replace the corn stock she has borrowed, one is paid to Joy as interest on the loan, and Prudence keeps the remaining bushel.

Joy is exploiting Prudence in this example. She does no work herself and lives entirely off the labor of Prudence. On the other hand, both people prefer the revised arrangement over the original scheme, and Prudence is much wealthier than Joy. Evidently the correspondence between wealth and exploitation breaks down in this case (but the correspondence between class and exploitation still holds true). Although Joy is an exploiter and Prudence is exploited, we do not feel sympathetic with Prudence or hostile toward Joy.

Roemer relies heavily on such examples to impugn exploitation as a moral concept. But these examples are far less telling than Roemer imagines. The Joy and Prudence situation derives its force from the radically different preference orderings of the two protagonists. Though neither preference ordering is implausible, generating odd outcomes by endowing actors with widely disparate utility functions does not prove much. With so many degrees of freedom, many curiosities can appear. These outcomes reveal more about eccentricities of interaction at cross-purposes than about the logic of exploitation.

But there is a deeper reason why the Joy and Prudence example does not tell against exploitation as a moral concept. Joy's response in this artificial situation shows why the reproduction of capitalism requires a propertyless proletariat. When people have any choice, it becomes difficult—and hence expensive—to discharge the really nasty tasks of production. If a person can become a surgeon or a molecular biologist, what reward would induce her to be a ditch digger? The reproduction of capitalism requires the existence of people having no such choice: a propertyless proletariat.

When discussing the introduction of a labor market into a subsistence economy in Chapter 3, in the section "Exploitation in a Subsistence Economy With a Labor Market," we showed that the availability of wage labor depended on the existence of people with not enough property to support themselves as independent producers. If Joy's preference orderings and productive resources were widespread, sustaining any realistic capitalism would be impossible. The interaction between Joy and Prudence is not a kernel of exploitation from capitalist society but an inadvertent demonstration of relations undermining such exploitation.

What about the claim that moral focus should be on property inequality rather than exploitation? The problem here is that we cannot determine the significance of property inequality independent of exploitation. Is property inequality, however achieved, immoral if it brings no advantage to the property owner?

That the significance of the property distribution should depend upon the extent of exploitation is analogous to Piero Sraffa's finding that the quantity of capital depends upon the rate of profit (Sraffa 1960). Roemer implicitly recognizes this analogy in his discussion of the SE2 economy. Here he gives an example of a two-person SE2 economy where the direction of exploitation reverses depending upon the reproducible solution in effect, and he associates this with the reswitching phenomenon first identified by Sraffa (Roemer 1982a, pp. 44-47).[18] Because the property distribution does not determine who exploits whom, what can be said about the fairness of the distribution in this example?

Almost all Roemer's theorems about exploitation are conditioned on the reproducible solution in effect, not simply on the distribution of property and the structure of markets. This constitutes mathematical recognition that the moral meaning of property inequality is ambiguous. Indignation about exploitation stems from the idea that rewards from and contributions to society should be in reasonable balance. But what constitutes balance?

Exploitation is not easy to measure, but the measurement of inequality in the ownership of property is no less difficult. As the famous capital controversy has shown (see note 18), difficulties in measuring the value of property arise on conceptual as well as practical grounds (Harcourt 1972). Most systems of production allow more than one economic equilibrium, and different equilibria value property very differently. Measurement of property is indispensable if the moral focus is to be on property inequality. Yet it is not evident to me that permanent equality in the ownership of alienable resources is a better or more practical moral principle than equivalence between the labor a person gives to society and the labor she receives in return.

The labor model of exploitation remains useful as a tool of normative analysis. Think about the venerable idea that freedom lies in emancipation from necessity, and that labor is the uniquely human way of shaping the world. A truly free person might dislike working but value the products of human labor in proportion to the amount of labor embodied in them. Let us call this the *liberated utility function.*

Given people endowed with the liberated utility function, operation of any economy involving exploitation would be impossible: the economic rewards would never induce performance of the necessary labor. The fundamental Marxian theorem implies that no profit-making economy is feasible given producers with the liberated utility function. The moral significance of labor exploitation may lie in measuring how much an existing economy must change in order to accommodate truly free people.

Conclusion

Controversies between Marxist and non-Marxist social scientists often revolve around the concept of exploitation. Exploitation may not be the manifest subject of controversy, but frequently it constitutes the subtext. The Marxist arguments in such a controversy boil down to the claims that exploitation exists as an objective reality and will profoundly influence the trajectory of the social order. Similarly, the non-Marxist arguments are reducible to disputes about the existence, causal efficacy, avoidability, or immorality of exploitation. Its continuing association with the analysis of exploitation is a principal reason why Marxist theory still finds adherents. As long as the advantages experienced by some people in society seem causally related to the disadvantages endured by others, observers seeking a systematic explanation will be drawn toward Marxism or something very much like it. Few contending social theories recognize the existence of, let alone explain, exploitation.

Given its importance to the continuing appeal of Marxism, it is surprising that the conceptual foundations of exploitation analysis stagnated for so long. The classical Marxist concept of exploitation, as all serious scholars knew, could not cope with the theoretical burden placed upon it. As a result, the analysis of exploitation in modern society became increasingly rhetorical and increasingly vulnerable to the charge of being mere ideological prejudice.

Analytical Marxism can take credit for turning this situation around. John Roemer and his colleagues have freed the concept of exploitation from the constraints imposed by the labor theory of value and placed it on a more solid theoretical foundation. They have specified different types of exploitation, clarified the circumstances under which it arises, related exploitation to a variety of other social processes, including imperialism and the capitalist business cycle, and showed how game theory can be used to elaborate exploitation theory. Perhaps most impressively, Roemer has given mathematical proof of a systematic relationship between class position and exploitation status.

But exploitation analysis, notwithstanding the achievements of Analytical Marxism, is not out of the theoretical woods. A fully adequate definition of exploitation is still not available. The ethical status of exploitation remains open to question, as does its salience for causal explanations of historical events. Some social relations that seem exploitative, such as gender relations and race relations, remain largely outside the purview of exploitation theory.[19]

A major challenge facing Analytical Marxism is constructing empirical measures of exploitation. Without empirical measurement it is virtually impossible to test specific propositions about exploitation. Even so fundamental a result as the Class Exploitation Correspondence Principle remains an analytical truth about models of society rather than an empirical truth about the social world.

The branch of Analytical Marxism that has progressed furthest in constructing empirical measures is the study of class. Class analysis and exploitation analysis, as is obvious from the Class Exploitation Correspondence Principle, are deeply connected. Empirical measures of class might even suggest promising approaches to the measurement of exploitation. The next chapter surveys Analytical Marxist thinking about class.

Notes

1. Due to the absence of mathematical reasoning in this book, claims about logical rigor are usually not substantiated. I can think of no other way of making the ideas of Analytical Marxism accessible to a large audience. This strategy of exposition has some unfortunate consequences because the value of certain contributions to Analytical Marxism derives more from the method of argument than from the originality of the claims. Readers who want a demonstration of logical rigor should consult the sources I have cited.

2. These relationships between class and exploitation, it should be emphasized, are not simple tautologies. By Roemer's definition of exploitation, a person is exploited if she necessarily gives to society more labor than she gets in return, and a person is an exploiter if she necessarily gets more labor than she gives (see Chapter 3). This definition says nothing about the sale or purchase of labor power. The systematic connection between labor power and exploitation arises as a deep and surprising theorem, lending credibility to the theoretical premises from which it is derived.

3. This is the simplest production technology considered by Roemer. It assumes constant returns to scale and a single process for producing every commodity. The Leontief technology is sometimes referred to as a *linear production technology*.

4. A *cone technology* is more complex than a Leontief technology. A cone technology allows several different ways of producing a single commodity, as well as production processes with several different outputs.

5. When considering a credit market economy, we modify the (x,y,z) notation used for SE3 so that x signifies production activities using one's own resources, y designates resources loaned to other producers, and z means production resources using borrowed resources.

6. Kalecki summarizes his theory of the business cycle as follows: "[The] rate of investment decisions is an increasing function of the level of profits and a decreasing function of the stock of capital equipment. This is the relationship which was the basis of the theory of the business cycle" (Kalecki 1971, p. 117).

7. "The reserve of capital equipment and the reserve army of unemployed are typical features of capitalist economy at least throughout a considerable part of the cycle" (Kalecki 1971, p. 137).

8. Kalecki develops a theory of mark-up pricing applicable when the degree of monopoly is high. When perfect competition does not prevail, prices are set by marking up costs to achieve designated profit margins. The extent of the price mark-up is directly related to the existing degree of monopoly (Kalecki 1971, pp. 160-63).

9. This section is slightly more technical than most of the others. I considered making it an appendix but decided to leave it in the main text. Although virtually everything that follows can be understood without reading this section, as with the appendices, I urge readers to give it a try.

10. A classic and still useful exposition of multiperson game theory appears in Luce and Raiffa, *Games and Decisions* (1957). Anatol Rapoport's *N-Person Game Theory* (1970) provides an elementary and engaging introduction to the subject. A more recent treatment is found in Martin Shubik, *Game Theory in the Social Sciences* (1982). Chapters 9 and 10 in Roger Myerson's *Game Theory* (1991) give an advanced and mathematically oriented discussion of coalition formation and uncertainty in multiperson cooperative games.

11. Appendix A4.2 discusses a variation of this definition in which Roemer replaces the domination condition stated in (c) with the requirement that exploiters depend upon the people they exploit. *Dependence* is understood to mean that exploiters would suffer if the exploited withdraw from society (Roemer 1982a).

12. The elimination of socialist exploitation does not require an equal division of talent or capacity to work. It only requires that differences in these abilities not command differential economic rewards (Roemer 1988a, p. 140).

13. To become more familiar with the concept of the core, consider the following example. Persons A, B, and C must divide $600 between them. This is a majority rule game: any majority of the three people can decide how to allocate the entire $600. An allocation of $200 to each person might seem to be optimal, but this equal allocation is not in the core of this division game. It is easy to see why not. A coalition of any two people has the power to allocate the entire $600 to themselves and cut out the third person entirely. Thus the equal allocation is vulnerable to defection by a two-person subgroup.

It turns out that no possible allocation of the $600 among the three people is invulnerable to defection. No matter how the money is divided, there is always a coalition that can improve the income of all its members. Hence no allocation is in the core, and thus the core of the division game is empty.

Suppose we modify the division game in a way that emphasizes the importance of unanimity. If A, B, and C achieve unanimity about an allocation, then they distribute $1,200 among themselves instead of $600. If unanimity is not achieved, however, then only $600 is distributed. Call this the unanimity game. An equal allocation of $400 to each person is in the core of the unanimity game: no coalition can do better for all its members. But this is not the only allocation in the core of the unanimity game. An allocation of $300 to A, $400 to B, and $500 to C is also in the core because—although not an equal distribution—no coalition can improve upon it for all coalition members.

The reader should convince herself that any allocation summing to $1,200 and giving at least $600 to each pair of players is in the core of the unanimity game.

14. A constant return technology is sometimes called a *linear technology*. Such a technology gives no advantages or disadvantages to changing the scale of production: the ratio of inputs to outputs remains constant. If one doubles all inputs to production (including labor), then the production outputs are also doubled. Similarly, if one halves inputs, then outputs are cut in half.

15. See Appendix A4.1 for further discussion of the problems posed by nonlinear production technologies for defining exploitation.

16. Increasing returns to scale means that large-scale production is more efficient than small-scale production.

17. The three-person unanimity game described in note 13 is a convex game. This is so because the coalition of three people can get $1,200, any coalition of two people can get $600, and any coalition containing just one person cannot be certain of getting any money under the rules of the game. It follows from this distribution of rewards that any coalition can get more than can be obtained by the sum of its constituent subgroups acting independently. This property defines a convex game.

18. Reswitching is important because it indicates a paradox in the concept of capital. The reswitching phenomenon refers to shifts in the value of capital, and can arise when capital consists of a heterogeneous assortment of goods. As a simple illustration of what reswitching means, consider two physical bodies of capital (i.e., collections of capital goods) labeled A and B. The value of capital, Sraffa hypothesized, depends upon the rate of profit. When the rate of profit is low, let the value of A exceed the value of B. When the rate of profit rises, suppose that the relative value of the two capitals switches, making B more valuable than A. When the rate of profit gets still higher, suppose that the relative value switches a second time so that A is again worth more than B. This double switch is reswitching.

The reswitching phenomenon gave rise to an extended debate about the theory and measurement of capital. Although the debate was conducted largely in technical economic terms, the underlying issue seemed to be the justice of capitalist property relations (Harcourt 1972).

19. Alan Carling tries to theorize gender and ethnic exploitation in parts V and VI of his book *Social Division* (1991). Some of Carling's models are discussed in the next chapter.

APPENDIX A4.1 TECHNOLOGY AND EXPLOITATION

Technology is extremely important in Analytical Marxism, and many theoretical results concerning exploitation assume a *Leontief technology* (i.e., a linear relationship between production inputs and production outputs and a single process for making every economic good). What happens to exploitation with more complex production technologies? We shall divide this question in two: What happens to exploitation with technologies allowing several different ways to make a good? What happens to exploitation under technologies with nonlinear relationships between inputs and outputs (e.g., increasing return technologies)?

Consider the first question. More specifically, consider a *cone technology,* which differs from a Leontief technology by tolerating several different ways of making a good and several different outputs for a single production process. A Leontief technology is actually a particularly simple cone technology. Because several different ways of making the same object may exist, as well as several different products of the same labor process, how can we define embodied labor with a cone technology?

The usual approach has been to define embodied labor as the minimum amount of direct labor needed to produce a good as a net product, considering all available production processes. We call this the *technological definition of embodied labor* because it depends entirely on the available technology and not upon prices. Unfortunately, this definition invalidates the Class Exploitation Correspondence Principle: it eliminates any systematic relationship between class position and exploitation status in economies with a cone technology.

To cope with this difficulty, Roemer suggests an alternative way of defining embodied labor under a cone technology. Roemer's alternative confines attention to production processes yielding maximum profit. Given any particular economic equilibrium, only some of the methods available for producing a specific good yield the maximum profit rate. These processes are the only ones rational producers will operate. Roemer defines the labor embodied in a good as the minimum amount of direct labor needed to produce it as a net product *considering only maximum profit production processes.* With this definition of embodied labor the Class Exploitation Correspondence Principle remains true in economies with cone technology (Roemer 1982a, pp. 147-64).

We call this the *social relations definition* because it makes embodied labor depend on the reproducible solution and on capitalist social relations. According to the social relations definition, the labor embodied in a commodity is not a technological fact but something that shifts according to the prevailing economic equilibrium. Goods that rational capitalists will not produce because they bring suboptimal profit margins are not really commodities and have no labor value. This argument also implies that the distribution of exploitation shifts with the going economic equilibrium.

The social relations definition has major theoretical consequences. This definition makes it impossible to explain equilibrium prices through embodied labor. At least in the case of a cone technology, equilibrium prices become logically prior to labor values. These prices control which production processes are maximum profit, and only then is embodied labor determined. Different price equilibria render different production processes maximum profit, and labor values shift accordingly. With a Leontief technology, however, the technological and social relations definitions of embodied labor are equivalent because all production processes operate at maximum profit.

Now consider the second question posed above: How are theories of exploitation affected by technologies allowing nonlinear relations between input and output and, in particular, by increasing return technologies? We shall examine this question in the context of the comparative exploitation model (discussed in Chapter 3, in the section "Models of Exploitation"), which defines exploitation by comparing an existing income distribution with the distribution expected if property relations changed in some specified way.

For example, Roemer proposes defining capitalist exploitation by comparing capitalist income distribution with the income distribution expected if alienable endowments (Roemer's term for means of production) were divided equally among all producers. A producer is a capitalist exploiter if her income declines under the egalitarian property distribution, whereas she suffers from capitalist exploitation if her income increases. The hypothetical income distribution is determined by assuming that technology remains constant and that competitive markets exist (Roemer 1988a, pp. 131-35).

The defects of the comparative approach to capitalist exploitation become apparent if we assume a nonlinear technology. With an increasing returns technology, all producers—whether rich or poor—could have reduced income under an egalitarian distribution of alienable endowments. In this extreme case, everyone is an exploiter and no one is exploited. But even if this outlandish situation does not occur, the comparative approach misrepresents exploitation with an increasing return technology: it inflates the number of exploiters and deflates the number of victims.

Roemer recognizes this problem and proposes several different remedies. One remedy is the game theoretic approach to exploitation discussed in this chapter. Another remedy involves modifying the property distribution by changing the holdings of a single producer to the social average and keeping everything else constant. If the producer's income increases with this change she is presumably exploited, and if it decreases she is exploited. But this procedure is not satisfactory because it changes the overall amount of alienable property in society, which would presumably change the volume of economic production. And why should an increase or decrease in income following an increase or decrease in property ownership be attributed to exploitation?

APPENDIX A4.2 EXPLOITATION AS A CONFLICT OF INTERESTS

In some of his writings, John Roemer claims that true exploitation requires that the exploiters be *dependent* upon the people they exploit (Roemer 1982a). He interprets exploitation dependence to mean that exploiters would suffer if the people they exploit disappeared from the scene, taking the things they own with them. This dependence requirement has interesting consequences for what counts as exploitation. To understand these consequences, consider two of the examples given by Roemer.

All the seed corn in a corn-producing society is owned by a few people. The owners hire one-third of the remaining population to work up their seed corn, paying these workers only a subsistence wage and securing a large profit for themselves. The other two-thirds of the nonowning population, whom Roemer calls peasants, must use inefficient agricultural technologies to eke out an existence. These peasants end up working exactly as long as the hired laborers. Are the peasants exploited? Roemer concludes that the peasants in this situation are unfairly treated but not exploited because the owners do not depend upon them. The peasants could disappear from society without reducing the income of the owners, who would continue hiring workers at the same subsistence wage.

Roemer also discusses a variation of this situation in which ownership of seed corn is distributed equally among half the population while the other half owns none. Once again the owners of seed corn can use an efficient technology while nonowners must adopt a highly time-consuming method of agricultural production. The owners work independently, relying entirely upon their own labor. Are the nonowners in this situation exploited? Although owners would lose and nonowners would benefit from a redistribution of seed corn, the dependence requirement once again excludes nonowners from exploitation. The nonowners could depart without harming the economic position of the owners.

The dependence requirement suggests an alternative approach to analyzing exploitation under nonlinear technologies. At the beginning of Chapter 3, exploitation was said to involve a fundamental conflict of interest between exploiter and exploited: what is good for the exploiter is bad for the exploited and vice versa. If rich people are exploiters, then augmenting the property of the poor should reduce the welfare of the rich, holding everything else constant. Conversely, if poor people are exploited, then diminishing the property of the rich should increase the welfare of the poor, again holding other things constant.

As a blatant example of how such exploitation might work, consider a modification of the Norma and Murray situation presented in Chapter 1. Again we have a two-person subsistence economy producing corn and berries, with each person requiring one unit of corn and one unit of berries, in this case per month, to survive. To differentiate this more elaborate example from the earlier one, let us call the participants Nancy and Milton.

Two kinds of land produce berries and corn: low-quality public land accessible to everyone and prime-quality land owned privately. No labor market exists, and in the first situation we investigate (Situation 1) Milton owns no land and must produce with public land, whereas Nancy owns prime berry-producing and prime corn-producing land. They produce and exchange goods so as to minimize the amount they must work. An equilibrium exchange rate arises, and we compute how much Milton and Nancy must work to acquire their berries and corn at this exchange rate.

We then vary Situation 1 by having Milton acquire prime berry-producing land but holding other things constant (Situation 2). The foremost question is whether Nancy needs to work more when Milton's situation improves. Next we change Situation 1 in a different way by confiscating Nancy's prime berry-producing land, thus compelling her to produce berries on public land (Situation 3). The question here is whether Milton can work less when Nancy's productive resources diminish. The details of this example appear in Table A4.1.

In Situation 1 the reproducible solution has one unit of berries exchange for two units of corn. At this exchange rate, Milton works 12 days and Nancy works $1\frac{1}{2}$ days. In Situation 2 a new reproducible solution arises, with one unit of corn exchanging for three units of berries. Now Milton works only $4\frac{2}{3}$ days and Nancy works $2\frac{2}{3}$ days.

Thus Nancy must work longer following Milton's property gain, showing that she is an exploiter in Situation 1. In Situation 3 one unit of berries exchanges for three units of corn, Milton works $10\frac{2}{3}$ days, and Nancy works $5\frac{1}{3}$ days. Milton works less after Nancy loses her prime berry-producing land, showing that he is exploited in Situation 1.

The inverse relationship between property change and welfare suggested by the opposing interest exploitation concept sets a stringent condition for the existence of exploitation. Not many conflicts of interest are quite so clear-cut as that in the Milton and Nancy example. The opposing interest concept, like Roemer's use of the dependence requirement, means that some dubious situations are implausibly exonerated of exploitation. But the advantage of this idea lies in separating exploitation from the mere fact of inequality and viewing it instead as a consequence of structural antagonism that inequality may or may not induce.

Roemer's dependence requirement and the opposing interest interpretation of exploitation both emphasize connections between exploiters and exploited. The connections entailed by the opposing interest interpretation are even deeper and less common than those needed to satisfy dependence.

Table A4.1 An Example of Exploitation as a Relationship of
Opposing Economic Interests–Berry and Corn
Production by Milton and Nancy

_____

Technology

Public land

    8 days labor → 1 unit berries

    4 days labor → 1 unit corn

Prime berry-producing land

    1 days labor → 1 unit berries

Prime corn-producing land

    2 days labor → 1 unit corn

Subsistence Requirements

1 unit berries per month

1 unit corn per month

Utility Functions

Producers want to minimize their labor. They seek to obtain subsistence requirements but nothing more.

Situation 1 (baseline situation): Milton only has access to public land while Nancy owns prime berry- and corn-producing land.

    Milton's technology

        8 days labor → 1 unit berries

        4 days labor → 1 unit corn

    Nancy's technology

        1 days labor → 1 unit berries

        2 days labor → 1 unit corn

    Reproducible solution for Situation 1

        1 unit berries exchanges for 2 units corn

    Milton's rational action in Situation 1

        a) Works 8 days, producing 2 units corn. 1 unit of corn is traded to Nancy for $\frac{1}{2}$ unit berries. 1 unit of corn is kept for own consumption.

        b) Works 4 days, producing $\frac{1}{2}$ unit berries for own consumption.

        c) Total labor time: 12 days.

    Nancy's rational action in Situation 1

        a) Works $1\frac{1}{2}$ days, producing $1\frac{1}{2}$ units berries. $\frac{1}{2}$ unit berries is traded to Milton for 1 unit of corn. 1 unit berries is kept for own consumption.

        b) Total labor time: $1\frac{1}{2}$ days.

Table A4.1 Continued

Situation 2: Milton gains prime berry-producing land. Otherwise Situation 1 remains unchanged.

    Milton's technology

        1 days labor → 1 unit berries

        4 days labor → 1 unit corn

    Nancy's technology

        1 days labor → 1 unit berries

        2 days labor → 1 unit corn

    Reproducible solution for Situation 2

        1 unit corn exchanges for 3 units berries

    Milton's rational action in Situation 2

      a) Works 2 days, producing 2 units berries. 1 unit berries is traded to Nancy for $\frac{1}{3}$ unit corn. 1 unit berries is kept for own consumption.

      b) Works 2 $\frac{2}{3}$ days to produce $\frac{2}{3}$ unit corn for own consumption.

      c) Total labor time: 4 $\frac{2}{3}$ days. This is an improvement over Situation 1, but it does not indicate that Milton was exploited in that situation because he has gained productive resources.

    Nancy's rational action in Situation 2

      a) Works 2 $\frac{2}{3}$ days, producing 1$\frac{1}{3}$ units corn. $\frac{1}{3}$ unit corn is traded to Milton for 1 unit berries. 1 unit corn is kept for own consumption.

      b) Total labor time: 2 $\frac{2}{3}$ days. This is a loss over Situation 1. It indicates that Nancy is an exploiter in Situation 1 because she is hurt by an improvement in Milton's property holdings even though her own property remains constant.

Situation 3: Nancy loses prime-berry producing land. Otherwise Situation 1 remains unchanged.

    Milton's technology

        8 days labor → 1 unit berries

        4 days labor → 1 unit corn

    Nancy's technology

        8 days labor → 1 unit berries

        2 days labor → 1 unit corn

    Reproducible solution for Situation 3

        1 unit berries exchanges for 3 units corn

Milton's rational action in Situation 3

a) Works 10 ⅔ days, producing 1⅓ units berries. ⅓ unit berries is traded to Nancy for 1 unit corn. 1 unit berries is kept for own consumption.

b) Total labor time: 10 ⅔ days. This is an improvement over Situation 1. The improvement indicates that Milton is exploited in Situation 1 because he becomes better off when Nancy loses property even though his own property holdings remain constant.

Nancy's rational action in Situation 3

a) Works 5⅓ days to produce ⅔ unit berries for own consumption.

b) Works 4 days to produce 2 units corn. 1 unit corn is traded to Milton for ⅓ unit berries. 1 unit corn is kept for own consumption.

c) Total labor time: 9⅓ days. This is a loss over Situation 1, but it does not indicate that Nancy is an exploiter in Situation 1. She has lost productive property, and hence a reduction in her welfare is to be expected.

5

CLASS

Class Analysis and Analytical Marxism

Class analysis need not be Marxist in theoretical inspiration. There exists an energetic group of neo-Weberian class analysts who, as we shall see, have made cogent criticisms of the Analytical Marxist approach (Goldthorpe et al. 1987; Marshall et al. 1988; Goldthorpe and Marshall 1992). What differentiates Marxist from other forms of class analysis is (a) the connection Marxists make between exploitation and class, and (b) their use of class analysis to explain historical development.

Erik Wright describes the basic theoretical quandary confronting Analytical Marxist class analysis with these words:

> The historical record of the past hundred years has convinced many Marxists that [the] image of a pervasive tendency towards radical polarization of class relations within capitalist societies is incorrect. . . . Among wage-earners, the growth of professional and technical occupations and the expansion of managerial hierarchies in large corporations and the state have at least created the appearance of a considerable erosion of a simple polarized structure. (Wright 1985, pp. 8-9)

Wright deals with the conceptual problems arising from the absence of radically polarized class relations by (a) refining the theoretical questions Analytical Marxists should ask, (b) strengthening the linkage between class analysis and theories of exploitation, (c) formulating testable Marxist theories at an intermediate level of abstraction, and (d) conducting empirical studies of class

using modern research methods for purposes of evaluating theoretically derived hypotheses.

The Marxist concept of *class*, says Wright, has four essential
properties. First, it is a relational concept, meaning that classes
are defined in relation to each other rather than through gradations of some attribute like income or status. Second, classes are
intrinsically antagonistic because they have opposing interests.
Third, relations of exploitation between classes are the structural
basis for their opposing interests. Classes are antagonistic, that is,
because the affluence of one is causally related to the deprivation
of another. Finally, class relations are rooted in the process of
social production, which provides the objective foundation of
exploitation (Wright 1985, pp. 34-37).

Class analysis means systematic examination of the causes,
transformations, and consequences of class structure. It deals
with four related phenomena: class structure, class formation,
class consciousness, and class struggle.

Class structure refers to a set of class positions that exist
independently of the specific people who occupy them but that
nevertheless determine the class interests of the occupants.
Because class, as understood by Marxists, is a relational concept,
class positions are defined in relation to each other. Wright
emphasizes the distinction between the class position and the
particular occupant by referring to the position as an empty
place. Thinking about positions rather than people involves a
difficult process of abstraction. After one becomes familiar with
the idea of class positions, however, it actually simplifies the task
of theorizing about classes.

Similar or identical material interests are attributed to positions within the same class, and divergent material interests are
imputed to positions in different classes. In fact, Wright regards
material interests as the most important commonality among the
positions constituting a class. His empirical work treats class
locations as more or less equivalent to jobs, and class structure
as something like a map of the job structure. This identification
creates certain theoretical problems because the job a person
holds may not determine her material interests.

Classical Marxist theory asserts that class structure is the basic
cause of class formation, class consciousness, and class struggle
but that it does not determine these things in any precise or

definitive way. The determination exercised by class structure simply limits the variations that can occur but does not specify which one will happen. Class structure also influences the broad trajectory of social change.

Class formation refers to the existence of organized collectivities established on the basis of material interests defined by the class structure. It measures the corporate coherence of a class and its organizational capacity to function as an active participant in society. Although class formation can wax and wane without changing class structure, collectivities organized along class lines sometimes transform class structure through the process of class struggle. Wright emphatically rejects the view that class formation can be deduced in any simple way from class structure. In fact, a major goal of Analytical Marxist class analysis is to explain the highly contingent relationship between class structure and class formation.

Class consciousness is a dual awareness of needs: awareness by persons in subordinate class locations of needing to transform class structure, and a corresponding realization by members of superordinate classes of needing to preserve it. *Class struggle* is the process by which formed and conscious classes transform the class structure of society. The links between class structure, class formation, class consciousness, and class struggle—as understood by Erik Wright—are diagrammed in Figure 5.1.

Analytical Marxism has already produced a wealth of ideas on the subject of class. This chapter dwells extensively upon the work of Erik Wright, who has formulated a comprehensive Analytical Marxist theory of class and has conducted empirical investigations of class relations in several advanced capitalist countries for purposes of testing his theory. Wright may be the most prominent student of class among the Analytical Marxists, but he is certainly not the only one. The germinal contributions of John Roemer to class analysis were discussed in Chapter 4, and, as we shall see, Roemer's ideas have influenced Wright deeply. Nevertheless, profound differences exist between these thinkers. They both engage in class analysis, but they engage in quite different kinds of class analysis.

Roemer is first and foremost a deductive thinker concerned with the logical connection between concepts. His method of analysis boils down to proving theorems from clearly stated

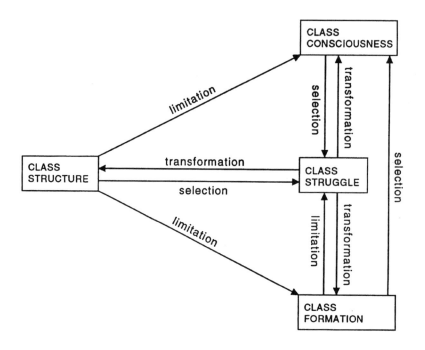

Figure 5.1. Causal Links Between Class Structure, Class Formation, Class Consciousness, and Class Struggle

SOURCE: Wright (1985), Figure 2.1, p. 30

assumptions. For example, he strives to establish the correspondence between class and exploitation as a mathematical theorem. Any important relationship between class and exploitation, Roemer's method suggests, should be a necessary consequence of plausible assumptions about these two phenomena. If empirical measures of class prove uncorrelated with empirical measures of exploitation, then so much the worse for empirical measurement: logical connections still hold. The absence of correlation only means that the intricacy and confusion of social life obscures the deep relationships that science ought to detect.

Wright, on the other hand, though philosophically sophisticated and logically precise, is fundamentally an inductive thinker. Disjunctures between theory and observation—such as the absence of polarized class relations or the presence of a large middle class—are the driving force in his work. Clarity is central to his methodology, but axiomatic reasoning is not. Wright's brand of analysis involves nuanced elaboration of what concepts mean, usually stimulated by an empirical problem of some sort. The theoretical structures he creates are ingenious and accessible but often lack the splendid self-sufficiency of axiomatic systems.

Wright has been amazingly willing to modify his thinking in response to empirical evidence and theoretical criticism. His exemplary intellectual honesty should be emulated by other social scientists, whether Marxist or not. Yet there is also a certain hubris implicit in building and abandoning a succession of elaborate theoretical structures. Being an inductive thinker, Wright usually treats relationships between variables as contingent rather than necessary. To explore the relationship between class and exploitation, for example, he would not try to prove theorems à la Roemer. Rather he would form a contingency table and study the properties of incongruous cells: for example, exploited capitalists or exploiting proletarians.

Although the boundaries of Analytical Marxism remain a bit fuzzy, they certainly include other important analyses of class. Adam Przeworski has studied class formation as a political process, focusing on the conditions influencing the emergence of the proletariat as a political actor (Przeworski 1985a). Samuel Bowles and Herbert Gintis develop a theory of class structure based on the idea that exchange is contested because the enforcement of economic claims is costly (Bowles and Gintis 1990). Alan Carling uses cooperative and noncooperative game theory to analyze class, gender, and ethnic divisions (Carling 1991). David Abraham studies the relationship between class structure and the rise of German fascism (Abraham 1986).

This chapter explores Erik Wright's version of Analytical Marxist class analysis, including some issues raised by critics, and then discusses several of the contributions mentioned above.

Exploitation and Class Structure

Erik Wright's intellectual odyssey has involved a shift from a theory of class emphasizing contradictory class locations to an interpretation founded upon the concept of exploitation (Wright

1985, chap. 2).[1] Wright absorbed Roemer's theory of exploitation but modified it in several ways, arriving at a distinctive image of class structure in capitalist societies based upon exploitation understood as a fundamental conflict of interest.

One way Wright modifies Roemer is by distinguishing between exploitation and *economic oppression*. Economic oppression results from property inequality but does not require an ongoing relationship between the rich oppressor and the poor oppressed. The oppressor simply wants to defend her property and does not much care what happens to the oppressed. Due to the absence of an ongoing relationship, rational self-interest does not moderate the actions of oppressors toward the oppressed, and the former can be extremely vicious toward the latter, even to the point of committing genocide.

Exploitation entails both economic oppression and appropriation of the *surplus product* of one class by another.[2] Appropriation of the surplus product means that the exploiting class depends upon the labor of the exploited class and would not seek its elimination. The prosperity of an exploiting class is causally related to the poverty of the class it exploits (Wright 1985, pp. 73-77). The two components of exploitation are separable. For example, children appropriate the labor of their parents but do not oppress them. Conversely, unemployed people are economically oppressed, but no one appropriates their surplus product.

Wright reformulates Roemer's "status exploitation" as exploitation based upon unequal control of organizational assets: *organizational exploitation*. This form of exploitation permeates state socialist societies but is also important under capitalism. The possessors of organizational assets (often called managers) cannot buy and sell them, but they exert substantial control over how these assets are transmitted and who can use them.

Wright renames Roemer's socialist exploitation as *skills/credential exploitation* because it derives from unequal distribution of skills and credentials and because it occurs in nonsocialist societies.

The main exploitation in capitalist society emerges from unequal distribution of ownership of means of production, but organizational exploitation and skills/credential exploitation are also important. The class structure of capitalist society results from the intersection of these three forms of exploitation. Table 5.1 shows

Wright's proposed typology of class locations in capitalist society. The main division in this typology is between owners and nonowners of means of production. Owners are divided according to how much capital they possess but not by organizational or skill/credential assets. Wright does not think organizational or skills/credential exploitation is relevant within ownership class locations. However, these forms of exploitation do define nine different class locations of nonowners.

For purposes of simplicity, Wright assumes that the three forms of exploitation constituting the capitalist class structure are independent and do not reinforce each other. This assumption seems especially dubious in the case of managerial class locations, and Wright acknowledges that capitalist exploitation often does enhance organizational exploitation. The assumption of independence between types of exploitation gives Wright's map of capitalist class structure the flavor of a mechanical cross-classification, an impression reinforced by the attribution of three levels to each mode of exploitation.

Although Wright tries to root his conception of class structure within relations of production, his view of organizational assets and skills/credential assets as class-generating forms of productive property remains troublesome. Organizational assets do not seem much like productive property, and skill/credential assets do not appear to create a class type of relationship. Wright's framework shows marvelous conceptual ingenuity but tends to substitute multiple dimensions for real class relationships. It resembles a gradational Weberian analysis of stratification cloaked by the Marxian rubric of exploitation.

In his own critique of the multiple exploitation framework, Wright freely acknowledges a Weberian temptation:

> Once you adopt a fairly differentiated Marxist class concept of the sort I have advocated, then in practice there is not actually all that much difference in the nature of the empirical class structure "variables" that are generated in neo-Marxist and neo-Weberian frameworks: after all, both acknowledge in one way or another that differences in property, skills/credentials/autonomy, and authority are bases for differentiating locations in the class structure. . . . The reason for adopting a Marxist strategy . . . has to rest on a commitment to the theoretical constraints that Marxist theory imposes on class analysis. More specifically, unless one sees the

TABLE 5.1 Class Locations in a Capitalist Society, Based Upon the Intersection of the Three Forms of Exploitation

Assets in the means of production

	Owners of means of production	*Nonowners (wage laborers)*			
Owns sufficient capital to hire workers and not work	1 Bourgeoisie	4 Expert managers	7 Semicredentialed managers	10 Uncredentialed managers	+
Owns sufficient capital to hire workers but must work	2 Small employers	5 Expert supervisors	8 Semicredentialed supervisors	11 Uncredentialed supervisors	>0
Owns sufficient capital to work for self but not to hire workers	3 Petty bourgeoisie	6 Expert nonmanagers	9 Semicredentialed workers	12 Proletarians	−
		+	>0	−	*Organization assets*
			Skill/credential assets		

SOURCE: Wright (1985), Table 3.3, p. 88

value of embedding the concept of class structure in an abstract model of modes of production in which classes are fundamentally polarized around processes of exploitation, then there would be no reason to accept the difficulties this abstract framework generates for the concrete analysis of classes. (Wright, Becker, et al. 1989, pp. 318-19)

Wright remains committed to the Marxist framework because it clarifies the possibilities for emancipatory social change, helps explain both major historical change and social conflict within specific societies, and renders research more cumulative by providing a well-articulated theory of society.

He concedes, however, that organizational and skill/credential exploitation are better conceptualized as rents levied on the property-owning classes.[3] Organizational and skill/credential assets provide a basis for strata within classes rather than outright class divisions.

Middle Classes and Contradictory Class Locations

Whatever its limitations, the exploitation-based concept of class structure does illuminate the nature of nonpolarized class locations. These class locations come in two varieties. Nonpolarized class locations of one sort neither exploit nor suffer exploitation because they have the per capita share of the relevant asset. Wright calls such positions the *old middle class* and gives the petty bourgeoisie (Category 3 in Table 5.1) as an example.

The new middle classes consist of class positions that are exploiting with respect to one type of exploitation but exploited with regard to another. Expert nonmanagers (Category 6) and uncredentialed managers (Category 10) are examples of new middle-class positions. These jointly exploiting and exploited positions are truly contradictory class locations, indicating that Wright's adoption of Roemer's exploitation theory may not entail any drastic departure from his previous theoretical outlook. Of course, all managerial and all expert positions are in a certain sense contradictory in that they possess organizational and/or skill assets without owning means of production.

Incumbents of contradictory class locations are important for historical change. Social revolutions, according to both Wright and Roemer, do not eliminate all forms of exploitation simultaneously: they eliminate only one particular kind of exploitation. Therefore the principal beneficiary of a social revolution will not be the most exploited class but rather a class occupying a contradictory location in prerevolutionary social structure. This analysis works well for revolutions against feudal property relations, whose main beneficiaries were not the comprehensively exploited serfs but the bourgeoisie, a class that held a contradictory position in feudal society.

Wright's theory has interesting implications about the future of capitalism. The most formidable rival of the bourgeoisie is not the completely exploited proletariat, but either the class of experts or—more likely—the managerial class, both of which are jointly exploiting and exploited. The successor to capitalism is likely to be not socialism but a society where organizational assets provide the chief underpinning for exploitation. By the same logic, the leading rival of the dominant bureaucratic class in state socialist societies is not the working class but the contradictorily located class of experts, which will be the exploiting class in a fully socialist society (Wright 1985, pp. 89-91, 114-18).

This conception implies that the managers under capitalism have some material interest in the emergence of statist society, whereas experts have a class interest in the achievement of socialism. These implications run counter to all available evidence. Both managers and experts appear fully committed to the continuation of capitalism, which enables them to capitalize their incomes and enter the property-owning classes. The class position of individual managers in a statist society is far less secure than under capitalism, for they can neither capitalize their position nor transmit it to their offspring. And the same is true of experts in a socialist society.

The collapse of Communist regimes, which occurred long after the publication of *Classes*, emphasizes the problems with this theory of history. The theory treats state socialism as a possible successor to capitalism, but the history of Communist societies suggests that state socialism may be a temporary substitute for capitalism, not an advance beyond it. Recent events indicate that state socialist societies lack long-term stability and frequently devolve toward capitalism (see Chapter 8). Yet by Wright's analysis, this transition resurrects a previously abolished exploitation and thus runs against the main thrust of historical development. If the collapse of Communism is seen as a deviation rather than the main thrust of history, then—to use Joan Robinson's ([1942] 1966) phrase—the exception becomes more important than the rule. Even "nomenklatura capitalism," the disparaging name bestowed upon the form of capitalism emerging in once-Communist countries, insinuates that the managers of state socialism hanker for private ownership of means of production to stabilize and expand their class privileges.

Class Structure

The Analytical Marxist approach concerns social research as well as social theory. It denies the existence of any specifically Marxist research methodology. Marxists can and should use all legitimate scientific methods. No Analytical Marxist has followed this advice more energetically than Erik Wright, and nowhere is the wisdom of the advice more evident than in Wright's empirical studies of class structure.

Since 1977, Wright has organized and coordinated a massive international study of class structure and class consciousness (Wright 1989a). The Comparative Project on Class Structure and Class Consciousness uses modern sample survey methodology and multivariate statistical techniques to investigate class relations in 11 capitalist countries: the United States, Sweden, Canada, Norway, Finland, New Zealand, Great Britain, Denmark, Germany, Australia, and Japan. Most of the results reported by Wright concern the United States and Sweden, and are based on data collected in 1988. Some monographs on other countries have been published, however, and further reports are expected (Marshall et. al. 1988).

The United States and Sweden, as Wright points out, afford a useful contrast. Both are advanced capitalist countries with similar average living standards and similar levels of technological development. Major differences exist, however: Sweden has less income inequality, more employment by the state, and far more frequent social democratic governance than the United States. Using his exploitation-centered concept of class, Wright compares the distribution of employed people over class locations in Sweden and the United States (see Table 5.2).

The class structures of Sweden and the United States have many commonalities. Proletarians are much the largest class, and the bourgeoisie is very small in both countries. The percentage of the labor force in each class location is roughly similar. The United States has more supervisory class locations as well as a stronger association between skill/credential exploitation and organizational exploitation. But the crucial difference between the class structures of Sweden and the United States, Wright believes, lies in the U.S. tendency to vest supervisory functions in positions that otherwise would fall into the working class (Wright 1985, p. 223).

Wright's analysis creates some confusion between class locations and people who occupy them. In the theoretical sections of his work, Wright carefully distinguishes between the position and its occupant, but when reporting empirical results the distinction is often obscured. Suppose that the distinction between people and locations is tenable, and also suppose that class locations exist independent of their occupants. The distributions reported in Table 5.2 can still differ from the corresponding distribution of class locations: some locations may be unfilled, and some people may not occupy a class location even if they work. A methodology allowing direct investigation of class locations would be more congruent with the theoretical position Wright articulates and would also maintain a sharper distinction between Marxist and non-Marxist ways of doing class analysis.

A strong relationship between class location and income exists in both Sweden and the United States. Members of the bourgeoisie earn much more than members of the working class, and income tends to increase along each dimension of exploitation. Although relevant data are only available for the United States, an even stronger relationship holds between unearned income (measured as income from investments) and the three dimensions of exploitation.

Marxists often characterize current capitalism as monopoly capitalism, but in both Sweden and the United States more

TABLE 5.2 Distribution of Employed People Over Capitalist Class Locations in the United States and Sweden

Owners	Nonowners (wage laborers)			
Assets in the means of production				*Organization assets*
1 Bourgeoisie U.S. 1.8% Sweden 0.7%	4 Expert managers U.S. 3.9% Sweden 4.4%	7 Semicredentialed managers U.S. 6.2% Sweden 4.0%	10 Uncredentialed managers U.S. 2.3% Sweden 2.5%	+
2 Small employers U.S. 6.0% Sweden 4.8%	5 Expert supervisors U.S. 3.7% Sweden 3.8%	8 Semicredentialed supervisors U.S. 6.8% Sweden 3.2%	11 Uncredentialed supervisors U.S. 6.9% Sweden 3.1%	>0
3 Petty bourgeoisie U.S. 6.9% Sweden 5.4%	6 Expert nonmanagers U.S. 3.4% Sweden 6.8%	9 Semicredentialed workers U.S. 12.2% Sweden 17.8%	12 Proletarians U.S. 39.9% Sweden 43.5%	–
	+	>0	–	
	Skill/credential assets			

SOURCE: Wright (1985), Table 6.1, p. 195

workers have jobs in firms with under 50 employees than in giant corporations with over 10,000.[4] Moreover, the most proletarianized companies—in the sense of having the largest share of working-class employees—are those of medium size.

Employment by the state has a strong impact on the class structure of advanced capitalist societies and constitutes a much larger share of the Swedish than of the American labor force. Much of the expansion of middle-class positions in both countries is attributable to the growth of state employment. State employment is relatively low among the working class, especially in the United States, and this, Wright hypothesizes, may be the structural source of antistatist sentiment among American workers.

Analysis of the links between class structure and the family also yields some interesting findings. In both Sweden and the United States most workers live in households containing only workers. However, middle-class people in Sweden are more likely to live in families with a working-class member than are middle-class people in the United States. The middle-class family, Wright concludes, is structurally more isolated from the working class in the United States than in Sweden. This structural isolation could influence the feasibility of political alliances between the middle and working classes. In both Sweden and the United States, working-class women are more likely to live in families deriving some income from exploitation than are working-class men (Wright 1985, p. 232).

Wright and Cho (1992) study the effect of class structure on friendships, using data from Canada, Norway, Sweden, and the United States. More specifically, they study the likelihood of friendships between members of different classes. The exploitation-centered model of class structure defines class boundaries of three kinds: differences in property ownership, differences in organizational authority, and differences in expertise. Cross-class friendships are least likely to occur across the property boundary and most likely to happen over the organizational authority boundary. The same pattern of cross-class friendships appears in all four countries despite deep cultural and political differences between them, implying that class boundaries have similar permeabilities in each one.[5] Wright and Cho view these findings as broadly consistent with Marxist theory but interpret the similarity between these four politically diverse countries to mean that relative permeability of class boundaries cannot explain class formation or political alliances between classes.

In his book *Classes* (1985), Wright interprets the differences between the class structure of Sweden and the United States largely in political terms. These differences arise chiefly from variations in state economic policy and variations in the political mobilization of the working class. The association between state employment and the expansion of middle-class positions has already been mentioned. The more extensive supervision of work in the United States may reflect an effort by capital to fragment the working class by giving some potentially working-class positions supervisory responsibilities, thereby weakening the union movement. Conversely, the greater power and centralization of the Swedish labor movement may mean that unions can themselves perform many supervisory functions.

An Alternative Approach to Class Structure

When criticizing his own work, Wright identifies two theoretical impulses within contemporary Marxist class analysis (Wright, Becker, et al. 1989, pp. 269-70). One impulse is to keep the concept of class structure simple and to remedy the resulting theoretical deficiencies by introducing other explanatory principles. The other impulse involves making the class structure concept more complicated so it can carry a greater explanatory burden. Wright identifies himself with this second theoretical impulse and explains—quite eloquently, I think—why he has made this choice.

Wright also mentions that his way of analyzing class structure has been criticized for being excessively static (Wright, Becker, et al. 1989, pp. 329-31). He defends his approach by noting that the concept of material interests is inherently forward looking (and hence dynamic) and by suggesting that, in certain cases, *job* might be replaced by *career* (a concept that has a temporal dimension) as the operational embodiment of class location. However, Wright asserts the conceptual primacy of structure over process because a concept of class structure is necessary to define the very meaning of class dynamics.

What Wright may not fully recognize is the connection between his choice of the second theoretical impulse and the criticism that his approach is excessively static. For many Marxists the theoretical purpose of the class structure concept is to analyze the forces propelling historical change. By complicating the concept of class structure, Wright may have weakened its capacity to explain historical change. The 12-class typology presented in Table 5.1 gives little insight about how class dynamics might transform capitalist society. By making the concept of class structure more useful for answering questions arising in a context of social stability, Wright may have lessened its power to explain the things of primary interest to Marxists.

Wright's defense of the conceptual priority of structure over process indicates a cognitive orientation attributing greater reality to static relationships than to dynamic processes. The conceptual priority of structure over process is surely not a law of thought. Wright's advocacy of this position only means that he finds the structural dimensions of class more vivid and intuitively accessible than the dynamic dimensions.

These issues emerge quite clearly in a paper by Wright and Shin (1988) contrasting class analysis based on a structural concept of class, like that used by Wright, with class analysis based on a process concept, like that of E. P. Thompson (1963). Although Wright and Shin report some interesting empirical findings, their theoretical interpretation is not entirely on target. They interpret a process approach to class analysis as oriented toward how past events have molded present class identity. They interpret a structural approach as oriented toward how present material interests shape preferences about the future. A crucial assumption of the structural approach is that class relations objectively determine material interests.

The process approach to class analysis, as interpreted by Wright and Shin, may provide invaluable guidance for Marxist historiography, but it can hardly furnish a theoretical understanding of the possibilities for change imminent within a given class context. It may be able to explain the present in terms of the past, but it would be helpless to illuminate the future using both the present and past. Yet illuminating the future is the main concern of Marxist social theory.

On the other hand, Wright and Shin's interpretation of the structural approach to class analysis remains oblivious to criticisms that could emerge from within Analytical Marxism. Property relations themselves do not always determine material interests. Material interests are determined only when property relations give rise to a fully articulated economic system, which under capitalism includes a schedule of wages and prices. The transformation of property relations into a fully articulated economic system happens through a process of class struggle. If material interests are indeterminate apart from class struggle, then so is class structure. The indeterminacy of class structure apart from class struggle is analogous to the indeterminacy of labor values apart from commodity prices that Roemer found under complex production technologies.

The analogy between the indeterminacy of class structure and the indeterminacy of labor values suggests an alternative approach to class structure, but an approach still firmly based on Roemer's theory of exploitation. The crux of the difference between Wright's concept of class structure and this alternative lies in the treatment of contradictory class locations and the middle class. Wright allows multiple forms of exploitation and defines a location as contradictory if it exploits on one dimension but suffers exploitation on another. The alternative approach recognizes only one form of exploitation under capitalism and defines a location as contradictory if its exploitation status is indeterminate (i.e., the location could exploit or be exploited).

The alternative approach to class structure rests on the idea that a capitalist economy can have several different reproducible solutions. Who is exploited and who is an exploiter depend upon which reproducible solution is in effect. Suppose we define class locations as follows: (a) a capitalist location exploits under all possible reproducible solutions allowing positive profits, (b) a proletarian location is exploited under all possible profit-generating reproducible solutions, and (c) a middle-class location sometimes exploits and is sometimes exploited, depending upon which reproducible solution exists.

Although we cannot discuss this alternative approach to class structure in any detail, let us distinguish two forms of class struggle: revolutionary class struggle, which contests property relations, and status quo class struggle, which accepts property relations but contests the reproducible solution that will hold. Assuming that the reproducible solution is determined by status quo class struggle, it follows that class structure is not given by property relations but actually emerges through a process of class struggle. The material interests of the middle class are not defined in advance but are formed through status quo class struggle. Sometimes the material interest of a middle-class location will lie in higher wages and sometimes in higher profits. Indeed, this ambiguity is what makes a location middle class.

The alternative approach suggests a different way of looking at the structural contradictions of middle-class location. A middle-class person is not torn between her differing status on various forms of exploitation. Her class situation is defined by a single exploitation, but she faces a continual struggle over whether she will be exploited or exploiter. This approach has a certain affinity with Adam Przeworski's ideas about class analysis discussed later in this chapter.

Class Consciousness

Analytical Marxist treatments of class consciousness derive from the theory of rational choice. The connection with rational choice theory occurs in several ways. Consciousness, as understood by Analytical Marxists, is a characteristic of individual people, not of supraindividual entities like classes. Class consciousness, therefore, is a characteristic of individual class members, not of classes taken as a whole.

Second, class consciousness concerns how individual class members make choices: what alternative actions they consider, how they assess the consequences of these actions, what preferences they hold among the outcomes. The choices involving class consciousness include things like whether to join a union, whether to merge with another corporation, whether to start an independent business: choices relevant to a person's class location. Analytical Marxists usually assume that action is rational in the sense of maximizing preference, given a class member's perceptions of alternatives and their consequences.

Rationality enters the picture in another way as well. Some Analytical Marxists think it possible to impute specific class interests to a class location on the basis of rational choice. These are the interests that a rational incumbent of the location would have if she fully understood the structure and dynamics of the class system and had no concerns other than those defined by her class location. Jon Elster defines class consciousness as "the ability to overcome the free rider problem in realizing class interests" (Elster 1985, p. 347). Thus Elster views class consciousness as an expression of class solidarity.

The free rider problem for classes occurs in two different shapes: individual versus class and short-term versus long-term class interest. The first of these arises because individual class members are tempted to seek the benefits of class struggle without enduring the costs of participation. The second manifestation of the free rider problem happens when class struggle focuses exclusively on relatively easy-to-obtain, short-term objectives rather than on difficult but decisive long-term goals.

Everyone, says Erik Wright, has a "desire for freedom and autonomy," and class interests arise, very naturally, from the wish to remove limitations on freedom based on class location (Wright 1985, p. 249). But Wright, in contrast to Elster, distinguishes class formation from class consciousness and does not use class interest to define the latter. Class consciousness refers to all class-pertinent beliefs, regardless of how these correspond to class interests. He conceives class consciousness in relation to class structure and class struggle:

> If class structure is understood as a terrain of social relations that determine objective material interests of actors, and class struggle is understood as the forms of social practices which attempt to realize those interests, then class consciousness can be understood as the subjective processes that shape intentional choices with respect to those interests and struggles. (Wright 1985, p. 246)

Wright's empirical work investigates the influence of class structure on class consciousness. To measure class consciousness in a capitalist society, Wright gets responses to six statements about relations between workers and capitalists, of which the following are typical:

Corporations benefit owners at the expense of workers and consumers.

It is possible for modern society to run effectively without the profit motive.

During a strike, management should be prohibited by law from hiring workers to take the place of strikers. (Wright 1985, pp. 146, 252-54)

In both Sweden and the United States, class consciousness is polarized between the capitalist class and the working class. As Wright's exploitation-based theory of class predicts, class consciousness in both countries changes in a largely monotonic way along each of the three dimensions of exploitation: holding constant any two dimensions of exploitation, proworking-class consciousness increases with increases along the remaining exploitation dimension.

Notwithstanding these similarities, the polarization of class consciousness is much greater in Sweden than the United States. Swedish capitalists are quite similar to American capitalists, but Swedish workers hold much stronger proworking-class beliefs than American workers. In the United States, procapitalist beliefs penetrate deeply into the wage-earning population, whereas in Sweden such attitudes occur extensively only within bourgeois, small employer, and expert manager class locations.

In both Sweden and the United States, union members within each wage-earning class location have stronger proworking-class beliefs than nonunion members. But the basic relationship between exploitation and class consciousness holds among union members as well as nonunion members in both countries. Men exhibit more polarized class consciousness than do women, but again the basic relationship between exploitation and consciousness is true of both genders in both countries.

Using the same data, Wright and Cho (1992) undertake a somewhat more elaborate analysis of the relationship between class structure and class consciousness. For purposes of this analysis, they divide all wage-earning positions into working-class and middle-class (i.e., contradictory) locations. They further divide these class positions between those located in the private sector and those located in the state sector. In addition to the proworking-class (i.e., anticapitalist) attitudes discussed above, Wright and Cho also consider prostatist attitudes, which concern support for state intervention in various social issues.

Within both the private and state sectors, the working class is more anticapitalist and more favorable to state intervention than the middle class. This result holds in both Sweden and the United States. Within the private sector, class differences in anticapitalism are much stronger in Sweden than in the United States. In general—in both countries and on both dimensions of class consciousness—there is more ideological polarization in the private sector than in the state sector.

The consciousness of the Swedish working class is much more homogeneous across the private-state sector division than is the consciousness of the United States working class. For example, the working class in the United States private sector is significantly more prostatist than the working class in the state sector. But this situation is reversed with respect to the middle class: the United States middle class is somewhat more ideologically homogeneous than the Swedish middle class.

As in the case of class structure, Wright explains differences between class consciousness in Sweden and the United States largely in political terms. The social democratic movement in Sweden has reinforced certain elements of working-class consciousness and placed a variety of class issues on the political agenda. The feebleness of the labor movement in the United States stands in sharp contrast to the vitality of the Swedish labor movement, which has succeeded in unionizing most white-collar employees and even a substantial number of managers. When dealing with issues of power and property, the political system in the United States eliminates all but a tiny range of alternatives. The upshot of these political developments is that incumbents of wage-earning class locations in the United States do not feel any real sense of unity vis-à-vis owners of capital. Instead, internal divisions, ultimately based upon organizational and skill/credential exploitation, loom overriding and insurmountable in their class consciousness.

Women and Class: Carling's Interpretation

Is the social division between men and women a class division? The answer to this question depends on how one defines class. Jon Elster proposes a rather general definition of class based on the relationship between a person's possessions and rational economic behavior. "A class is a group of people who by virtue of what they possess are compelled to engage in the same activities if they want to make the best use of their endowments (Elster 1985, p. 331). If the idea of endowments is understood broadly, then Elster's definition of class makes gender a class division.

The Analytical Marxist who has examined the relationship between gender and class most carefully is Alan Carling (1991). After pondering how to conceptualize properly the class position of women, Carling adopts the following definition of class:

> Class position is about the range of options a person has as a result of the distribution of social access to forces of production. A class division exists between two agents whose welfare differs systematically at an equilibrium of social interaction, as a result of differential possession of forces of production, differential behavior with respect to the production process or both. (Carling 1991, p. 275)

The innovative thing about this definition is Carling's insistence that class division can result from unequal behavior as well as unequal endowments.

The major economic division between men and women in a capitalist society, says Carling, derives from unequal wages in the workplace plus the unequal division of labor within the household. Husbands systematically exploit their wives within domestic production, and the gender split constitutes a bona fide class division. A viable Marxist class analysis must link the public domain of capitalist production with the private domain of household labor (Carling 1991, p. 276).

Carling uses two game theory models to analyze the class position of women. The first model, based upon cooperative game theory, treats the economic process by which marriages between working class people—people who must sell their labor to secure a living—are formed.[6] The second model, based upon noncooperative game theory, considers how housework is divided between wife and husband.

The fundamental assumption of the first model is that men get higher wages than women. Each person must obtain a certain amount of money and perform a certain quantity of domestic labor in order to survive. Marriage is conceptualized as an economic agreement in which each party agrees to provide a certain amount of money and to perform a certain amount of housework for the marital unit. People get married for the purpose of reducing the amount of time they must work, and a marriage will not happen unless both husband and wife work less than they do when living alone.

Given these assumptions, what kind of households are formable through marriage? Economic rationality requires that the couple take advantage of the higher wages available to men. Hence every viable household has the husband doing at least some wage labor and the wife doing at least some domestic labor. Moreover, the wife always works longer hours than the husband (though less than she would work if living alone). According to this model, the wife receives a shadow wage for her domestic labor; and a necessary and sufficient condition for a viable household is that this shadow wage be greater than the market wage available to women but less than the wage paid to men (Carling 1991, p. 165).

Carling identifies four kinds of viable households: (a) symmetrical households, in which husband and wife each do some paid labor and some domestic labor; (b) houseworker households, in which the wife does all the domestic labor, but both husband and wife do paid labor; (c) breadwinner households, in which the husband does all the paid labor, but the domestic labor is shared; and (d) traditional households, in which the husband does all the paid labor and the wife does all the domestic labor. The surprising result is that symmetrical households—the only viable households that seem relatively egalitarian—are never Pareto optimal and thus would never be formed by economically rational men or women.[7] By contrast, all other formable households are Pareto optimal and hence real options for rational people.

Using this relatively simple cooperative game model, Carling derives a variety of sometimes counterintuitive results. If the wage paid to women increases, then households of the breadwinner type (in which husbands do all the paid labor) become more frequent. Conversely, if the wage paid to men decreases, then houseworker households, where women do all the domestic work, become more common. When children enter the picture, greatly expanding the time required for domestic labor, breadwinner households become the preponderant and sometimes the only economically rational form (Carling 1991, pp. 168-74).

Within any formable household, women work longer then men. Does this constitute exploitation? Carling considers this question with painstaking care under several different assumptions about the legitimacy of the wage differential and the coerciveness of the exchange between husband and wife. But even under the most benign assumptions—with the wage differential deemed just and the exchange noncoercive—there are compelling reasons to think the wife's labor overload is exploitative. For example, there always exist formable households where the difference between the amounts of labor performed by wife and husband exceeds the difference that would happen if they lived apart. And because the domestic relationship between wife and husband entails irreducible exploitation, Carling concludes that Analytical Marxists—who generally advocate exploitation-based concepts of class—must consider it a class relationship.

Carling's first model concerns the nature of the marriage contract and the economic conditions under which a conjugal household comes into being. His second model, based on noncooperative game theory, deals with the strategic interaction between husband and wife over who actually does the housework.

With regard to any housework, a spouse can either contribute or not contribute to doing the task. Assuming that both husband and wife dislike housework, the most preferred outcome is having the other spouse do the job while doing nothing oneself. The next most preferred outcome is doing the housework together. Because workers want to have neat and orderly homes, the worst outcome is if neither spouse does the housework.

Interaction defined in this way generates a game of Chicken, named after the suicidal teenage driving contest of the 1950s. The payoff matrix for this household version of Chicken appears in Figure 5.2. Each cell of the matrix designates an outcome of the game. The first symbol in the cell gives the payoff of that

Husband

	Contributes to doing housework	Does not contribute to doing housework
Contributes to doing housework	b, b	c, a
Does not contribute to doing housework	a, c	d, d

Wife (appears at left, spanning both rows)

$$a > b > c > d$$

Figure 5.2 Payoff Matrix for Chicken Game Generated by Interaction Between Wife and Husband About Who Does the Housework

outcome for the wife (the row player), and the second symbol gives the payoff to the husband (the column player).

The household Chicken game has two radically different solutions. In one solution the wife does the housework and the husband does nothing. The second solution is just the reverse: the husband does the housework and the wife does nothing. No other solutions exist: that is, no other combination of strategies is stable. Both of these solutions involve extreme exploitation, but from the abstract game model alone we cannot determine which solution, if any, will occur.

Although the solution of the game model is indeterminate, Carling argues that the weight of convention and just about everything else favors the wife doing the housework and the husband doing nothing. In most cases the husband will have a stronger position in the job market. A messy household diminishes the status of the wife more than that of the husband. Men have learned how to contrive insensitivity to domestic chaos as a means of evading household chores.

To support this argument, Carling reviews Susan McRae's study of 30 British couples among whom the wife had higher occupational status than the husband (McRae 1986). If these cross-class families were motivated by the kind of economic rationality assumed in the first model, they would reverse the conventional distribution of housework to accommodate the wife's greater earning power. But McRae found that gender role reversal rarely happens, even among couples ideologically committed to gender equality.

The Chicken game supports Carling's claim that relations between men and women involve systematic exploitation of the latter by the former and are therefore class relations. It also indicates that exploitation can be the unavoidable outcome of social interaction even when endowments are completely equal. The Chicken game is entirely symmetric, yet the only sensible solutions involve one player egregiously exploiting the other. This is why Carling insists that class divisions can result from unequal behavior as well as from unequal endowments. The theoretical motivation underlying Carling's definition of class is clear, but it threatens to make every inequality, no matter how it happens, a class division.

Women and Class: Wright's Interpretation

> "Class" is not equivalent to "oppression," and so long as different categories of women own different types and amounts of productive assets, and by virtue of that ownership enter into different positions within the social relations of production, then women *qua* women cannot be considered a "class." (Wright 1985, pp. 129-30)

Women do not constitute a class, says Erik Wright; the tendency to conceptualize the oppression of women as a class relationship reduces the intelligibility of the class concept and also shrouds the true nature of women's oppression.

To analyze the place of women in the class structure, Wright formulates the concept of mediated class relations (Wright 1989c, p. 41). Real people are linked to production not only by their direct relations to productive resources but also by other social relations such as connections with the state and family ties. Wright calls these indirect relations with the system of production *mediated class relations* and reconceptualizes class structure as the sum of direct and indirect class relations. Although capitalist class structure shows considerable variation, mediated class relations are usually more important for defining the class locations of women than of men.

Where are housewives located in the capitalist class structure? With respect to capitalism, says Wright, their material interests and their exploitation status do not differ from those of their husbands. Though husbands may exploit their wives within the context of household production, Wright doubts that this usually happens. That is, he doubts that the normal economy of the working-class family involves a net transfer of labor from housewives to their working husbands, and he doubts that working-class wives would toil less if the division of labor within home and workplace were completely equal (Wright 1985, p. 129). Part of Wright's skepticism about the prevalence of household exploitation reflects the existence of gender discrimination in the labor market. Being subject to discriminatory wage rates and hiring practices, housewives might not benefit from a completely egalitarian division of family labor.

Turning from housewives to employed women, Wright finds that men and women who participate in the labor force have very different class distributions. Women in both Sweden and the United States are a clear majority of the working class but are underrepresented in class locations exercising exploitation. Surprisingly, the difference between the class distribution of employed men and women is greater in Sweden than the United States, and Swedish women experience more underrepresentation within exploiting-class locations. One cause of gender differences in class distribution is that men are much more likely to gain promotion from working- to middle-class positions, especially during the first half of their working careers (Wright 1985, p. 199).

The family incorporates both direct and mediated class relations and is vital for understanding the class structure of any society. In both Sweden and the United States, most working-class people live in households containing only workers. However, marriages between working-class and middle-class people are less common in the United States than in Sweden, from which Wright concludes that the U.S. middle class is structurally more isolated. Because women constitute a majority of the working class (of people occupying consistently exploited-class locations), working-class women are more likely to live in families that get some income from exploitation than are working-class men. This disparity in family context may explain differences in the class actions taken by working-class men and women (Wright 1985, p. 232).

Within both Sweden and the United States, the same basic relationship between class location and class consciousness holds among women and among men: for each gender, procapitalist attitudes increase along each dimension of exploitation. However, women in both countries exhibit less ideological polarization then do men: differences in class consciousness between women in exploiting- and women in exploited-class locations are smaller than for men. Women in expert manager positions prove distinctly less favorable toward capitalism than their male counterparts, which accounts for much of the gender difference in ideological polarization. Female expert managers are less enthusiastic about capitalism, Wright hypothesizes, because they usually occupy lower positions on the managerial hierarchy than their male counterparts (Wright 1985, pp. 266-67).

An important element of class consciousness is subjective class identification. Into which, if any, class does a person place herself? Wright studies the relative influence of own class location and husband's class location on the subjective class identification of married employed women. In theoretical terms, this amounts to investigating the comparative impact of direct and mediated class relations on female class consciousness. In the United States, it turns out, the class location of a woman's job does not affect either her own subjective class identification or that of her husband. In Sweden, however, the class location of a woman's job influences her husband's class identification as well as her own. Mediated class relations seem to affect female class consciousness in both countries, but direct class relations only influence the consciousness of Swedish women (Wright 1989c, p. 52).

Within the United States, observes Michael Burawoy (1989), class location influences class consciousness mainly through its effects on material consumption, whereas in Sweden class location shapes class consciousness at least partly through daily interactions at work. This difference might explain the results reported in the previous paragraph. In the United States—but not in Sweden—an employed wife's class identity derives mainly from her family's level of material consumption, and hence mainly from the earnings of the chief breadwinner. Because the chief breadwinner is usually the husband, an employed American wife—but not an employed Swedish wife—tends to identify with her husband's class location (Wright 1989c, pp. 59-60).

Eric Wright consistently emphasizes the distinctions between class and gender, and between exploitation and oppression. With equal consistency, however, he recognizes that class exploitation and gender oppression interact with each other in important ways. The nature of this interaction is highly variable, and Wright cannot yet formulate a systematic theory of how it operates. The concept of mediated class relations provides a materialist foundation for addressing the relations between class and gender without compromising the essential distinctions between the two and without subordinating one to the other.

Proletarianization

Classical Marxism claimed that capitalist development entailed a systematic process of proletarianization. As commodity production expands, capitalist relations invade every form of economic activity, and the organization of production becomes increasingly centralized. The spread of capitalist relations ruins small producers and independent artisans, forcing them into the working class, which becomes steadily larger. The process of proletarianization, it is argued, also transforms the character of labor under capitalism. The activity of labor becomes increasingly routinized, the autonomy of the worker becomes increasingly restricted, and technical knowledge becomes increasingly concentrated in an ever-diminishing share of the labor force. The thesis of a continuing proletarianization of labor under modern capitalism is powerfully advocated in Harry Braverman's influential book *Labor and Monopoly Capital* (1974).

Analytical Marxists tend to be agnostic about the thesis of continuing proletarianization under modern capitalism. Because Roemer identifies unequal ownership of property rather than domination of the labor process as the source of capitalist exploitation, the proletarianization thesis is not essential to his analysis of capitalism. Capitalist exploitation occurs equally well under credit markets involving little proletarianization as under labor markets that involve a great deal. Moreover, any real capitalist society contains a combination of different exploitations rather than the growing monopoly of a single form. This is significant because some varieties of exploitation do not proletarianize labor.

Important empirical research on the progress of proletarianization in recent decades is reported in two papers by Erik Wright and his collaborators (Wright and Singelmann 1982; Wright and Martin 1987). Among other things, these papers exemplify the self-critical spirit and willingness to acknowledge error admired by Analytical Marxists.

The earlier paper (Wright and Singlemann 1982) uses a combination of survey and census data to examine proletarianization in the United States class structure between 1960 and 1970. The authors break down changes in proletarianization into two components: (a) an *industry effect* that alters proletarianization by changing how the labor force is distributed between different industries, and (b) a *class effect* that alters proletarianization by changing the nature of particular industries.

These two components of proletarianization counteracted each other during the 1960-1970 decade. A strong and consistent proletarianizing tendency occurred within particular industries, but this was hidden by the growth of industrial sectors—such as state services—with low proletarianization. On the basis of these findings, Wright and Singelmann anticipated an increase in proletarianization in subsequent decades. Class effects causing proletarianization within industries would continue and perhaps even accelerate, they predicted, while industry effects reducing aggregate proletarianization through labor force redistribution would diminish.

The second paper (Wright and Martin 1987) uses the same method to analyze proletarianization in the United States over the 20-year period from 1960 to 1980 and utterly refutes the predictions made in the first. Contrary to expectations, the authors found that *deproletarianization* occurred within almost all industrial sectors during the 1970s and that changes in the relative size of industrial sectors during this decade continued to favor deproletarianization.[8] They also discovered a pronounced acceleration in the growth of managerial class locations within almost all industrial sectors.

How can Marxist theory explain such deproletarianization? Capitalist development, argue Wright and Martin, fosters the emergence of postcapitalist class relations, which rest upon organizational and skill exploitations. The growth of classes controlling organizational assets and skill assets in various combinations explains the process of deproletarianization observed during the 1970s.

Whether Wright and Martin intend this as a theoretical explanation of the observed deproletarianization or merely as a redescription of the finding using the language of exploitation is not quite clear. But if it is intended as an explanation, then it seems tainted by tautological reasoning. Wright and Martin claim knowledge about the postcapitalist development of human society and try to explain present happenings through the imminence of this hypothetical future. Their explanation also implies that deproletarianization is a protracted tendency rather than a temporary fluctuation. Any significant resumption of proletarianization during the 1980s or 1990s would invalidate the Wright and Martin explanation of how class structure evolved during the 1970s.

A Neo-Weberian Critique of Analytical Marxist Class Analysis

The British team associated with the Comparative Project on Class Structure and Class Consciousness reach theoretical conclusions very different than those of Erik Wright. Although they do not doubt the existence or the causal importance of class structure in British society, Gordon Marshall and his colleagues believe that a neo-Weberian perspective provides a better basis for class analysis than does the Analytical Marxist approach of

Erik Wright (Marshall et al. 1988, pp. 136-40; Rose and Marshall 1989; Goldthorpe and Marshall 1992).

Some of the criticisms made by the British team are methodological in nature:

> [The] Wright classifications are not generally reliable in terms of what they themselves purport to be measuring. There are too many instances of managers who are not really managers, supervisors who are not really supervisors, and workers who are not really workers. The categories are extremely heterogeneous—even in their own terms. . . . On practical grounds alone his schemes are of doubtful value. Nor is it clear that Wright's class algorithms generate meaningful categories—irrespective of the reliability with which they operationalize the theory. (Marshall et al. 1988, p. 139)

Other criticisms are more substantive. The theoretical categories used by Wright artificially diminish the number of intermediate class locations and thus greatly exaggerate the degree of polarization in British class structure. The artificial elimination of intermediate class locations also exaggerates the amount of social mobility in British society, making it seem much more open than it really is.

Marshall and his colleagues conclude that the neo-Weberian framework suggested by John Goldthorpe offers a more robust and reliable way of analyzing British class structure than Wright's Analytical Marxism. Goldthorpe, in contrast to all Marxist approaches, does not interpret class as an antagonistic relationship or derive it from the system of economic production. Instead, he views a person's class as a combination of her market situation and her work situation. In a subsequent paper, Goldthorpe and Marshall advocate treating class analysis as a research program rather than a theoretical position of any sort, and conjecture that class structure may be irrelevant to social change (Goldthorpe and Marshall 1992).

How devastating are these criticisms? The methodological problems identified by the British team afflict virtually every form of empirical research on social class. Their evidence does not establish that Wright's scheme creates more egregious methodological difficulties than other possible class categories. At least some of the methodological problems can be handled without a major theoretical overhaul. For example, improved ways of operationalizing autonomy and authority on the job would reduce apparent misclassifications.

Some of the substantive criticisms made by the British team seem to reflect prior commitments about the nature of British class structure. The results of applying Wright's class categories may be surprising, but are they wrong? Perhaps British society is both more polarized and more open than Marshall and his colleagues want to believe.

The most important difference between neo-Marxism and neo-Weberianism concerns the theory of history. Neo-Weberians are highly skeptical that any general theory of history is possible, whereas for neo-Marxists understanding history is the main purpose of scientific inquiry. Given such differences, it is only natural that neo-Weberians should want to detach class analysis from broad concepts of history. But is anything gained by such detachment? The polarization hypothesis may be entirely wrong. The chief causal impact of class structure may be, as Goldthorpe and Marshall suggest, resisting rather than compelling change. Yet the effort to connect class analysis and history greatly enriches the propositions social scientists are inclined to investigate. Indeed, this connection has been the main motivation for class analysis and the main source of its continuing fascination.

Class Struggle and Class Formation

A Marxist method of class analysis entirely different from that of Wright is developed by Adam Przeworski and his coworkers (Przeworski 1985a; Przeworski and Sprague 1986). Przeworski denies that class structure is prior to class formation and class struggle:

> *Classes are not given uniquely by any objective positions because they constitute effects of struggles, and these struggles are not determined uniquely by the relations of production. . . .* Class struggles . . . are structured by the totality of economic, political, and ideological relations; and they have an autonomous effect upon the process of class formation. . . . Positions within the relations of production . . . are no longer viewed as being objective in the sense of being prior to class struggles. . . . Positions within

social relations constitute limits upon the success of political practice, but within these historically concrete limits the formation of classes-in-struggle is determined by struggles that have class formation as their effect. [author's italics] (Przeworski 1985a, pp. 66-67)

Classes, according to this conception, are the results rather than the causes of class struggle, and class struggle is a continuous process leading to the organization and disorganization of classes. Eventually, class struggle becomes a conflict between different classes, but before that it is a struggle about which classes will be formed.

The formation of classes is not inevitable. Class formation emerges from political conflict when various organizations are able to instill the masses with a particular vision of society. But collective identity need not congeal along class lines; it could also take shape on the basis of race, ethnicity, nationality, or religion. And even if classes are formed, the character of this formation is not uniquely determined: several different class constellations are feasible under any historical circumstances.

The subtleties of Przeworski's class analysis are illustrated by his interpretation of political relations between workers and bourgeoisie under capitalism. Political organizations associated with the working class typically try to organize politics on a class basis. That is, they try to develop political structures based on the image of a class-divided society, each class having its own particular political interests. Bourgeois ideology, on the other hand, interprets society as a classless collection of individuals with no structurally induced conflicts of interest. In contrast to workers, the bourgeoisie seldom relies upon a separate political party. Rather it operates through many different parties, each claiming to represent the universalistic interests of all individuals.

Due to these political relations, ideological class struggle under capitalism focuses on whether the concept of class is essential for understanding society. It turns out that

class is important in a society if, when, and only to the extent to which it is important to some political parties, which organize workers as a class. Workers are the only class which is a potential proponent of the class image of society: when no political party seeks to organize workers as a class, separately from and in opposition to all other classes, the class image of society is absent altogether from political discourse. (Przeworski 1985a, p. 102)

Przeworski is interested in why capitalism has been so resilient and why socialism has never been established through an electoral process. He uses his class struggle concept of class to argue for two main conclusions: (a) In order to participate effectively in the process of electoral competition, socialist parties are compelled to undermine the organization of workers as a class; and (b) economic conflict under capitalism is not a zero-sum game. Economic compromises between workers and capitalists are possible and are often preferred by workers over more radical strategies (Przeworski 1985a, p. 3). Przeworski and Sprague conclude that socialism is something of an embarrassment to modern left-wing parties that function in a democratic capitalist context (Przeworski and Sprague 1986, p. 185).

We shall say more about these assertions in the next chapter. But let us briefly consider why Adam Przeworski's iconoclastic ideas about class fall into the domain of Analytical Marxism. Although strongly at odds with Analytical Marxists like Wright and Roemer who place class structure at the heart of class analysis, Przeworski's thinking relies heavily upon the concept of rational action. It is this concept that makes him doubt that class structure can be defined apart from class struggle, and it is this concept that reveals insuperable barriers to the achievement of socialism by electoral means. He advocates the principle of methodological individualism and makes extensive use of game theory to model the interaction between classes. Moreover, Przeworski has developed his theories of class in dialogue with leading Analytical Marxist thinkers like John Roemer and Erik Wright.

If class is an effect of class struggle, as Przeworski claims, then what causes class struggle? Although Przeworski has much to say about political parties, trade unions, and the state, this question never receives a convincing answer. When pressed to distinguish class struggle from other conflict, he boldly defines it as "any struggle that has the effect of class organization or disorganization" (Przeworski 1985a, p. 80), thus consigning the entire relationship between class and class struggle to the realm of tautology.

Przeworski's class struggle interpretation of class is original, provocative, and insightful regarding the durability of capitalism.

Taken as a general doctrine, however, it weakens the capacity of class to explain either historical transformations or the social organization of noncapitalist economic systems. If class divisions do not derive from fundamental social relations but are continually formed and deconstructed in response to ill-defined struggles, then what can class tell us about the evolution of human society or the prospects that lie ahead?

Przeworski does not think the class structure of society is infinitely malleable or that class formation is free of exogenous constraints. But he is not very clear about what these constraints might be and what real possibilities of class formation exist in any concrete situation. Przeworski's research practice seems far less iconoclastic than his theoretical pronouncements. Judging from the latter, his concept of class should be something entirely novel. But when gathering data or doing specific historical interpretations, he talks about the usual capitalist classes and defines them in very standard ways. Perhaps this notable disjuncture between theory and practice reflects the inadequacy of available evidence, but it could indicate an extravagant mode of theoretical expression.

The Collapse of German Democracy: A Class Analysis

Consider the application of class analysis to an important historical problem: the collapse of the Weimar Republic and the ascendance to power of German fascism. David Abraham, a social historian influenced by the ideas of Adam Przeworski, makes extensive use of class analysis to explain the collapse of German democracy during the 1930s (Abraham 1986). Perhaps the most distinctive feature of Abraham's interpretation is his application to the German bourgeoisie of Przeworski's notion that classes are continuously organized and disorganized through class struggle. Difficulties in achieving bourgeois class unity are central to his interpretation of why the Weimar democracy collapsed.

Abraham explains the disintegration of the Weimar Republic as a conflict between the conditions required to reproduce social democracy and the requirements of capital accumulation:

> At a certain point of its history, Weimar Germany could no longer tolerate the conflict between the costs of integration in a political system that was based on a mixture of strife and cooperation between social classes, and the necessity of private accumulation and control in a capitalist economy. . . . The eventual recourse to an alliance with the fascist movement, or what might charitably be described as a surrender to the Nazis by the majority of the representatives of Germany's dominant class fractions, issued from the perceived inadequacy of the republican political system: based on tenuous coalition building among fragmented parties it could not unite the interests of the dominant classes and could aggregate no base of popular support other than the costly one represented by social democracy. Industrial and agrarian leaders were convinced that post-Depression Germany had to be spared the costliness and unreliability of a democratic political constitution and profit-devouring social-welfare system. Support of fascism was thus not simply an attempt to survive the Depression; it was a way of using the crisis. (Abraham 1986, pp. lii-liii)

The German bourgeoisie consisted of three principal class fractions with somewhat divergent class interests: owners of agricultural estates, capitalists based in heavy industry relying upon domestic markets, and capitalists within newer industries oriented toward production for export. A stable system of capital accumulation must achieve a minimal degree of bourgeois unity, establish a coherent routine of economic reproduction, and provide sufficient popular support for capitalist relations. Given the fragmentation of the bourgeoisie, establishing and maintaining such a system was highly problematic and usually required extensive political mediation.

The process of class struggle in German society generated shifting class coalitions, and these coalitions placed severe constraints on how capital accumulation could be accomplished. Prior to World War I, the dominant coalition in German capitalism was a union between the landowning class and heavy industry, giving political supremacy to large landowners and supporting industrial profits by constraining the working class. The class struggles that erupted at the end of World War I destroyed the political supremacy of the landowners and eliminated many constraints formerly placed on the working class. Hence these struggles shattered the viability of the prewar class coalition.

The social foundation of the Weimar Republic, according to Abraham, was a coalition between capitalists in the more dynamic, less cartellized, export-oriented industries (e.g., chemicals, textiles, electrical equipment, machine goods), salaried employees, and the industrial working class. Under this coalition, the non-property-owning classes gained various welfare benefits but accepted the inviolability of capitalist property and abandoned efforts to participate in managing capitalist industry. The export industries secured state support for peaceful penetration of foreign markets (often at the expense of agricultural interests). The export industries could afford this class compromise during the mid-1920s because they enjoyed technological superiority over foreign competitors and had relatively low labor costs.

The economic crisis of the late 1920s undermined the working class-export industry coalition. Profit margins in the export industries declined, as did their political dominance over other fractions of the capitalist class. Neither the export industry capitalists nor any other fraction of the bourgeoisie felt they could afford the welfare system that was the heart of the Weimar social contract. Yet the German bourgeoisie could not institute a viable regime of capital accumulation on some other basis. The politically fragmented nature of Weimar democracy made it difficult to establish the necessary degree of capitalist class unity and to mobilize popular support for the capitalist system.

Meanwhile the Nazi movement gained impressive support among the beleaguered middle classes of German society. This, together with the fragmented nature of the bourgeoisie and the absence of a popular base for capitalism, created a situation rife with fascist possibilities.

> The conditions were present for a polarization of political conflict and its removal from the parliamentary theater, as well as for a possible capitalist-fascist alliance: (1) an economic crisis . . . in which the national product was insufficient to satisfy both labor's minimal wage demands and the minimally necessary level of profit; (2) a socialist (and a communist) movement, which showed no signs of backing away from costly and successful economic demands; (3) a mass authoritarian populism (especially within the

petite bourgeoisie and peasantry), which could be organized and harnessed politically despite the absence of any substantial economic unity; and (4) a politically weak capitalist class frustrated with liberal institutions and prepared to support imperialist and antisocialist movements in league with preindustrial statist elites. (Abraham 1986, p. 275)

The fragmented German bourgeoisie neither created nor controlled the Nazi movement. But Abraham maintains they eventually welcomed Hitler's rise to power as a means of overcoming their own disunity and establishing stable routines of capital accumulation: "It would be an alternative through which the interests of the dominant classes might be represented less directly but more effectively than they had been" (Abraham 1986, p. 36).

Abraham's class analysis of the collapse of the Weimar Republic has been highly controversial among students of German history. Many of the criticisms reflect differences between Marxist and non-Marxist historical perspectives.[9] While appreciating the ingenuity of Abraham's interpretations and his use of theoretical principles suggested by Analytical Marxists, we can still raise questions about the plausibility of his analysis. Was the division between heavy industry and export industry as clear and decisive as he suggests? Would difficulties in achieving bourgeois unity, even when combined with frustrations about parliamentary democracy, be sufficient to panic large parts of the capitalist class into alliance with a radical and volatile fascist party? Even if such an alliance were formed, could it propel the fascist party into power and accomplish the demolition of democracy?

Conclusion

The study of class has been one of the most fruitful activities of Analytical Marxism: a ground for sustained interaction between theoretical conception and empirical research. Space limitations prevent us from discussing all the meritorious work on class produced by Analytical Marxists. We are compelled to pass over the Bowles and Gintis theory of contested exchange (Bowles and

Gintis 1990) and Philipe Van Parijs's analysis of the class structure of welfare-state capitalism (Van Parijs 1989), among others.

The strategy of class analysis pursued by most Analytical Marxists involves the following elements: (a) theoretical integration between the concepts of class and exploitation; (b) use of rational action to establish a linkage between individual and class; (c) a multidimensional concept of class allowing complex specification of class locations, (d) use of class dynamics to explain major historical transitions, and (e) testing hypotheses derived from class analysis through multivariate statistical analysis. Analytical Marxists are not converging toward a unified theory of class, but their shared assumptions facilitate useful dialogue. Such dialogue greatly enriches each separate formulation even when it does not generate theoretical convergence.

The intense interest exhibited by Analytical Marxists in problems of class analysis is not very surprising. Most of the pressing issues in Marxist theory can be formulated in terms of class. What explains the reluctance of the proletariat to function as the revolutionary undertaker of capitalism? Why do class locations that are neither bourgeois nor proletarian proliferate in capitalist society? How does the class structure of underdeveloped capitalism differ from that of advanced capitalism, and what does this imply about the historical trajectory of the former? What is the class structure of state socialist societies, and can these societies evolve toward genuine socialism?

These questions are in no way unique to Analytical Marxism. They constitute a challenge to traditional Marxist theory and demand consideration by serious Marxists of all theoretical stripes. What may be unique to Analytical Marxism is how its practitioners address these questions. They do so by trying to combine standard methodologies of modern social science, revisionist inclinations toward Marxist theory, and fidelity to the emancipatory project of Marxism.

If Analytical Marxism has a general strategy for doing science, then class analysis must lie at the heart of that strategy. The heart of Analytical Marxist class analysis involves reformulating the concept of class in a manner that affirms its link to exploitation, improves its capacity to explain historical events, and suggests plausible answers to crucial social questions of our epoch.

Notes

1. In recent publications, Wright appears to retreat a bit toward a concept of contradictory class locations (Wright, Becker, et al. 1989, pp. 269-348). I cannot discern whether this retreat is tactical or strategic.

2. *Surplus product* has received various definitions in the Marxist literature, none of which is entirely satisfactory. Analytical Marxists try to define this concept without resort to the labor theory of value. They understand surplus product as that part of a society's total economic product not required to sustain the producers or to replace means of production used up in the production process. A slightly more abstract version of this same idea defines surplus product as the difference between the value of the total economic product and the cost of producing it.

3. A rent is a payment made to the owner of an asset for the privilege of using it. Thus skill/credential exploitation might consist of payments to the possessors of skills or credentials for the privilege of using them in the production process. Similarly, organizational exploitation might involve payments to persons in positions of administrative authority to insure their loyalty to the organization. Loyalty, in this formulation, is conceived as an asset owned by the incumbent.

4. This finding does not conflict with Marxist theories of monopoly capitalism. These theories rarely claim that most workers are employed in large firms. Their main claims concern the overall dynamics of capitalist development. Under a monopoly capitalist system, giant corporations and relations between them are thought to be the main determinants of political and economic development (Baran and Sweezy 1966; Foster 1986).

5. This finding brings to mind a remark by Bernard Shaw in the last chapter of *The Intelligent Woman's Guide to Socialism, Capitalism, Sovietism, and Fascism*: "I cannot afford the friendship of people much richer than myself: those much poorer cannot afford mine" (Shaw [1928] 1972, p. 491).

6. A cooperative game permits players to form coalitions, within which they coordinate game-playing strategies. A noncooperative game does not allow coalition formation.

7. Pareto optimality refers to the welfare of a group of people. An outcome is Pareto optimal if no other possible outcome is unambiguously better for the group as a whole. More specifically, an outcome is Pareto optimal if there is no other outcome under which some members of the group do better and everyone else does equally well. The concept is named after the Italian economist Vilfredo Pareto (1848-1923).

8. Deproletarianization, as measured by Wright and his coworkers, refers to decline in the relative number of working-class positions. Both the industry effect and the class effect contributed to deproletarianization during the 1970-1980 decade.

9. For an anti-Marxist critique of Abraham's work see Henry Turner, *German Big Business and the Rise of Hitler* (1985).

6

STATE

The Strategic Conception of the State

The leading Analytical Marxist theorist of the state, Adam Przeworski, makes the following comment about Marxist political theory:

> The central and only distinctive claim of Marxist political theory is that under capitalism all governments must respect and protect the essential claims of those who own the productive wealth of society. Capitalists are endowed with public power, power that no formal institutions can overcome. People may have political rights, they may vote, and governments may pursue popular mandates. State managers may have interests and conceptions of their own. But the effective capacity of all governments to attain whatever goals is circumscribed by the public power of capital. The nature of political forces that control the state institutions does not alter this situation, for it is structural: a characteristic of the system, not of occupants of governmental positions or the winners of elections. (Przeworski 1990, p. 65)

The work of Przeworski and his collaborators has revolved around the question of whether capitalists really do have public power that no political institutions can overcome. Almost all Marxist political thinkers, from Engels through Gramsci, have claimed they do. Przeworski is not so sure. He rejects the functionalist Marxism of Claus Offe (1985) and Nicos Poulantzas (1973, 1975), who explain the public power of capitalists by arguing that the state in a capitalist society is institutionally committed to reproducing the capitalist economic system. He also rejects the instrumentalist interpretations of William Domhoff (1983) and Ralph Miliband (1969), who derive the political power of capitalists from direct penetration of the state by capitalist personnel, values, and/or resources.

While wrestling with such questions, Przeworski evolves what I shall call the *strategic conception of the state*. This concept attempts to avoid the twin snares of determinism (which makes political action irrelevant) and voluntarism (which renders all political results contingent) by interpreting the state as the institutional terrain upon which strategic interactions concerning the domain of political affairs take place. The state as an institution consists of all structures defining the conduct of strategic political interactions. These interactions can be conflictual, cooperative, or any combination thereof. For theoretical purposes, the participants are usually conceived as rational actors, and they may be individuals or social aggregates like parties, classes, bureaucracies, or pressure groups.

The political outcomes that are the object of strategic interaction in the state include formation of public policy, occupancy of positions within the state structure, transformation of the state institutional terrain itself, and specification of who can participate in politics. Calling the interaction process "strategic" does not mean it is fair, equal, or orderly. State-organized political interaction is typically loaded in favor of some social classes and against others. Indeed, one or more classes may be entirely excluded from the political interaction process. The strategic concept of the state does not exclude the possibility of a class-dominated state. For example, a capitalist state could be defined as one where the political interaction process systematically shields capitalist relations of production and/or gives special advantage to the capitalist class in the interplay of political strategies.

Political outcomes have well-defined utilities for the political contenders, giving strategic interaction on the terrain of the state a game-like character no matter how grave the issues under contention. Consequently the methodology most appropriate for elaborating the strategic conception of the state is *game theory*.

Przeworski's strategic conception of the state is similar to the view set forth by Jon Elster (1985, pp. 398-428). The cardinal question in the Marxist theory of the state, says Elster, concerns whether the state can be understood as an expression of class interest. This question gained momentum from the crucial shifts in the thinking of Karl Marx induced by the revolutions of 1848. Prior to that year, Marx considered the state simply an instrument of the economically dominant class. But when the French, English, and German bourgeoisie each rejected the readily available reins of state power, Marx concluded that states—at least in capitalist societies—could be more autonomous of the dominant class than he had previously believed possible. The autonomy of the state, however, was not complete and could itself be deduced from the properties of class structure.

Elster uses the *Prisoner's Dilemma* game to explain Marx's thinking about the state. Relations between members of a class resemble the Prisoner's Dilemma situation: common class interests exist, but there is also a strong temptation to seek individual advantage by defecting from the cooperative class strategy. If many class members defect, the entire class suffers—sometimes egregiously. "The task of the state is to provide a cooperative solution for the Prisoner's Dilemma faced by members of the economically dominant class, and, as part of this task, to prevent the members of the dominated class from solving *their* dilemma" [author's italics] (Elster 1985, p. 400). According to Marx's pre-1848 instrumentalist conception, the state undertook this task because it was a tool of the dominant class. Subsequently he recognized that the state could organize the dominant class and disorganize the dominated class more efficiently by having some autonomy from the former. However, Marx held a narrow pre-strategic conception of power, says Elster, which prevented him from recognizing the full extent of state autonomy under capitalism.

The strategic conception of politics articulated by both Przeworski and Elster stands at the center of Analytical Marxist thinking about the state, but other theories have been proposed. Gerald Cohen's version of historical materialism suggests a functionalist theory in which the characteristics of the state are explained by the effects they have on the economic base of society (Cohen 1978). Erik Wright also adopts an essentially functionalist position, explaining the form of the state under various modes of production through its consequences for class relations and for maintaining the dominant pattern of exploitation (Wright 1985, pp. 122-23). A Weberian conception of the state, which is defined as monopoly of the legitimate means of coercion plus the institutions regulating the power flowing from this monopoly, is proposed by Samuel Bowles and Herbert Gintis in their book *Democracy and Capitalism* (1986, p. 99). They combine this, somewhat incongruously, with enormous faith in the liberating potential of radical democracy.

This chapter concentrates upon the strategic conception of the state not only because it is preponderant among Analytical Marxists but even more because it embodies the distinctive features of the Analytical Marxist approach to politics. As we shall see, this approach tries to integrate class analysis with the theory of rational action in explaining the formation of public policy. The strategic conception of the state carries this program a step further by deriving a deep structure of political affairs from strategic interactions of nominally autonomous actors on a terrain of tolerated strategies, institutionalized rules, and expected payoffs called the state.

State Autonomy

A state is considered *autonomous* if the policies it implements are not determined by forces outside the state itself. Under capitalism the two external forces most likely to determine state policy are the citizens of the state and the capitalist class. The executives of an autonomous state have objectives of their own and the institutional capacity to pursue these objectives. State autonomy does not mean that state policy is unconstrained by external forces, uninfluenced by public opinion, or independent of the wishes of the capitalist class. It does mean that the state is able to contravene public opinion and act against the desires of the dominant economic class.

Despite the impact of 1848 on the political thinking of Karl Marx, until fairly recently most Marxists regarded state autonomy in a capitalist society—although theoretically feasible—as an exceptional situation. Since the 1960s, however, Marxists of all varieties have usually considered state autonomy as the normal political condition of a capitalist society. But they are not of one mind about why the state is autonomous from the capitalist class. The specific contribution of Analytical Marxism has been to explicate the logical foundations of various explanations and offer sympathetic criticism. We shall discuss three different theories of state autonomy: (a) capitalist class abdication, (b) capitalist class weakness, and (c) class balance (Elster 1985, pp. 411-28; Przeworski 1990, pp. 36-44).

According to the *capitalist class abdication theory*, the capitalist class could control the state but finds it advantageous not to do so. Why might political abdication be advantageous to capitalists? Because money making is their overriding concern, capitalists might avoid all distractions from the pursuit of profit, including politics. Such abandonment of politics for money making is especially feasible if the state is constrained, by fiscal dependence and other considerations, against following policies hostile to capitalist interests.

Alternatively, the capitalist class may consider itself systematically unsuited to govern. The unquenchable appetite for profit vital to a successful capitalist could have disastrous results in a state manager, yielding hard times for the entire capitalist system. Capitalists may want an autonomous state able to function as a neutral party for resolving conflicts between them. Control of the state by the capitalist class could undermine the legitimacy of state policy, thereby embroiling capitalists in exhausting and avoidable struggles with other classes, particularly workers. This possibility could furnish another incentive for political abdication by the capitalist class.

The capitalist class abdication theory has two fundamental weaknesses. A plausible claim of abdication requires proof that the capitalist class really could control the state, but no compelling arguments to this effect are forthcoming. The capacity to rule is simply assumed as a consequence of capitalist social relations. There is also a problem of confidence. State policy is highly relevant to the fortunes of capitalist enterprise. How can the capitalist class acquire sufficient confidence in the good will and competence of an autonomous state to motivate collective political abdication? Occasionally the state does adopt policies that seem contrary to the wishes and interests of the capitalist class.

According to the *class weakness theory*, the state is autonomous only if the capitalist class lacks sufficient strength to govern. A contrast is sometimes drawn between the center and periphery of the capitalist world system, with the former having a strong bourgeoisie and a dependent state, and the latter having a weak bourgeoisie and an autonomous state. Unfortunately, the available evidence does not support the class weakness theory. The state is customarily autonomous in capitalist societies regardless of whether the bourgeoisie is weak or strong. And by the same token, the polarity between the center and periphery of the capitalist world does not correspond to a division between dependent and autonomous states.

The *class balance theory* attributes state autonomy to a class equilibrium within civil society. Workers and capitalists (along with their respective allies) are so equally matched that neither can become politically dominant over the other. Efforts by either side to seize control of the state could precipitate civil war, and recognition of this possibility encourages mutual restraint. The class stalemate removes the usual constraints on government activity creating a situation of state autonomy. A balance between a strong capitalist and a strong working class encourages the emergence of a fascist state, whereas a balance between two weak classes precipitates a less strident authoritarianism.

Class balance theory may illuminate authoritarian versions of the capitalist state, but it does not provide a general explanation of state autonomy, which often exists even without anything approaching a class equilibrium.

Przeworski poses the interesting question of whether state autonomy exists under democracy. State autonomy is not inevitable under democratic conditions, he concludes, but it can happen largely because state officials are not perfect agents of the people. To illustrate this point, Przeworski develops a simple rational choice model based on the idea that state officials derive satisfaction from state activity. The model predicts that these officials, if not closely monitored, will initiate more state activity than is best for the public (Przeworski 1990, pp. 57-64).

Jon Elster gives the following example of interaction between an autonomous state and a strong capitalist class (Elster 1985, pp. 406-07). The government can select a policy from a set of alternatives, but the capitalist class can exclude any alternative that it finds particularly bad. If the government gets too outrageous, the capitalist class can remove it from office, but the capitalists must then rule directly, something they hope to avoid doing.

If the worst alternatives are excluded, reason the capitalists, it matters little which of the remaining policies the government selects. Because the government knows its tenure in office depends upon "good" behavior, capitalists probably need not trouble themselves to eliminate the worst alternatives: rational state managers will not select them anyway. And if the government does not choose the alternative most favored by the capitalists, this shields the class from political resentment without inflicting significant harm.

The government, in this hypothetical interaction, recognizes that its own power rests upon the reluctance of the capitalists to rule directly and is therefore conditional. But such reluctance still gives the government considerable decision-making leeway. Though conditional, the power of the state is very real and—depending on the circumstances—may match that of the capitalist class.

Parties and Political Strategy

Political parties are an essential component of democratic capitalism. An effective party system, some would say, makes the difference between government constrained by popular will and rule by plebiscite. Marxist theory poses two major questions about parties under democratic capitalism: Can the electoral process accomplish a transition from capitalism to socialism? What kind of political strategy should a socialist party adopt under democratic capitalism? The most incisive work on these questions has been done by Adam Przeworski and his colleagues (Przeworski 1985a; Przeworski and Sprague 1986; Przeworski and Wallerstein 1988).

The organization of democratic politics in terms of class, points out Przeworski, is not inevitable and sometimes does not happen. The relevance of class to the political process depends upon the strategies adopted by leftist and socialist political parties because these are the organizations that can benefit from politics organized along class lines. Individual voting behavior of all descriptions results largely from the activities of political parties.

Political parties are not reducible to either class or state. They maintain relative autonomy from entities of both kinds and actually participate in the constitution of each. As indicated above, Przeworski regards class as the effect of class struggle, which, under conditions of democratic capitalism, is largely organized by political parties. Similarly, the identity of the state depends heavily upon the party structure it incorporates.

Under democratic capitalism, socialist political parties face a unique dilemma. Manual wage workers, the traditional core of the working class, never have been and never will be the numerical majority in any capitalist society. Hence manual wage workers cannot, on their own, carry a leftist party to electoral victory. Nevertheless, socialist and leftist parties in virtually all democratic capitalist societies are based upon manual wage workers. Leaders of these parties must choose between being (a) homogeneous in class composition and with a straightforward class-based ideology, but with no chance of winning elections; and (b) a broader party with a diluted class orientation and some hope of winning elections (Przeworski 1985a, p. 103).

What makes this choice particularly difficult for socialists is that becoming a mass party (rather than a class party) significantly weakens the organization's appeal to workers. By becoming a mass party and adjusting its propaganda for that purpose, the socialist party reduces the relevance of class for politics, reduces the likelihood that manual wage workers will adopt a working-class identity, and reduces the internal cohesion of the working class. Thus the gain in non-working-class voters is often counterbalanced by the loss of working-class adherents. Socialist parties, observes Przeworski, remain minority parties even after becoming parties of the mass.

To investigate these ideas further, Przeworski and Sprague develop a simple model of strategic action and apply it to Western European leftist parties in post-World War II elections. Of particular interest is the tradeoff between losing working-class votes and gaining votes from other classes when a leftist party shifts from a class to a mass base. When a social democratic party faces competition from other parties that appeal to workers on a particularistic basis—Communist, religious, or ethnic parties—then the tradeoff for becoming a mass party is quite severe (i.e., the ratio of votes lost to votes gained is relatively high). On the other hand, if labor unions are strong, then the tradeoff is more favorable because unions keep class politically salient even when the leftist party opts for a mass base.

Przeworski and Sprague find a definite tradeoff between the political recruitment of manual wage workers and salaried employees. Manual workers in post-World War II Europe simply do not consider salaried employees to be working class. When left-wing parties abrade the salary-wage distinction, then class becomes less important as a basis for voting and manual workers become less likely to vote socialist.

The overall strength of a socialist party, conclude Przeworski and Sprague, depends mainly upon its strength among workers. Among other things, socialist leaders are more willing to use nonclass political strategies when their parties receive strong support from manual workers. But most leftist parties could have won more votes by using somewhat different electoral strategies than they actually did. For example, the Przeworski-Sprague model indicates that the French Socialist Party would have improved its electoral performance by adopting a more working-class orientation. On the other hand, Swedish Social Democrats erred by excessive concern with the working class.

Their study of electoral socialism makes Przeworski and Sprague rather pessimistic about using elections to accomplish radical change:

> Regardless of their strategies, left-wing political parties were unlikely to win an overwhelming majority of votes. Their prospects were limited by the fact that they compete in societies in which there exist real conflicts of interests and values. Whether parties deliberately restrict their appeal to specific groups or attempt to conquer the entire electorate, their opportunities are limited by the heterogeneity of developed capitalist societies. In a heterogeneous society, no party can win the support of everyone without losing the support of someone, because some other party will put in the wedge. Thus no political party can win elections over whelmingly in a way that could be taken as a clear mandate. Elections are just not a vehicle for radical transformations. They are inherently conservative precisely because they are representative, representative of interests and values in a heterogeneous society. (Przeworski and Sprague 1986, p. 183)

But is it really true that elections are inherently conservative? In the situations studied by Przeworski and Sprague, most people did not want radical change. Elections quite properly registered this reality by repeatedly denying left-wing political parties an overwhelming majority of votes. This does not demonstrate the inherent conservatism of elections. Establishing that requires examining situations in which the majority really does want radical change, and showing that the electoral process itself prevents them from getting it. The rapid reunification of Germany and what John Feffer calls "East Germany's sprint to the market" (Feffer 1992, p. 85) are certainly radical transformations, and they were mandated by electoral processes.

Class Conflict and the State

If capitalism is characterized by deep and structurally irreconcilable class conflict, and if the capitalist class constitutes a small minority of the population, then why does the state in a democratic capitalist society consistently act to reproduce capitalist social relations? Functionalist versions of Marxism explain this as a consequence of the functional relationship between the economic base and the political superstructure of society. But if functional relations integrating various social institutions are so prevalent, how can class conflict be a fundamental component of capitalism?

The consistently procapitalist policies of the state, thinks Przeworski, result from a basic compromise between workers and capitalists. The state acts to reproduce capitalist social relations because this is the choice of both workers and capitalists in democratic capitalist societies. Why do workers and their political representatives choose capitalism? Not from false consciousness, or leadership treachery, or the abolition of class conflict. The choice of capitalism and the compromise with the capitalist class express the real material interests of the working class under democratic capitalism (Przeworski 1985a, pp. 171-203).

Socialism, assumes Przeworski without argument, is better for the working class than capitalism. But this does not mean that workers hoping to improve their material welfare should struggle

for socialism. Any realistic transition from capitalism to socialism involves massive economic and social dislocations with
severe negative consequences for the welfare of workers. Hence
economically rational workers, even if they desire the socialist
outcome, will shy away from the onerous transition:

> Between the capitalist path and the socialist one there is a valley
> which must be traversed if workers move at any time toward
> socialism. If such conditions indeed exist and if workers are
> interested in a continual improvement of their material welfare,
> then this descent will not be undertaken or, if it is undertaken, will
> not be completed by workers under democratic conditions. (Przewor-
> ski 1985a, pp. 176-77)

With socialism out of the picture—at least in terms of practical
politics—the class struggle continues but takes place entirely
within the framework of capitalist institutions. The economic
class struggle under capitalism concerns the use made of capitalist profits. The capitalist class controls investment and decides
how to divide its income between consumption and investment.
The working class cannot make investments, but through trade
union activities and political organizing it can determine what
share of profits becomes higher wages and what share becomes
capitalist income.

The volume of investment governs the future growth of the
capitalist economy, and thus both capitalists and workers want
investment to happen. This consideration prevents the working
class from seizing all profits. If they did so, the immediate
income of workers would increase dramatically, but the capitalist economy would soon plunge disastrously, with workers suffering severe material deprivations. What share of profits should
the working class take? This depends upon the strategic interaction between workers and capitalists. If the working class takes
too large a share of profits, then capitalists will find little benefit
in entrepreneurial activity and will consume their income rather
than investing it. On the other hand, if workers take too small a
share of profits, they will lose the benefits of economic growth.

A parallel strategic dilemma afflicts the capitalist class. If they
invest too high a share of their income, the economic product
will grow rapidly, but capitalists will miss out on consumption—
which Przeworski sees as the ultimate goal of both workers and

capitalists. If they invest too little of their income, economic growth will be extremely slow and capitalist consumption will expand little. Moreover, the working class—whose material interests suffer from capitalist investment lethargy—will soon retaliate by appropriating a larger share of profits.

Przeworski and Wallerstein (1982) construct a game theory model to study the strategic interaction between workers and capitalists, and particularly the possibilities of class compromise that emerge from the process. Important elements of this model are the respective rates at which capitalists and workers discount the future. If a class discounts the future at a high rate, it focuses on short-term costs and benefits and largely ignores the long-term situation. If a class discounts the future at a low rate, then appraisals of long-term outcomes are important in its calculations.

The future discount rates are not understood as psychological properties of the workers and capitalists. Rather they reflect the degree of uncertainty that class members have about the future, and this depends largely on the existence of social institutions able to defend class interests and protect any class compromise reached. Foremost among these institutions is the state; but the state has different relations with different classes, which is one reason why classes discount the future at different rates.

The working class must decide how much profits to appropriate for higher wages and how much to leave as capitalist income. The optimal working-class decision depends on both the rate at which capitalists invest and the rate at which workers discount the future. If the growth of output exceeds the rate at which workers discount the future, then the working class should adopt a strategy of class compromise allowing capitalists to retain as income a large share of profits. This strategy hitches the material welfare of the working class to long-term growth of the economy, not to redistribution of capitalist income. But if lagging capitalist investment causes the growth of output to fall below the workers' future discount rate, then the working class should struggle militantly against appropriation of profits by the capitalist class.

The capitalist class must decide whether to invest or disinvest, and this will depend on the share of profits appropriated by the working class and on the capitalists' own future discount rate. If the maximum possible growth of profits exceeds the capitalists' future discount rate, then capitalists should make positive investments. However, if this condition is not satisfied, then the optimal capitalist strategy is to disinvest.

What is the predicted outcome of the strategic interaction between workers and capitalists? The standard way of analyzing noncooperative games involves finding the *Nash equilibria*, and typically the worker-capitalist game has only one: workers struggle militantly against capitalist appropriation of profits and capitalists disinvest. This outcome signifies unmitigated class conflict, but Nash equilibrium approach is not the only way of analyzing the worker-capitalist game.

An alternative approach, called the *Stackelberg solution*, requires specifying one participant as the dominant or leading player. The dominant player assumes her opponent will make the optimal response to whatever strategy the leader chooses. Using this best-response assumption, the dominant player then selects her optimal strategy, and the resulting strategy combination (leader: optimal strategy assuming best response, follower: best response to leader's strategy) is the Stackelberg solution corresponding to that particular dominant player. A second Stackelberg solution results if the other player is specified as dominant. The Stackelberg approach generates interesting possibilities of class compromise and an important role for the state.

Przeworski and Wallerstein consider four cases, each defined by the amounts of uncertainty (rate of discounting the future) characterizing workers and capitalists respectively:

	Workers' Uncertainty	Capitalists' Uncertainty
Case 1:	high	high
Case 2:	high	low
Case 3:	low	high
Case 4:	low	low

They discuss these four cases using elaborate symbolism and graphs, but it is possible to convey the same general ideas with simple two-by-two noncooperative games. In each of these games, workers must choose between strategies of militance (high profit appropriation) and nonmilitance (low profit appropriation), whereas capitalists must choose between strategies of investing and disinvesting.

Uncertainty represents doubt felt by class members about whether they can actually secure the potential benefits arising from a compromise between classes. Hence the respective uncertainty levels of workers and capitalists influence how they assess the outcomes of various strategy combinations.

Consider Case 1: both workers and capitalists feel uncertain about whether any class compromise would hold, and hence discount the future strongly. An example of this might be the political situation in France during 1936 when elections put the "Popular Front" coalition of the left into office. The strategic interaction between workers and capitalists under these circumstances is modeled by the game depicted in Figure 6.1.

This is a classic Prisoner's Dilemma. Militancy is a dominant strategy for workers, and disinvestment is a dominant strategy for capitalists. Together they result in the Pareto inferior Outcome D, which is also the only Nash equilibrium of the game, as well as both Stackelberg solutions (worker dominant and capitalist dominant). With so much mutual distrust and so much uncertainty about the future, no class compromise between workers and capitalists is possible.

If Outcome A (workers compromise, capitalist invest) is Pareto optimal, why doesn't the state impose this solution upon the contending classes? According to Przeworski's theory, the state cannot create a class compromise if the material basis for it does not exist. The foundation of state action in democratic capitalist societies is class compromise or at least the possibility of it. Moreover, the condition of the state is reflected in the uncertainty felt by both workers and capitalists. If a government had the capacity to broker a class compromise, then either workers or capitalists (or both) might not discount the future so strongly.

Consider Case 2: workers have high uncertainty about the future, but capitalists are confident they could secure the benefits of class compromise. Such class consciousness would arise with low unionization, weakly institutionalized labor relations, and little working-class influence on the state. A situation of this sort currently exists in the United States. Figure 6.2 presents a simple game that models strategic interaction between workers and capitalists under the conditions of Case 2.

Although Figure 6.2 resembles Figure 6.1, this game is not a Prisoner's Dilemma. Disinvesting is not a dominant strategy for

Capitalists

	Invest	Disinvest
Compromising	A 2, 2	B 4, 1
Militant	C 1, 4	D 3, 3

Workers

Figure 6.1 Strategic Interaction Between Workers With High Uncertainty and Capitalists With High Uncertainty (Case 1)

NOTE: The first number in each box indicates the value of the outcome for workers, and the second number indicates its value for capitalists. 1 indicates the most preferred outcome, 2 indicates the second most preferred outcome, and so forth. The letter in the upper right-hand corner of each box is for purposes of identification.

capitalists because their evaluations of Outcomes A and B have switched, and this change creates an opportunity for class compromise. Outcome D is still the only Nash equilibrium, and it is also the capitalists' dominant Stackelberg solution. However, Outcome A (workers compromise, capitalists invest) is now the workers' dominant Stackelberg solution, and this outcome represents class compromise. The workers, under Outcome A, come off relatively worse than the capitalists and live with a constant temptation to become militant. However, the militancy impulse is held in check by recognition that it would be met by capitalist disinvestment, to the disadvantage of all. Such awareness is precisely what is imputed to the Stackelberg leader. If a class compromise is to happen under these conditions, it is the working class that must shoulder its costs.

Consider Case 3: workers confident about the future and capitalists uncertain. This is exactly the reverse of the previous situation. It could happen if trade union organization were strong and centralized, labor relations were highly institutional-

Capitalists

		Invest	Disinvest
Workers	Compromising	A 2, 1	B 4, 2
	Militant	C 1, 4	D 3, 3

Figure 6.2 Strategic Interaction Between Workers With High Uncertainty and Capitalists With High Uncertainty (Case 2)

NOTE: The first number in each box indicates the value of the outcome for workers, and the second number indicates its value for capitalists. 1 indicates the most preferred outcome, 2 indicates the second most preferred outcome, and so forth. The letter in the upper right-hand corner of each box is for purposes of identification.

ized, and the effective political parties represented the working class. Such conditions existed in the heyday of Weimar Germany, within Italy during much of the 1970s, and at various–but not recent–intervals of post-World War II English history. The matrix of a game representing strategic interaction in Case 3 appears in Figure 6.3.

Now the shoe is on the other foot. Outcome A–the class compromise outcome–is the capitalists' dominant Stackelberg solution and is relatively more advantageous for workers than for capitalists. If a class compromise, orchestrated by the state, happens in Case 3, the capitalist class will bear the costs of achieving it. Outcome A is not a Nash equilibrium, and the capitalist class languishes under the constant temptation to disinvest, a temptation curbed only by fear of provoking working-class militancy.

We come finally to Case 4, in which both workers and capitalists feel they have the capacity to get the benefits of class compromise. Conditions propitious for such consciousness are

Capitalists

	Invest	Disinvest
Compromising	A 2, 2	B 4, 1
Militant	C 2, 4	D 3, 3

Workers

Figure 6.3 Strategic Interaction Between Workers With Low Uncertainty and Capitalists With High Uncertainty (Case 3)

NOTE: The first number in each box indicates the value of the outcome for workers, and the second number indicates its value for capitalists. 1 indicates the most preferred outcome, 2 indicates the second most preferred outcome, and so forth. The letter in the upper right-hand corner of each box is for purposes of identification.

effective economic organization by both workers and capitalists, highly institutionalized labor relations, and a strong position within the international market. Sweden between the mid-1930s and mid-1960s meets these desiderata. The structure of strategic interaction, given bilateral confidence about the future, is represented in Figure 6.4.

The prospects for class compromise seem bright. The class compromise outcome (Outcome A) is a Nash equilibrium and is also both types of Stackelberg solution. Outcome D (unmitigated class struggle) is also a Nash equilibrium, but it is Pareto inferior. If bilateral confidence prevails, a government should have scant difficulty implementing compromise between workers and capitalists and reproducing capitalist social relations on that basis.

The class compromise state is Przeworski's way of acknowledging state autonomy without cutting the state entirely loose from its class moorings. The principal weakness of the models outlined above emerges from the substitution of Stackelberg solutions for Nash equilibria. If a class compromise is not a Nash

Capitalists

	Invest	Disinvest
Compromising	A 1, 1	B 4, 2
Militant	C 2, 4	D 3, 3

Workers

Figure 6.4 Strategic Interaction Between Workers With Low Uncertainty and Capitalists With Low Uncertainty (Case 4)

NOTE: The first number in each box indicates the value of the outcome for workers, and the second number indicates its value for capitalists. 1 indicates the most preferred outcome, 2 indicates the second most preferred outcome, and so forth. The letter in the upper right-hand corner of each box is for purposes of identification.

equilibrium, it is not self-enforcing: at least one class, whatever its level of political maturity, routinely encounters enticements to defect from the compromise. If the state plays an essential role in preventing such defections, then it surely operates in a more class-biased way than Przeworski wishes to acknowledge.

Structural Dependence of the State

In 1973 the mathematical economist Kelvin Lancaster published an article entitled "The Dynamic Inefficiency of Capitalism" analyzing capitalism as a dynamic conflict between workers and owners of capital. Lancaster's differential game model of capitalism was inspired by both Marx and Keynes. From Marx he got the idea that workers and capitalists can be regarded as homogeneous classes with common interests that each pursues collectively. From Keynes he got the notion that savings decisions and

investment decisions are often separated and that this separation can disturb the process of capitalist accumulation. Lancaster's original contribution was to locate savings decisions with
the working class and investment decisions with the capitalist
class, and to analyze capitalism as an interaction process in
which each class used those decisions under its control to
advance its collective interests.

If each class acted rationally, Lancaster concluded, the capitalist accumulation process would have two phases. During the first
phase, the working class would save as much as possible and the
capitalist class would invest all its income. During the second
phase, the working class would save as little as possible and the
capitalist class would invest nothing. Although this so-called
"bang-bang" solution expressed rational interaction between
the classes, it was inefficient from the perspective of the capitalist system as a whole. The first phase of the accumulation
process, during which savings and investment occurred, did not
continue long enough. Had it continued longer, the welfare of both
workers and capitalists would have increased. The essential reason
for the inefficiency lies in the separation of the savings and investment decisions. Because capitalists receive only a fraction of the
income increments generated by their investments, they value
these investments less than does society as a whole.

Lancaster's model of class interaction under capitalism has
been highly influential. Among other things, it has had a formative effect upon the analyses of class conflict and the state
discussed in the previous section. More recently Przeworski and
Wallerstein (1988) have adapted this model to examine the
Marxist theory of structural dependence, which was mentioned
in the quotation near the start of this chapter.

Structural dependence theory asserts that any government of
a capitalist society, even a radical or socialist government, must
respect the essential interests of the capitalist class. For if the
government interferes with the capacity to make profits, then
capitalists will automatically reduce their investment rate, economic growth will fall, and all classes will suffer. This relationship between profit making and investment derives from the
basic structure of the capitalist economic system and requires
neither political organization of the capitalist class nor any
particular form of capitalist class consciousness.

Przeworski and Wallerstein simplify the Lancaster model by assuming that the wage share of national income (controlled by the working class) and the rate of investment (controlled by the capitalist class) remain constant over the entire time period considered. They also assume that workers and capitalists discount the future at the same rate, and, for purposes of solving the model, they treat the working class as the Stackelberg leader within the interaction process. After considering strategic relations between workers and capitalists without government intervention, they introduce a state and analyze what happens under various forms of taxation.

In the absence of a state, the rate of investment optimal for capitalists is inversely related to the share of wages in national income: the higher the wage share, the lower the optimal rate of investment. This severely limits the capacity of workers to redistribute national income. Rational workers can only hope to obtain a fixed share of national income even though the working class controls wages. This result confirms structural dependence theory: in the absence of a state the working class must respect capitalist profits.

What happens when a state sympathetic to the working class enters the picture? Suppose the state imposes an income tax on all capitalist income and transfers the proceeds to the working class. This policy changes nothing. The workers' and the capitalists' shares of national income remain exactly the same. A government cannot change the income distribution between workers and capitalists by means of a tax upon capitalist income. This result also confirms structural dependence theory: a state armed with an income tax policy must also respect capitalist profits.

But things change dramatically if, instead of taxing all of capitalist income, the state only taxes that part of profit earnings used for capitalist consumption (i.e., no tax upon investment funds). Przeworski and Wallerstein obtain the remarkable result that the rate of investment is completely unaffected by the tax on capitalist consumption. This tax policy seems to give the state a means for escaping structural dependence on capital. A government can increase the workers' share of national income by taxing capitalist income and transferring these revenues to the working class. By coordinating wage demands with taxation policy, the state can achieve virtually any income distribution

desired—including driving capitalist consumption to near zero—
without reducing the rate of investment.

From these results, Przeworski and Wallerstein conclude that
the state in a capitalist society is not structurally dependent
upon capital in any static sense. A government sympathetic to
the working class is not powerless in the face of capital. There
exist policies by which it can redistribute income without wreck-
ing the capitalist economy. Przeworski and Wallerstein do say that
structural dependence may exist in a dynamic sense (as a result
of capitalist anticipations about changes in state policy), but the
thrust of their argument is entirely in the opposite direction.
This refutation of structural dependence theory vindicates the
claim of social democrats and Keynesian liberals that a proworker government can manage a capitalist economy to give
workers as much as they would get under socialism. Hence
socialism becomes ethically unnecessary and politically unlikely
in democratic capitalist societies.

In his recent book *Democracy and the Market*, Przeworski
reaffirms his critique of structural dependence theory:

> The controversial question is whether this dependence is so bind-
> ing on all democratically elected governments that the democratic
> process can have no effect on the policies followed by govern-
> ments. My view is that all governments are to some degree depend-
> ent on capital but that this dependence is not so binding as to make
> democracy a sham. There is room for the democratic process to
> affect the outcomes. (Przeworski 1991b, p. 14n.)

Nor does he think structural dependence will stay the hand of
dictatorial governments in capitalist societies:

> Contrary to Marx, the last constraint [structural dependence of
> the state on capital] may turn out to be insufficient to protect the
> bourgeoisie from the state. In fact, several military regimes in Latin
> America did enormous damage to some sectors of the bourgeoisie:
> Martínez de Hoz destroyed one-half of Argentine firms, and the
> Brazilian military built a state sector that competed with private
> firms. (Przeworski 1991b, p. 68n.)

Przeworski appears to be jousting with a straw man. Structural
dependence theory does not claim that democracy is a sham or

that structural dependence will always protect the bourgeoisie against the ravages of a military regime. The claims of the theory are much more modest. Any policy that limits profit making without transforming the institutional structure of capitalist production, asserts the theory, will generate severe economic consequences rendering it extremely difficult to continue the policy.

The theoretical argument against structural dependence is not nearly as overpowering as Przeworski and Wallerstein claim. Their model allows capitalists only extremely limited ways of responding to state policy: they cannot react in intelligent ways to severe attacks upon profit making. By theoretical fiat, capitalists are rendered short-sighted and essentially passive about state policy, to which they adjust rather than maneuver to change. By treating the working class and/or the proworker state as Stackelberg leader, Przeworski and Wallerstein deprive capitalists of even that limited strategic initiative available within their model.

Also weakening the argument against structural dependence is the tension between the limited sovereignty of the nation-state and the international mobility of capital. The nation-state cannot hope to control economic policy all over the capitalist world. This reality gives capitalists an obvious and powerful rejoinder to heavy taxation or other state policies unfavorable to profit making.

The Lancaster-Przeworski-Wallerstein formulation is a supply-side model that—notwithstanding Lancaster's salute to Keynes—neglects effective demand. It misrepresents class relations because it neglects another form of structural dependence: dependence of the capitalist class on working-class consumption. As the model now stands, the capitalist class would happily cut working-class consumption to zero, taking all national income as profit.

Mayer and Mott modify the Lancaster-Przeworski-Wallerstein formulation by making economic growth depend upon effective demand (Mayer and Mott 1990). This alters what had been a monotonically declining relationship between wages and investment. Now manipulating income distribution through taxation becomes extremely complicated if not impossible. And if the capitalist class is permitted a more active role—for example, treated as Stackelberg leader or allowed to maximize something other than short-term capitalist consumption—then structural dependence of the state reappears with a vengeance.

Democracy

Virtually all Analytical Marxists place a high value upon democracy, not only as a means for the attainment of social and economic objectives but even more as an end in its own right. Several have criticized classical Marxism for its instrumental attitude toward democracy and theoretical indifference to human rights. Marxism, write Samuel Bowles and Herbert Gintis, lacks a firm dedication to democracy: "Classical Marxism is theoretically anti-democratic in the same sense that any political philosophy that fails to conceptualize the threat of state authoritarianism, and the centrality of privacy and individual liberty to human emancipation, provides a haven for despots and fanatics" (1986, p. 20).

The overriding theoretical question concerns the relationship between capitalism and democracy. Modern liberalism maintains that a capitalist economy is necessary for stable democracy because capitalism makes productive property an effective base of individual power, thereby limiting the domain of state authority. Most Analytical Marxists think otherwise. They see an inherent tension between capitalism and democracy because wealth is a form of domination and the capitalist economic system is profoundly undemocratic. Capitalist democracy involves an unstable balance between democratic and authoritarian forces, with the former represented by the growth of individual rights and the latter by the expansion of capital.

How can the citizen rights of a democratic polity be reconciled with the property rights of a capitalist economy? Why aren't citizen rights used to eliminate property rights or, vice versa, property rights to abolish citizen rights? Bowles and Gintis (1986, pp. 41-47) identify four ways in which citizen rights and property rights have been reconciled during the history of capitalism. The first reconciliation—named the *Lockean accommodation* by Bowles and Gintis—involved disenfranchising the working class because it might challenge the dominance of property. This arrangement gradually eroded because the capital-owning classes sought to ally themselves with the property-less masses against the bastions of aristocratic privilege.

The second reconciliation between citizen rights and property rights, stimulated by the American Revolution and called the *Jeffersonian accommodation*, became important mainly within the United States, with its abundance of land. The Jeffersonian accommodation gave, or proposed to give, all citizens—that is a subset of white men—some productive property. Citizen rights and property rights would be reconciled by making everyone who really counted a property holder. The Jeffersonian accommodation was entirely unfeasible in most regions of emerging capitalism, and even within the United States the immense concentration of property induced by capitalist development soon undermined any possibility of carrying it out (Bowles and Gintis 1986, pp. 47-51).

The idea behind the third or *Madisonian accommodation* was divide and conquer: social fragmentation of all potential challengers to property. Numerous cross-cutting cleavages, it was argued, would prevent the masses from achieving enough unity to endanger the property-owning classes. Eventually, however, the growth of the working class and of working-class organizations invalidated the premises of the Madisonian accommodation (Bowles and Gintis 1986, pp. 51-55).

The most recent effort to reconcile the prerogatives of citizenship and property, the *Keynesian accommodation*, used mediation by the state to achieve an alliance between democracy and capitalism. By combining limited social welfare with prudent macroeconomic management, state policy could satisfy the interests of both labor and capital. In the United States and elsewhere, the state mediated a compromise by which capital accepted labor unions, guaranteed minimum living standards, and provided relatively full employment, while labor conceded capitalist control over production and investment and acknowledged profitability as the basic guide to resource allocation.

The Keynesian accommodation deradicalized the labor movement and weakened right-wing capital. It did not, however, abolish the basic contradiction between economic privilege and democratic rights. Eventually the Keynesian accommodation sabotaged itself by fostering a profit squeeze crisis, which was also brought on by the revival of international economic competition during the 1970s and 1980s (Bowles and Gintis 1986, pp. 55-62).

Like several other Analytical Marxists, Bowles and Gintis interpret democracy very broadly: it is a characteristic of all social relations, not of the state exclusively. They deny any inherent

opposition between democratic practices and economic efficiency. Without democratic organization of the workplace, economic security conflicts with willingness to work: under hierarchical management, the economically secure resist working. But
worker-owned and democratically controlled firms can avoid this
conflict. Without the structural opposition between workers
and management, they have lower surveillance costs and can
actually achieve greater efficiency than traditional hierarchically organized capitalist firms.

To accommodate this broad interpretation of democracy, Bowles
and Gintis propose a synthesis of the Jeffersonian and Marxian
social visions, which they call *postliberal democracy*. This stresses
workplace democracy and community empowerment rather than
expansion of the state. Four important elements of postliberal
democracy are (a) democratic accountability of major economic
actors, whoever these actors may be; (b) secure access to economic livelihood; (c) development of a truly democratic culture;
and (d) a range of democratic institutions standing between the
individual and the state (Bowles and Gintis 1986, pp. 204-05). In
certain respects, postliberal democracy resembles the classical
Marxist concept of socialism, but it takes liberty and popular
sovereignty as the ultimate objectives of social organization.
Whether an economy operates through markets or through planning is not of fundamental theoretical or moral significance and
should be decided on pragmatic grounds.

Fearing democratic institutions will become ineffectual or unstable if they attempt too much, Adam Przeworski gives a more
circumspect account of what democracy means (Przeworski
1991b). The essence of democracy is pervasive uncertainty
about the outcome of the political process and determination of
political results by "the people," or rather by competition between organized forces promoting popular interests and values.
Uncertainty about outcomes arises because democracy is a system of decentralized strategic action in which available knowledge is local rather than global. The crucial step in the formation
of democracy is the transfer of power from a group of people to
a set of rules.

Przeworski recognizes the vulnerability of democratic institutions and tries to identify the conditions making them stable.
The stability of democracy depends upon the loyalty of the losers

in democratic competition. What makes these losers comply with outcomes unfavorable to themselves rather than subverting the democratic process?

Several time-honored explanations of compliance by losers are explicitly rejected by Przeworski. Democratic compliance could not result from adherence to a prior social contract. Contracts are by nature enforced from outside, and nothing stands above the will of the parties establishing the democratic system. Nor can the concept of legitimacy explain compliance with democratic decisions. Legitimacy pertains to individual values, and democracy is threatened not by isolated individuals but only by organized political forces. Normative commitments to democracy certainly exist and probably influence political action, but Przeworski thinks they are unnecessary for explaining the stability of democratic institutions.

Stable democracy is a self-enforcing system: an equilibrium of contending political forces. The abstract conceptual foundation for this view comes from recent developments in game theory showing that cooperation can be enforced even in the absence of central authority. More specifically, if games involving choices between cooperation and noncooperation (e.g. Chicken, Prisoner's Dilemma) are played repeatedly and if the outcome of each game is observed, then cooperative behavior can be enforced as an equilibrium, provided the players are sufficiently patient. The mathematical results implying the existence of cooperative solutions to interactive situations are known as folk theorems for repeated games (Fudenberg and Tirole 1991, pp. 150-97).

Democracy is a self-enforcing system when losers in the democratic competition find it advantageous to accept their defeat and try again in the future and disadvantageous to overthrow or undermine democratic institutions. This happens because the cost of losing is not overwhelming (effectiveness prevails), and losers think they have a reasonable chance of winning in the future (fairness exists). If either of these conditions do not hold—if the costs of losing are prohibitive (lack of effectiveness), or if chances of winning in the future seem very small (lack of fairness)—then democratic institutions are endangered. The greater the effectiveness of a democratic system, the less fairness is required to preserve its existence, and vice versa (Przeworski 1991b, pp. 26-34).

But there remains a certain tension between what Przeworski calls fairness and effectiveness. Fairness requires protecting all major interests, but effectiveness may demand harming some of these interests to make the democratic system work reasonably well. In particular, any significant economic transformation entails damage to some important political interests. Enough tension between fairness and effectiveness can destabilize a democratic system; thus it would seem that a democratic system is not well suited for making economic revolutions: "A stable democracy requires that governments be strong enough to govern effectively but weak enough not to be able to govern against important interests" (Przeworski 1991b, p. 37).

Uncertainty is central to Przeworski's understanding of democracy, but he also acknowledges that uncertainty exists under dictatorship. Democratic uncertainty and dictatorial uncertainty are, however, quite different. The uncertainty characteristic of democracy derives from the decentralized nature of the system. Citizens of a democracy are very clear about the political possibilities but uncertain regarding the outcome of the democratic decision process. By contrast, the uncertainty of dictatorship stems from ignorance about the wishes of the dictator, and means a more fundamental confusion about what possibilities exist.

Przeworski draws a very sharp contrast between democracy and dictatorship, making it hard to see how he would characterize intermediate political systems such as limited franchise democracy or oligarchic rule. The interaction between factions in an oligarchy might have some of the characteristics Przeworski attributes to democracy. Conversely, the relationship between those without franchise and the state in a limited democracy resembles dictatorship.

Przeworski's earlier work pioneered sophisticated ways of combining class analysis with theories of the state, but class relations are strangely absent in his recent thinking about democracy. Although the democratic state must not govern against important interests, it has no explicit class identity and is not specially constrained by class relations. In contrast to Bowles and Gintis, Przeworski finds no strong antagonism between citizen rights and property rights. The perils confronting democracy are problems of institutional organization, not problems emanating from class struggle. Far from being a contradictory system, democratic capitalism may be the only viable form of democracy in the modern world.

Political Aspects of Full Employment

An early application of what amounts to a strategic conception of the state is Michał Kalecki's analysis of government policy toward full employment. Published during World War II, Kalecki's assessment still provides relevant insights about the strategic relationship between government leaders and the capitalist class, and about differences between how democratic and fascist states function within a capitalist economic context (Kalecki [1943] 1971, pp. 138-45).

Kalecki asks why capitalist states do not routinely adopt policies insuring full employment:

> The assumption that a Government will maintain full employment in a capitalist economy if it only knows how to do it is fallacious. In this connection the misgivings of big business about maintenance of full employment by Government spending are of paramount importance. This attitude was shown clearly in the great depression of the thirties, when big business opposed consistently experiments for increasing employment by Government spending in all countries, except Nazi Germany. This attitude is not easy to explain. Clearly higher output and employment benefits not only workers, but businessmen as well, because their profits rise. (Kalecki [1943] 1971, p. 138)

Kalecki gives three general reasons why business leaders tend to oppose full employment accomplished through government spending: (a) intrinsic dislike of government interference with employment, (b) dislike of public investment and government-subsidized consumption, and (c) opposition to political changes resulting from full employment.

Under a laissez-faire capitalist system, government relies upon business confidence to maintain decent levels of employment. Hence the state must avoid doing things that might undermine business confidence: that is, the state is dependent upon capital.

But when the government learns how to increase employment through its own spending, state dependence upon capital declines, and political leaders need not accept the policies favored by big business. Business leaders oppose government intervention in the economy partly because it reduces their leverage upon the state.

The capitalist class opposes public investment because it might compete with private investment, and opposes subsidized consumption because it might subvert the work incentive. Full employment may boost profits but is hardly an unmixed blessing for captains of industry: it weakens labor discipline and renders the working class more aggressive.

The arguments above pertain to a democratic capitalist state. Many things change under fascism. Business opposition to full employment is vastly reduced because the absence of democracy allows stronger and more stable capitalist control over government economic policy. Under fascism, the working class can be disciplined through political pressure; unemployment is no longer necessary for this purpose. Soon, however, the economic objectives of the fascist state shift from achieving full employment to securing armaments. The upshot is decreased consumption by the masses and ultimately war.

How do business leaders propose dealing with an economic slump within a democratic polity? In the absence of a firm alliance with the government, the capitalist class favors combating the slump by stimulating private investment through tactics like lowering the interest rate or reducing the income tax. Kalecki believes that stimulating private investment in these ways will rarely prevent mass unemployment. These processes create what Kalecki calls a "political business cycle."

During an economic slump, the government of a democracy, encountering stiff pressure from workers suffering from or threatened with job loss, tries to increase employment through public investments financed by borrowing. This policy, if pursued aggressively, will be successful and will initiate an economic upswing. Soon, however, the capitalist class and its rentier allies will feel severely threatened by the prevailing combination of government economic intervention, deficit financing, and rising prices. The capitalists and rentiers successfully lobby the government to revert to an orthodox policy of cutting the budget deficit. This eventually leads to a renewed slump, and then a renewal of deficit-financed government spending. This business cycle is specifically political because its main dynamics flow from class-generated political pressures upon the state.

One may question whether the economic dynamics of capitalism are as straightforward as Kalecki suggests, but his analysis does identify a recurring political interaction between the classes of a democratic capitalist society. Although originally conceived to explain what happened during the Great Depression of the 1930s—an event that now seems like ancient history—the relevance of Kalecki's model to capitalist politics during the final decade of this century is evident.

Conclusion

Analytical Marxism has no political line. The politics of its practitioners vary, if not all over the map, at least enough to make impossible any coherent party platform. Nowhere is this political diversity more evident than in discussions about the state, which show far less mutual consistency than Analytical Marxist work on exploitation or class. One cannot even say whether Analytical Marxism vindicates or refutes the structural dependence of the state upon capital, sometimes called the central claim of Marxist political theory.

The diversity of Analytical Marxist political analysis may reveal the limitations of the strategic conception of the state. Although this conception provides theoretical flexibility, circumvents the twin pitfalls of voluntarism and determinism, and facilitates the use of game theory for modeling political action, it gives very little guidance about how theories of the state should be formulated. The strategic conception is uncomfortably reminiscent of a blank slate upon which almost any theory of the state can be inscribed. It offers far less direction to political theorists working within the Marxist tradition than did the functionalist notions of classical historical materialism.

On the other hand, the heterogeneity of Analytical Marxist theorizing about the state may be an unwitting reflection of a skepticism about state power induced by the sordid history and

recent collapse of Communist regimes. Most contemporary Marxist thinkers are dubious about or outrightly hostile to the idea that
state power can remake society, the central proposition of the
Leninist theory of revolution. Historical experience, viewed
from the last decade of the 20th century, seems to indicate that
total reliance upon state power is a horrendously costly and
ultimately ineffective approach to social change. The state cannot be everything, but denying it any role in transforming
society would also fly in the face of historical evidence and
common sense. What should that role be? Is a democratic state
a potential catalyst of revolution, a guardian of the status quo, a
contradiction in terms, or none of the above?

If Analytical Marxism is anything more than a theoretical flash
in the pan, it cannot neglect these questions and others like
them. Answers to questions about the role of the state in transforming society, or at least enlightenment about such issues, are
what serious students of society expect from a Marxist theory.
I expect to see much Analytical Marxist writing about the state
in the next few years; and political relevance is not the only
reason why.

A guiding theme of Analytical Marxism has been connecting
class analysis with theories of strategic rationality. Political affairs, the domain par excellence of strategic rationality, must be
central to such an endeavor. In politics one confronts not an
impersonal objectified market, not a sequence of actions dictated
by technological rationality, not the emotionally overburdened
confrontations of family life, not the routinization commanded by
bureaucratic authority, but rather a cunning interplay between
calculating agents for highly valued and tolerably well-defined
political stakes.

Chapter 5 discussed the idea that classes are formed by class
struggle. The strategic conception of the state, on the other
hand, makes politics a central domain of class struggle and thus
an important source of class formation. Following this logic, the
state should be a place where the primordial elements of class
get converted from "might be" to "is" or "is not." Here lies a
possible nexus between class, state, and rationality. If efforts to
connect class analysis with strategic rationality make any sense
at all, they should help us understand the structure of states and
the dynamics of political action.

7

REVOLUTION

Analytical Marxism and the Theory of Revolution

Revolution is a hazardous enterprise both for revolutionaries and for a revolutionized society. The penalties for unsuccessful revolutionary action are severe, and the prospects of changing society for the better—if reckoned optimistically—are extremely slim. Whatever benefits an accomplished revolution may have do not belong exclusively to those who shoulder the risks; in fact, activists are prone to be victimized by the astonishing vicissitudes of revolutionary power. In view of these realities, how do revolutionary movements happen? Why would any rational person undertake such an unrewarding activity?

Social theory has responded to these questions in two different ways. One response acknowledges the importance of individual volition but denies that rationality has much to do with revolutionary action. The second response minimizes the importance of volition and relies upon a comprehensive structuralism to explain revolution. This structuralist approach characterizes Jeffrey Paige's pathbreaking work on agrarian revolution in the underdeveloped world (Paige 1975) and is carried even further in Theda Skocpol's comparative study of the French, Russian and Chinese revolutions (Skocpol 1979). Social revolutions, Skocpol argues, only make sense from a structuralist and nonvoluntarist perspective that is attentive to institutionally determined relations between groups. Revolutionary outcomes are perpetually different from those intended by any participants, and this is taken as clinching evidence against voluntarism of any sort.

Neither of these responses is persuasive to Analytical Marxists. Most human action is purposive, and the concept of rationality is indispensable for understanding purposive action. Forsaking the use of rationality in explaining revolution means treating this vital social phenomenon idiosyncratically—as a consequence of emotional outbursts or jerry-built social structures—thereby renouncing efforts to construct a unified theory of society. Although structuralism sometimes provides keen insights about how revolutionary processes work, and although Analytical Marxists have learned a great deal from the writings of Skocpol and Paige, structuralist analysis is hopelessly incomplete without an explanation of why individuals undertake revolutionary action. Structuralism pure and simple lacks microfoundations. In the study of revolution as in the study of other social processes, Analytical Marxists want an integrated analysis of institutional structure and strategic rationality.

Analytical Marxist work on revolution differs from that of rational choice theorists like Jack Goldstone or Michael Hechter in at least two important ways. Although both groups emphasize the importance of strategic rationality in explaining revolution, Analytical Marxists stress the centrality of class dynamics for understanding revolutionary processes. They use strategic rationality to explicate revolutionary class dynamics. As indicated in previous chapters, Analytical Marxists avoid assuming the existence of social classes, and they also avoid assuming a specific form of class dynamics. The goal is to derive both class structure and class dynamics from the distribution of productive property and social rules specifying how this property may be used. A further objective is to explain the occurrence of revolution with these minimal assumptions.

A second difference between Analytical Marxists and rational choice theorists of revolution concerns the relation between revolution and development of productive forces. Rational choice theorists make no particular connection between these phenomena, but Analytical Marxists try to theorize revolutions (not always successfully) as crises in the development of productive forces.

The theory of revolution poses a special challenge to Analytical Marxism for at least three different reasons. The first reason derives from the special place occupied by revolution in the moral universe of Marxism. The idea of revolution expresses the unresolved tension between freedom and determinism in the Marxist view of the world. Although revolution is not the end of social evolution or even the ultimate goal of Marxist strategic action, its occurrence is taken as material evidence that a classless society has some practical possibility.

Although the theory of historical materialism is based on inexorable development of productive forces, the act of revolution expresses pure potentiality: a new beginning, a social rebirth only lightly constrained by what came before. For these very reasons, revolution affirms the power and fecundity of the social community: its capacity to escape the incubus of the past and establish itself as author of its own future. Due to this odd juxtaposition of revolutionary romanticism and hard-boiled materialism, Marxism is sometimes called the science of revolution. Any comprehensive reconstruction of Marxist thought cannot avoid addressing the issue of revolution.

The second reason for the challenge posed by the theory of revolution is far more mundane. Any phenomenon broadly regarded as the quintessence of nonrational action will naturally constitute a theoretical test for an approach emphasizing rationality. The urgency of the challenge is greatly amplified if, as with revolution, the event is intrinsically important.

The third reason Analytical Marxists address the theory of revolution is more or less the inverse of the first two. The reputation of revolution has suffered severely in the last few years. The Russian Revolution is widely seen as a catastrophic failure, even by people who once touted its achievements; ditto the Chinese, Cuban, and Vietnamese revolutions. The main current of radical thinking about revolution is highly self-critical: we have exaggerated the formative power of social revolutions while drastically underestimating their human costs. Are such judgments valid? Do they represent a temporary disorientation of radical thinking or a spineless capitulation to intellectual fashion? Should the value of revolutions be assessed on a case by case basis, and if so by what criteria?

These questions permeate the intellectual milieu from which Analytical Marxism has emerged. The answers Analytical Marxists have so far given are few, tentative, and certainly not uniform. But the questions will not disappear and will surely motivate continuing Analytical Marxist attention to the theory of revolution.

A Critique of Karl Marx's Theory of Revolution

A natural starting point is the theory of revolution proposed by Karl Marx. Using the principle of methodological individualism, Jon Elster makes an incisive critique of Marx's ideas about revolution (Elster 1985, pp. 428-46; Elster 1988). Although Marx has many striking insights about revolution, Elster claims that teleological reasoning subverts much of his systematic thinking on the subject:

> I want to emphasize the a priori nature of his reasoning—the speculative, teleological strand in his thought. The summit in this respect is reached in the assertion that these classical revolutions [the English Revolution of 1640-1688, the French Revolution of 1789] "reflected the needs of the world at that time rather than the needs of those parts of the world where they occurred, that is England and France." . . . [This statement] fits in very well with Marx's general tendency to explain the classical revolutions in terms of final causes—by looking at their achievements rather than at the social forces that set them in motion. (Elster 1985, p. 432)

According to the general theory of historical materialism, revolutions occur when "the material productive forces of society come into conflict with the existing relations of production" (Marx [1859] 1987, p. 263). Marx's more specific ideas about revolution, which appear in bits and pieces throughout his voluminous writings, are not always consistent with this general theory. He finds deep contrasts between bourgeois and communist revolutions and offers different explanations of each.

Although its main achievements are abolition of feudal privilege and creation of free competition, the political form of bourgeois revolution is transition from absolute to constitutional monarchy, with a temporary republican interlude between: "two steps forward and one step back" (Elster 1985, p. 429). The achievement of a stable bourgeois republic usually occurs considerably after a successful bourgeois revolution. During the brief republican phase of a bourgeois revolution, a radical communist movement often appears. But because the material conditions for communism do not exist, the fledgling communist movement unconsciously acts in the service of the bourgeoisie.[1]

In his more historically focused writings, Marx explains the occurrence of bourgeois revolutions through interactions between the bourgeoisie and the absolutist state. To promote economic development and thereby strengthen itself against the feudal aristocracy, the monarchy encourages growth of the bourgeoisie. Eventually, however, the bourgeoisie becomes so strong it threatens monarchy, which then tries to limit further bourgeois development. This is when revolution is likely to occur.

To achieve all its political objectives, however, the bourgeoisie must ally with the lower classes of society. Thus the bourgeoisie must choose between establishing a democracy more radical than it wishes—a democracy that might soon turn against capitalism—or reaching a compromise with the former rulers of the state. Given such a choice, the bourgeoisie has consistently rejected radical democracy. Marx railed against the cowardice of the bourgeoisie in the German Revolution of 1849, but eventually came to see its capitulations as a rational defense of bourgeois interests.

The writings of Marx on bourgeois revolutions exhibit a continuing tension between causal analysis, treating classes as rational actors, and teleological thinking, with classes functioning simply as puppets of an imputed historical destiny. Moreover, he does not answer the main question raised by his theory of revolution: Why would any person or any class engage in revolutionary struggle merely to establish social relations optimal for developing productive forces? (Elster 1988, p. 207).

Having no historical examples to guide his thinking, Marx's ideas about communist revolution are even more flawed than his theories of bourgeois revolution. Communism requires a revolutionary transition because it is economically superior only if established on a nationwide scale. Partial or miniature versions of communism cannot compete successfully with capitalism. Elster thinks it implausible—for reasons he never articulates—that a communist society could be more technologically innovative than capitalism. But even if it were, the costs of transition, the free rider temptation, risk aversion, and myopia would thwart any concerted working-class movement for communism.

Occurrence of a successful communist revolution requires juxtaposition of both the objective and the subjective conditions for communism, and deep historical reasons make this unlikely to happen. As Marx predicted, these conditions do appear, but they appear in opposite poles of the capitalist world. The objective conditions for communism—high labor productivity, large-scale production enterprises, rapid technological innovation, and so forth—occur in advanced capitalist countries. The subjective conditions for communism—alienation from capitalism, cooperative consciousness, revolutionary movements, and so forth—happen in backward parts of the capitalist world. Although Elster understands that Soviet Communism differs drastically from the communism of Marx, he carefully notes that Communist revolutions have occurred only in underdeveloped countries (Elster 1988, p. 225).

Some of Marx's writings on communist revolution, conjectures Elster, may not express his real views on the subject. The writings in which he deals with the topic were often produced on behalf of a working-class organization (e.g., the First International) and may reflect the political compromise reached therein. This makes it difficult to interpret what Marx says about the possibility of a nonviolent transition to socialism. A number of his later writings on England and the United States suggest a peaceful transition could happen. However, Elster thinks the views expressed several decades earlier in *The German Ideology* ([1845-1847] 1976) are more authentic. Here Marx asserts that revolution is necessary to transform the slave mentality of a subordinate class.

Elster finds theoretical reasons for doubting the plausibility of communist revolution even under the most favorable circumstances. Because capitalism develops productive forces to previously unprecedented heights, the capitalist class has both the wherewithal and the incentive to make whatever material concessions are necessary to diffuse a threatening revolutionary movement. Similarly the state, equipped by modern technology with overwhelming coercive force and presumably acting on behalf of the capitalist class, would anticipate and energetically crush any budding communist revolution.

According to Elster's analysis, Marx violates the cardinal principle of political rationality: never assume your adversary is less rational than yourself (Elster 1988, p. 222). Only by violating this principle can Marx conclude that communist revolution will breach the formidable bulwarks of advanced capitalism. The classical Marxist theory of communist revolution assumes that workers and/or capitalists and/or governments will behave irrationally. It is based more on wishful thinking than on sober social analysis.

Elster unquestionably identifies serious weaknesses in Karl Marx's theories of revolution. Yet his critique seems to imply that all revolutions are impossible, or that human beings are profoundly irrational about exactly those issues that concern them most. As matters now stand, communist revolution is extremely unlikely in any advanced capitalist society. But this results rather more from beliefs about the undesirability of communism than from the impregnable defenses of the capitalist state or capitalist class. Elster underestimates the constraints placed by the logic of capitalism upon both the capitalist state and the capitalist class. He assumes that both will maintain internal unity in face of any serious challenge to their power. Consequently he overestimates the likelihood of flexible, timely, and steadfast resistance to revolutionary movements against capitalism.

In light of his own opinions, it seems strange Elster should belabor Marx for insufficient attention to the rationality of capitalists and their allies. Toward the end of his essay on revolution, Elster allows that the enormous complexity of modern political decisions renders rational choice theory quite useless. He recommends—perhaps in a jocular spirit—using Keynes's notion of "animal spirits" to explain the strategic behavior of labor, capital, and government (Elster 1988, p. 228).

Rebellion and Revolution in Preindustrial Contexts

Many important revolutionary movements occur in preindustrial settings with peasant economies and low levels of urbanization. Yet classical Marxist theory did not anticipate extensive revolutionary activity in such contexts. How can revolutionary movements overcome the demographic decentralization and social isolation found in preindustrial societies? How can revolutionary consciousness arise among peasant classes supposedly imbued with narrow and highly individualistic outlooks? How are such classes able to overcome the free rider problem?

Insightful studies of the Vietnamese Revolution using rational choice theory have been made by Samuel Popkin (1979, 1988). Though Popkin is not usually identified as an Analytical Marxist, his work exhibits the joint awareness of class structure and individual decision making that characterizes this approach. Popkin argues that community organizers, whom he calls political entrepreneurs, were the crucial facilitators of collective action among the Vietnamese peasantry. These organizers acquired credibility and support through practical village-level activities and used these local bases to launch revolutionary struggles on a national level.

More surprisingly, he contends that the organizational methods used by the Cao Dai sect (a Vietnamese merger of Confucianism, Buddhism, and Taoism), the Hoa Hao religion (a millenarian, anticolonial, egalitarian belief system), and the Catholic Church of Vietnam bear many similarities to those of the Communist Party. The success of each depended heavily upon the activities of local community organizers who helped Vietnamese peasants escape their longstanding dependence on large landowners and village officials. In all four cases, most benefits to peasants came from reforming market institutions rather than redistributing land. Allegiance to each of the organizations emerged mainly from a network of small group ties rather than belief in a revolutionary ideology (Popkin 1988, p. 10).

Exactly how do political entrepreneurs overcome free riding and facilitate collective action by decentralized peasant communities? The entrepreneurs link individual peasants, thereby rendering their actions interdependent. This makes each person feel that her individual contribution to collective action is significant, thus reducing the temptation to free ride. Even more important, the political entrepreneurs expedite detection of free riding when it does occur, and simplify infliction of community sanctions against these defectors. Under these conditions, free riding is not so free: it forgoes community approval and carries definite penalties. Organizers also help peasants understand what collective actions are feasible and how they would benefit the entire community.

Agrarian movements, says Popkin, are not giant leaps carried out by hordes of outraged peasants, but a multitude of small steps whose cumulative impact on society can be massive. Effective revolutionary leadership depends mainly upon communication skills. It disaggregates large political goals into many small steps, a tactic that also enhances the perceived importance of contributions by individual community members. The apparent disinterestedness and self-sacrifice of political entrepreneurs is vital to establishing their credibility within the peasant village. Their subsequent role is not mainly coercive or authoritarian, but that of providing the information and coordination needed to make collective action possible (Popkin 1988, pp. 60-61).

The approach pioneered by Popkin is extended by Michael Taylor (1988b) in a paper responding to Theda Skocpol's starkly structuralist theory of revolution (1979). Taylor argues for a methodology that is both structuralist and individualist. Social structure and individual attitude determine each other: individualist explanations of structure and structuralist explanations of attitudes are both necessary. Although social structure is not the same thing as individual action, structures emerge from, are maintained by, and change through the actions of individuals (Taylor 1988b, pp. 94-95).

According to Skocpol, peasant revolution in China took far longer than comparable agrarian revolutions in France and Russia because prerevolutionary agrarian society had less structural solidarity in China than in France or Russia. The weakness of the peasant community compelled the Chinese Communist Party to organize collective action on a village by village basis.

Taylor does not reject this analysis; he merely finds it incomplete. The peasant community, most historians agree, provides the social basis and organizational framework for agrarian revolution, but this does not eliminate the importance of analyzing individual choice. Social structure did not compel the Communist Party to organize collective action by Chinese peasants. Moreover, the influence of structure operates through the modality of individual choice. Membership in a strong community can make rebellious action rational for a peasant, whereas absence of binding community ties typically undercuts the rationality of insurrectionary behavior.

Revolutionary collective action, Taylor wants to show, is often rational action and can be explained by a standard theory of rationality: the "thin theory of rationality." This theory, which provides the basis of neoclassical economic theory, makes four basic assertions: (a) individuals are egoistic, (b) rationality is relative to the attitudes and beliefs held by the individual, (c) individual actions are instrumental for achieving given aims in light of a person's beliefs, and (d) the range of incentives motivating a person's actions is quite limited (Taylor 1988b, p. 66).

Social pressure is much more potent in small stable groups where people know each other well. This being so, the thin theory of rationality predicts that cooperation is more likely to be rational (a) in small groups than in large ones, and (b) when people live together in a community rather than when they have only casual relationships. The importance of primary groups for inducing cooperation is a principal reason why revolutionary organizations mobilize support through local branches.

Not all collective action can be explained by the thin theory of rationality. Taylor thinks the theory is likely to apply when the following conditions hold: (a) the options available to a person are strictly limited, (b) the person's incentives are well defined and substantial, (c) a great deal depends upon the choice in question, and (d) the person has had many similar choices in the past (Taylor 1988b, p. 90). These conditions suggest the theory will be more applicable to the poor than the rich. Hence it should do a better job explaining when peasants rebel than accounting for the actions of rural elites. The destruction of community in modern societies, Taylor conjectures, removes the most important basis for collective action, making the thin theory of rationality less relevant.

James Tong uses a rational choice model to explain banditry and rebellion during the Ming Dynasty of China (1368-1644). Tong uses data from local gazetteers to examine the occurrence of these phenomena in 1,097 counties over a period of 277 years (Tong 1988). Finding that banditry and rebellion are directly related to the danger of starvation and the uncertainty of punishment, he interprets them as rational responses to subsistence crises. Many more of these outbursts occurred during the second half of the Ming Dynasty (1506-1644) than during the first, a fact not lost upon observers at the time, one of whom commented: "The demise of the Ming was due to banditry. The rise of banditry was due to famine" (Tong 1988, p. 116).

Tong rejects both Durkheimian and Marxist interpretations of rebellious activity in Ming China. A Durkheimian perspective might conceptualize this activity as anomic violence and attribute it to the social disintegration resulting from rapid change. However, contrary to the expectations of Durkheimian theory, Tong finds no association between collective violence and either commercialization or urbanization, the dominant forms of social change in Ming China.

A Marxist interpretation is considered inadequate because "class conflict approaches cannot adequately account for political violence in a premodern society where intraclass solidarity and interclass antagonism have not yet been intensified by urbanization and industrialization" (Tong 1988, p. 105). The incidence of banditry and rebellion in Ming China is not explained by class conflict between aristocrats and peasants, at least not by the measures of rural class conflict available to Tong.

Tong's findings are not nearly so incompatible with Marxist theory as he thinks. He gives an admirable materialist account of how banditry and rebellion happen, yet tells us very little about the social origins of starvation. Class relations and the development of productive forces can explain a great deal about the occurrence and distribution of famine. Research on the occurrence of famines in the modern world shows that avoidance of mass starvation is associated with both development of productive forces and, even more, with political emancipation of the subordinate classes. Amartya Sen points out that "no democratic country with a relatively free press has ever experienced a major famine" (Sen 1993, p. 43).[2]

Ming China may present a situation of conditional independence. Given the overall agricultural practices and land tenure systems in that society, local variations in class structure appear statistically independent of frequency of outlaw actions. This implies that class structure is not the immediate or direct cause of banditry in Ming China. But what causes agricultural practices and land tenure systems? Class structure could be implicated at this level. How often, during the Ming dynasty, did aristocrats practice banditry and rebellion against peasants?

A Game of Revolution

An ingenious game of revolution has been developed by John Roemer (1985, 1988b). The game involves a two-person interaction between a revolutionary and a counterrevolutionary strategist, symbolically designated as Lenin and the Tsar respectively. Lenin's purpose—that is, the purpose of the revolutionary strategist—is to build a coalition with the maximum probability of making a successful revolution. The Tsar wants to prevent the formation of any such revolutionary coalition. Lenin tries to build a coalition by proposing a redistribution of income among the people, but the redistributions he can propose are constrained by the assumption that total income remains constant. Lenin's strategic problem is to determine what proposed redistribution will form the most effective revolutionary coalition.

To prevent formation of a revolutionary coalition, the Tsar threatens to impose income penalties (i.e., fines). These penalties will be enacted upon anyone who joins the revolutionary coalition if the attempt at revolution proves unsuccessful (otherwise they could not be enforced). The penalty specified by the Tsar cannot be larger than a person's income. Moreover, larger penalties tend to increase the probability that a coalition that is able to form will make a successful revolution. Hence the Tsar may not want to impose the largest possible penalties.[3] The counterrevolutionary strategic problem is deciding what list of penalties most seriously inhibits the probability of revolution.

A person wants to be a member of a revolutionary coalition if the income she can expect from joining exceeds her current income. This expectation depends upon the income the person is promised by Lenin, the penalty threatened by the Tsar, and the probability the coalition will make a successful revolution. A coalition is said to be formable if every person included wants to be a member according to the above criterion. Given a proposed income redistribution and a proposed penalty list, Roemer shows there exists a unique formable coalition with maximum probability of revolutionary success. It turns out that every other formable coalition is included within this maximum success coalition.

Roemer interprets this game between Lenin and the Tsar not as a model of how revolutions really happen but as a means of examining the rational foundations of revolutionary ideology. The leaders of revolutions rarely adopt their ideologies for strategic reasons, but if an ideology precludes acting rationally in revolutionary situations, then the person holding it is not likely to lead a successful revolutionary movement. A process of natural selection, Roemer conjectures, favors revolutionary leaders with strategically rational ideologies and eliminates others. An analogous process selects defenders of the status quo with sensible counterrevolutionary strategies. The game between Lenin and the Tsar helps Roemer identify rational components of revolutionary and counterrevolutionary ideologies.

It is assumed that the Tsar acts first by publishing his schedule of penalties, after which Lenin proposes an income redistribution. Thus the Tsar functions as a Stackelberg leader in this game of revolution, and Lenin acts with full knowledge of the penalties selected by his opponent. Roemer proves that the game so constructed has a solution: a set of penalties minimizing the probability of revolution, and a proposed redistribution of income constituting a best response to these penalties. If Lenin and the Tsar were to act simultaneously rather than sequentially, then the game might have no solution.

Roemer works with five assumptions about the probability of revolution. First, he assumes that adding people to a revolutionary coalition never diminishes the probability of revolution. This is called the *Coalition Monotonicity* assumption. Second, he assumes that increasing the penalties imposed for participating in a revolutionary coalition never decreases the probability that a fixed coalition will successfully make a revolution. This is called the *Penalty Monotonicity* assumption.

The third and fourth assumptions are closely related to each other. The fourth assumption (Symmetry) is actually an extreme case of the third (Lean and Hungry) and figures only occasionally in Roemer's analysis. The *Lean and Hungry* assumption says that adding a poor person to a revolutionary coalition increases the probability of revolution at least as much as adding a rich person. The *Symmetry* assumption makes the stronger assertion that—given a fixed penalty schedule—the probability of revolution depends only upon the size of the revolutionary coalition and not upon the particular people who are in it.

Relative Severity is the name of Roemer's fifth and final assumption. A penalty is thought to be more severe if (a) it is larger or (b) the person upon whom it is inflicted has less income to begin with. Increasing a penalty that is more severe boosts the probability of revolution more than increasing a penalty that is less severe. Increasing a more severe penalty presumably induces greater anger and resistance than increasing a less severe penalty.

Roemer derives an impressive array of results from this model, some of which are difficult to state in nontechnical language. The main gist of his findings is that the Tsar's optimal strategy involves penalizing poor people more than rich people, whereas Lenin's optimal strategy entails redistributing income from the rich to the poor. This happens because Lenin can build an effective revolutionary coalition at lesser expense among poor people and because the Tsar must concentrate his reprisals upon those people most likely to be recruited for revolution. Keep in mind that Lenin and the Tsar are acting strategically and not ideologically in this game: Lenin's sole purpose is to make a revolution, whereas the Tsar's single intent is to prevent one. Yet acting strategically, they converge toward positions that make ideological sense. Discovery of this unanticipated convergence between strategy and ideology is perhaps the main contribution of Roemer's formidable mathematical analysis.

If the probability that a coalition will successfully make a revolution is unaffected by the penalties imposed, then tyranni-cal behavior—meaning confiscation of all income belonging to people participating in revolutionary coalitions (i.e., maximum possible penalties)—is optimal for the Tsar. But if the probability that a coalition will make a revolution is sensitive, even in the slightest way, to the penalties imposed, then a rational Tsar will never be tyrannical.

A revolutionary coalition consisting of everyone with less than a certain income is said to be *poor connected*. If the probability of revolution is unaffected by penalties, then the revolutionary coalition will be poor connected. But this is not the only circumstance leading to a poor-connected revolutionary coalition. If the probability of revolution is sufficiently high, then the revolutionary coalition will also be poor connected. To generate a poorconnected revolutionary coalition, Lenin can propose a "progressive" redistri-bution of income, meaning a redistribution such that people above a certain income get less than they previously did and people below that level get more.

Under all circumstances society breaks down into three classes based upon income: everyone below a certain income x belongs to the revolutionary coalition, no one above income level y belongs to the coalition, and people with incomes between x and y may or may not be in the coalition. If the revolutionary coalition is poor connected, then the middle class (as defined here) is entirely empty. A revolutionary coalition is poor connected if and only if all its members suffer exactly the same penalty severity. The penalties threatened against rich people, in this case, are distinctly less severe than those threatened against the poor.

Despite the mathematical fertility of this game of revolution, Roemer is keenly aware of its theoretical limitations. Most importantly, the game does not cope with the free rider problem. Why do people join the revolutionary coalition in the first place? The income Lenin promises is not contingent upon joining the coalition, so almost every individual would gain by avoiding the risk of being penalized by the Tsar. Roemer makes a few rather lame points about how Lenin's charisma or the class consciousness induced by identical severity of punishment might overcome the free rider problem. Mostly, however, he chooses to ignore the issue.

Although Roemer's game of revolution is already fairly complicated, various technical modifications are needed to create a fully satisfying model. The probability of revolution depends exclusively upon the identity of the revolutionary coalition and the schedule of penalties. It should also depend upon the existing and the proposed income distributions. The Tsar can only defend the status quo by making threats. Realism—not to mention strategic parity—suggests he should be able to use positive incentives by offering income redistributions of his own.

Whatever its limitations, Roemer's game of revolution does achieve an important objective of Analytical Marxism. Rather than assuming a particular class structure and deriving revolutionary dynamics from this class structure, Roemer succeeds in deriving revolutionary class dynamics from more elementary assumptions about the distribution of income and rational pursuit of material gain. This is an important step toward converting the famous proposition stated in the very first lines of *The Communist Manifesto*—"the history of all hitherto existing society is the history of class struggle" (Marx and Engels [1848] 1976, p. 482)—from an axiom of Marxist theory to one of its foremost theorems.

Transition to Democracy

Classical Marxist theory considered revolutionary transitions from feudalism to capitalism and from capitalism to socialism. It acknowledged the possibility of thrusts in the opposite directions, but these were seen as reactionary movements, not as bona fide revolutions in the main line of human emancipation. Events of the last decade challenge this outlook upon revolution. It is evident that movements against bureaucratic state socialism can mobilize immense popular support, accomplish emancipatory tasks, and bring sweeping changes in the organization of society. Although the economic aspect of these movements against state socialism usually involves establishing (or reestablishing) capitalism, their ideological core and a major basis of their popular support revolves around creating democratic institutions.

Movements against state socialism in Eastern Europe and the former Soviet Union are by no means the only transitions to democracy in recent decades. Transitions of this general nature also occurred in parts of southern Europe and Latin America. Democratic revolutions are surely the most important political transformations of the current historical period and cry out for theoretical analysis.

The most interesting treatment of this subject from something like an Analytical Marxist perspective is provided by Adam Przeworski (1986, 1991b). Because Przeworski's discussion of transitions to democracy makes little use of historical materialism, or class analysis, or exploitation theory, or virtually any recognizable element of Marxist analysis, including it within a book on Analytical Marxist requires some justification. I choose to discuss Przeworski's analysis of the transition to democracy because it bristles with insights, because it makes frequent reference to Marxist theory, because it links with Przeworski's other, more clearly Marxist writings, and because it is better to err on the side of inclusion rather than exclusion when talking about Analytical Marxism.

Przeworski uses a very simple definition of democracy. It is a system with (a) free elections in which a majority of the population can vote, and (b) a government responsible to an elected parliament or president (Przeworski 1991b, p. 86n.) Three aspects of democracy are crucial to the process of transition:

> First, democracy is a form of institutionalization of continual conflicts. Second, the capacity of particular groups to realize their interests is shaped by the specific institutional arrangements of a given system. Finally . . . outcomes of conflicts are not uniquely determined either by the institutional arrangements or by places occupied by participants within the system of production. Outcomes that are unlikely can and do occur. (Przeworski 1986, p. 58)

The uncertainty of democratic outcomes and the possibility that the unexpected will happen are particularly salient to the dynamics transition.

Modern authoritarian regimes have different kinds of vulnerability. Regimes based upon ritualized speech that no one really believes are vulnerable to public expressions of the honest truth that everyone already knows. Regimes based upon fear are vulnerable to mass movements that end individual isolation through the safety of numbers. Regimes based upon a tacit exchange of prosperity for acquiescence are vulnerable to economic crises. But the breakdown of an authoritarian regime may not lead to democracy. Whether it does depends largely upon the context in which the authoritarian regime collapses.

The process of transition has two phases: liberalization of the authoritarian regime and transition proper. The second phase occurs in two general forms, which Przeworski considers separately: (a) the authoritarian regime does not collapse but extricates itself from power through negotiation; (b) the authoritarian regime does collapse, so the opposition is entirely free to construct new political institutions.

By the time transition to democracy has become even a remote possibility, the rulers of the authoritarian regime are divided into hardliners and liberalizers. The liberalizers hope to strengthen their position within the regime by instituting changes that would relax social tensions. If liberalization does occur, it results from interactions between these splits within the regime and popular mobilization: mobilization (up to a certain point) strengthens the hand of the liberalizers, and the existence of a liberalizing faction encourages and protects the popular mobilization.

Przeworski analyzes the liberalization phase by considering the decisions liberalizers must make. First they must decide whether to remain aligned with the hardliners or to embark seriously upon the path of change. The second decision arises only if the liberalizers opt for change and the popular movement then tries to eliminate the authoritarian regime entirely. Under these circumstances, the liberalizers must decide whether to attempt repression of the movement or to allow transition to a different form of society. When making this decision, liberalizers are uncertain about how successful an attempted repression would be. Unsuccessful repression leads to insurrection, assumed by Przeworski to be the worst outcome for everyone. This conceptualization leads to the decision tree given in Figure 7.1.[4]

Given this decision tree, the outcome depends heavily upon the preference structure of the liberalizers. Suppose the liberalizers rank the alternatives as follows:

1. broadened dictatorship (most preferred)
2. status quo dictatorship
3. transition to democracy
4. narrower dictatorship
5. insurrection (least preferred)

Suppose further that these preferences are known to everyone. To analyze the outcome, we first consider the end of the decision tree and move backward from there.

At their second decision, liberalizers will surely choose transition because they prefer it to either of the alternatives that can arise from repression. Hence civil society (i.e., the popular movement) faces a choice between a transition to democracy and participation in a broadened dictatorship, and will surely choose transition. From this it follows that liberalizers, in their first decision, must choose between transition to democracy and a status quo dictatorship. Given the preference structure above, they will choose the status quo dictatorship; so liberalization does not get started even though the liberalizers prefer a broadened dictatorship over all the alternatives.

How can a transition to democracy occur with such a decision tree? Przeworski identifies two ways it could happen. The first way assumes that liberalizers are closet democrats or close to it. For example, their preference structure might be the following:

1. broadened dictatorship (most preferred)
2. transition to democracy

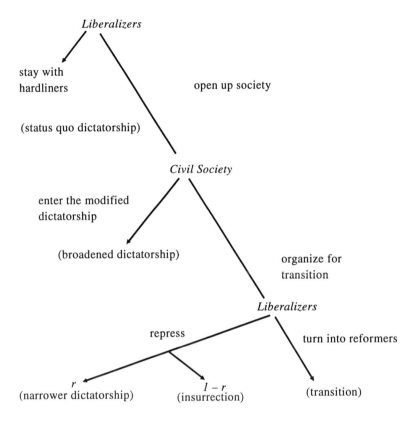

Liberalizers

stay with
hardliners

open up society

(status quo dictatorship)

Civil Society

enter the modified
dictatorship

(broadened dictatorship)

organize for
transition

Liberalizers

repress

turn into reformers

r
(narrower dictatorship)

$1 - r$
(insurrection)

(transition)

Figure 7.1 Decision Tree of the Liberalizers
SOURCE: Przeworski (1991b), p. 62

3. status quo dictatorship
4. narrower dictatorship
5. insurrection (least preferred)

If the popular movement knows about these preferences, then the outcome will be transition to democracy, as the reader can verify by repeating the steps above. The problem with this scenario is that hardliners will step in if they think liberalizers are actually closet democrats.

The second alternative involves a change of outlook by the liberalizers during the course of the decision process. For example, they might initially think that repression could be successful, but change their mind as a result of interaction with the popular movement. Or the liberalizers might fantasize—contrary to all reason and evidence, thinks Przeworski—that they could compete successfully in elections. Given such wishful thinking, they might come to view transition to democracy in a more favorable light, rejecting the repression they originally planned on using.

Liberalization may not eventuate in transition to democracy, but Przeworski views liberalizers as either ludicrous or tragic figures.

> The perennial tragedy of Liberalizers was described by Marx as early as 1851: They want democracy that will keep them in power, and they are stung when it turns against them. They try to hold on as long as they can, but at some point they must decide whether to go backward to authoritarian restoration or forward to democratic emancipation. (Przeworski 1991b, p. 66)

The Two-Front Struggle for Democracy

The struggle for democracy takes place on two fronts. One front concerns the struggle against the authoritarian regime. The other front—becoming increasingly important as the regime weakens—concerns the struggle among members of the anti-authoritarian coalition for position within the anticipated democracy. This two-front struggle greatly complicates the politics of transition.

Przeworski identifies four actors centrally involved when democracy emerges through extrication from an authoritarian regime. Within the regime, there are hardliners and political reformers (who may or may not be the same as the liberalizers discussed above). Within the antiauthoritarian coalition, there are moderates and the radicals: the former being more risk averse, but perhaps not less ideologically radical, than the latter.

Extrication requires an understanding between reformers on the regime side and moderates on the coalition side. Such an agreement calls for a limited type of democracy preserving the social position of authoritarian elites and usually exempting the military from civilian control. If the moderates ally themselves with the radicals behind a program of sweeping democratic change, including civilian control of the military, then a negotiated exit from authoritarian rule becomes extremely unlikely. Conversely, if the reformers join forces with the hardliners, they will try to maintain the authoritarian regime.

The extrication process can be represented as a simple two-person game between reformers and moderates. Political reformers can choose to ally with hardliners behind a preserve-the-regime strategy, or with moderates behind a strategy of limited democracy. Moderates can choose to join with radicals asking for complete democracy, or with reformers on behalf of a limited democracy. Przeworski provides several slightly different interpretations of the Extrication Game, one of which is reproduced in Figure 7.2.

This version of the Extrication Game has no pure strategy equilibrium, but some indication of its strategic dynamics can be obtained from the Stackelberg solutions. If reformers are the Stackelberg leaders, the outcome will be survival of the authoritarian regime with some reforms. If moderates are the Stackelberg leaders, the outcome will be limited democracy.[5] Because liberal democracy is better for both players than a reformed authoritarianism, this could well be the outcome of an extrication interaction structured along the lines of Figure 7.2. A great deal seems to depend upon the resourcefulness of the moderates.

The relationship between moderates and radicals tends to be ambivalent. Moderates need radicals, Przeworski (1991b) observes, to pressure the reformers; but moderates also fear that intransigent radicals will not consent to the deal they eventually negotiate with the reformers. Most moderates would prefer a democracy in which the political tendencies represented by reformers have an important role over one dominated by the radicals. This sheds further light on why the extrication route from authoritarianism to democracy often keeps the military free of civilian control and allows it to exercise a baleful tutelage over democratic politics.

Some democratic politicians prefer an autonomous military because it can be relied upon to repress popular mobilizations and

		Group with whom Moderates try to ally themselves and strategy which they chose:	
		Radicals and a strategy of complete democracy	Reformers and a strategy of limited democracy
Group with whom Reformers try to ally themselves and strategy which they chose:	Hardliners and a strategy of preserving the authoritarian regime	Authoritarian regime, survives with no change 2,1	Authoritarian regime, survives with some reforms 3,2
	Moderates and a strategy of limited democracy	Complete democracy established, including civilian control of the military 1,4	Limited democracy established, without civilian control of the military 4,3

Figure 7.2 A Version of the Extrication Game Between Reformers (Row Player) and Moderates (Column Player)

SOURCE: Przeworski (1991b), p. 71

thus support established political parties. Nationalism, a belief that military institutions somehow embody the national spirit, and fear of leaving the nation defenseless also discourage determined efforts to curtail military autonomy. Given the limited range of institutional possibilities, the choice confronting realistic democrats may be between tolerating military autonomy or destroying the military establishment entirely (Przeworski 1991b, pp. 76-77).

Although democracy emerged in parts of Eastern Europe (e.g., Poland) through an extrication process, the role of the military in these places differs sharply from that sketched above. Communist regimes almost always maintained exceptionally tight civilian control over the military. Thus it is hardly surprising that Eastern European military establishments should ardently support abolition of the Communist monopoly on power. But despite the absence of a military overlord à la Argentina and Brazil, Przeworski fears that several Eastern European countries will end up fervently anti-Communist, but not democratic.

The extrication route to democracy seems inherently unstable to Przeworski. It produces a polity with certain institutional vestiges of dictatorship, and with powerful incentives to eliminate these authoritarian legacies. Efforts to do this are sometimes successful, as in Poland and Spain, but they can also undermine the limited and fragile democracy.

Przeworski's analysis of what happens when the authoritarian regime simply collapses (e.g., East Germany, Czechoslovakia, Romania) is less penetrating than his discussion of extrication. When authoritarianism collapses, the basic political questions concern what democratic institutions will emerge and whether these institutions will be self-enforcing. Przeworski's most striking conclusion is that stable democracy emerges most easily when the balance of political forces is unknown to the democratic institution builders: that is, when they function behind a Rawlsian veil of ignorance. When this happens, the institutions chosen usually incorporate many checks and balances, which constrain the exercise of power and the advantages of having it. With such institutions, losing is not a catastrophe. Losers are induced to comply with unfavorable decisions and to continue participating in the democratic process (Przeworski 1991b, p. 88).

Przeworski has modest expectations of democracy: it is only a system for processing conflicts without violence. Although democracy is imperative in a world with so little consensus and so much possibility of violence, the nitty-gritty texture of democratic politics hardly inspires confidence in human rationality or good will. The same is true about the transition to democracy: "In spite of Vaclav Havel's eloquent eulogies to the subversive power of truth, the lasting source of opposition to communism was not a yearning for liberty (as distinguished from independence from the Soviet Union), but religion and nationalism; indeed the historically specific amalgam of the two" (Przeworski 1991b, p. 93).

Since 1985, if not earlier, the trajectory of Adam Przeworski's thought has been away from Marxism of all sorts, including Analytical Marxism. One senses in his writings a declining optimism about the creative potential of revolution and even about the possibility of radical reform in the style of left-wing social democracy. Declining optimism about the possibility of forward leaps in human emancipation is hardly unusual in these last years of our century. Yet Przeworski has not completed the transition away from Marxism: he still makes use of Marxist concepts, defines his own position with reference to classical and contemporary Marxism, and chooses Marxists as his main intellectual antagonists. Moreover, his divergence from Marxism has not been a unidirectional movement but an uneven sequence of attractions and repulsions. Przeworski's ability to combine intuition with logic and historical interpretation with model building is extremely rare. No serious student of revolutionary transitions to democracy, whether Analytical Marxist or other-wise, can afford to ignore his ideas.

Conclusion

By no stretch of the imagination is Analytical Marxism a science of revolution in the sense of providing scientifically certified advice about how and when to make revolutions. Nor does any Analytical Marxist I know about aspire to such a role. Several seem dubious about the value of violent upheavals under any circumstances, and many tend to think that classical Marxist theory greatly exaggerated the historical importance of revolu-tion. Analytical Marxism has made definite progress on why rational people engage in revolutionary action, yet the question remains disturbing.

The issue of revolution has always been a difficult one for Marxists. This is the place where theory and practice intersect. This is the issue on which Marxists must declare themselves, indicating what they stand for and what they stand against. Most deep schisms within Marxist theory and Marxist politics concern the issue of revolution. The commitment of Analytical Marxism to scientific rigor and methodological openness will not shield them from the ethical and political problems posed by revolution.

As suggested in the discussion of Adam Przeworski, there may be a connection between optimism about the future and enthu-

siasm for revolution: optimistic thinkers generally welcome revolutions whereas pessimists do not. Despite the intellectual
promise of Analytical Marxism, this is not a very optimistic
period in the history of Marxist theory. Since its high-water mark
in the late 1960s or early 1970s, serious Marxism has lost adherents everywhere, and it now exercises only a fraction of the
intellectual appeal it did when I was a young man. Marxists of
every description feel chastened in their ability to predict the
future and radically uncertain about how human emancipation
is best served.

For the first time in over a century the revolutionary left lacks
a project that could give a semblance of common purpose to its
disparate and frequently antagonistic minions. It is meaningless
to be revolutionary in the absence of a revolutionary purpose.
Yet the outlook is not entirely bleak, and Analytical Marxism may
be one source of revolutionary optimism. There is a definite link
between the insistence of Analytical Marxism on rigorous deductive explanations and the theoretical importance it gives to
individual rationality on the one hand, and the reappearance of
a plausible emancipatory project on the other. To be sure, this
link may remain unconsummated. Analytical Marxism could
degenerate into a meaningless academic scholasticism; but it has
far more liberating potentialities as well.

One of the achievements of classical Marxist theory was to
forge an alliance between a significant fragment of the intelligentsia and those social classes identified as victims of exploitation. The ideological foundation of that alliance was an
intellectually credible emancipatory project. The project had
intellectual credibility partly because it was fashioned with the
most credible methods of intellectual production available at the
time. If a new project can be formulated and if a new alliance
between progressive intellectuals and victims of exploitation
can be forged, then the most broadly credible contemporary
methods of intellectual production have a vital role to play.

For the past century or more, the unifying project of the
revolutionary left has been building socialism. Leftists disagreed
about what constituted socialism and how to build it, but not
about the project itself. What went wrong with these attempts
to build socialism? Does their failure demonstrate the inadequacy of Marxist theory in all its incarnations? Is socialism still

a plausible objective? Or is it perhaps a utopian dream, the implementation of which induces totalitarianism? The next two chapters consider Analytical Marxist contributions to these vital questions.

Notes

1. This insight suggests that the Communist revolutions of the 20th century may be extended, drastic, and unintentional preparations for bourgeois hegemony in the underdeveloped countries where the revolutions occur. But even if historical events consistently follow this pattern, it does not explain why the Communist revolutions happen.

2. Sen uses the example of Maoist China to show that growth of national income alone may not prevent famine:

In India . . . famine ceased with independence. A multiparty democratic system and a relatively unfettered press made it obligatory for the government to act. In contrast, even though postrevolutionary China has been much more successful than India in economic expansion and in health care, it has not been able to stave off famine. One occurred between 1958 and 1961, after the agricultural program of the Great Leap Forward failed. The lack of political opposition and a free press allowed the disastrous policies to continue for three more years. The death toll consequently climbed to between 23 million and 30 million people. (Sen 1993, pp. 43-44)

3. See the discussion of Penalty Monotonicity below.

4. Uncertainty about the success of repression is represented in the decision tree by two possible outcomes that repression can produce: with probability r, repression is "successful" and leads to a narrower dictatorship; with probability $1 - r$, it is "unsuccessful" and induces insurrection.

5. The reader should check her understanding of the Stackelberg concept by verifying that these are indeed the two Stackelberg outcomes.

8

THE COLLAPSE OF
COMMUNIST SYSTEMS

A chapter on the collapse of Communist systems was not included in the first draft of this book. None of the main works on Analytical Marxism address this subject in a systematic way, and it is hard to identify distinctively Analytical Marxist positions on the issue. Yet when discussing this manuscript with friends and colleagues over the last 2 years, the subject of Communist collapse frequently arose. My interlocutors wanted to know how Analytical Marxism explained the amazingly rapid demise of Communist systems in Eastern Europe and the Soviet Union. Some of them thought this phenomenon so thoroughly contradicted the fundamental expectations of Marx and Engels as to invalidate any theory even remotely derived from their writings. In light of the stunning turn taken by history during the waning years of the 20th century, they wondered why any alert student would want to study any version of Marxist theory.

These discussions convinced me that a book on Analytical Marxism published in the 1990s must deal with the breakdown of Communist systems. It was not only a matter of placating other people; I also felt internally challenged to build a coherent explanation of Communist collapse that fit within the broad outlines of Analytical Marxism. If this perspective really advances our understanding of historical dynamics, it should elucidate the most momentous, but least predicted, socioeconomic transformation of recent times.

Predicting is not the same as anticipating. Although no Analytical Marxist predicted the collapse of Communism, several anticipated this possibility. In Chapter 2, I quoted a passage from G. A. Cohen claiming that "premature attempts at revolution, whatever their immediate outcome, will eventuate in the restoration of capitalist society." Other Analytical Marxists have written in a similar vein. Jon Elster discussed the likelihood of premature communist revolutions with disastrous outcomes (Elster 1985, pp. 293-99, 451-52). The possibility (but not the necessity) of a retreat from Communist social organization lies implicit within John Roemer's concept of socially necessary exploitation (Roemer 1988a, pp. 143-47). These rather casual anticipations do not make Analytical Marxists any more prescient about historical events than other social scientists. I cite them only to suggest that Analytical Marxism has a theoretical basis for explaining the collapse of Communist states.

A methodological comment is appropriate here. A theory of history should not aim at predicting historical events. Even the most valid historical theory will not be able to do this with any degree of precision. Historical prediction on a scientific basis is impossible not only because causal variables are numerous, random factors are present, and free will exists. It is also impossible because of the severely nonlinear relationship between historical cause and historical effect: a very small change in the cause can sometimes produce a very large change in the effect.

The appropriate objective of a theory of history is identifying fundamental principles operative in the historical process and using these principles to interpret historical evidence. Application of valid principles can explain or at least illuminate what happens in history. Rigorous methodology and conscientious collection of evidence make it feasible to distinguish between valid and invalid historical principles. Yet none of these activities enable historical prediction in any meaningful sense. The situation is analogous to how the principle of natural selection functions in explaining biological evolution. Natural selection elucidates a great deal of biological evidence, but it does not support predictions about the future evolution of life.

This is the spirit in which I discuss some Marxist interpretations of why many Communist systems have collapsed.

Basic Causes

Communist revolutions, almost without exception, occurred in poor countries with weak capitalist relations and lacking modern forces of production. Through a combination of military conquest and political domination, Communist social organization spread to other countries that experienced no indigenous revolution, but no formidable Communist insurgency has ever occurred in an advanced capitalist society. Within these historical circumstances lies the basic cause of the collapse of Communism.

A fundamental principle of historical materialism is a tendency toward congruence between the level of productive forces and the nature of productive relations (Cohen's Primacy Thesis) (Cohen 1978, p. 134). According to this principle, an economic system based upon public ownership of means of production, guaranteed employment, restricted income inequality, and planning of production assumes highly developed forces of production. Yet the flow of historical events will not be detained by theoretical propositions. A revolutionary party can sometimes abolish private ownership of the means of production and establish a collectivized system of production in an economically backward society. The resulting economic system may even accomplish some impressive feats of production. These facts, however, do not annul the tendency toward congruence. The social cost of exemplary economic achievements proves extremely high, and the political institutions that propel them bear little resemblance to any kind of democratic socialism. The prematurely collectivized economic system cannot sustain its successful performances and becomes increasingly unstable.

Unless forces of production are already highly advanced, Communist relations do not facilitate sustained growth of the productive power of society. On the contrary, they establish numerous microeconomic inefficiencies and soon impede the development of productive forces. Hence the continued existence of Communist systems violates another principle of historical materialism: productive forces have a tendency to develop (Cohen's Development Thesis). This violation is particularly egregious in the context of a capitalist world system. The capitalist system experiences cycles of accelerated and retarded economic growth, but sooner or later the protean dynamism of capitalist property relations offers an obvious and galling contrast to long-term Communist stagnation.

How does all this happen? A Communist party that seizes power in a backward society undertakes tasks of economic accumulation elsewhere accomplished by capitalism. Under capitalism (in its classical forms) the agent of accumulation is the bourgeoisie, and the accumulation process involves extensive coercion of various sorts. Under Communism the agent of accumulation is the state, and the political and economic environment within which accumulation unfolds is unpropitious at very best. Even with the greatest luck, Communist accumulation can scarcely avoid coercion, and in several cases the coercion has reached staggering dimensions.

The specific instruments of Communist accumulation are a dictatorial state, a disciplined party, and an ideologically galvanized population. These instruments can be effective during the first part of the accumulation process, which depends mainly on mobilizing underutilized economic resources (e.g., labor power, raw materials) using well-known productive techniques. They are far less effective at subsequent phases of accumulation, partly because the instruments themselves break down, and partly because the target-oriented campaign style mobilization process for which they are suitable loses relevance once full utilization of economic resources is achieved. Advanced accumulation entails a continuing qualitative transformation of the production process (e.g., new technologies, new products, new methods of work, new approaches to management) for which state dictatorship, party discipline, and ideological conviction are at best blunt tools.

And these blunt tools become corrupted. Any population has a limited capacity for ideological mobilization. Indifference and disillusionment eventually render ideological appeals ineffective. The once-disciplined party becomes cynical, self-serving, and incompetent. The dictatorship recoils from its own deeds and forswears the use of terror but is increasingly hamstrung by bureaucratic inertia. The former instruments of accumulation become barriers to accumulation. Communist elites lose confidence in their historical mission, and a large share of the intelligentsia fostered by Communist accumulation eventually view the Party as a parasite upon society. Socialism, once considered the hope of the future, seems a turgid inefficient system stifling individual initiative and vastly inferior to capitalism for most practical purposes.

Leaders of Communist revolutions are usually well versed in historical materialism and freely acknowledge that socialism cannot arise under conditions of economic backwardness. They have coped with this dilemma in one of two ways. One strategy involves aggressive promotion of revolution in economically advanced societies, hoping that transition to socialism can occur on an international basis even when some of the participants are initially underdeveloped. This approach invites military intervention by powerful defenders of the status quo and founders on the absence of revolutionary motivation within advanced capitalist societies. The second and more common strategy involves developing the forces of production required by socialism within the revolutionary society itself. As we have seen, however, revolutionary momentum exhausts itself long before sufficient forces of production are developed.

The basic reasons for the collapse of Communist systems are readily deducible from the theory of history proposed by Karl Marx. For all their military power and economic achievements, Communist regimes never overcame the limitations inherent within their origins. Given the weak impulse toward economic development within pre-Communist social structure, and given their ideological hostility towards private property, the accumulationist visions of Communist leadership required political dictatorship. Comprehensive economic planning and high rates of surplus appropriation within basically poor societies entail political dictatorship. Whatever economic dynamism Communist societies could muster came not from the institutional structure of the Communist system but largely from the political momentum generated by the authoritarian leadership. The comprehensive nature of Communist dictatorship—reflecting the goal of transforming society comprehensively—masked, but could not eliminate, its political fragility.

The ultimate causes of political fragility were the impossible tasks that the system was organized to accomplish and by which it was justified. When the dictatorship finally lifted, the entire politically driven Communist system collapsed amazingly quickly.

The Tendency Toward Economic Stagnation

The economic analysis of the collapse of Communism involves answering two questions: (a) why the long-term tendency of Communist economic systems is toward stagnation, and (b) why efforts to reform the system often lead to economic crisis.

Consider the first question. The strengths of Communist economic systems lie in their capacity to mobilize underutilized resources, to function under emergency conditions such as war, and to organize for the achievement of specific goals. These strengths are evident in chaotic postrevolutionary situations and during early periods of "extensive" economic development that concentrate on heavy industry and building basic infrastructure of production. The weaknesses of Communist systems are the obverse of their strengths: improving economic performance when most readily available resources have been mobilized, making progress on a steady orderly basis, and advancing on a broad front rather than towards particular objectives. The weaknesses, although never absent, become more obvious and insufferable during subsequent phases of "intensive" economic development, when progress requires qualitative transformation of production methods and when mobilizing people on the basis of ideological commitment and dedication to the community becomes more difficult.

Several structural characteristics of Communist economic systems are important for explaining their tendency toward stagnation. Centralized management creates a hierarchical and inflexible decision-making structure depriving regional and local economic units of initiative. Central management relies upon information provided by regional and local units, yet the latter often have strong incentives to withhold or distort crucial pieces of information. The effort to plan centrally generates a bias favoring large production units that simplify the tasks of centralized planning and management. This reduces the sources of supply, often creating regional production monopolies, and eliminates any real possibility of competition between production units. In addition, Communist ideology regards competition as a wasteful aspect of capitalism to be abolished under socialism. The absence of competition weakens incentives toward efficiency and technological innovation. It also renders the price structure established by the central planning board largely arbitrary and hence of limited utility for evaluating economic performance.

Communist economic systems are sometimes said to have a "soft budget constraint" blunting responsiveness to price signals (Kornai 1992, pp. 140-48). The massiveness of production units, the absence of alternative sources of supply, and the commitment to full employment all make political authorities reluctant to allow a production unit to fail even if it is performing badly. There is also the problem of determining when a unit actually is performing badly. The arbitrary character of prices renders price-based evaluations of performance (e.g., profit margins) highly suspect, suggesting that exaction of serious economic penalties on the basis of such indicators entails gross injustice. The doubtful validity of sophisticated performance indicators causes plan fulfillment to mean achieving a certain volume of production irrespective of how wasteful the production process may be. During normal times (i.e., in the absence of a national emergency) Communist managers can usually keep their production obligations well within their plant capacity through political maneuvering of various sorts.

Because of all this, Communist managers know they operate under very little risk. The absence of risk weakens both incentives toward efficiency and responsiveness to consumer demand. It also induces insatiable demands for productive resources. Acquisition of these resources creates no significant economic peril but does enhance (a) the ease with which the firm can fulfill its production targets, (b) the firm's strategic influence within the Communist economic system, and (c) the status of its managers. These insatiable demands for productive resources are an important source of the shortage phenomenon frequently observed in Communist economies.

Problems associated with motivations to work are another source of the tendency toward stagnation. Over the course of their existence Communist societies have used three methods (in various combinations) to motivate work: ideology, terror, and reward. Ideology can be effective for limited periods of time but is not an enduring inducement to productive effort. Terror is expensive and difficult to control (often being hazardous to its perpetrators and to the dominant groups in society), and propagates work of dubious quality. The efficacy of reward as a work motivator depends upon the range of rewards available and on the correlation between effort and reward. Communist economies are lacking on both counts. Shortages and political limitations on the range of permissible incomes limit positive rewards for working. Commitments to full employment and the individual's right to have a job often prevent dismissing or even disciplining inept or uncooperative workers. These practices, along with the emphasis on political reliability evident in the "nomenklatura" promotion system, deeply attenuate the correlation between effort and reward, and ultimately discourage endeavors beyond the ordinary.

The accelerating complexity of a modern economy overwhelms all efforts at comprehensive planning, even those undertaken with the assistance of modern computers. Next year's plan, remarked the Russian academician Federenko, if fully checked and balanced, would be ready in about 30,000 years (quoted in Nove 1990, p. 189). The Communist response to the impossibility of comprehensive planning has been to focus upon a few priority targets while neglecting other sectors (usually consumer goods and social services). This leads to imbalanced and unsustainable growth, and also contributes to the shortage phenomenon.

John Roemer (1994) conceptualizes the issues raised above in terms of relations between a principal (e.g., the owner of a business) and her economic agent (e.g., the hired manager). Although first studied in the context of capitalist corporations, principal-agent problems arise in numerous economic contexts (Stiglitz 1987). Naturally the principal wants her agent to act in the principal's interest. However, the principal is not fully informed about the agent's activities and thus has difficulty determining whether the agent has really done so. How can the principal motivate the agent to obey her interests? More precisely, what compensation scheme will motivate an economically rational agent to act in the principal's interests?

Centrally planned economies, Roemer believes, face three critical principal-agent problems: (a) the manager-worker relationship, (b) the planner-manager relationship, and (c) the public-planner relationship. In each of these relationships the first party is conceived as the principal and the second as the agent. The manager-worker problem arises because managers have difficulty motivating workers, whom they can neither fire nor reward with additional consumer goods, to carry out the manager's production plan. The planner-manager problem exists because managers in Communist societies become immune to the sanctions of planners. Managers routinely develop cozy relationships with local politicians who protect them from anything the economic planners might do. The public-planner problem is a result of political dictatorship, which prevents the public from compelling economic planners to act in its interests. Failure to solve these three principal-agent problems, argues Roemer, is responsible for at least some of the difficulties encountered by economies of the Soviet type.

Communist economic systems also have problems with technological innovation. To be sure, they can sometimes appropriate existing technologies and sometimes acquire military technologies known to be feasible (e.g., nuclear weapons and ballistic missiles). But they consistently lag behind advanced capitalist economies in the routine development and exploitation of new technologies. This weakness obviously hinders economic progress. Why do Communist economies, supposedly organized around the idea of rational planning, have such a deficiency?

One cause is overcentralization. Considerable evidence suggests that decentralized authority is associated with both scientific and technological progress (Basalla 1988; Wuthnow 1980). Centralized economic organization fosters monopoly situations in which the operational procedures of central management remain unchallenged. Innovation is certainly not imperative—and may be resoundingly suboptimal—within an economic strategy aimed at maintaining monopoly. A small economic unit operating in the context of other small units, on the other hand, cannot aspire toward monopolist supremacy. Innovation is a natural way to gain advantage over competitors.

Technologically innovative ideas can strike almost anywhere. An economic structure congenial toward technological progress will allow agents with innovative ideas relatively easy access to production. The formidable barriers to entry characteristic of Communist economic organization largely eliminate spontaneous innovation as a source of technological progress.

Nor does the target approach to economic planning facilitate technological innovation. The obligation of each production unit is to reach its production target, not to make innovations.

The production target is typically a modest increment above the previous year's production level. Technological innovation creates uncertainties that could actually endanger achievement of the production target. Even if successful, an innovation may not be welcome. It brings a corresponding leap in subsequent targets, possibly making life harder for both managers and workers, and it may cause unwelcome changes in the structure of employment.

Consumer demand is an important source of technological innovation in capitalist economies, but consumers have little leverage within Communist economic systems. Producers are responsible to planners, not to consumers, and the shortage environment means that virtually anything produced will be sold. These circumstances obliterate most consumer-generated pressure toward innovation.

These factors jointly explain why Communist economic systems have a weak impulse toward technological innovation. This deficiency, along with the other conditions discussed above, creates an habitual tendency toward stagnation. Stagnation, it must be emphasized, is not the same as economic collapse. Communist economies mired in stagnation still muddle along in suboptimal fashion. Sooner or later everyone sheds his or her ideological illusions: the notion that centralized planning is rational or that planning even exists is understood to be a farce. The economy functions through a network of ad hoc agreements between workers, managers, and planners. Realistic objectives are stability, doing just a bit better than the year before, and avoiding any serious economic calamity. A general sense of inferiority toward leading capitalist countries becomes prevalent among intellectuals of Communist society, and even among Party members the hope of overtaking capitalism withers away.

Sources of Economic Crisis

We turn now to the second question posed at the start of the previous section: Why do efforts to reform the Communist economic system often lead to economic crisis? If, as I claim, Communist economies tend toward stagnation, it is easy to see why reform efforts might occur. The most important attempts to reform Communist economic institutions without abandoning state socialism altogether occurred in Yugoslavia after Tito's break with Stalin, in Hungary in 1968 and later, in China following the death of Mao, and within the Soviet Union under Gorbachev. Although these reforms were by no means identical either in content or in outcome, they all involved varying degrees of economic decentralization, market relations, private entrepreneurship, and economic inequality. The outcome in China still remains in doubt and is discussed later in this chapter. The Yugoslavian, Hungarian, and Soviet reforms (not to mention more limited changes elsewhere in Eastern Europe) did not succeed in preserving any recognizable version of socialism. Why is this so?

One kind of answer is given by the Hungarian economist Janos Kornai:

> Stalinist classical socialism is repressive and inefficient, but it constitutes a coherent system. When it starts reforming itself, that coherence slackens and its internal contradictions strengthen. In spite of generating a whole series of favorable changes, reform is doomed to fail: the socialist system is unable to renew itself internally so as to prove viable in the long run. So the time for really revolutionary changes does come in the end, eliminating the socialist system and leading society toward a capitalist market economy. (Kornai 1992, p. xxv)

The difficulty with Kornai's answer lies in the nature of the postulated incoherence of reformed Communism. His analysis freely mingles structural components of the Communist system with particular aspects of Communist history. Although he discusses several kinds of incoherence, the really decisive one derives from the political history of the Communist movement. Reformed Communism allows some freedom of speech and some political democracy, which naturally encourages desires for full civil liberties and complete democracy. Yet the Communist Party that initiated the reforms will not want to abandon its monopoly of power. If it should do so and allow the establishment of complete democracy, then the entire socialist system—which Kornai regards profoundly unpopular—is rapidly swept into the ash can of history.

Kornai is probably correct about the actions of Communist parties and the feelings of people in many Communist societies, but this is an historical and not a structural argument. It may reveal something about the nature of Communist history since 1917, but it does not demonstrate the structural incoherence of reformed Communism. That a society with the economic institutions Kornai attributes to reformed Communism should be ruled by a dictatorial party governing over a resentful and disgruntled population is surely not inevitable.

Focusing on the case of the Soviet Union, Ellman and Kontorovich offer a somewhat similar explanation of why the Soviet economic system disintegrated after Gorbachev's political reforms:

> The economic collapse has been in part an unintended by-product of the political changes Gorbachev has introduced. These political changes (the withdrawal of the Communist Party from a direct role in the economy, the transfer of substantial powers to the Soviets, detotalitarianization, an expansion of the independence of enterprises) were expected to release the human factor in economic development and thus lead to rapid economic growth. In fact they removed the motive force (pressure from above) which had propelled the Soviet economy in previous decades, without replacing it by an adequate substitute. Hence, as the political reforms became more radical, the economy went into a tail-spin. (Ellman and Kontorovich 1992, p. 7)

The role of pressure in a command economy, they argue, is analogous to the role of competition in a capitalist economy, providing the main source of dynamism. Gorbachev's fundamental error was believing that the Soviet system could be democratized without collapsing.

Any retreat from a command economy is likely to involve reduction of pressure from above, but such reduction did not send the post-Maoist Chinese economy into a rapid tailspin. And even though state socialism ultimately collapsed in Hungary and Yugoslavia, market reforms did not cause economic crisis in these countries. Perhaps explanations of the Soviet economic collapse should emphasize reduction of pressure from above less and failure to provide an adequate substitute more. Reform of a Communist economy, even when diminishing pressure from above, need not induce economic crisis. Whether this happens depends largely upon the circumstances under which the reform occurs. Three considerations are especially important: (a) the political credibility of the government undertaking the reform; (b) the attitudes of the various classes within Communist society, particularly their willingness to support fundamental reforms; and (c) the coherence of the reform programs.

None of these considerations boded well for Gorbachev's reforms. After years of economic stagnation and widespread alienation from the regime, the political credibility of the Soviet government was weak at best. The coherence of the reform program also left much to be desired. Although the Gorbachev team seemed reasonably clear about its economic objectives— greater consumer sovereignty, technological development, use of markets, and open participation in the world economy—they tinkered with the traditional Soviet economy rather than boldly fashioning a new democratic socialist structure. Tinkering not founded upon a lucid and consistent social vision soon created structural conflicts. For example, Gorbachev weakened the Communist Party and touted the importance of democracy, but continued to base his own rule on Party dictatorship and did not seek a genuinely democratic mandate.

I shall have more to say about class dynamics and the collapse of Communism. To indicate some of the problems encountered by Gorbachev's reforms, it will be sufficient to quote the conclusion reached by Burawoy and Krotov in their recent study of class relations within the Soviet wood industry:

> Far from becoming militant or radical, the workers in Arctic City became more and more demoralized as perestroika unfolded. They were humiliated by the way they have to live. . . . Certainly, for most the future looks bleaker than the past. . . . So while in the West we celebrate the "collapse of communism," at Polar workers mourn for the past and despair for the future.[1] (Burawoy and Krotov 1992, pp. 36-37)

Contrary to Kornai's interpretation, the relationship between reform and economic crisis does not indicate the absence of a third path different from either state socialism or corporate capitalism. Nor does the relationship stem from the democratic illusions of reforming Communists, as Ellman and Kontorovich seem to think. Gorbachev's efforts to reform Soviet Communism suffered from insufficient democracy, not from too much.

The crux of the relationship between reform and crisis turns around politics. Economic reform is not a cure for the political weakness of Communist regimes. When a discredited government attempts to reform a Communist economy mired in stagnation, it may well destabilize society and touch off an acute economic crisis. But this is not likely to happen when a politically robust Communist government initiates a coherent reform program.

The Yugoslav reforms of 1949 and afterward are instructive on this point. These reforms constituted a radical initiative toward market socialism carried out in a relatively poor, war-devastated, ethnically divided country facing severe international political pressures. These radical departures from orthodox Stalinist economic relations neither destabilized Yugoslav society nor created an economic crisis. The fact that Yugoslavia is currently something of a basket case should not obscure that for several decades it experienced fast growth and significant welfare gains without the shortages characteristic of many command economies. The crucial factor was that the Communist government carrying out the reforms enjoyed considerable political support.

Although the long-term vulnerability of Communist societies has economic roots, the sudden collapse of Communism in Eastern Europe and the Soviet Union requires a political explanation. Wherever attempts at reform induced economic crisis, they did so because the governments undertaking reform were politically weak, not because Communist economic systems are impossible to reform. If this hypothesis is correct, then Asian Communism—having a quite different political background—need not follow its Eastern European counterpart into historical oblivion.

Cuba presents a very interesting test case. With the demise of Soviet Communism, it is hard to imagine a more politically and militarily exposed society. If the Communist economic system is both unviable and unreformable, then Cuban Communism should fall in short order. But if the roots of economic crisis are largely political, then Cuban society may indeed reform without experiencing economic collapse.

Political Analysis of Communist Collapse

The basic cause of Communist political structure is the effort to revolutionize society without sufficiently deep and durable political support. The disparity between the monumental revolutionary endeavor and the modest political base impels Communist leadership to evolve a political structure with certain distinctive features. These features have sometimes been a vital source of Communist strength, but they have become, I shall argue, an important cause of Communist collapse. I emphasize four related features of Communist political structure: totalitarianism (by which I mean the comprehensive unbounded nature of the Communist state), ideological cohesion, dictatorship, and the disciplined party. I do not try to explain the origin or operation of these characteristics, only their role in the collapse of Communism.

The totalitarian or comprehensive state cannot organize every aspect of social life, but it recognizes no limitation on its permissible sphere of action. The distinction between state and civil society collapses, and the state assumes responsibility for many activities—from place of residence to family size—usually lying outside the political domain. Such deep penetration of social life sometimes enables the state to mobilize unexpected social energy, yet it also creates vulnerability.

Total sovereignty implies total responsibility. The totalitarian state explicitly or implicitly assumes responsibility for all social, economic, cultural, and even personal problems. Every organizational malfunction and individual dissatisfaction can be, however circuitously, laid at the state's door. Resentment is not diffused through recognition of multiple responsibility; on the contrary, it is compiled and concentrated. During periods of system decline, malfunctions and dissatisfactions accumulate rapidly, creating a disruptive potential that can be triggered by relatively minor events. Thus the totalitarian nature of Communist political structure creates the possibility of organizational overload and sudden political collapse.

This is more than a quantitative predicament. Totalitarian structure unifies the control of social activities thereby facilitating transmission of pathology between different social institutions. Such extreme interdependence makes social problems become inordinately difficult to quarantine, further increasing the vulnerability of the political system.

Totalitarian structure explains the capacity for rapid and complete system failure but does not account for the exact timing of Communist collapse.

Consider the consequences of ideological cohesion. All modern societies have ideologies, but Communist societies use ideology for internal integration and social change far more than most. Communist ideology differs from other social ideologies in several important respects: it is self-consciously constructed, it is highly exclusive and not readily amalgamated with other ideological positions, and it is imposed upon society by an identifiable political process rather than being an outcome of diffuse historical experience. A social ideology can be considered *utopian* if it promises attainment of a social condition qualitatively superior to any previously realized. Because Communist ideology aims at revolutionary transformation of society, it tends to be utopian: utopian objectives are needed to justify the sacrifices entailed by revolution.

A society whose social integration and political dynamism depend upon ideology, especially a utopian ideology, will be highly susceptible to ideological failure. Disbelief threatens the capacity of the system to function and precludes durable reproduction of the social order. Utopian claims, to say the very least, have a high propensity to fail. In a society founded upon ideological cohesion, such failure endangers stability of the state and requires elaborate ideological rectification. A certain number of ideological failures are tolerable, but continual failure invites disbelief and social disintegration. The significance of ideological failure is evident in the following account of disillusionment with Leninism by the Soviet general, Dimitry Volkogonov:

> I began asking myself questions about Lenin, how, if he was such a genius, none of his predictions came true. The proletarian dictatorship never came to be, the principle of class struggle was discredited, communism was not built in fifteen years as he had promised. None of Lenin's major predictions ever came true. (quoted in Dallin 1992, p. 287)

A society dependent upon ideology will shield its ideology in various ways. An elementary but important protective method involves restricting the flow of contradictory information. Such restriction, however, prevents any serious social reform, which requires accurate delineation of institutional malfunctions and careful specification of alternatives. The reform of Communist societies and the flow of information connected with it can undermine the ideological foundations of the social order. When this happens, controlled reform becomes political debacle, as it did in the Soviet Union after gruesome details of Stalinist repression became broadly known.

Cynicism becomes rampant in ideologically dependent societies when the ruling ideology no longer commands widespread belief but is still kept in place by institutional fiat and political power. Fully developed cynicism involves contempt for all ethical systems and disbelief in the very possibility of moral action. It corrodes official ideology and, more importantly, obstructs the emergence of alternative social values. The Soviet Union and the countries of Eastern Europe under late Communism were often described as highly cynical societies where officials disbelieved the words they spoke and lying reached virtually epidemic proportions (Simis 1982). An ideologically coordinated society infected by cynicism is unlikely to remain stable even when facing only normal historical shocks.

A still more elusive relationship exists between ideological cohesion and personal identity. When an ideology finds broad social acceptance, it automatically exerts a powerful influence on the formation of personal identities within that society. Ideologically integrated societies foster relatively homogeneous personal identities. This has major consequences for both political mobilization and political stability. Heterogeneous personal identities imply both resistance to political mobilization (because symbols have different meaning to different people) and high political stability (because no sequence of events will devastate everyone's sense of identity). Homogeneous personal identities, on the other hand, have the opposite implications: high mobilization capacity due to similar political understandings, but correspondingly low political stability due to the possibility of pervasive disillusionment should the common identity lose viability.

The collapse of Communist ideology is also a collapse of personal identity for a significant fraction of people in these societies. These parallel breakdowns induce a general skepticism about all universalistic belief systems, which appear dangerously utopian and impossible to fulfill. They also initiate frantic searches for alternative sources of personal identity. The natural tendency is toward particularist belief systems like nationalism because these were suppressed under Communism and also because they counter the abstract utopianism of Communist ideology.

The collapse of Communist ideology has a material foundation. It derives from the economic failures analyzed in the previous sections and from increasingly unfavorable comparisons with capitalist societies. Quite possibly, however, the coherence of Communist ideology is intrinsically linked with political mobilization and the revolutionary transformation of society. When the strategy of class warfare is forsaken and political mobilization slackens, and when the pace of social change declines while further revolutionary transformations recede into the mists of the future, Communist ideology loses plausibility, and disintegration of the ideologically dependent Communist system sets in, first slowly but later at breakneck speed.

Yet ideological collapse in Communist societies may be less complete than the interpretations above suggest. A careful survey of opinions about political change conducted within the Soviet Union in 1989 found continuing support for socialism, particularly among those people most eager for change:

> That many advocates of change continue to support the socialist view that the state, rather than individuals themselves, is responsible for the well-being of the citizenry, suggests that contrary to much popular belief in the West, there has not been a wholesale abandonment of socialist principles. On the contrary, there may even be more support for these ideas among those who are the strongest believers in individual free expression and rapid change. What many Soviet citizens pressing for change may want is a more efficient and productive state, rather than a state shorn of social obligations. The Communist Party, as the engine of that obligated state was rejected, but not the obligation itself; the institution failed, but not the norm. (Finifter and Mickiewicz 1992, p. 861)

The third aspect of Communist political structure responsible for the sudden collapse of the system is dictatorship. Fear is a powerful motivator. The fear inspired by ruthless dictatorship contributed to Communist military and economic achievements beside forestalling, for several decades at least, corruption in Communist bureaucracies.

Yet dictatorship remains a two-edged sword, even when evaluated on strictly instrumental grounds. Fear deters the flow of critical information. Dictatorial power enables a leader to overcome resistance and persist with the implementation of unpopular policies. A policy initiated by a dictatorial leadership can have terrible results without corrective measures being taken. Communist dictatorships have sometimes persisted with truly catastrophic policies. It is no accident that the two worst famines in modern history occurred during the course of Communist-led agricultural collectivization campaigns: the Soviet famine of 1929-1931 (10 million deaths estimated; see Volin 1970, chap. 10) and the Chinese famine of 1958-1961 associated with the Great Leap Forward (30 million deaths estimated; see Ashton et al. 1984). Aside from the moral dimensions of these policy-induced catastrophes, they created profound structural problems and ineradicable hatred that plagued the regimes ever afterward.

Communist dictatorship usually eases long before the system collapses. Easing means the elimination of arbitrary terror, but other forms of coercion continue, and honest public criticism remains a perilous activity. Corruption spreads rapidly because fear no longer deters people able to use power for personal gain. Several other factors also spur corruption: the concurrent weakening of ideology, knowledge of terrible crimes committed by the dictatorship, the emptiness of public discourse and the routine practice of lying propagated by absence of civil liberties, and the contagious nature of corruption itself. Corruption, even more than cynicism, breeds contempt for the Communist social order among both the corrupt and those who witness the corruption. When other methods for controlling bureaucratic iniquity fail, a reforming Communist leadership experiences a nagging temptation to use terror. Renewed terror, however, is thoroughly incompatible with other elements of reform.

Why not complete abolition of dictatorship? Communist reformers believe this would mean abandoning the goal of socialism for which so much sacrifice had been made. The political dilemma on which Gorbachev foundered was how to democratize Soviet society without fully abandoning the privileged position of the Communist Party, supposedly the indispensable instrument of socialist transformation. Apparently Gorbachev's long-range strategy was to replace the Party with a broad coalition of Soviet citizens committed to socialism. But economic decline weakened support for socialism as well as the credibility of the reformist strategy. In the teeth of ideological confusion and political crisis, Ukrainian, Georgian, Lithuanian, and Russian national identities proved more meaningful than Soviet citizenship.

What role did the Communist Party have in the collapse of the Communist system? The vanguard party is surely the most important political innovation of the 20th century. It made possible Communist revolutions where they occurred, and even in the absence of revolution it provided the vital organizational apparatus of Communist takeover. When Communism came to power, the support provided by a disciplined vanguard party sustained Communist rule much longer than would otherwise have been possible.

Yet the very existence of the Party hindered full democratic reform under Communist aegis. Even when the will to initiate political democracy existed, Communist leaders found it difficult to curtail Party power, let alone to govern without it. Gorbachev, for example, understood that democratization required reducing the Communist Party's economic authority, but his elimination of direct Party participation in the economy seriously aggravated the Soviet economic crisis.

The relationship between party and state in Communist societies constitutes a structure of dual power. Under certain circumstances this structure increases the control available to the central political authority. However, when the twin columns of power are not fully united—as often happens during major policy changes—the dual structure can cause organizational gridlock within the political system. In recent decades it has diminished the flexibility of Communist societies in responding to internal and external changes. The resulting rigidity temporarily preserved the traditional institutions of Communism but vastly enhanced the likelihood of sudden collapse. Yet to expect a different relationship between party and state is to ignore the basic cause of Communist political structure: the glaring disparity between the requirements of revolution and the obtainable political base.

Class Analysis of Communist Collapse

The class relations involved in the collapse of Communism differ from one country to the next. Resentment against state socialism was spread throughout Communist social structure, but the class foundation of the transition from Communism to capitalism—insofar as such a transition is happening[2]—lies in the more privileged sectors of Communist society. In a perceptive paper dealing with class factors in Soviet economic reform, David Kotz offers the following analysis:

Like capitalism, state socialism evolved a ruling group that ran the system and had a privileged position within it. But, unlike that of capitalism, the ruling group of state socialism did not own the means of production. Furthermore, according to the official ideology, the ruling group of state socialism was supposed to operate the economy and government selflessly for the direct benefit of working people. Since the system was undemocratic and authoritarian, the workers who were the supposed beneficiaries of the system had no power to enforce their official status as the ruling class. . . . [The] ruling group had no continuing structural tie to the state socialist system, other than tradition. The real democratization of the system would probably have displaced the great majority of the ruling group from their high-level positions, and would also have reduced the privileges that went along with leadership positions. The group that stood to benefit from democratizing socialism was the working class, but they lacked the power to direct the process. . . . [The] underlying structural factor at work was the failure of undemocratic state socialism to develop a ruling class with an abiding interest in protecting and defending the system over which it presided. Once the system went into a moderately serious social and economic crisis, the bulk of the ruling group deserted the system and opted for capitalism. (Kotz 1992, pp. 23-24)

The class coalition supporting the transition to capitalism in the Soviet Union includes three main groups, according to Kotz: (a) small-scale entrepreneurs who emerged under state socialism and now want to enlarge their business opportunities; (b) intellectuals who chafe about their integration with the working class and think their relative class position would improve under capitalism; and most importantly (c) the political and economic elite of state socialist society, most of whom merely pursue wealth and power, and now hope that capitalism will expand and solidify their privileges.

This class analysis of Communist collapse rests upon four simple propositions: (1) state socialism creates a ruling class; (2) this ruling class lacks an abiding interest in defending the state socialist system; (3) state socialism experiences social and economic crises; (4) when these crises become sufficiently severe, the ruling class abandons state socialism and tries to establish capitalism. Propositions (1) and (3) are not particularly controversial, although one might quibble about whether the ruling group under state socialism should be considered a ruling class. The even-numbered propositions are more problematic. Why would a ruling class lack an abiding interest in the system that created it? And why should that class push for capitalism of all possible economic systems?

State socialism may create a ruling class, but the ideology of state socialism refuses to acknowledge its existence or legitimize its rule. Hence the position of the ruling class remains precarious, and reproduction of the class over time is not assured. Such institutionalized insecurity diminishes the interest of the ruling class in defending the state socialist system. This is further diminished by suspicions that state socialism is a sinking ship, suspicions stimulated by its intractable social and economic crises and its losing competition with advanced capitalist societies. Transition to capitalism has serious risks for the ruling class of state socialism, but perhaps no greater risks than trying to maintain a stagnating economic system ideologically uncongenial to class rule.

Why capitalism? The ruling class of state socialism, like any ruling class, wants a system in which class rule is legitimate. This excludes all varieties of socialism. It would be pointless, and probably impossible, to establish a mode of production seriously incompatible with the modern world economy. This excludes all precapitalist economic systems.

These arguments are probably correct, but not really to the point. The successor to state socialism is not chosen by the ruling class. The modern world economy is a capitalist world economy. When challenges to capitalism are defeated, the resulting system will be capitalism—though probably an underdeveloped type of capitalism—and not some other logically conceivable economic structure. The defeat disorganizes opposition to capitalism, convincing most if not all potential challengers that further resistance is futile.

Capitalism, in contrast to state socialism, does not require establishment; it grows whenever the terrain is suitable. The process lies implicit in classic definition of capital: value used for the purpose of increasing value. Any social terrain allowing economic value to be used for purposes of increasing value can be congenial to the growth of capitalism. This can happen in countless different ways within a surplus-producing economy, which explains why capitalist development is so hard to contain under these conditions. To one degree or another, capitalist relations grew within the body of state socialism. Sometimes capitalist relations were fostered as the most acceptable means of coping with the pathologies of Communist economic organization. The emergence of capitalist relations probably hastened the demise of state socialism, but even if they did not, they certainly influenced the orientation of its renegade ruling class and the identity of its successor.

If the transition from Communism to capitalism favors and is supported by the privileged classes of state socialist society, why is there so little working-class resistance to the change? Although workers in Communist societies may have, as Michael Burawoy (1989) suggests, considerable power on the shop floor,[3] on a societal level the working class is assiduously demobilized and structurally fragmented by Communist social organization. Because Communist parties claim to rule on behalf of the working class, absolute quiescence of the latter is of the utmost importance. Whenever the working class develops an autonomous political voice, as with Polish Solidarity, Communist party rule is in serious jeopardy. Solidarity is the exception. Demobilization and fragmentation of the working class over many decades usually preclude any coherent working-class response to Communist collapse and transition to capitalism.

Why should workers resist these developments? Has Communism been good for the working class? Although certain social indicators suggest it has (Navarro 1993), the accumulationist preoccupation of virtually all Communist states involves systematic exploitation of the working class. Workers in Communist societies do not feel like rulers of society. Anecdotal evidence suggests they feel no less alienated from political power than do workers in capitalist societies. If a Communist worker could compare herself to a French, German or Swedish counterpart, she would not feel especially privileged.

On behalf of what economic system should workers resist a transition from Communism to capitalism? Many contemporary Marxists would propose democratic socialism. As matters now stand, democratic socialism is little more than a slogan with few organizational roots in Communist or post-Communist societies. Embracing such an alternative means embarking on a new visionary experiment with little idea of how to proceed and even less assurance of success. Virtually all classes in post-Communist societies hanker for security rather than innovation. Nor is it evident that democratic socialism can be organized by even the most benevolent central authority. Very likely it must grow, through working-class initiative, from the grassroots to the political center. Historical experience cautions the working class of post-Communist societies against pinning its hopes upon great leaps forward.

With no clear vision of an alternative, with little confidence in its own existence as a corporate entity, and with few institutions it can collectively embrace, coherent working-class resistance to a capitalist transition is almost unthinkable.

The Case of China

Despite the debacle of Communism in Eastern Europe and the Soviet Union, a Communist party remains in power in the world's most populous country, China. According to many indicators, the Chinese economy is currently flourishing. Some experts consider it "the world's fastest growing economy."[4] Although Party dictatorship persists and is sometimes brutal—as in the Tiananmen massacre of 1989—sweeping economic reforms happened after the death of Mao in 1976 and the political defeat of his chosen successors. These reforms dismantled collectivized agriculture, fostered small-scale private enterprise, encouraged investment in China by foreign enterprises, encouraged foreign trade, reduced state price controls and, since 1990, facilitated the emergence of a Chinese stock market. The Communist Party seems to be organizing the restoration of capitalism in China.

In view of Communist collapse elsewhere, why does the Chinese Communist Party remain in power and even retain a measure of popular support? The Chinese journalist and social critic Lin Binyan (1992) gives four reasons for continued Communist rule. First, the Party still gets much credit for achieving national independence, defeating the parasitic landlord class, and initiating serious modernization of China. Second, totalitarian control of information prevents emergence of any broadly based organized opposition. Third, the improvement of living standards during the period of economic reform strengthens the position of the Party. Finally, there is popular reaction to the disintegration of Communism elsewhere:

> For many people . . . the crackdown on the student movement of 1989 marked the end of Communist legitimacy. Yet the collapse of Communism in the former Soviet Union has done the Chinese regime a great service. Afraid of chaos, the breakup of the country, and the economic hardship that characterizes the current situation in the former Soviet empire, the Chinese people are now giving Communist government another chance. (Binyan 1992, p. 7)

None of the above suggests that Communist rule or a managed economy will remain in China very long. Deng Xiaoping and the reigning Communist leadership claim that anything that expands production automatically helps socialism, and that individual self-interest and modern technology are the best means to expand production. Yet the present Chinese economy is rapidly diverging from any known species of socialism and rapidly converging toward capitalism, most probably in its underdeveloped incarnation.

Communist Party dictatorship in Eastern Europe and the Soviet Union proved much more fragile than it appeared. Although Communist rule in China has very different roots, the position of the Party is also fragile. The Chinese Party has never fully recovered from the blows to its esteem and authority delivered by the Cultural Revolution. It is rife with corruption and riddled with cadre cynicism. Adherence by Party branches to the directives of the center is often only approximate. During the recent period of economic reform, Western capitalist culture has deeply penetrated Chinese society, eviscerating ethical codes long used by the Party to maneuver the population.

These symptoms strongly suggest the Chinese Communist Party lacks the political and ideological resources to perpetuate its dictatorship. Is a total disintegration of Chinese Communism in the offing? This could happen, but there is also some chance of transition to a progressive democratic society with a mixed economy and a comprehensive social welfare system. China lacks any significant tradition of political democracy, and Party elites understand recent history to mean that democratic reform invites national disintegration and the collapse of Communism. Nevertheless the educated classes on whom China's subsequent economic development depends are thoroughly opposed to arbitrary authoritarianism and seem to favor democracy. Because the economy is doing well and because the Communist Party retains some political credibility, future Party leadership may exhibit flexibility and initiative. If the present economic momentum continues, such a leadership will be in a far stronger reforming position than was Gorbachev. Because China has been unified for several thousand years and 95% of the population is of Han nationality, it will not face a disintegration crisis.

That a capitalist economy is reemerging in China seems evident. That Communist Party dictatorship will not endure long seems very likely. Any further predictions are pure speculation. If China adopts democratic capitalism, preserves the main social achievements of the revolution, institutionalizes civil liberties, and sustains the present economic momentum, it might be misleading to say that Communism collapsed there as it did in Eastern Europe. One could argue that the Communist revolution in China successfully fulfilled its historical mission, acknowledged the limits placed on its development by social structure, and devolved into the best feasible system of political economy.

This would seem to be the most positive conceivable outcome of the great Chinese Revolution. Many observers will view the above scenario as wildly implausible. William Hinton, for example, thinks that "China is rapidly returning to a semifeudal, semicolonial, comprador capitalist status" (Hinton 1991, p. 15).

Is Communist Collapse Inevitable?

Overweening ambition is the Achilles heel of Communist revolutions. This comes in both a political and an economic form. The political variant of overweening ambition revolves around the effort to revolutionize society without adequate popular support. This generates political dictatorship, not as a temporary response to revolutionary crisis and not in the tempered form of genuine class dictatorship but as a permanent method of rule exercised by a narrow and self-selected elite. It can lead to horrendous acts of tyranny, but even in its most moderate mutation, overweening political ambition institutionalizes a preposterous contradiction between economic cooperation and democracy.

Communist dictatorship presents itself as an advance over capitalism. Yet any advanced form of social equality requires democracy. Dictatorship perforce establishes a radical inequality of power and social status and must be considered a primitive type of social organization. Democracy as currently practiced may have serious limitations such as instability, difficulty achieving consensus, and avoidance of important issues, but the appropriate response is developing better forms of democracy. If this is not possible, then it seems preferable to abandon revolutionary power in favor of democracy rather than mutilating the inner meaning of the revolutionary movement.

The economic variant of overweening ambition involves undertaking economic tasks for which the forces of production are not sufficiently developed (e.g., building a planned economy when the productivity of labor remains low). When energetically pursued, this aberration squanders human effort and creates distorted increasingly dysfunctional economic systems. Through prodigious exploitation of human labor and natural resources, remarkable results can be temporarily achieved, but the relation between output and input remains unsatisfactory, and economic reproduction of the system becomes increasingly difficult.

The Stalinist system consisting of a centrally managed economy and a totalitarian state coordinated by ideology and propelled by terror is not viable over any long time interval. It is not inevitable, however, that Communist revolutions evolve into

Stalinist systems. When not molested by external enemies, other paths of development are available. The key is to resist revolutionary hubris and the overweening ambition that it conveys. Marxist theory implies that revolution is sometimes possible and sometimes necessary to unleash the forces of production. It also implies that the evolution of human society cannot be determined by sheer volition, regardless of how fierce and relentless that volition is.

Nor is it inevitable that a Stalinist system, once established, will frustrate all reforming efforts short of capitalist restoration. The chance of reforming a Stalinist system depends more upon political than upon economic circumstances. The main structural pathology of Stalinism is the complete absence of democracy combined with the unbounded power of the state. The main objects of successful reform must be full democracy, limited state power, and creation of a balanced, decentralized, efficient economic system. Several reform efforts have foundered on the absence of a coherent and practical vision of the economic structure to be created. The economic system should, among other things, encourage cooperation without relying excessively upon the altruistic motivation of economic actors.

A great deal depends upon the political credibility of the reforming agent. Successful reform will rarely, if ever, be accomplished by a severely compromised political authority. Nor can the reform endeavor be undertaken with any guarantee of success; this would violate the spirit and letter of democracy. The accumulated crimes of the regime, when fully exposed, may preclude any possibility of reform. The point at issue is not the certainty of successful reform. The point is only to deny the inevitability of failure. Stalinism cannot and should not succeed; but the Communist project conceived in a larger sense need not perish along with it.

Conclusion

The general context for comprehending the collapse of Communist systems is the classical historical materialist proposition that a socialist society can be created only with highly developed forces of production. This principle doomed the effort to build socialism in one (economically backward) country from the very start. Communist revolutions cannot, through their own independent efforts, develop forces of production sufficiently to make socialism feasible. The optimism and human energy mobilized by the revolution exhaust themselves long before the necessary forces of production exist. The economic system designed to accomplish the herculean tasks of "socialist accumulation" lacks both macroeconomic balance and microeconomic efficiency. Eventually it slumps into a condition of stagnation from which its economic inferiority to advanced capitalism becomes plainly evident.

The political structure begotten in the effort to build socialism in a backward society is inevitably dictatorial. The impulse toward socialism has weak roots in precapitalist societies. In the absence of a revolutionary class committed to socialism, the socialist impulse must come from a state determined to impose its will upon the population it rules. The extent and brutality of the revolutionary dictatorship can vary a great deal, but without an extreme concentration of state power, socialist construction would never start in an underdeveloped country.

The Communist dictatorship, once thoroughly established, is very difficult to reform. It fragments and demobilizes the subject population and repels democratizing efforts by Communist elites. Hence the dictatorial political structure remains intact long after belief in Communist ideology declines, and the state bureaucracy adds cynicism to its longstanding incompetence. Deprived of honest conviction and without hope of achieving its original goals, the state evolves into an imposing but rigid shell lacking resilience or recuperative power. When that shell is fractured— as eventually it must be in the normal course of social affairs—the entire superannuated political edifice falls to the ground.

The roots of Communist collapse may lie in its economic structure, but the timing and abruptness of the breakdown requires a political explanation. Four distinctive characteristics of Communist political organization have been emphasized: totalitarianism, ideological cohesion, dictatorship, and the disciplined party. These characteristics explain why Communist systems are subject to sudden and complete breakdowns. By studying them carefully—a task that has not been undertaken in this chapter—one gains certain insights about when breakdowns are likely to happen.

The demise of Communism in Eastern Europe and the Soviet Union does not mean that all Communist systems will collapse in the near future or that reform of Communist systems is impossible. A Communist system is unlikely to collapse when governed by systematic terror, or when the economy is performing well and the ruling party has reasonable political credibility. The possibility of successful reform depends upon establishment of a balanced, decentralized, efficient economic system that encourages cooperation but also allows a variety of different property forms. It depends even more on the emergence of full democracy, which requires a deep and unlikely shift in the orientation of the Communist Party. The Party must countenance a transition from its secure position as an institutionalized part of the state apparatus to a contingent status as one of several contending political parties. A reform that preserves the real social achievements of Communism in realms such as health, education, and employment and that is not just a polite surrender to capitalism is much more likely when the economy is not in crisis condition and when the agent of reform is not universally despised.

The interpretation of Communist collapse presented in this chapter may be consistent with the precepts of Analytical Marxism but is certainly not unique to it. Nor will it command consensus among Analytical Marxist theorists. I venture to say that none of the major figures in the field will agree with this interpretation in its entirety. The theory of Communist collapse is still in its infancy. Analytical Marxists can make at least three distinctive contributions to this vital subject. They can apply an axiomatic reformulation of historical materialism to Communist social formations. They can use the general theory of exploitation to explain why economic systems with Communist productive capabilities and Communist property relations experience difficulty reproducing themselves. Finally, they can employ what I describe as class-conscious general equilibrium theory to study the viability of various proposals for reforming Communism.

Notes

1. *Arctic City* is the name given by Burawoy and Krotov to the northern Russian city where their field work occurred. *Polar* is their name for the large furniture-making factory they studied.

2. The withering away of the party state in the Soviet Union, argue Burawoy and Krotov (1992), does not constitute a revolution but actually exaggerates the longstanding pathologies of the Soviet economic system. Insofar as any movement toward a market economy has occurred, it is a movement toward merchant capitalism, blocking bourgeois industrial capitalism and fomenting underdevelopment.

3. The power of workers on the shop floor results from two characteristics of a shortage economy: (a) managerial dependence on the cooperation of workers to accommodate the habitual uncertainty of production inputs, and (b) shortage of labor power increasing the capacity of workers to resist managerial encroachments (Burawoy and Krotov 1993).

4. See the *New York Times*, May 9, 1993, Business Section, p. 6.

9

SOCIALISM

Anyone who is not confused does not understand the situation.
—anonymous aphorism

The Socialist Project in Crisis

For well over a century, socialism has been the shadow alternative to capitalism. Criticisms of capitalist institutions on behalf of freedom, justice, or equality explicitly or implicitly posit socialism as the systemic alternative. The critics may disagree about what socialism means or whether it already exists, but socialism has nevertheless been the specter giving practical relevance to movements against capitalism.

Now the status of socialism as a feasible and desirable alternative to capitalism is in jeopardy. Numerous intellectuals in every part of the globe now regard it as either infeasible or undesirable or both. By far the most important cause of disaffection from socialism is the brutal history and stunning collapse of Communist regimes in eastern Europe and the former Soviet Union. The reasons for the collapse were discussed in the previous chapter. Although few scholars regard Communist regimes as anything more than distant relatives of socialism, their precipitous demise still suggests that socialist institutions are unstable, inefficient, and inherently authoritarian. Capitalism, for all its flaws, appears to many as the best social system available at the end of the 20th century.

Analytical Marxism arose prior to the fall of Communist systems in 1989 and afterward. Analytical Marxists uniformly opposed the tyrannical aspects of Communism and sought to redeem scientific Marxism from the banalities of official Soviet ideology. Although none predicted the collapse of Eastern European Communism, there is no logical reason why this collapse should pose an intellectual or moral crisis for persons with an Analytical Marxist perspective.

I have emphasized the theoretical openness and political diversity of Analytical Marxism. Yet virtually all Analytical Marxists embrace the emancipatory intent of classical Marxist theory and do not want the socialist project buried beneath the rubble of dictatorial Communism. Several energetically reaffirm the feasibility and desirability of socialism and are now constructing practical models of how it might work (Cohen 1991; Roemer 1991, 1992b, 1994).

Recent Analytical Marxist theorizing tends to focus on market socialism. Communist societies, points out John Roemer, differ from Western capitalist societies in three fundamental ways: dictatorial politics, central allocation of resources, and public ownership of means of production. Theoretical considerations as well as recent history suggest that this particular combination is economically inefficient, politically unstable, and morally catastrophic; but they certainly do not show that public ownership of productive facilities, if combined with a democratic polity and decentralized resource allocation via markets, is infeasible or undesirable (Roemer 1991, 1992b, 1994). A society organized along these latter lines is called *market socialist.*

Not all Analytical Marxists are enthusiastic about market socialism. In a touching article discussing the sadness he feels about finally abandoning all hope for the Bolshevik experiment, Gerald Cohen warns that a process of "adaptive preference formation" (1991, p. 12)—preferring an alternative merely because it is available—has induced some socialist intellectuals to wax enthusiastic about market socialism. Cohen himself regards market socialism as inherently unjust and "at best second best" (1991, p. 14):

> Market socialism is socialist because it abolishes the distinction between capital and labor: there is no separate class of capitalists facing workers who own no capital. But it is unlike traditionally conceived socialism in that its worker-owned firms relate to one another and to consumers in standard market-contractual fashion. . . .

> Market socialism remains deficient from a socialist point of view . . .
> because . . . there is injustice in a system which confers high rewards
> on people who happen to be unusually talented and who form highly
> productive cooperatives. (Cohen 1991, pp. 14-15)

The most systematic attempt to address such critiques of market socialism is David Miller's (1989) book, *Market, State and Community*, which carries the subtitle *Theoretical Foundations of Market Socialism*. Miller, like Cohen, is firmly committed to socialism and strongly influenced by the methods of analytical philosophy. We shall consider Miller's arguments and conclusions after briefly reviewing the history of ideas about market socialism.

The Classic Model of Market Socialism

In his latest book on the future of socialism, John Roemer (1994) identifies five stages through which the idea of market socialism has progressed.[1] The first stage involved recognition that labor time and other natural units were not adequate for rational economic calculation. Socialism, if it had any pretense of being a rational economic system, had to establish meaningful prices that conveyed vital economic information. The second stage revolved around the insight that general equilibrium theory was relevant to socialist economic calculation. This insight suggested that prices appropriate for socialism could be obtained by solving a very large and complicated set of equations.

The third stage in the evolution of thinking about market socialism came about when Oskar Lange, Abba Lerner, and a few others saw that strictly theoretical calculations would not suffice. Obtaining prices suitable for socialism required using a real market. Even assuming the availability of powerful computers, a central planning board could never have all the information needed for proper price calculations. Lange (1936-1937) developed a model showing how markets and planning could be integrated under socialism. The model indicated what policies the central planning board should follow to converge upon equilibrium prices. Lange subsequently modified this model on the basis of suggestions by Lerner (1936), and the Lange-Lerner formulation is generally regarded as the classic paradigm for market socialism.

The fourth stage of thinking about market socialism emerged from market reforms in Communist societies. The most important of these reforms occurred in Yugoslavia after Tito's break with Stalin, in Hungary after the introduction of the "New Economic Mechanism" in 1968, in China after the death of Mao, and in the Soviet Union under Gorbachev. None of these reforms were perfect implementations of the Lange-Lerner model, but they did compel socialist thinkers to acknowledge many previously unrecognized barriers toward a workable market socialism, especially if an over-weening state routinely rescues enterprises that perform badly.

Roemer labels current theories as the fifth stage of thinking about market socialism. Current theories have moved beyond the Lange-Lerner model by eliminating most public ownership of productive enterprises and virtually all price setting by a central planning board. Roemer's own blueprint for market socialism (discussed later in this chapter) provides a good example of current thinking.

Before discussing contemporary thinking, it will be useful to examine more closely the Lange-Lerner formulation, the classic model of market socialism. According to this model, branches of industry where perfect competition prevails remain in private hands, but the remaining sectors become publicly owned. Two branches are distinguished within the publicly owned industry: units producing consumer goods, and units producing capital goods. The prices of consumer goods are determined by the market, but the prices of capital goods are set by a central planning board.

To set prices, the central planning board uses a trial and error procedure patterned upon the Walrasian concept of *tâtonnement*. The board establishes an initial set of prices for capital goods and then observes the relation between supply and demand under these prices. If the supply of a capital good exceeds the demand, then the price of that good decreases in the next round. Conversely, if the demand exceeds the supply, then the price increases in the subsequent price iteration. This is precisely what happens in a free market economy, so the central planning board appears to emulate the market. Through this trial and error process, claims Lange, prices converge to an optimal equilibrium.

Price convergence is assisted by the two rules that managers of publicly owned enterprises are instructed to follow: choose production methods that minimize average cost, and choose the level of production output at which marginal cost equals product price (Lange and Taylor 1938, pp. 75-78). Wages should be proportional to the disutility of the labor being performed. Thus disagreeable labor is rewarded more generously than enjoyable work.

A socialist economy of the Lange-Lerner type is claimed to have three main advantages over a private enterprise economy. It distributes income in a manner that attains maximum social welfare. It converts social overhead costs into prime costs, thus eliminating much of the social waste connected with private enterprise. Capitalist monopolies hinder introduction of new technologies, whereas socialist enterprise should—at least in theory—encourage innovation. Against these advantages, Lange sets two drawbacks of his market socialism: the rate of accumulation is politically determined and hence arbitrary, and economic life has a tendency to become bureaucratized under socialism. The latter disadvantage is mitigated, however, because tendencies toward bureaucratization are said to be equally strong or even stronger under monopoly capitalism.

Before discussing the theoretical foundations of market socialism, I shall mention a few of the more frequent criticisms about the Lange-Lerner model. It is not evident why a central planning board is needed at all. Why not determine all prices in the public sector by market mechanisms? Although Lange and Lerner do not favor comprehensive economic planning, the price-setting tasks they give to the central planning board are still well beyond its capacities. Even if such problems are ignored, there are strong theoretical and practical reasons for doubting that the trial and error procedure will converge to an equilibrium.

Given the important functions of the central planning board, it will be difficult to hold managers responsible for economic failures. Thus a tendency toward protecting inefficient enterprises will emerge. The central planning board could conceivably mimic the price-setting functions of a market, but it could not induce the genuine competition upon which economic efficiency depends. Hence Lange-Lerner market socialism, even when implemented faithfully, would be a cumbersome, wasteful, and inefficient economy.

Having sketched the classical model and some criticisms of it, we shall now consider the theoretical foundations of market socialism followed by some recent Analytical Marxist thinking about how socialism might be implemented.

Theoretical Foundations of Market Socialism

The image used by David Miller to explore the ethical underpinnings of market socialism is a synthesis of traditional socialism and the radical individualism found in libertarian philosophies. The basic aims of his market socialism are (a) obtaining economic efficiency by using markets in production, (b) making democracy feasible by limiting the role of the state, (c) achieving a more equal distribution of primary income, and (d) protecting the autonomy of workers (Miller 1989, pp. 9-10). To achieve these aims, the ownership of capital is socialized, but a market mechanism is used to provide most goods and services.

In Miller's version of pure market socialism, all productive enterprises are workers' cooperatives, and each enterprise is democratically controlled by its workers. The enterprise sells its products on an open market and pays its workers from the receipts of these sales. The cooperative decides how to distribute income among its workers, how much and in what to invest, what prices to charge for its products, and on all other matters pertaining to itself. Under pure market socialism, the income of a worker depends entirely upon the economic success of her cooperative. Socially owned capital is managed by a number of public investment agencies from which workers' cooperatives lease capital. The public investment agencies decide which projects to support and how much interest to charge.

Considerations of justice and practicality require modifications in this model of pure market socialism. Though workers' cooperatives remain preponderant, various forms of productive enterprise must coexist, and a democratic state has an important role to play. The functions of the state under market socialism include (a) protecting the system against external encroachment, (b) setting ground rules for social and economic relations, (c) managing the economy so that all markets work efficiently,

(d) modifying the income distribution to achieve distributive justice, and (e) supplying public goods (Miller 1989, pp. 18-19, 295-98).

Miller does not try to present a detailed plan for market socialism. His purpose is not designing societies but defending the concept of market socialism against criticisms raised by libertarians and traditional socialists. Compared to the feasible alternatives, market socialism provides the greatest attainable amounts of economic and political freedom. It offers more economic and political choices than state socialism, and offers choices to more people than capitalism does. Market socialism, claims Miller, can equal competitive capitalism in economic efficiency, yet generates far less income inequality than either capitalism or state socialism.

Is market socialism just? Social justice, argues Miller, means not strict economic equality, but each person getting what she deserves. A just economic system bases rewards upon personal desert; yet measuring desert is no simple matter. A sensible measure of personal desert must be public, nonarbitrary, and reasonably easy to implement.

A controversial feature of Miller's analysis is the role he assigns to equilibrium prices. If a situation of relative equality exists and if a price equilibrium has been achieved, then Miller regards market value superior to other practical methods of judging a person's economic contribution to society. But market socialism creates relative economic equality and approaches or attains a price equilibrium. Thus the economic rewards distributed under market socialism usually correspond to personal desert and are reasonably just. In the minority of cases where economic reward departs drastically from personal desert, the socialist state intervenes to make amends. The appropriate standard of justice, keep in mind, is not some hypothetical ideal but what can be attained in the real world.

The constraints imposed by practicality are essential to Miller's argument for the justice of market socialism. Even under ideal circumstances, market value is not an accurate measure of effort or competence (or any combination thereof) unless one resorts to tautology. Market value might be the best *practical* measure of personal desert, but one needs to show that a highly inaccurate measure of desert is still more just than strict equality. Of course, strict equality might sabotage economic efficiency, but is this relevant to the issue of justice?

Furthermore, the degree of equality attained by market socialism may not approximate the ideal circumstances mentioned in the previous paragraph. The economic advantages attributed to markets require extensive inequality of reward. However, income distribution affects the structure of demand, and demand affects equilibrium prices. How can a market value, prejudiced by both income inequality and the prices resulting from this inequality, constitute a plausible measure of personal desert? Yet if market value does not measure desert, then Miller's argument for the justice of market socialism collapses.

Does exploitation exist under market socialism? Miller considers a transaction exploitative if (a) the transaction is more advantageous to the exploiter and less advantageous to the exploited than some appropriately chosen benchmark transaction, and (b) the transaction occurs because the exploiter has some prior advantage over the exploited party (Miller 1989, p. 186). The benchmark Miller favors for measuring economic exploitation is the set of equilibrium prices entailed by morally defensible economic entitlements.

A surprising consequence of this idea is that no exchange at equilibrium prices can be exploitative. Nonequilibrium exchange is a necessary but not sufficient condition for exploitation. Unfortunately Miller's benchmark encounters the problem of multiplicity: many morally defensible regimes of economic entitlement may exist, and many price equilibria may correspond to each one. Multiplicity of price equilibria renders assessment of exploitation entirely indeterminate.

If workers do not have access to capital and if private ownership of capital is deemed morally indefensible, then capitalist economic transactions are inherently exploitative. This is so because the scarcity of capital enables its owner to command a premium. But a nonexploitative capitalism is theoretically possible: capitalism would be nonexploitative if all workers had easy access to capital. Although this is unlikely, to say the least, Miller uses the hypothetical possibility to argue that capitalist exploitation derives not from the form of the relationship between workers and capitalists but from their unequal bargaining power.

According to Miller, the situation is entirely different under market socialism. Here people can acquire valuable resources only by undertaking productive activity, and these resources cannot be made into private capital. The absence of giant corporations means that perfect competition occurs more readily under market socialism than under advanced capitalism. The absence of private capital and the existence of perfect competition greatly reduce the likelihood of exploitation under market socialism. Exploitation can still occur but, contrary to capitalism, it need not. With an economy based upon workers' cooperatives and public ownership of capital, a properly crafted public policy can successfully prevent exploitation.

Miller wants to establish that market socialism is not "at best second best," as Gerald Cohen claims, but the optimal economic system for the current historical epoch. Hence he offers a critique of communism (with a small c), a form of society Marxists usually regard superior to socialism. He defines communism as

> a negation of the leading features of capitalism. Wage labor, commodity production, and the market are all abandoned. Production takes place according to a socially determined plan, though each person is allowed to choose the kind of work he performs. The division of labor is broken down, each person being permitted to work at a succession of different tasks. People are allocated goods from the common stock according to need. Economic competition disappears, and social relationships become communitarian. (Miller 1989, p. 201)

Miller makes three basic critiques of communist society: (a) it does not eliminate all possibility of exploitation, (b) it may not allow people to develop their own individuality, and (c) it lacks the inherent dynamic thrust of capitalism.

These are not overpowering criticisms. Eliminating the very possibility of exploitation may be excluded by the indeterminacy of human institutions. That communism would prevent people from developing their individuality is highly conjectural at best. And in an age of environmental peril, a society not wedded to growth by the logic of its social relations could be considered an unmitigated blessing. Naturally Miller's critique of communism is closely associated with his defense of markets. Markets are needed to develop human individuality and to institutionalize social dynamism.

Markets in any form do generate alienation, but market socialism, Miller insists, eliminates some alienation present in other market societies. Market alienation is further mitigated if the market economy has been democratically chosen. And not all alienation comes from markets. Some is deeply rooted in the nature of work as a social activity and will survive any conceivable economic reorganization. Miller believes the competitive features of market socialism should be tolerated because they serve cooperative purposes, an argument rather similar to Adam Smith's defense of capitalism.

The ubiquity of markets under capitalism tends to isolate individuals and produce antagonistic relations between them. Socialists hope to create an active and mutually supportive community that augments a person's sense of efficacy, security, and happiness. Can market socialism facilitate the emergence of a strong community?

Miller is dubious about the traditional socialist concept of community. Such a community must be small, intense, and highly exclusive. Yet if overall social integration is desired, a more inclusive but less intense form of association must emerge. Miller also sees tension between communal solidarity and individual self-development. Self-development is easily stifled by the ministrations of an overweening community. Reconciling the legitimate claims of individuality and solidarity requires a looser form of community than is usually favored by socialists (Miller 1989, pp. 232-33).

These caveats notwithstanding, a vital community remains an important element of market socialist society. A vital community enriches personal identity, helps individuals influence the world, and provides cultural underpinning for the socialist principle of distribution according to need. According to Miller, however, citizenship—understood as active and disinterested participation in the political affairs of society—is the only universal form of community viable in the modern world. While recognizing that citizenship is a pale shadow of what socialists have meant by community, Miller still thinks it embodies elements of the radical vision. Citizenship helps constitute personal identity, expresses equality of political status, and can provide an ideological basis for distribution according to need.

Associated with citizenship in constituting a viable socialist community is the phenomenon of nationality. Socialists are often hostile to nationality, viewing it as an ominously divisive identification indicative of a nonrational orientation toward social life. Miller regards this position as short-sighted. The nation is the only context within which an overarching and inclusive community can form in modern societies. Nationality provides enough common culture to underwrite social solidarity, but not so much as to suffocate individual autonomy. Thus, like the market, it can achieve an optimal blend of opposing tendencies. The perils of nationalism cannot be ignored, but a strong sense of nationality remains indispensable for building a socialist community.

Politics carries a particularly heavy weight under David Miller's conception of market socialism. Politics must make good the unjustified inequalities, the deficiencies in spontaneous community, and the residual alienation and exploitation characteristic of pure market socialism. Politics under market socialism should be distinguished by its emphasis on consensus-creating dialogue.

Dialogue politics is an alternative to interest aggregation politics. Under interest aggregation politics, actors are irredeemably egoistic and have essentially immobile opinions grounded in fixed interests. The essence of politics is reconciling interests to forge a coherent majority coalition. Dialogue politics, on the other hand, assumes that political actors seek the common good and that opinions can change drastically as a result of communication. Political dialogue succeeds when a proposal not only commands majority support but can be accepted by the minority as well. Legitimacy of decisions in dialogue politics derives not mainly from adherence to proper procedure but from honestly presenting the reasons behind a decision, thus making it easier for opponents to accept.

Miller's notion of dialogue politics connects with his ideas about community. A tightly knit community is not optimal for political dialogue because it obstructs the social distance needed for objective discussion. Conversely, however, vigorous political dialogue can occur even in large countries. Miller speaks warmly of political representation as a mechanism allowing a certain kind of dialogue to happen.

He also has definite ideas about the kind of state required by market socialism and dialogue politics. It must be a constitutional state rather than a majoritarian democracy. For purposes of establishing an effective system of checks and balances, decision-making rights must be carefully divided. The market socialist state should institutionalize the rule of law rather than the rule of the majority and should confer specific rights upon all its citizens. Investment banks function as guardians of socially owned capital in Miller's version of market socialism. Many such banks should exist, and they must be highly autonomous from the central government. Welfare goods are distributed according to need, and access to these goods is a constitutional right rather than a means-tested privilege.

One has to admire the ingenuity of Miller's arguments and the doggedness of his efforts to separate practical from utopian elements in the theory of socialism. His basic theoretical strategy is to link socialism with the development of individuality and to link the latter with markets. By this device he tries to synthesize libertarianism with traditional ideas about socialism.

While recognizing Miller's creativity and complete sincerity, I doubt that libertarianism and socialism are nearly so compatible as his approach would require. Miller sacrifices most of the distinctive aspects of socialism to a static concept of individualism. Markets are the historical progenitor of the individualism he touts and indeed may be indispensable for its continuation. That such hermetical imprisonment within the acquisitive self is the highest form of human development of which the current historical epoch is capable, or that it conveys human happiness in copious amounts, seems dubious and is certainly not established by Miller.

An even deeper problem with *Market, State and Community* is the tendency to make a virtue of necessity: if market socialism is the only politically feasible version of democratic socialism, then perhaps it is also the most desirable variety. This practice badly confounds normative and strategic judgments, obscuring the important distinction between cherished ideals and concessions to political reality. David Miller, I must agree with Cohen, does engage in adaptive preference formation.

A Blueprint for Socialism

John Roemer's ideas about market socialism differ from those of David Miller in three important ways: (a) his thinking is more operational and less philosophical than Miller's (he presents an operational "blueprint" for a market socialist economy), (b) control of enterprises by their workers is not an essential part of Roemer's blueprint, and (c) he makes no claims about the justice of market socialism (Roemer 1991, 1992b). On the latter issue, Roemer says:

> It is wrong, in my view, to maintain that any market system, with or without capitalists, allocates resources and incomes justly. What perfectly working competitive markets do is pay people according to the evaluation that other people in society put on their contribution. . . . Under market socialism, people will receive differential wages, and that will reflect their differential economic value to society. But they will not deserve those wages nor be entitled to them, because I do not believe they deserve or are entitled to returns to their arbitrarily assigned genetic compositions and familial and social environments, which largely determine their skills. . . . I view the differential wages that will accompany a market socialist system as justifiable for only one reason: they are a by-product of using a labor market to allocate labor, and there is no other known way to allocate labor more efficiently in a large, complex economy than by use of a labor market. (Roemer 1992b, p. 462)

Roemer conceives market socialism as an economic system with market allocation of most private goods and services, public ownership of economic enterprises, democratic control over how economic surplus is used, and significant state control over major economic institutions. The state control advocated by Roemer differs entirely from the command/administrative allocation found in Communist societies. Market socialism need not be Pareto inferior to capitalism in providing material goods, and will surely beget greater income equality. Roemer makes his market socialism as much like successful capitalist economies as possible.

The decisive operational characteristic of Roemer's market socialism is that publicly owned firms are managed by individuals who try to maximize profits at going prices. As we shall see, several important institutions are designed to insure that enterprise managers do try to maximize profits. Managers are not appointed by the state: they may be elected by workers or hired by a board of directors. Labor markets exist, and workers are hired at wages set by supply and demand. Even when workers have the power to hire and fire managers, they still need labor unions to protect them from managerial zealotry. Private goods and services are allocated by markets, and the government provides public goods.

Market socialism as conceived by Roemer has two important socialist characteristics: profits are divided equally among all adult citizens (i.e., they are a social dividend), and the government intervenes to control the overall nature of investment.

The nature of government intervention represents Roemer's most original contribution to the theory of market socialism. By simply regulating the interest rates at which firms borrow money, government planners can, as Roemer and his colleagues show, achieve virtually any technically feasible composition of investment (Ortuño-Ortin, Roemer, and Silvestre forthcoming). Such regulation of interest rates is a nonintrusive but effective form of central planning. Neither output nor prices nor the distribution of labor is centrally planned—only the composition of investment. Investment planning is not the arbitrary imposition of a government bureaucracy: the broad features of investment are decided by democratic political processes. Roemer considers political determination of investment necessary to avoid various possible market failures. For example, equilibrium investment levels often fall below the social optimum.

While recognizing that workers' control may be helpful in limiting the power of managers, Roemer remains ambivalent about this practice. Workers must not appropriate the profits of the enterprises at which they work. These firms belong to everyone, and direct profit appropriation would create large and unjustified income inequalities. More generally, workers' control could interfere with profit maximization, thereby undermining the efficiency of the market socialist economy. For example, worker-controlled firms might protect jobs by resisting labor-saving technology or pad wages by refusing to hire additional workers when production should expand.[2]

Market socialism, if it hopes to be a dynamic economic system, must encourage innovation. To provide incentives for "lonely inventors" and other creative entrepreneurs, Roemer allows small private firms to exist. If these firms exceed a certain size, they are nationalized, with ample compensation to the owners.

He thinks this arrangement will inspire the entrepreneurial spirit.

In the absence of the discipline imposed by a stock market, what will induce market socialist managers to maximize profits? Originally suggested by Pranab Bardham (1991), the system of managerial control outlined by Roemer is based on the role of banks in Japanese capitalism. The essential problem is to find or create agents with both the motivation and the capacity to monitor managerial performance in market socialist enterprises.

For this purpose, Roemer organizes his market socialist economy into groups of firms producing related products (but with no direct competitors in the same group). Each group is clustered around a bank that arranges financing for the associated firms. Each firm owns shares in the other firms of its group, and the board of directors of each firm includes representatives from the other firms and the bank. Part of the social dividend received by workers derives from the profits of other firms within their own group, giving workers a material interest in the economic performance of these firms. Roemer hopes this arrangement will give each firm the incentive and capacity to monitor the managers of other firms in their group.

Although bank monitoring of firms has been a successful alternative to the stock market in both Germany and Japan, the Bardham-Roemer proposal has certain drawbacks as a means of enforcing managerial efficiency under market socialism. It would surely increase the already substantial income inequality resulting from differential wages. The clusters could easily become quasifeudal domains restricting the efficient flow of capital and allowing managers to protect rather than monitor each other. Nor is it evident how workers could effectively participate in the monitoring process.

Is such an elaborate monitoring system really necessary? Would not tying the salaries and continued employment of managers to profits induce the desired profit-maximizing behavior?

Superior managerial monitoring could conceivably result from participation in international trade. Except for the protection of infant industries, Roemer recommends adopting a free trade policy. Market socialist firms should be exposed to the regimen of international competition, but stringent limitations must be placed upon the political power of foreign capital. The legal system must prevent foreign capital from exercising undue political influence within market socialist society.

How does market socialism stack up against other economic systems? We have already compared it to unadorned capitalism. Within highly productive economies, Roemer conjectures, social democracy of the Scandinavian sort would equalize income about as well as market socialism. But this would not happen in less productive economies. Here market socialism would prove distinctly more egalitarian than social democracy. Yet income equality is not the fundamental goal of socialism. It is only a means to the more basic objective of equality in opportunity for self-realization. Whether opportunity for self-realization can be even roughly equalized under market socialism remains an open question.

In this era of disaffection from socialism, John Roemer's message remains remarkably optimistic: "What the left must learn from the last seventy-five years is not that socialism is impossible, nor even that planning is unnecessary or harmful, but rather that the transition to socialism will be less dramatic than we had hoped" (Roemer 1991, p. 568).

Circumventing Socialism

David Miller claims that market socialism is preferable to communism. Robert van der Veen and Philippe Van Parijs take a different tack. They ask whether socialism is really necessary to attain communism and conclude that it is not (van der Veen and Parijs 1987). If socialism means collective ownership of the means of production and if communism means distribution according to need, then communism, or something very much like it, can be reached without going through socialism.

Socialism, argue van der Veen and Van Parijs, is not necessary to produce material abundance because capitalism creates abundance at least as quickly as socialism. Nor is socialism needed to develop altruistic social consciousness: communism does not require altruism. Although the left has traditionally favored socialism, historical experience indicates it is neither an effective means of human emancipation nor the exclusive route toward communism.

Van der Veen and Van Parijs recommend circumventing socialism by introducing an unconditional income grant to each adult
within a capitalist society. This grant gives each adult exactly
the same amount of money irrespective of whether she works or
has other income sources. Referred to as basic income, the
unconditional grant is gradually expanded until it provides most
of the income a person needs. By this process, income is increasingly distributed according to need: that is, society approaches
communism.

Gradually expanding basic income, argue van der Veen and
Van Parijs, is superior to other ways of transforming capitalism.
For example, it is better than guaranteed income programs
because it does not subvert incentive to work. It also has beneficial effects on the direction of technological progress. Workers
provided with basic income are less willing to take extremely
unpleasant jobs, thus spurring development of technology needed
to eliminate such work.

In his more recent papers Van Parijs offers a revised argument
for basic income capitalism (Van Parijs 1992a, 1992b). Though
strongly defending such a system, he no longer touts it as a road
to communism. When evaluating the justice of a social system,
a major consideration should be how well it treats the person
with least opportunity. The most just system is that providing
the greatest opportunity to the member with least opportunity—
the system maximizing minimum opportunity. This, Van Parijs
tries to show, is approximately equivalent to providing the highest basic income. The choice between socialism and capitalism
should be made not on abstract theoretical grounds but largely
on the basis of which can provide the highest basic income. A
mixed economy would probably be optimal for this purpose, but
Van Parijs believes its main characteristics should be capitalist.

Erik Wright takes issue with the claim that expanding basic
income is a feasible route from capitalism to communism (Wright
1987). Basic income, maintains Wright, will reduce the rate of
profit, causing both capital flight and capital strike. To render
basic income policy viable, the state must energetically block the
flight and strike of capital, but this activity automatically gives
society important socialist characteristics.

A transition to communism requires socialism for political
even more than for strictly economic reasons. Under capitalism,

meddling with the income distribution can be extraordinarily divisive. Without socialism, Wright doubts that adequate political support could be mustered for expanding basic income toward eventual distribution by need. A basic income policy would, however, strengthen the working class and assist a transition toward (not a circumvention of) socialism.

Van Parijs deals with Wright's critique by attacking the assumption that basic income will lower the rate of profit. On the contrary, provision of basic income will, at least temporarily, increase capitalist profits by reducing industrial conflict and creating a more flexible and dynamic economy. Politically speaking, this effect is of the essence. The political possibility of basic income capitalism hinges largely upon the practicality of making capitalism more profitable via a basic income policy. Van Parijs acknowledges that when pushed far enough, basic income will be incompatible with capitalist incentives. But that eventuality lies far in the future and need not constrain present policy.

At a time when socialist, social democratic, and even welfare state ideas are under severe attack, the basic income approach offers a glimmer of hope for people on the left. The basic income concept is both disarmingly simple and attractively bold. Its implementation within an advanced capitalist system seems far more feasible than any transition to socialism. Yet, as Wright points out and Van Parijs seems to recognize, a basic income policy could not go very far without requiring profound changes in capitalist property relations.

The meaning of work would also require sweeping transformation. A large share of the work performed in advanced capitalist societies remains exhausting, tedious, and/or irksome. People only do it because they need the money. Most of these tasks cannot be automated within the foreseeable future, and given alienated capitalist relations of production, very many will remain undone if adequate basic income becomes available. If the spur of necessity is retired as a major motivation for doing unpleasant labor, something else must take its place. Primary income theorists indicate this something else will not be sheer altruism, but say little about what it could be. Without physical or economic compulsion, could the motivation for doing unpleasant labor be something very different than integration into an egalitarian socialist community?

The Basic Income Game

Alan Carling uses game theory to study the basic income proposal (Carling 1991, pp. 377-411). Adapting Michael Taylor's ideas on the social foundations of cooperation (Taylor 1976, 1987), Carling formulates what he calls the Basic Income Game (BIG). This game addresses the question of whether people would work if they received an unconditional basic income.

Each person in the Basic Income Game decides whether or not to work. If a person works, she produces a fixed amount of economic value but also suffers the personal cost of laboring (assumed to be less than the value she produces, that is, a net surplus results from working). In accordance with the basic income principle, the value a worker produces is distributed equally between all members of society whether or not they work; the worker receives no special compensation for her labor. If a person does not work, she gets an equal share of what is produced by those who do work, and she does not endure the disutility of working. Of course, a person who does not work sacrifices that small share she would have received when her own economic product was divided equally among all members of society.

The population playing the Basic Income Game is partitioned into a group that works and a group that does not. Is this particular division stable or unstable? Suppose a person is currently working. To decide whether she will work in the future, the worker compares the reward she now receives with the reward she would receive if she stopped working (but everything else remains the same). If this reward is greater than what she now gets, she stops working. Otherwise she continues working. Thus she will continue working only if the personal cost of working is less than the small fragment of value she gets when her own economic product is divided equally among the entire population. Unless the population is minuscule, this is extremely unlikely.

Suppose a person is currently not working. She will work in the future only if the net rewards she can expect from working—assuming nothing else changes—exceeds what she currently gets. Once again, this happens only when the cost of working is less than her proportionate share of the value she produces.

Under all reasonable assumptions about population size and the productivity of labor, the only equilibrium of Carling's Basic Income Game is no one working. Yet all members of society would be better off if everyone worked. The Basic Income Game is actually a multiperson generalization of Prisoner's Dilemma.

This is a disheartening conclusion. Can anything be done to make a basic income policy workable? Using ideas suggested by Michael Taylor, Carling reconceptualizes the Basic Income Game as an infinitely repeated game or supergame. Anticipated future plays of the BIG supergame influence current strategic thinking, but because people weigh the future less than the present, these plays are discounted at a fixed rate. The supergame conceptualization greatly ups the ante because participants must now contemplate the entire sequence of plays. It also makes possible much more sophisticated strategies of play.

Consider a conditional strategy in which a person works in the next time period if at least n people worked in the last time period but does not work next time if fewer than n people worked last time. Carling shows that an equilibrium of the BIG supergame exists when exactly n people adopt this strategy and everyone else never works. This equilibrium—named by Carling the *greenstick equilibrium* because its graphical representation resembles a greenstick bone fracture—assumes that n is sufficiently large and that future plays of the game are important to people (i.e., the future is evaluated at a high rate).

The greenstick equilibrium exists only because the n people who adopt the conditional strategy see that if any one of them stops working in the next period, then absolutely no one will work thereafter. The work of each, one might say, is motivated by the combined work of all coalition members and by considering the entire future evolution of the BIG supergame.

The greenstick equilibrium may sustain a basic income policy, but if the number of nonworkers is large it can hardly be considered an egalitarian solution. We then have what amounts to a class division between workers and nonworkers, even though these classes are not based upon ownership of property. It does make sense for workers to continue working, but their own welfare remains distinctly inferior to that of nonworkers. The lazy, to use a phrase of Jon Elster, are exploiting the industrious.

Can the Basic Income Game be reformulated to retain the basic income idea but allow for a more egalitarian solution? Carling presents two such variations, which may be called Gotha Programme socialism (after the 1875 unification program of German socialists criticized so trenchantly by Marx) and police socialism.

Gotha Programme socialism takes off from the idea of rewarding work appropriately and then distributing the rest of the economic product equally among all members of society. Thus each worker is paid exactly the amount commensurate with the disutility of her labor, and everything else is distributed by the basic income principle. With this method of payment, the only equilibrium turns out to be everyone working and thus receiving exactly the same income.

Gotha Programme socialism preserves the basic income principle only by introducing wages in a big way. By assuming all jobs have the same disutility, it assumes away a paramount problem with the basic income approach: the tendency for the worst work to remain undone. Carling himself identifies a "major snag in this solution": as population increases, the advantage of working over not working becomes vanishingly small. Gotha Programme socialism provides rather cold comfort to advocates of basic income.

Police socialism is even less reassuring. The idea behind police socialism is distributing income equally but then punishing people who do not work. This punishment is implemented through a police force—or the functional equivalent of a police force—financed by taxes upon working people. The effectiveness of a punishment is directly related to its cost. The authoritarian implications of this process are supposedly mitigated because punishments will seldom if ever be used.

The rationale for this institutional structure is to implement basic income without resorting to wages and with incentives that remain intact as population increases. The mechanism of the punishment imposed upon nonworkers and the form of taxation paid by workers are both important for achieving the desired effects. Without belaboring the details of Carling's police socialism model, we can observe that the tax paid by each worker is proportional to the number of nonworkers, and the punishment suffered by each nonworker is proportional to the number of workers. If the number of workers is small, they will be swamped by the costs of punishment. But if the number of workers is large, the power of the punishment will be overwhelming.

As one might expect, police socialism has two equilibria: everyone working and no one working. The system also defines a critical number of workers. If the initial working population exceeds this critical number, then the game approaches the everyone-working equilibrium. If the initial working population is less than the critical number, then the no-one-working equilibrium is reached.

Most socialists, Carling understands, will be repulsed by the coercive nature of police socialism. He defends his formulation in two ways. The presentation is intentionally provocative, but the character of the "police force" and the nature of the sanctions upon nonworkers remain flexible and need not entail elemental coercion. And whatever authoritarianism police socialism truly implies is simply that needed to stabilize any system of market relations: "If the case of [police socialism] entails an authoritarian solution to the problem of social order, then capitalism is an inherently authoritarian system" (Carling 1991, p. 404).

Whatever policy implications can be drawn from Carling's game theoretic analysis are not particularly favorable to the basic income approach: "It seems very unlikely that a Basic Income scheme is workable without some system of sanctions against free-riders. . . . Whatever social apparatus is devised to administer these sanctions—formal or informal, moral or material, centralized or decentralized—there will have to be externally applied discipline in the society" (Carling 1991, pp. 404-05).

Market Socialism and Social Democracy

Some Analytical Marxists favor market socialism as the best practical alternative to corporate capitalism. Others, like Adam Przeworski,[3] embrace social democracy. The principal claim of social democracy is that the irrationality of capitalism can be overcome without socializing the means of production. This can be done by strengthening the working class within capitalist society through building vigorous trade unions and a popular social democratic political party. Whereas market socialists understand worker's control to mean abolishing capitalist property and establishing workers' cooperatives, social democrats interpret it as the existence of strong, democratically run unions within capitalist society.

Social democratic strategy involves making the capitalist economy as efficient as possible—mainly by using Keynesian economic policies—while simultaneously increasing the income and financial security of the working class. Advanced social democracy, some theorists claim, is an embryonic form of socialism and will steadily evolve into a full-blown socialist society. Others make no prediction about the future but simply regard social democracy as a more rational and less conflictual form of capitalism.

The appeal of social democracy is easy to understand. It does not require a violent revolution or even a profound reorientation of capitalism. It does not propagate utopian—and hence potentially dangerous—visions of the future, but suggests practical means by which a capitalist state can eliminate poverty without courting economic inefficiency. It builds upon the actual achievements and proven capabilities of advanced capitalism, and can be implemented (or at least initiated) within a bourgeois republic. Social democracy has impressive accomplishments to its credit—including almost complete abolition of poverty in Scandinavia—and seems a low-risk way of making social and economic change.

How can we compare social democracy and market socialism? Jon Elster and Karl Ove Moene address this question in their introduction to the volume *Alternatives to Capitalism* (Elster and Moene 1989). The short-term performance of a social system can be misleading: new systems sometimes commence with blazing success but then falter badly and remain mired in the doldrums. Really useful comparisons are based upon the endogenous steady-state properties of the systems being compared.

Elster and Moene also discuss the difference between static efficiency (optimal use of existing resources) and dynamic efficiency (optimal creation of new resources). Systems that maximize static efficiency rarely maximize dynamic efficiency. The patent system, to use one of Elster's favorite examples, hinders spread of existing knowledge but strongly motivates creation of new technology. Elster and Moene consider dynamic efficiency more important than static efficiency when comparing economic systems.

Comparisons between social democracy and market socialism usually center on the issue of workers' cooperatives. Many writers conceive of market socialism as a system of workers' cooperatives that relate to each other primarily through the market. They regard the existence of such cooperatives as the major difference between market socialism and social democracy. All firms in a market socialist economy need not be workers' cooperatives. It is sufficient that the cooperatives, even if not in the majority, constitute a strong and coherent block within market socialist society. Such a mixed economy has definite advantages. Cooperative organization may be ill suited for certain lines of production, and workers not wishing to participate should not be dragooned into producer cooperatives.

Moene defines a workers' production cooperative as an organization in which (a) production activities are performed jointly by workers, (b) workers have a hand in managerial decisions and these decisions reflect their interests, (c) net income is divided among workers by some agreed-upon method, and (d) members have equal rights, so really important decisions are made democratically on a one-person one-vote basis (Moene 1989, p. 84). Workers' cooperatives sound good, yet in most situations where firms can form freely, the great majority are not cooperatives. Why is this so?

Most Marxists deny that firms can ever form freely under capitalism. In a capitalist society, people who want to establish producer cooperatives usually have a hard time getting reasonable financing. As Elster and Moene point out, there is often a scale trap when assessing the viability of social innovations. It is hazardous to infer how an innovation will work when instituted on a large scale on the basis of how it functioned on a small scale. The scarcity of cooperatives in an economic environment emphasizing competitive relationships is no evidence that producer cooperatives are inherently flawed or that market socialism is unworkable.[4]

The few workers' cooperatives that manage to survive under capitalism have attractive characteristics: low absenteeism, low labor force turnover, no production losses from strikes, and high labor productivity. Within large cooperatives, efficiency requirements make extensive worker participation in management impractical, but representative democracy at the workplace plus periodic election of managers might remedy this problem (Elster and Moene 1989, p. 25).

The issue of innovation poses an even more serious quandary for workers' cooperatives. Workers in producer cooperatives lack strong economic incentives to innovate since the innovator only gets a small share of the gains resulting from a successful innovation. A low innovation rate soon becomes a low rate of economic growth, and the weakness of innovation is sometimes called the Achilles heel of workers' cooperatives and market socialism.[5]

However, there are forces pushing in the opposite direction. Incentives to innovate can be structured into workers' cooperatives, and, as we shall see, the absence of labor-capital conflict under market socialism often results in a higher rate of investment boosting economic growth.

Because they try to maximize income per worker and make employment decisions on this basis, workers' cooperatives are sometimes said to act in economically irrational ways (Ward 1958). When the price of its product increases, a cooperative will supposedly reduce the number of workers (to increase income per worker), thus supplying less of the product to the market.

In an article comparing the economic effects of strong unions and workers' cooperatives, Karl Moene analyzes the irrationality hypothesis (Moene 1989). As a description of what cooperatives actually do, he finds it quite absurd. The hypothesis is based on a faulty understanding of the social and economic relations prevailing within workers' cooperatives. These organizations do strive to increase the average income of their workers, but this is certainly not their only nor even their most important objective. They also strive to provide security for their workers and to assure them equal treatment.

Moene considers two methods by which cooperatives can protect their workers in the face of unemployment. Both methods assume that the state provides some unemployment benefits to workers who lose their jobs. Under one method, the cooperative compensates the workers it discharges so that the sum of state unemployment benefits plus cooperative compensation equals the income of employed workers. Under the second method, the cooperative provides no compensation, but workers to be discharged are chosen on a completely random basis. Moene shows that guaranteed income in the first case exactly equals expected income in the second.

Given security providing methods like these, layoffs affect both employed and unemployed workers. Employed workers are affected because they must pay benefits to the unemployed or because they have to face an equal risk of becoming unemployed themselves. Major decisions are made democratically in workers' cooperatives, and without adequate security, workers will not vote to fire themselves. More to the point, it does not make economic sense to sack workers after a price increase when those fired will have the same income, or at least the same expected income, as those who are not. Thus workers' cooperatives will not respond to price increases in the perverse way of reducing the amount supplied.

However, unemployment can result from a steep drop in prices. If prices fall so sharply that unemployment benefits exceed the value of a worker's marginal product, then an economically rational cooperative will lay off workers. But the discharged workers will presumably be rehired if and when prices increase sufficiently. Because democratically run cooperatives cannot easily fire their members—it rarely makes economic sense to fire workers, given the rules under which they operate—they will also hesitate about taking new members.

This points out an important difference between capitalist firms with strong unions (social democracy) and workers' cooperatives (market socialism). Strong unions negotiate rigid wage schedules, and the firms in which they operate respond to output reductions by maintaining wages but reducing employment. Conversely, workers' cooperatives usually share the burden of hard times among all members: they tend to maintain employment and absorb economic fluctuations by adjusting wages. Starting from a position of full employment, Moene thinks market socialism would be less recession prone than social democracy.

Moene also thinks the continuing conflict between capital and labor within social democracy induces a tendency toward underinvestment, the strength of which is more or less proportional to the power of the trade union movement. The underinvestment tendency arises because the bargaining power of unions increases with the amount of fixed capital a firm installs. Thus investments drive up wages, and capitalist firms hesitate to make them. Capitalists underinvest precisely to limit the wage demands of workers. And when they do invest, owners may choose less productive but more mobile and resalable equipment just to reduce the bargaining leverage gained by workers.

The conflictual relationship between capital and labor causes yet other forms of waste and inefficiency within social democratic capitalism. Truth is hard to come by under conditions of intense conflict. To deter wage demands, firms may conceal their true profitability. Workers, expecting such deception, do not believe what they are told, and false perceptions about company profits can motivate high wage demands and even strikes. Given the nature of this strategic interaction, a rational union may strike just to establish a reputation as a tough bargainer.

The discussion above is largely theoretical. What does empirical research tell us about the actual performance of social democracy? In a recently published review article, Gosta Esping-Anderson and Kees van Kersbergen (1992) summarize and evaluate several decades of social scientific research on social democracy. The general thrust of research findings is that social democratic movements, if sufficiently strong and operating under congenial circumstances, can reduce income inequality and significantly improve the welfare of the working class under capitalism. There is little indication, however, that social democracy does or can transform capitalism into socialism.

Successful social democracy requires both strong left-wing political parties exercising government power and a strong centralized trade union movement. Parties or unions alone have little effect upon capitalist society. An important—and perhaps surprising— function of trade unions is imposing wage restraint upon the working class in pursuit of macroeconomic objectives such as full employment or monetary stability. Other conditions are also necessary for successful social democratic change: (a) the political right must be weak, (b) coalitions between urban workers and agricultural producers must exist, and (c) the country must have a favorable position in the international economy.

The Polish Marxist Michał Kalecki doubted the possibility of sustaining full employment under capitalism. He thought sustained full employment would induce serious inflation and wages so high they would threaten the existence of capitalist profits. But social democracy has been able to achieve full employment over long periods of time with neither runaway inflation nor a bankrupt capitalist class. Research suggests that full employment under capitalism is best achieved if the left is either very weak or very strong. If the left is weak, the capitalist class does not fear the effect of full employment on working-class militancy. If the left is strong, social democratic style full employment becomes feasible.

Neoclassical economic theory implies that income redistribution by the government depresses economic growth. But empirical research indicates this effect can be reduced or entirely limited if trade unions are strong enough to moderate wage demands. Scandinavian countries with strong social democratic movements have been able to increase economic equality without depressing economic growth.

Yet the findings reported above are based upon a small number of unambiguously social democratic societies. The sparsity of such societies makes distinguishing nation effects from true social democratic effects extremely difficult. Social democratic theory may be a theory about Scandinavia alone, and the Swedish example may not be relevant elsewhere.

But even if the Swedish case is relevant elsewhere, we have ample reason to doubt that social democracy provides a durable solution to the problems of capitalism. Scandinavian social democracy has weakened considerably since about 1980. The rise of social democracy is often linked to the emergence of "organized capitalism," a version of capitalism featuring mass production methods, oligopolist industries, stable relations between corporations and unions, and the management of demand by the state. However, organized capitalism has declined significantly since the mid-1970s due to postindustrial production methods requiring greater flexibility and increased international mobility of capital. Both political pundits and social scientific research suggest that the decline of organized capitalism has weakened social democracy, especially in its traditional Scandinavian strongholds.

Yet the prospects for social democracy are not entirely bleak. In a world of sharply curtailed political expectations, Scandinavian social democracy—or at least Scandinavian social democracy at its apex—is widely considered the most desirable form of social organization with any realistic chance of being implemented. And social democracy is gaining strength in southern Europe just as it weakens in the north. Judgment on this development must be postponed: southern European social democracy has so far produced only a few of the results that made Scandinavian social democracy so appealing.

Participatory Economics

Not everyone whose work might fall within the Analytical Marxist fold advocates market socialism, social democracy, or market economies of any sort. In three interrelated books, Michael Albert and Robin Hahnel propose "participatory economics," a democratic form of socialism based upon egalitarian organization of work and highly decentralized economic planning (Hahnel and Albert 1990; Albert and Hahnel 1991a, 1991b). Albert and Hahnel are not usually regarded as Analytical Marxists; in fact they are usually considered closer to the anarchist tradition than to Marxism of any variety. Nevertheless their reliance upon assumptions of rationality, use of neoclassical economic theory for radical purposes, and attention to class analysis justifies locating their important work within the realm of Analytical Marxism.

Participatory economics lies in the tradition of council communism and anarchosyndicalism, but is more thoroughly elaborated than previous visions of this sort. The elaboration takes two forms. On the one hand, Albert and Hahnel present detailed hypothetical examples of socialist production units (e.g., a book publisher, an airport, a steel plant), carefully indicating how participatory economics might function in these particular cases (Albert and Hahnel 1991a). On the other hand, they use sophisticated mathematical models to demonstrate the desirability and feasibility of their proposed system (Hahnel and Albert 1990; Albert and Hahnel 1991b).

A good economic system, say Albert and Hahnel, should provide equity, participatory self-management, community solidarity, and variety of economic outcomes. Neither capitalism nor centralized planning (which they call "coordinatorism") nor market socialism provides all of these things. Hence socialists must find another system. Albert and Hahnel are particularly eager to refute socialist theorists like Alec Nove who claim there can be no third way between markets and centralized planning (Nove 1983).

Participatory economics assumes that (a) all productive property is publicly owned, and (b) income is distributed according to effort (modified somewhat by need) but definitely not on the basis of personal contribution (i.e., effort amplified by luck and talent). Applying the principle of payment for effort to the situation depicted in the film *Amadeus*, Albert and Hahnel conclude that Salieri, a hard-working but plodding composer, should receive more than Mozart, an irresponsible musical genius.

Participatory economics rests upon three institutional pillars respectively determining how decisions are made, how work is organized, and how economic planning is accomplished. Economic decisions are made through a network of workplace and community councils, each run democratically and each exercising dominion over those matters mainly of concern to its participants. Local or enterprise councils are linked with community councils, which are linked with regional councils, and so forth; but broader councils (not considered to be higher) do not have authority over more provincial ones. The relation between councils at different levels entails much discussion and negotiation, and reaching a decision for a broad constituency can be an extremely time-consuming process.

One of Albert and Hahnel's most original ideas is the balanced job complex, an innovation designed to make work relations nonhierarchical. A balanced job complex is a collection of different tasks—some mental and some manual, some creative and some repetitious, some easy and some hard—that together constitute a job description. Balanced job complexes are designed to be equivalent in prestige, power, and desirability not only within their own productive unit but between such units as well. This is why they are balanced. Albert and Hahnel carefully explain how equivalence within productive units is achieved but are rather vague about how job complexes located in different units can become equivalent. They argue strenuously, if not entirely convincingly, that balanced job complexes will not impair (and may enhance) productive efficiency.

Decentralized economic planning happens through a series of iterations relying heavily upon the use of computer technology. An individual person's economic plan consists essentially of what she intends to produce and what she intends to consume over the course of a year. Normally the value of productive contribution should equal the value of consumption within an individual's plan.

During the first stage of the planning process, each adult forms an individual economic plan using the price levels that prevailed in the previous year. Relevant information and user-friendly planning forms are furnished through an extensive computer network. These individual plans are evaluated and aggregated by the local council (with computer assistance), which adds inputs for its own projects to the combined individual plans. These local council plans are then evaluated, aggregated, and supplemented at the next level of the council network. This process continues until a first approximation national plan is formed. The balance between supply and demand is determined for each product in the national economy, and proposed price levels are calculated accordingly. The planning process begins again using these new price levels. The iterative process continues until the supply of each good matches the demand (or is slightly larger than the demand to avoid shortages). Albert and Hahnel propose various institutional interventions to facilitate convergence of supply and demand within a reasonable number of iterations.

The iteration process proposed by Albert and Hahnel is a modern socialist adaptation of the equilibrium-seeking process (*tâtonnement*, "groping," or recontracting) first described by Leon Walras in the middle of the 19th century (Walras 1954). It is similar in spirit to the Lange-Lerner model of socialism developed in the 1930s and described earlier in this chapter. Granting certain assumptions, Albert and Hahnel prove that the iteration process converges toward a Pareto-optimal allocation of goods. The deviation between the formal model of participatory economics and how a real participatory economy would function is much smaller, they argue, than the corresponding gap between formal model and reality for either market economies or central planning.

One has to admire the boldness and originality of Albert and Hahnel's participatory economics. They try to demonstrate the existence of an alternative to lukewarm reformism and discredited authoritarianism. They try to rally socialists and give them inspiring vision and renewed self-confidence. They try to change the terms of contemporary political dialogue now so heavily stacked against radical thought. But despite their audacity and admirable intentions, Albert and Hahnel's endeavor is only partially successful: the vision of participatory economics is not entirely compelling. Reservations mainly concern the feasibility of participatory economics, but even its desirability is not beyond question.

Participatory economics, as conceived by Albert and Hahnel, places seemingly impossible demands on the time and knowledge of almost everyone. Both as workers and as community members, persons are caught up in an endless round of meetings and computer sessions. How meaningful are the multiple decisions people are required to make? How valid is the information on which the decentralized planning process proceeds? Will the net result be more democracy or pervasive frustration at the intrusion of politics and participation into every nook of social life? Their acute fear of authority in any form causes Albert and Hahnel to undervalue time, to compromise efficiency, and to neglect the legitimate claims of private life.

The model of production advocated by Albert and Hahnel rests upon balanced job complexes, but this concept is not unproblematic. With balanced job complexes, introduction of new technology—the Achilles heel of market socialism—could be difficult because many people must approve the change and learn the technology. Balanced job complexes, in the language of computer science, are not a modular design. The intense interdependency resulting from this cross-cutting organization of labor may reduce control over one's own work. Any significant change in a balanced job complex ramifies through the entire organization and could significantly disrupt production. By the same token, labor mobility creates serious problems. Replacement workers must have multiple skills and, in the limiting case, departure of a single person could abruptly stop even a large enterprise.

The mathematical theorems about the welfare properties of participatory economics are less persuasive than Albert and Hahnel hope. The theorems assume what needs to be proved:

that individuals can act quickly and rationally in the required decision-making roles.

Ironically and inadvertently, participatory economics may invite authoritarianism of a certain sort. The potential for authoritarianism derives from the homogeneity of the antiauthoritarian vision. Can we establish and maintain a detailed and substantially uniform conception of economic relations without using coercive authority? If a person becomes frustrated with balanced job complexes, decentralized iterative planning, and numerous council meetings, and if she wants to start her own business, must some external authority prevent her from doing so?

Conclusion

It is sometimes said that political defeat engenders deeper and more lasting social theory than does political victory. This may be an unfounded myth or merely a sop thrown to intellectuals on the losing side. Yet if there is some truth in this adage, then the years just ahead should yield profound Marxist theory since most Marxists I have encountered recently feel rather defeated.

Some of my nonradical friends think it strange that principled Marxists should feel defeated by the collapse of repressive unpopular Communist regimes that they themselves had consistently opposed. Gerald Cohen, in the essay cited at the start of this chapter, offers this explanation of his own paradoxical feelings:

> Although I have long since sustained little hope that things in the Soviet Union might get substantially better, in a socialist sense, there is, in certain domains . . . a vast difference between nourishing little hope and giving up all hope. The small hope that I kept was, as it were, an immense thing, since so much was at stake. And now that residual hope has to be forsworn. So a feeling of loss is not surprising.
>
> And there is also another and perhaps less rational motif here, which I would do well to avow. It is true that I was heavily critical of the Soviet Union, but the angry little boy who pummels his father's chest will not be glad if the old man collapses. As long as the Soviet Union seemed safe, it felt safe for me to be anti-Soviet. Now that it begins, disobligingly, to crumble, I feel impotently protective toward it. (Cohen 1991, pp. 9-10)

I do not know how many Analytical Marxists share Cohen's feelings, but he is surely not alone. Nor are such sentiments irrelevant to the kinds of problems currently studied by Analytical Marxists. Issues pertaining to the nature of socialism are at or near the top of their research agenda. Some fascinating and even brilliant results have been obtained, but as the contents of this chapter amply demonstrate, no theoretical consensus about the meaning or feasibility of socialism has emerged among the Analytical Marxists.

What has emerged is a set of questions likely to guide future Analytical Marxist research pertaining to socialism. These questions include the following:

1. What is the role of markets (i.e., commodity production) in a feasible socialism? Can markets exist without alienation, inequality, and the emergence of capitalism?

2. What is the role of economic planning in a socialist society? Is decentralized planning possible? Is centralized planning inherently inefficient and/or authoritarian? What is the relationship between economic planning and political democracy?

3. Is worker control desirable? Is it consistent with economic rationality? Does worker control undermine equality and growth? Can meaningful worker participation in enterprise management be sustained over time?

4. How much social and economic equality is feasible? How much is desirable? Will a feasible socialism be more egalitarian than capitalism? Is there an unavoidable tradeoff between equality and efficiency?

5. How can a socialist society cope with race and gender inequality? Is socialism more effective than capitalism in coping with such problems? Does elimination of racism and sexism require a strong state?

6. Is a democratic socialist society inherently developmentalist? Can it be ecologically rational? Is socialism any better than capitalism in caring for the environment?

7. Are neoclassical models of general equilibrium or neo-Keynesian models of effective demand of any use in designing or managing a socialist society? Is classical Marxist theory of any relevance to modern socialism?

Most of these questions far transcend the boundaries of Analytical Marxism and are of deep concern to intellectuals of many different theoretical identities. In the years ahead we can expect to get a stream of sharply divergent answers. But within this torrent of contestation Analytical Marxism has a distinctive contribution to make. Only Analytical Marxists propose a class analysis of socialist society premised upon assumptions of individual rationality. Only Analytical Marxists identify structural sources of exploitation within all forms of socialism without growing complacent toward the continued existence of global capitalism. Only Analytical Marxists build new models of socialism using both the libertarian critique of collectivism and systematic consideration of the experience of Communist societies.

Notes

1. Roemer's five-stage interpretation extends and elaborates a scheme originally suggested by Friedrich Hayek (1940).

2. See the section later in this chapter, "Participatory Economics," for further discussion of this issue.

3. "I can see no grounds on which to choose between social democracy and market socialism," says Przeworski (1991b, p. 133), but elsewhere he identifies himself as a social democrat.

4. To illustrate the dangers of inferring from the local to the global, consider the practice of marrying for love. In former times, writes Tocqueville, most people regarded this as a very foolish practice because the love matches that were formed often ended badly. Obviously this does not mean marrying for love is inherently unsatisfying or impractical. Any practice that bucks social convention has two strikes against it, observes Tocqueville, and people who persist in doing so are probably bull-headed, a characteristic not particularly conducive to marital success (Elster and Moene 1989, p. 15).

5. Yet Lange (1936-1937) and Lerner (1936), in what I have called the classic model of market socialism, claim it is superior to monopoly capitalism in making technological innovations. See the earlier section in this chapter, "The Classic Model of Market Socialism."

10

SUMMARY, CRITIQUE, FUTURE DIRECTIONS

Analytical Marxism and Modern Social Science

Classical Marxism did not try to be part of mainstream social science, which was conceived as an intellectual product of the bourgeoisie. Instead, classical Marxists sought to abolish bourgeois social science and to reconstitute the science of society entirely anew.

Modern Analytical Marxists display less hubris than their classical predecessors and view mainstream social science in less starkly class terms. They want to be part of the mainstream so they can have an impact upon it. They believe that Marxist theory, properly formulated, can exert a beneficial influence within many domains of mainstream scholarship. They explicitly deny that Analytical Marxism—or any other type of Marxism—could or should engulf the whole of social science.

More controversially, Analytical Marxists embrace the methodological standards of modern social science. They accept the usual logical conventions on how scientific theory should be expressed and elaborated. They also accept the customary rules about gathering scientific evidence and evaluating hypotheses. Some observers interpret this wholesale acceptance of conventional social scientific norms as a yearning for academic respectability. Although Analytical Marxists may have such feelings, there are less pejorative reasons for embracing modern social scientific methodology.

The relatively tolerant relationship between Analytical Marxism and mainstream social science reflects neither acceptance of capitalism nor rejection of the emancipatory project of classical Marxism. However, it does indicate awareness that capitalism is more durable and emancipation less straightforward or immediate than Marxists of an earlier generation believed.

Increased humility toward the conventional norms of science coincides with diminished piety toward Marxist theory itself. Its objectives may be admirable, its practitioners courageous, and its enemies despicable, but Marxist theory plays in the same ballpark as, and must compete with, other social theories. Marxist theory and its competitors share certain concepts, often try to explain the same facts, and have influenced each other willy-nilly for many decades. If the practice of social science is indeed a common cultural heritage and if Marxist theory routinely competes with non-Marxist rivals, then why should it be subject to different intellectual standards?

Classical Marxism paid a high price for its overweening ambition and splendid isolation. Any collective intellectual endeavor, including science, develops in a context of dialogue and interaction. Separated from these social processes and insulated from serious challenge, a scientific doctrine suffers stagnation, loss of intellectual vitality, and decreasing appeal for creative minds. The stagnation of classical Marxism has several sources over and above grandiosity and intellectual isolation; but grandiosity and isolation, beside being liabilities in their own right, increased its vulnerability to the other impediments. By placing themselves squarely within the domain of modern social science and by accepting the conventional norms of scientific practice, Analytical Marxists hope to minimize tendencies toward conceptual sclerosis and to preserve intellectual vitality.

The Achievements of Analytical Marxism

As of this writing, the most distinctive contributions of Analytical Marxism lie in three related fields: the theory of history, the theory of exploitation, and class analysis. In each of these fields, its principal contributions have been clarifying the foundations of Marxist analysis, establishing which lines of reasoning are plausible and which are not, and casting Marxist theories in an axiomatic form. By building a bridge to mainstream social science, the Analytical Marxists have promoted empirical work within contemporary Marxism (though more empirical work is needed) and encouraged systematic testing of Marxist hypotheses.

Analytical Marxists usually defend the viability of a theory of history. That is, they defend the idea that history, taken as a whole, is a suitable object for scientific investigation and not a sequence of disjointed episodes with no internal logic. They also defend the idea that human history has a certain direction defined by the development of productive forces. The existence of a general historical direction does not presuppose a historical teleology, a fixed progression of stages, a terminal point toward which history is heading, or even the primacy of productive forces. On the contrary, the direction of history can be derived from general properties of human nature (e.g., rationality and disinclination to toil) and social organization (e.g., existence of hierarchical class structures based upon appropriation of economic surplus).

The theory of historical materialism, a pillar of classical Marxism, has been refurbished and revitalized largely through the efforts of Analytical Marxists. Restoration has not meant carte blanche support for the tenets of historical materialism. The crucial steps have entailed establishing the scientific legitimacy of theorizing about history, clarifying the specific meaning and implications of historical materialism, and pinpointing deep changes required to make the theory credible and coherent.

As I have indicated, the revitalized theory of historical materialism faces a new challenge to which Analytical Marxists must respond. The appeal of the theory rested largely on the conviction that capitalism was approaching the end of its historical tether and would soon be replaced by socialism. Historical materialism gave a general theoretical explanation of why this might be so and placed the transition away from capitalism in a broad historical context. Today it is not at all evident that capitalism has reached the end of its tether, either globally or within specific countries. How relevant will historical materialism seem—even the refurbished and revitalized historical materialism of the Analytical Marxists—if the demise of capitalism is nothing more than a distant hypothetical possibility?

The challenge posed by the continued vitality of capitalism, it could be argued, is political and ideological rather than scientific. Analytical Marxist theories of history do not indicate how or when the capitalist economic system will end, nor whether this will happen within our own lifetime.

If we hope to explain fundamental economic transformations through the fettering of forces by relations of production, this defense of historical materialism is much too facile. Under the aegis of capitalism, productive forces have experienced long and prodigious development, and the productive expansion shows no signs of abating. Yet despite five centuries of unparalleled productive expansion, despite wars, strikes, revolutions, revolutionary ideologies, revolutionary technologies, booms, busts, and vanguard parties, despite sound and fury and sociological earthquakes, capitalism remains firmly entrenched everywhere. Should a scientific observer remain unmoved? Is this not sufficient cause to doubt the fundamental dynamic of change postulated by Analytical Marxist theories of history?

Consider the theory of exploitation. Analytical Marxism can claim credit for rescuing exploitation theory from both the armories of ideological warriors and the fallacies of the labor theory of value. Exploitation is not the figment of a Marxist imagination but occurs, in one form or another, whenever productive assets are unequally distributed. It is not caused by the labor process, as many Marxists had previously thought, but results from the structure of property relations. Very weak assumptions about property relations suffice to prove the existence of exploitation.

Even more impressive is the linkage Analytical Marxists have established between the phenomena of class and exploitation. John Roemer's Class Exploitation Correspondence Principle is one of the great theoretical achievements of modern social science. By taking what was previously an unproved axiom and deriving it as a theorem, Roemer gives us a marvelous example of what rigorous theoretical analysis can accomplish. Erik Wright's use of exploitation concepts to construct a general framework for conducting empirical studies of class structure deepens the linkage between class and exploitation by locating it within observable social reality.

Yet just when the theoretical and empirical credibility of exploitation seem more firmly established than ever, its social relevance is challenged: exploitation does exist but may not be very important. The detractors say it is neither a fundamental moral category nor a sensible basis for criticizing society. These are serious critiques requiring serious consideration. Emerging as they do from the founders of Analytical Marxism, the critiques seem like snatching defeat from the jaws of victory. Whatever the fate of this controversy, Analytical Marxism has successfully resurrected exploitation—much as it did historical materialism — as a credible and enticing object of scientific inquiry.

The contribution of Analytical Marxism to class analysis is both theoretical and empirical. I have already mentioned the tighter theoretical integration between the concepts of class and exploitation. Another theoretical contribution is conceptualizing the complex linkages between class structure, class formation, class consciousness, and class struggle. Recognizing the impossibility of studying the modern capitalist middle class using the categories of classical Marxism, Erik Wright and his collaborators developed a sophisticated typology of class locations that has proved effective for investigating the class relations of contemporary capitalism.

Analytical Marxism has inspired a wave of Marxist empirical research on class. It has done so partly by legitimizing the use of formerly suspect empirical methodologies, such as survey research and multivariate statistical analysis, and partly by broadening the range of empirical questions Marxists want to ask. This broadening happens because the theories formulated by Analytical Marxists leave many more questions contingent. Moreover, the conceptual exploration advocated by Analytical Marxism punctures grandiose theoretical claims, expresses propositions in a lean or minimalist fashion, and increases the perceived complexity of the social world. Each of these developments enriches the realm of contingency. Analytical Marxist models are often consistent with several possible states of reality; precisely which state holds requires empirical determination.

The mainstream methodology appropriated by Analytical Marxism for empirical research on class relations works better for studying social statics than social dynamics. Consequently,

Analytical Marxist research on class has focused largely on issues of class structure rather than class struggle. Is the methodological tail wagging the Analytical Marxist dog? Does the quantitative methodology of mainstream social science constitute a "statics trap" that will inconspicuously divert the attention of Analytical Marxists away from class dynamics? Any such conclusion would be premature, but recognizing the temptation and acting to forestall it is entirely appropriate.

Critiques of Analytical Marxism

Analytical Marxism has received surprisingly many critiques, which may be backhanded testimony to its intellectual significance. Most of the critiques are written by other Marxists (e.g., Kieve 1986; Lebowitz 1988; Ruccio 1988; Weldes 1989; Wood 1989, 1990; Amariglio, Callari, and Cullenberg 1989; Devine and Dymski 1991, 1992), but some, such as David Gordon's (1990) libertarian critique of Analytical Marxism, come from outside the Marxist tradition.

As the reader is well aware, Analytical Marxism is not a unified or even an internally consistent body of thought. Gerald Cohen defends functional explanation, whereas Jon Elster vehemently attacks it. John Roemer advocates methodological individualism, but Erik Wright thinks it would hobble social scientific explanation. Cohen, Roemer, and Wright believe there is a general tendency for productive forces to develop over time, but Robert Brenner denies the existence of general historical laws and claims that development tendencies emerge from the specific class relations within a particular society. In view of this diversity, it is hardly surprising that critics usually address some but not all of the Analytical Marxists. Among the Marxist critics, John Roemer is the Analytical Marxist most frequently targeted for criticism. Roemer's work is not more vulnerable than others, but its deductive prowess, jarring inconsistency with classical Marxism, and bold prose seem to incite critics.

A good example of the criticisms leveled against Analytical Marxism by other Marxists are the comments made by Jutta Weldes in her paper "Marxism and Methodological Individualism":

The empiricist assumptions of rational choice Marxism violate the "hard-core" of the Marxist research tradition in at least three important ways: 1) most generally, its atomistic ontology directly contradicts the *relational* ontology of Marxist theory; 2) the empiricist conception of science undermines the Marxist conception of social science as *critique*; and 3) more specifically, rational choice and game theory mark a retreat from the social and relational philosophical anthropology of Marx back to the liberal individualist tradition initiated by Hobbes. [author's italics] (Weldes 1989, p. 372)

Weldes elaborates the consequences of these "violations" of Marxist research tradition for the development of Marxist theory and political practice:

The adoption of a competing ontological stance . . . results not in the reinvigoration of Marxist theory, but in its *replacement* with a competing research tradition. Rational choice Marxism thus cannot, as its practitioners would wish, be the means by which "what is true and important in Marxism [can] be more firmly established." . . . An individualist framework, by denying reality to social structures and relations and taking certain *social* institutions as natural, relegates social change to "piecemeal engineering" or incrementalism because it prestructures both the nature of the questions that can be asked about change and the answers that are possible. [author's italics] (Weldes 1989, pp. 372-73)

It is impossible to discuss all the serious criticisms that have been leveled against Analytical Marxism. I shall concentrate upon criticisms made by other Marxists because they seem most penetrating and because they include the more important non-Marxist criticisms. In the rest of this section I discuss six fundamental criticisms of Analytical Marxism: (a) atomism, (b) economic determinism, (c) disregard of history, (d) static analysis, (e) tautology, and (f) political conservatism. I state these criticisms as clearly and persuasively as I can. In the following section I give an Analytical Marxist rejoinder to each of these critiques.

Atomism

The atomist critique is directed mainly against those Analytical Marxists who practice methodological individualism, but it also pertains, if only to a lesser extent, to the entire microfoundations strategy. Analytical Marxism is said to practice atomism because it conceptualizes isolated individuals as the basic units of society. Social structures, be they families, production units, religious institutions, or states, are treated as combinations of individuals that exist only because they serve individual purposes. If an existing institution no longer satisfies individual intentions or, more exactly, is no longer an equilibrium of intentional action by individuals, then the institution will soon fade away or collapse.

The isolated individual is an abstract fiction that has neither historical reality nor conceptual justification. In many cultures humans do not even consider themselves as individuals separate from the rest of society. Even when they do, the intentions people have, the modes of feasible action, and the thought processes by which actions are evaluated depend almost entirely on the social context.

The idea of a separate rationally calculating individual is a product of capitalist culture. Using this concept to interpret all human history is tantamount to making all history the unfolding of capitalist relations or at least an extended preparation for capitalism. By the same token, taking the rationally calculating individual as the building block of society or the fundamental unit of social analysis covertly sabotages the capacity to conceive a desirable alternative to capitalism. All such conceptions are erected upon an image of human nature honed for consistency with capitalist social relations.

The theoretical primacy of the atomistic individual denies independent causal efficacy to social structures and social processes. Structures and processes are conceptualized as epiphenomena of individual action. This radically restricts the range of possible explanations for social phenomena and constitutes an unjustified a priori constraint upon the development of the social sciences. The causality exerted by social structures and social processes is less intuitively accessible than the causal force of individual intention. Hence prohibitions against theorizing such causality can be particularly difficult to throw off and can severely handicap scientific understanding of social relations.

Economic Determinism

Most Analytical Marxists think that the development of productive forces is key to explaining the main contours of human history. When put into practice, this belief amounts to economic or technological determinism. It completely overwhelms class struggle in Analytical Marxist explanations of social evolution. Analytical Marxists recognize the limitations of unilinear concepts of historical development, but their commitment to economic determinism prevents formulation of a truly multilinear or nonlinear alternative. Their interpretations of history are thus unidirectional, abstract, and dependent upon an implausible universal rationality.

When dealing with almost any subject, be it class, exploitation, or the state, Analytical Marxists frequently privilege economic considerations and treat human beings as narrow economic maximizers. Such economic determinism dovetails nicely with their emphasis on individual rationality and their fondness for abstract mathematical models. It sometimes seems dictated by methodological convenience rather than defensible beliefs about the mainsprings of social action. Without a reified interpretation of economic relations and with a more realistic interaction between economic base and social superstructure, it would be extremely difficult to take a rigorous deductive approach to theory development and prove elegant theorems after the fashion of John Roemer.

Economic determinism flies in the face of empirical evidence. Neither narrative history nor empirical research in the social sciences indicates that economic variables explain more than a small part of the things of interest to Marxists. In fact, economic determinism is one of the main reasons why neoclassical economics—which exerts a strong influence on Analytical Marxism—is so thoroughly irrelevant to the real economic life of society.

Disregard of History

Although Analytical Marxism is concerned with theories of history, its adherents show little inclination to study historical events and sometimes ride roughshod over historical evidence. The passion for generalizing characteristic of Analytical Marxism results in theories of little use to practicing historians because the concepts are excessively abstract and time scale is excessively long.

Analytical Marxists often show little interest in whether their models are consistent with historical research or empirical evidence of any kind. Real science is an empirical enterprise.

Analytical Marxism, despite its genuflections to scientific methodology, has a strongly a priori flavor. Its most impressive achievements are deductive explorations of models not derived from, not
tested by, and perhaps not amenable to testing by empirical
research.

Analytical Marxism implicitly rejects historical particularism.
The entire enterprise rests on the assumption that universally
valid principles of social relations exist and can be discovered.
This is, to say the least, a questionable assumption; yet it receives
almost no justification in the literature of Analytical Marxism. If
historical universalism is false or methodologically impractical,
then the entire approach falls on its face.

Static Analysis

Analytical Marxism has difficulty analyzing change. This difficulty is apparent in both the functional explanations favored by
Cohen and the general equilibrium models of Roemer. Cohen
finesses the issue of change by treating it from a standpoint of
Olympian remove. Change is bound to occur because the development of productive forces eventually brings them into conflict with productive relations. Questions of timing, agency, and
mobilization–the really interesting questions about revolutionary change–somehow slip through the cracks in Cohen's functional rendition of historical materialism.

Roemer is completely forthright about the problems of using
the equilibrium method:

> Like many economists of my generation, I am strongly influenced
> by the power of the equilibrium method: of examining a model
> when it is at rest . . . in the sense that all the rules that describe
> how its parts work are simultaneously fulfilled. What is disturbing
> about the equilibrium method is that it pictures the typical posi-
> tion of the system as a position the system rarely or never en-
> joys. . . . There seems to be a deep contradiction between using
> models whose main analytical trick is to postulate a position that
> is precisely at variance with the most interesting and important
> aspect of capitalist economy as described by Marxian theory–its
> incessant, contradictory motion. There is, therefore, the danger
> that . . . the equilibrium method will prevent one from seeing the
> most important aspects of the Marxian theory of capital. Knowing
> no other method, I use the equilibrium method, with the vague

thought that, when rereading these pages in twenty years, its obsolescence as a modeling tool for Marxian theory may be clear. (Roemer 1981, p. 10)

Having written this eloquent warning, however, Roemer proceeds to ignore the "deep contradiction" in his own methodology. How many readers remember that the Class Exploitation Correspondence Principle is not true of capitalism—not even a very simple form of capitalism—but only of a model depicting the system in a position it "rarely or never enjoys"? What can be learned from such a model? Why is the mathematical elegance achieved by the equilibrium method worth the disregard of reality that it requires?

By examining a system at rest, the equilibrium method leads Marxists in entirely the wrong direction. It is not a sensible way of abstracting because it negates the most essential feature of the system being studied: its incessant motion. Simplification is inevitable and can be highly informative. But surely a Marxist simplification should preserve the dynamic aspects of the system being studied. If such models are technically intractable at the current time, then Marxists should try to discover new techniques. If new techniques are not forthcoming, then we should dispense with the elegance of equilibrium modeling rather than ignoring the essence of reality.

Tautology

Several critics, but especially Ellen Wood (1989), claim that Analytical Marxism is often tautological in the sense of assuming what needs to be proved. The rigorously deductive theorizing in which Analytical Marxists take pride is only possible because the conclusions lie implicit within the assumptions. The essential circularity is apparent in the treatment of relations between individual motivations and social structures. Analytical Marxists like Elster, Roemer, and Przeworski try to explain social structures as consequences of individual motivations. These motivations were created by the structures to be explained even though they now function as assumptions within the formal theory.

The schematic simplicity of deductive theorizing as practiced by Analytical Marxists is deceptive. The seemingly simple assumptions require a whole set of unmentioned social relations to exist in the real world. For example, the existence of differential ownership of productive assets assumed in Roemer's models of class and exploitation requires elaborate economic and political infrastructure. Although this infrastructure remains in the background, its presence makes possible the differential ownership to which Roemer attributes the phenomena of class and exploitation.

Another example of assuming what needs to be proved is the historical evolution of exploitation as presented by Analytical Marxists. Never are new forms of exploitation born; they have always been present on the margins. The only creative feature of the historical process is the disappearance of old exploitations. An analogous problem occurs when explaining the emergence of capitalism from feudalism. Analytical Marxism does not explain the creation of capitalism, it simply assumes that capitalist relations existed within feudalism and even earlier.

A satisfactory account of historical dynamics must explain the transformation of a society using only elements present within it and without presupposing future social relations. Analytical Marxism consistently violates this requirement. It resorts to a deus ex machina from outside history—autonomous development of productive forces—to explain transformations of human society. One consequence of this theory is homogenizing history, which prevents Analytical Marxists from grasping the specificity of each mode of production.

Political Conservatism

Although Analytical Marxists differ in their individual political convictions, Analytical Marxism generally gives a sanitized interpretation of capitalism excluding the exercise of force and compulsion. This benign vision of capitalism emerges from the emphasis on property relations rather than production relations, and because Analytical Marxists insist on viewing the victims of necessity as optimizing decision makers. The image of opulent capitalism underlying Analytical Marxist theories derives from northern European societies rather than Africa or Latin America. All this seriously weakens the moral case against capitalism.

To be sure, Analytical Marxists do develop a moral critique of capitalism, but this critique lacks moral passion. Moreover, its separation from both the positive explanation of capitalist accumulation and practical struggles for socialism renders the moral critique politically harmless. The narrow abstract concept of capitalism favored by Analytical Marxists and the tendency to homogenize different modes of production (thereby exaggerating the similarity between capitalism and socialism) encourage reconciliation with capitalism rather than struggle against it. Assumptions about the irreducible individualism of the human species combined with abstract conundrums of rational action (e.g., the free rider problem, Arrow's social choice paradox) create a defeatist attitude toward all projects of radical change.

Defending Analytical Marxism

I now try to defend Analytical Marxism against the criticisms made above. Defending Analytical Marxism, I should emphasize, does not mean dismissing all the criticisms. Many of these are well taken and some are very telling. Defense means helping the reader see the issues from an Analytic Marxist point of view. A few of the criticisms can be dismissed, but more often I just try to soften the critical assault and indicate why it may not be fatal to Analytical Marxism.

Atomism

I can think of no Analytical Marxist who conceives people as isolated individuals or believes social institutions are formed through a compact between formerly atomized human beings. The search for microfoundations rests on the simple observation that most human action has a purpose and that theories requiring individual action without plausible individual purposes are at least incomplete.

In no society, not even the most thoroughly capitalist one, is all human action the result of rational calculation. Many actions are best understood as obedience to social norms involving little choice or calculation. It is also true, however, that rational calculation long antedates capitalism and is an important process in every human society. Metal coins have existed for at least

2,500 years, and surely the use of money indicates that rational calculation is a vital element in the life of society.

Analytical Marxists do not assume everyone acts rationally on all occasions. Yet usable models of society must be highly simplified; the question is only which simplifications to make. Analytical Marxists choose to explore models that assume that productive assets are unequally distributed and that people use their assets rationally. This simplification has not been a theoretical disaster. On the contrary, it has enabled Analytical Marxists to obtain extremely sharp theoretical results that often, though of course not always, agree with conclusions reached by other methods.

Nor do Analytical Marxists wish to deny the causal import of family, religion, class, state or other supraindividual social structures. But no matter how causally efficacious these structures may be, their continued existence depends entirely upon the actions of individual people. Why is such action forthcoming? How does institutional structure relate to the purposes of the individuals whose actions maintain that structure? To what extent do the structures lie implicit within the constellation of individual purposes and capacities? These questions fascinate Analytical Marxists.

As an example, consider the relationship between the individual and class. Rather than blandly assuming the existence of a particular class structure, Analytical Marxists would like to derive that structure as a logical consequence of elementary relations between individuals. One possibility would be to derive the class structure from the distribution of productive resources among individuals and the nature of permissible economic interactions between producers. Along these lines, John Roemer has established a necessary connection between a person's wealth and her class position. This is an impressive result, but it only partially explicates the relationship between individual and class. The questions of where the distribution of productive resources came from and why only certain forms of economic interaction are permissible remain unanswered.

Economic Determinism

Analytical Marxists, I emphasize again, take divergent views about the interplay between forces and relations of production, and about the importance of economic considerations in explaining social action. However, the preponderant tendency is to make development of productive forces critical for understanding the broad sweep of human history. This idea has excellent credentials within classical Marxism and is supported by empirical research in archaeology and economic history (Basalla 1988).

Such a position does not constitute economic or technological determinism. The primacy of productive forces is asserted only for the broadest stretch of human history and, even here, is not deemed the only causal process operative. When considering history on a scale of decades or even centuries (rather than millennia), the primacy of productive forces is not claimed. On these lesser time scales class struggle, power aggrandizement, demographic processes, nationalism, ideology, personality, or even sheer chance may have causal primacy.

Analytical Marxists often do emphasize economic motivations when building models of society. The less important reason for this emphasis is that economic concerns are, by common consent, significant causes of much social action.

The more important reason derives from the Analytical Marxist approach to developing scientific social theory. The object is to find basic principles of social action. The difficulty is that even when operative, these principles are thoroughly obscured by the enormous complexity of social life. Analytical Marxists proceed by identifying a candidate principle and incorporating it within a well-formulated model. A suitable model must be sufficiently realistic to provide insights about the thing being studied but sufficiently simple to generate clear and sharp results. The simplicity requirement encourages conceptualizing people as economic maximizers, even though this rarely describes how people act.

This methodology of theory development does not require the use of economic motivations or maximizing behavior. If alternative assumptions comparable in plausibility, simplicity, and deductive leverage can be found, then Analytical Marxists are quite prepared to use them. They are certainly not wedded to the image of persons—even persons in capitalist society—as single-minded economic maximizers. I anticipate many such innovations in the further evolution of Analytical Marxism.

The search for sharp and clear results and the use of mathematical methods to obtain them is not a personal conceit of Analytical Marxists or a capitulation to academic fashion. The point is to understand the logical consequences of basic principles. Unless the consequences are linked to the principles in the strongest possible way, they will have little credibility within a diverse and skeptical intellectual community. Unless the consequences are clear and sharp, they will not give much insight into reality being studied.

Disregard of History

Many Analytical Marxists think building a theory of history is a feasible and important project. But even a highly satisfactory theory of history would not allow predicting the future with any degree of accuracy or even specifying a reliable sequence of historical stages. Prediction and explanation are not the same. Rather than promulgating grandiose historical predictions, it is more sensible to seek general principles usable for explaining historical processes. A general principle is not necessarily a timeless principle or one relevant to all historical situations. A general principle is general only in the sense of being valid for all situations within some clearly specified domain. Analytical Marxists are committed to finding such principles, but they do not require propositions valid always and everywhere.

The neglect of history for which some critics fault Analytical Marxism results more from its newness and limited number of practitioners than from disinterest in particular historical events or devotion to a priori interpretations of history. Many Analytical Marxists do not think they can presently make useful contributions to explaining particular historical events. That would require having general principles applicable to such events. Such principles are rarely available and even more rarely securely established. Thus the main thrust of Analytical Marxism in its first 15 years has been to formulate and explore such principles. If and when they are firmly established, we can anticipate a surge of interest in explaining particular historical events.

Within all the social sciences there is some disjuncture between theory building and empirical research. Although frequently denounced, this disjuncture is hard to overcome probably because the fit between theory and empirical data is not tight in any social science. The hiatus between theory and research is as evident in Analytical Marxism as elsewhere, but surely not more so. So far, Analytical Marxism has concentrated on building theory rather than doing research. Nevertheless, important Analytical Marxists like Erik Wright and Adam Przeworski have worked hard to link the two endeavors, producing some very impressive empirical results. Nothing about Analytical Marxism discourages empirical research, and if the approach persists, much more empirical activity can be expected in the years ahead.

Static Analysis

Analytical Marxism has difficulty analyzing change because everyone has difficulty analyzing change in more than a rhetorical manner. All social theory is part of the intellectual culture of its times and is constrained by the limits of that culture. If a methodologically sound way of analyzing social change existed, then Analytical Marxists would certainly use it. No such technique currently exists, and Analytical Marxists energetically probe the limits of existing methodology in hopes of finding a defensible way of modeling change.

Given this reality, what is a sensible way of proceeding? Would it be wise to ignore functional explanation and the equilibrium method because they theorize change awkwardly or not at all? Can nothing of value to Marxism be learned by these methods or by statistical techniques such as structural equation modeling? Analytical Marxists reject this idea. Existing methodologies have their limitations, which should never be ignored, but rejecting them out of hand is an arrogant dogmatism Marxists can ill afford. Indeed, the achievements of Analytical Marxism prove that Marxists can learn a great deal from these methods. Nevertheless, the search for more suitable ways of studying change must continue undiminished.

Such methods, when they are found, will probably require modification of results previously obtained by Analytical Marxism. But they will surely not rehabilitate those tenets of classical Marxism rejected by the Analytical Marxists. They will surely not rehabilitate the labor theory of value, the falling rate of profit, the theory of capitalist breakdown, or the idea that capitalist exploitation requires wage labor.

The injunction to dispense with the elegance of equilibrium modeling rather than ignore the essence of reality is misleading because the prime purpose of the equilibrium modeling is to gain insight about that essence. To be sure, reality does entail deep and abiding change, but knowing this does not tell us how social dynamics work. To reach first base in theorizing social dynamics, we must understand how elements of a dynamic system interact. These interactions are what the equilibrium method, as used by Analytical Marxists, tries to study. It is clearly a flawed method for studying the structure of interaction, but it is far better than no method at all.

Tautology

All deductive reasoning has an element of tautology in that the conclusions lie implicit within the premises. This does not prevent deductive reasoning from being highly informative, because the conclusions are usually not obvious from the premises. A clever deductive argument is a thing of beauty and a source of delight precisely because it reveals entirely unsuspected consequences of the premises. When first encountering Roemer's Class Exploitation Correspondence Principle I was amazed, I doubted its truth, and I tried to construct a counterexample. Only after going through the proof several times was I persuaded that the principle followed from the assumptions about differential property and markets.

Roemer, Przeworski, and Elster often surprise attentive readers by deriving unsuspected propositions from seemingly innocent assumptions. Yet titillating readers is not the main reason for the use of deductive reasoning by Analytical Marxists. Deduction, it hardly needs saying, is fundamental to scientific explanation. An observation is scientifically explained if and only if it can be deduced from accepted scientific principles. Anything weaker than a deductive link between principle and observation is scientifically insufficient. Note, however, that deductive explanation does not require prediction.

Critics point out that the assumptions used in the deductions of Analytical Marxism are not generally accepted scientific principles but contentious assertions that themselves require demonstration. Differential ownership of property may imply exploitation, but the really interesting question is how and why the differential ownership came about. This is an important question, but its importance does not diminish the value of establishing a necessary connection between differential ownership and exploitation. Establishing this connection constitutes a giant leap toward explaining exploitation.

Critics also point out that the assumptions made by Analytical Marxists are hardly innocent: they contain a great deal more than meets the eye. As mentioned in the previous section, differential ownership can only occur in the context of an elaborate economic and political infrastructure. This may be so, but it does not weaken the deductive link between differential ownership and exploitation: the infrastructure is not logically necessary to explain the exploitation. And what accounts for the observed association between differential ownership and infrastructure? Is it possible that the infrastructure is itself a logical consequence of differential ownership? Even if no such logical connection exists, it is vital to recognize that a scientific principle need not explain everything to be useful and important. This is how principles function in every recognized science.

A quite different issue is whether Analytical Marxism can explain new things or must assume these things always existed. Consider the explanation of capitalism. Even if we assume that capitalist relations existed within feudalism and before, providing an explanation of why other relations of production fell by the wayside and capitalist relations became dominant constitutes major scientific progress. This way of explaining capitalism is analogous to accounting for the age of mammals within evolutionary biology. Apparently mammals existed for millions of years before they became the dominant species. How they first came into being is an interesting question, but explaining how mammals became dominant after an extended existence on the margins of the ecosystem is at least of equal importance.

Analytical Marxists do not assume capitalist relations existed prior to capitalism merely because they cannot explain the creation of the former. On the contrary, there are strong theoretical and empirical reasons for asserting the existence of capitalist relations under feudalism and before. If this were not so—if

capitalism and capitalist relations were born contemporane-
ously—then Analytical Marxists would try to formulate a theory
of how this happened. This theoretical enterprise might not be
successful, but its failure would not result from the metatheoreti-
cal commitments of Analytical Marxism.

Do Analytical Marxists like Gerald Cohen explain the transformation of society by resorting to elements external to that
society? Is the development of productive forces an autonomous
process impinging on society from outside? Or is it rather an
endogenous tendency constituted by the organization of society
itself and by the consciousness of people therein? Cohen sometimes takes the former position, but most other Analytical Marxists such as Carling (1993) and Wright (Wright et al. 1992) clearly
have the latter in mind. Why else would they acknowledge
radical variations in the rate at which productive forces grow
and even significant productive retrogressions?

Part of the development of productive forces is a process of
natural selection favoring more over less productive societies. If
this constitutes a force outside of history, then perhaps natural
selection in biology constitutes a force outside of nature.

Political Conservatism

Revolutionary ideology is on the defensive everywhere. The
great revolutions of the 20th century have been enormously
costly of human life and have spawned undemocratic, nonegalitar-
ian, and inefficient societies. When given an opportunity to choose,
the overwhelming majority of people in postrevolutionary societies
reject the revolutionary legacy. The almost inescapable conclusion
is that much better results could have been achieved by nonrevo-
lutionary methods. As might be expected, Analytical Marxists have
reacted to the often dismal outcomes of 20th-century revolution
in different ways: some have drifted away from political involve-
ment, some have become social democrats, some have reaffirmed
their commitment to socialism. None have joined in the celebration
of capitalism.

Analytical Marxists rarely emphasize force and violence in
their depictions of capitalism, but their models hardly white-
wash the capitalist system. Recall that the Analytical Marxist
approach tries to strip a subject to its bare essentials. Force and
violence are not emphasized because the processes of accumu-

lation and reproduction, in their mature capitalist forms, do not rely upon physical coercion. Analytical Marxists have, however, revealed the irreducible exploitation at the heart of capitalist society and the hollow choices available to people without property. The exclusion of force and violence does not weaken the moral case against capitalism but rather helps demonstrate that socialism is superior even to the least coercive capitalism.

Analytical Marxists are quite capable of moral passion, and what their moral critique of capitalism lacks in fervor it more than gains in accuracy and insight. As an example of both insight and ardor, recall the output expansion bias of advanced capitalism described by Cohen:

> *Capitalism inherently tends to promote just one of the options, output expansion, since the other, toil reduction, threatens a sacrifice of the profit associated with increased output and sales, and hence a loss of competitive strength.* . . . The boundless pursuit of consumption goods is a result of a productive process oriented to exchange-values rather than consumption-values. . . . The economic form most able to relieve toil is least disposed to do so. . . . As scarcity recedes the same bias renders the system reactionary. It cannot realize the possibilities of liberation it creates. It excludes liberation by febrile product innovation, huge investments in sales and advertising, contrived obsolescence. It brings society to the threshold of abundance and locks the door. For the promise of abundance is not an endless flow of goods but a sufficiency produced with a minimum of unpleasant exertion. The dynamic of advanced capitalism is, arguably, hostile to the prospect of balanced human existence. [author's italics] (Cohen 1978, pp. 304-07)

In subsequent work Cohen shows why the capitalist working class is collectively unfree even if workers, considered as individuals, are not strictly compelled to sell their labor power.

Like everyone else who contemplates human affairs, Analytical Marxists are subject to passionate feelings, yet they do not recognize passion as a desirable characteristic of moral critique. After all, passion can prevent careful reflection about alternatives and motivate imbalanced and impulsive judgments. Analytical Marxism bears no responsibility for the current weakness of social movements against capitalism, but when these movements do finally revive, they will find the moral critique of capitalism developed by Analytical Marxists judicious, penetrating, and politically useful.

The political and moral crises experienced by postrevolutionary societies have been a major motivation for the development of Analytical Marxism. Several prominent Analytical Marxists have repeatedly reaffirmed their commitment to socialism. As is evident from the discussion in Chapter 9, they are currently reconstructing socialist theory to eliminate the wishful thinking and conceptual errors that egregiously misled the first serious efforts to build socialist societies. The persistence and ingenuity of these theoretical initiatives hardly suggest a defeatist attitude toward all projects of radical change.

Future Directions

Analytical Marxists believe that reliable knowledge about the dynamics of human history is possible. This belief distinguishes them from most contemporary social thinkers, Marxist or non-Marxist. It explains their continuing enthusiasm for logical rigor and scientific methodology in a period of profound skepticism about the value of scientific approaches to human affairs.

Any strategy for gaining reliable knowledge about the dynamics of human history is bound to have serious flaws, and the critics of Analytical Marxism have identified some nontrivial shortcomings. Practitioners of Analytical Marxism recognize these shortcomings, but they also recognize and admire the results their strategy for gaining knowledge has made possible. Herein lies an essential difference between supporters and detractors of Analytical Marxism, at least among people attracted to Marxist thought in the first place. Supporters cherish the achievements of the Analytical Marxist strategy and endure the deficiencies to sustain these accomplishments. Detractors find the achievements less impressive and therefore are not inclined to tolerate the deficiencies. Divisions of this sort arise repeatedly in the intellectual, political, and intimate personal affairs of the human species.

Marxist social theory of any form bears a special burden: it is deeply torn between the desire to understand and the desire to transform the world. Sometimes these desires reinforce each other, but sometimes they are at odds. Non-Marxist thinkers also experience this conflict, but perhaps not as intensely because Marxism attracts people who sense the world desperately requires changing.

Marxist thought flourishes on the possibility of social change. If the next century is a time of sustained social stability, all forms of Marxism will probably seem irrelevant and wither away. If stability does not prevail, then Marxist ideas or recognizable successors will surely influence the social thought of our descendants. The fate of Analytical Marxism is tied up with the fate of Marxist thought as a whole. If Marxism continues as a living intellectual tradition, then Analytical Marxism or something similar will have a significant place within it. If the Marxist tradition peters out, then elements of Analytical Marxism will be absorbed within whatever remains of social science, but the general approach described in this book will lose coherence and fade away.

Most theorists automatically assume their approach has a future, and Analytical Marxists are no exception. To sustain their current theoretical vitality, Analytical Marxists must address at least some of the shortcomings identified by its critics. By way of conclusion, I briefly outline six challenges currently facing Analytical Marxism.

First and foremost, Analytical Marxism must become a more dynamic way of understanding society. Functional explanation and the equilibrium method have their uses, but the raison d'être of Marxist theory is explaining social change. Any version of Marxism unable to account for social dynamics cannot expect to flourish.

Many social scientists, both Marxist and non-Marxist, have expressed an increased concern with social dynamics. Moreover, there are technical developments that can facilitate improved comprehension of social dynamics. Differential equations have long been the most important means of modeling dynamics in the physical sciences. Increased understanding of nonlinear differential equations and development of a qualitative theory of differential equations have helped create a general theory of dynamical systems, which has already had important applications in the biological sciences and may be useful in modeling dynamic processes of interest to Marxists (Hirsch and Smale

1974; Perko 1991; Abraham and Shaw 1992). Coupled with this is the theory of chaos, elaborated over the last two decades, which provides insights about and techniques for analyzing complex forms of evolution like those observed in social systems (Thom 1975; Hale and Koçak 1991; Ott 1993).

Differential game theory—combining game theory and dynamical systems theory—offers some promise as a means by which Analytical Marxists can study dynamic interactions while maintaining their characteristic focus on logical rigor and rational choice (Başar and Olsder 1982; Mehlmann 1988). The challenge of becoming dynamic, however, is not mainly a technical problem. It requires more clarity about how society is changing and more substantive insight about why these changes happen.

One of the strengths of classical Marxism was its ability to address particular historical situations: wars, revolutions, booms and busts, changes of government, and so forth. Analytical Marxists show little inclination to engage with these issues. Particular historical events seem outside the purview of pure science, and the abstract concepts created by Analytical Marxism rarely clarify specific situations. Although reluctance to address political affairs is understandable—and infinitely preferable to pontificating about everything under the sun—Olympian detachment from current history is unlikely to facilitate intellectual progress. On the contrary, detachment leads to excessive abstraction and the narcissistic scholasticism to which academic scholarship is so vulnerable. I do not say that Analytical Marxism should abandon its general theoretical pursuits in favor of political commentary. The point is to create theories that illuminate specific historical events and to engage in discussions about present history, not least because interaction between abstract conception and concrete occurrence often provokes scientifically valuable ideas.

A related issue is the conduct of empirical research. Although a few Analytical Marxists engage actively in empirical research, the group as a whole leans heavily toward pure theory. The resulting imbalance between thought and observation is not conducive to sustained intellectual progress. Exclusive reliance upon empirical research conducted by others is not satisfactory; a coherent scientific school must design its own research projects adapted toward its own theoretical concepts. Among other things, endogenous empirical research establishes common points of reference that help unify a collection of intellectually volatile and disputatious theorists. Analytical Marxism needs many more research endeavors like Erik Wright's Comparative Project on Class Structure and Class Consciousness.

Analytical Marxism may not practice economic determinism, but it has focused upon economic issues and relied extensively upon the explanatory power of economic motivations. This economic emphasis must recede. Even if productive forces have causal primacy—and many Analytical Marxists reject this proposition—they certainly do not constitute the whole of human society. The economic preoccupation of Analytical Marxism restricts its appeal and sometimes obscures its differences from neoclassical economic theory. Analytical Marxism can make headway with problems of race, gender, politics, culture, and much more, but doing so requires cultivating a broader concept of social determination.

Little has been written by Analytical Marxists about the poor countries of the capitalist world, yet these countries contain most of humanity. An acceptable theory of capitalist development cannot focus exclusively upon advanced capitalism; it must also explain how exploitation and accumulation operate within peripheral capitalism. This poses a major theoretical challenge to Analytical Marxists. To vindicate their approach and deflate charges of Eurocentrism, they must show how their ideas can be successfully applied to the social formations of underdeveloped capitalism.

Marxist theory became important because many people thought capitalism was haunted by a specter and would soon be swept into the ash can of history. This prognosis seems less compelling today than it did in the halcyon days of the 1848 revolutions. Perhaps it is not capitalism but the specter haunting it that has fallen into the ash can of history. Ash cans and specters notwithstanding, the future of capitalism is anything but assured. No task has greater theoretical importance for Marxists than demonstrating that feasible alternatives to capitalism do exist. Analytical Marxists understand the stakes involved, and have already made impressive progress on this task. But the work on conceiving a feasible socialism is only beginning and must be sustained for many years to come. Both fortitude and imagination are of the essence.

If Analytical Marxism can meet these six challenges—if it can become more dynamic, explain specific historical events, expand endogenous empirical research, transcend economic motivations, theorize peripheral capitalism, and model feasible socialism—it will remain an important part of social science for many years to come.

GLOSSARY

accumulation

The use of economic surplus to increase the productive capacity of society.

advanced capitalism

A capitalist system that is at the monopoly capitalist stage of development or beyond.

Analytical Marxism

A branch of Marxist thought emphasizing careful analytical reasoning, including axiomatic logic, mathematical models, and statistical inference. Analytical Marxists view Marxist social analysis as a branch of social science and think Marxist scholars should use any legitimate scientific method rather than seeking a uniquely Marxist methodology. They are critical of many classical Marxist concepts, including the labor theory of value and the falling rate of profit, and often use analytical philosophy, game theory, rational choice analysis, and/or general equilibrium theory to elaborate Marxist ideas. The unity of Analytical Marxism exists on a methodological plane and does not extend to matters of substantive theory or politics.

analytical philosophy

A school of philosophical thought claiming that the proper task of philosophy is not extending knowledge but removing conceptual confusion and misunderstanding. Such clarification is to be accomplished by methods like choosing simple and parsimonious premises, adopting appropriate terminology, and using logically precise reasoning.

base

The economic structure of society. The term *base* is often used in contrast to superstructure (which refers to the noneconomic institutions of society).

basic income proposal

A strategy for approaching communism suggested by van der Veen and Van Parijs. The basic income proposal is to make an unconditional income grant to each adult in capitalist society, and to gradually expand this grant until it provides most of the income a person needs.

blocking coalition

A concept from the theory of cooperative games, defined with respect to a proposed allocation of rewards within a cooperative game. A blocking coalition is a coalition that can prevent the implementation of the proposed allocation.

business cycle

The cycle of fluctuations in levels of capitalist economic activity. It moves from periods of depression to periods of boom and back.

capital

Exchange value being used for the purpose of increasing exchange value. Different kinds of capital correspond to the different kinds of exchange value being used for purposes of self-expansion. Thus *merchant capital* indicates commercial facilities being used to generate exchange value, and *industrial capital* means industrial capacity being used to earn a profit.

capitalism

A form of economic organization in which all forms of wealth tend to be converted into capital (value used for the purpose of increasing value). A mature capitalist system is characterized by extensive wage labor and by a sharp distinction between people who own capital and people who perform wage labor.

capitalist class abdication theory

A theory of state autonomy in a capitalist society asserting that the capitalist class has the capacity to control the state but finds it advantageous not to do so.

capitalist exploitation

The kind of exploitation that occurs in capitalist society. Analytical Marxists believe it happens due to the unequal distribution of capitalist property. More specifically, capitalist exploitation reflects the unequal distribution of alienable means of production like land, machines, and patents.

Chicken

A simple game named after the suicidal teenage driving contest of the 1950s. The Chicken game models a contest of wills spurred by the desire to dominate but ending in disaster if neither party submits.

civil society

The private or nonstate realm of society, including the economy. The contrast between state and civil society is often emphasized.

class

A group of people who or a set of positions that all relate to the economic structure of society in the same way. Classes are defined in relation to each other rather than as gradations of some attribute like income. Classes are intrinsically antagonistic to each other because they have opposing interests. Analytic Marxists do not assume that relations of exploitation exist between different classes but derive this result through rigorous class analysis.

class analysis

Systematic examination of the causes, transformations, and consequences of class structure.

class balance theory

A theory attributing state autonomy under capitalism to class equilibrium within civil society.

class consciousness

Awareness by incumbents of class positions of the antagonistic relationship between their own class and others.

Class Exploitation Correspondence Principle

A mathematical theorem proved by Roemer concerning the relationship between class and exploitation in capitalist economies.

The theorem says that people whose optimal economic strategy requires them to hire labor will be exploiters, and that people whose optimal strategy requires them to sell labor will be exploited. This important result converts the relationship between class and exploitation from an axiom of Marxist theory to a logical consequence of more elementary premises.

class formation

The extent to which organized collectivities established on the basis of the material interests defined by class structure exist. Class formation measures the corporate coherence of a class and its capacity to be an active participant in society.

classical Marxism

Marxist thought that adheres closely to the ideas of Marx and Engels.

class structure

A set of class positions that exist independently of the specific people who occupy them but that determine the class interests of the occupants.

class struggle

The process by which formed and conscious classes transform the class structure of society.

class weakness theory

A theory asserting that the state is autonomous in a capitalist society only if the capitalist class lacks sufficient strength to govern.

commodity

An object or service produced for the purpose of being exchanged rather than for the purpose of being used by the producer.

communism

An economic system characterized by complete abolition of social classes. Under communism, income is distributed according to need, no permanent division of labor exists, and all coercive aspects of the state are eliminated.

Communism

A form of society that evolved from the Bolshevik Revolution especially after Stalin's ascension to power. Communism features a dictatorial state run by a hierarchically organized political party. It entails a centrally administered economy that claims to be building socialism. Communist social policy does not accept any important distinction between the state and civil society.

comparative exploitation model

A model of exploitation proposed by Roemer that measures exploitation by comparing the income distribution occurring under existing property relations with the distribution expected if a certain form of property were abolished. The comparative exploitation model is contrasted with the labor exploitation model.

cone technology

A model of production differing from a Leontief technology because it allows several different ways of making a good and several different outputs from a single production process.

contradictory class location

A concept developed by Wright indicating a class position simultaneously located in more than one class. Examples of contradictory class locations are managers, simultaneously located in the capitalist class and the working class, and small employers, simultaneously located in the capitalist class and the petty bourgeoisie.

convex game

A cooperative game defined by the idea that every coalition is more powerful than the sum of its parts. More exactly, every coalition in a convex game can get rewards greater than the sum of the rewards available to its subgroups acting independently.

cooperative game

A game permitting players to form coalitions within which they coordinate game-playing strategies. Noncooperative games do not allow coalition formation.

core

A concept from the theory of cooperative games used extensively in mathematical economics. An allocation of rewards is said to be in the core of a cooperative game if no coalition of players can improve upon the rewards received by the members of the coalition.

credit market

A credit is a loan to be used for purchasing something. A credit market is a market for loans where lenders and borrowers interact to determine the amounts of loans and the conditions under which they will be made.

culpable person

A concept from the game theoretic analysis of exploitation. A person is culpable if she belongs to a minimal exploiting coalition. A culpable person is contrasted with a vulnerable person.

Development Thesis

A hypothesis in Cohen's interpretation of historical materialism stating that productive forces tend to develop throughout history.

dialectics

A complex and elusive concept designating both a process of reasoning about change and the dynamic forces underlying change. Marx adopted the concept of dialectics from Hegel, and the relation between the Marxist and Hegelian ideas about dialectics is a matter of much dispute. Various interpretations of Marxist dialectical reasoning exist, but none commands general agreement. Analytical Marxists tend to be skeptical about the validity of dialectical reasoning.

differential game

A game played continuously in time and involving attempts by two or more players to control a system of variables. The rules to which the variables are subject are expressed as differential equations. Lancaster's dynamic conflict between workers and owners of capital is an example of a differential game.

economic oppression

A form of subjugation distinct from exploitation. Economic oppression results from property inequality but does not require a continuing relationship between the rich oppressor and the poor oppressed. Hence rational self-interest does not moderate the actions of the oppressors towards the oppressed.

economic structure

The distribution of effective ownership rights over producers and productive forces. The economic structure of society is often identified with its relations of production.

economic surplus

The amount by which the economic product of society exceeds the inputs required to create that product. Economic surplus might also be characterized as the difference between the value of the economic product and the cost of producing it.

emancipation

The removal of obstacles that prevent the full development of human capacity.

equal division core

The core of a socialist withdrawal game, so named because the only allocation it contains is an equal division of rewards.

equilibrium

A state of a real or theoretical system in which all the rules describing how the parts work are simultaneously fulfilled. When a system is in equilibrium, the variables characterizing its state show no tendency to change.

exchange value

A concept of classical Marxism indicating a social relationship between things and people. The exchange value of an object is its market value, the amount for which it can be exchanged. *Exchange value* is often contrasted with *use value*.

exploitation

An asymmetrical relationship in which one group of people (the exploiters) gains advantages from the activities of another group (the exploited) while this second group is somehow harmed, weakened, or deprived by the relationship. Classical Marxism understood exploitation as the appropriation by one class (the exploiting class) of the surplus labor of another class (the exploited class). Analytical Marxism conceives exploitation as differential income resulting from differential ownership of productive assets. With this conception, different types of exploitation correspond to the different types of productive assets on which exploitation can be based.

exploitation dependence

A condition sometimes said to be necessary for the occurrence of exploitation. The condition requires that exploiters suffer if the people they exploit disappear from the scene, taking the things they own with them.

exploited coalition

A coalition of people within an economic system for whom (a) there is a feasible alternative system under which all members of the coalition are better off, (b) people not in the exploited coalition are worse off under the alternative than under the existing system, and (c) coalition members are currently dominated by people not in the coalition.

exploiting coalition

The complement of an exploited coalition.

false consciousness

Awareness by incumbents of class positions that denies the existence of class divisions or denies the antagonistic relationship between their own class and others.

fetishism

The tendency to invest something with powers it does not have on its own. Marxists often talk about commodity fetishism, which refers to the illusion that commodities (i.e., things produced to be exchanged) autonomously have exchange value. Capital fetishism refers to the illusion that capital is intrinsically productive (i.e., that it is productive even apart from the productive activities of human beings).

feudal exploitation

The kind of exploitation that occurs in a feudal society. Analytical Marxists believe feudal exploitation results from the unequal distribution of feudal property. More specifically, it happens because property rights over labor power are unequally distributed. For example, lords in a feudal society possess part of the labor power of their serfs, whereas the serfs do not even possess all of their personal labor power.

fiscal crisis

A capitalist economic crisis that happens when taxation takes so much capitalist profit that the incentive to accumulate collapses.

free rider problem

A theoretical problem about why individuals participate in risky actions intended to achieve a collective good. The rational strategy in such situations would seem to be "free riding" on the collective: obtaining the benefits of the collective action (if it is successful) without enduring the risk of participating in it. Extensive free riding sabotages the possibility of collective action.

functional explanation

A method of social scientific explanation that tries to explain the existence of a social pattern through its effects on some other element of society. The legitimacy of functional explanation is hotly disputed among Analytical Marxists.

functionalism

The doctrine that all elements of social life are interconnected and reinforce one another, and that each element exists because of its contribution to the whole. Functionalism as a general theory of society is different than functional explanation as a special way of explaining particular social patterns.

Fundamental Marxian Theorem

A mathematical theorem asserting that the profit rate in a capitalist economy cannot be positive unless exploitation exists and vice versa. This theorem is due to Morishima, Okishio, and Seton.

game theory

A mathematical theory that studies the properties of rational interaction between agents, each of whom acts in her own interests. Game theory tries to determine what strategies rational agents (i.e., players) should use and what the logical outcome of the interaction (i.e., the game) will be. Many types of games have been studied including zero-sum and nonzero-sum games, cooperative and noncooperative games, static and dynamic games, and games with complete and incomplete information.

general equilibrium theory

An economic theory that derives an equilibrium price structure for an economy as a whole by analyzing the relations between economic agents who buy and sell goods and services to each other. General equilibrium theory should be contrasted with partial equilibrium theory, which seeks a price equilibrium only in one sector of the economy. Marxists have traditionally regarded general equilibrium theory to be inherently incompatible with Marxist economists. Some Analytical Marxists, however, have used it as a means of improving and extending Marxist economic theory.

Hegelian logic

A complex and obscure reasoning process involving the use of dialectics. Hegelian logic is intended as a way of thinking about change and as an alternative to static Aristotelian logic. It often entails a process through which a subject (e.g., individual, class, nation) achieves self-consciousness.

historical materialism

The theory of history advocated by Marx and Engels. It seeks the ultimate cause of historical events in the economic development of society. Economic structures rise and fall as they support or retard the development of productive forces. Legal and political institutions are decisively shaped by the economic structure of society.

ideology

An organized set of beliefs, values, and symbols associated with a particular class location. An ideology distorts reality in ways that can be understood by considering the class location with which it is associated.

imperialism

A form of domination enabling one nation to extract wealth from another.

labor exploitation model

A model of exploitation proposed by Roemer generalizing the idea that exploiters appropriate the surplus value of the people they exploit. According to this model, a person is exploited if she gives more labor to society than she receives in return. Conversely, she is an exploiter if she receives more labor from society than she gives to it. The labor exploitation model is contrasted with the comparative exploitation model.

labor market

The interaction between buyers and sellers of labor power that determines the amounts, the kinds, and the prices of the labor power sold.

labor power

The capacity to labor, as distinct from the exercise of labor itself. Classical Marxists believed the distinction between labor and labor power to be very important because it explained the creation of surplus value. Analytical Marxists consider this distinction much less important.

labor theory of value

The hypothesis that commodities will exchange at equilibrium prices proportional to the quantities of labor socially necessary for their production. Analytical Marxists are very critical of the labor theory of value.

Leontief technology

A simple model of economic production named after the Nobel-prizewinning economist Wassily Leontief. A Leontief technology posits a linear relationship between production inputs and production outputs and no fixed capital.

liberated utility function

The utility function characterizing a person who dislikes working but values the products of human labor in proportion to the amount of labor embodied in them.

marginalist economic theory

A version of mainstream economic analysis that proceeds by considering the effects of adding or subtracting one unit from some economic variable. Marginalist economic theory is an important component of neoclassical economics and was the main object of Piero Sraffa's famous critique.

market socialism

A socialist economic system that makes substantial use of market processes for purposes like setting prices, establishing wage levels, deciding the composition of output, and determining investment levels.

materialism

The doctrine that whatever exists is or depends upon matter. It is necessary to distinguish philosophical materialism from historical materialism. Philosophical materialism claims that matter exists independent of thought. Historical materialism asserts the causal primacy of productive forces in the determination of social relations.

material properties

A term used by Cohen to indicate elements of the interaction with nature that confront humanity as given: the exogenous constraints to which society must adjust. *Material properties* are often contrasted with *social properties.*

methodological individualism

A principle concerning the nature of satisfactory explanation of social phenomena. According to methodological individualism, an acceptable explanation must derive a social phenomenon entirely from the properties of the individual people involved. This principle is controversial among both Analytical Marxists and other social scientists.

microfoundations

A characteristic of some social scientific explanations. An explanation is said to have microfoundations if it gives a plausible account of why each individual person acts as she does. Some philosophers regard microfoundations as a necessary characteristic of satisfactory social scientific explanations. The microfoundation approach is similar to but not identical with methodological individualism. Functional explanations are often criticized because they lack microfoundations.

middle class

A set of class locations in capitalist society lying between the working class and the capitalist class. Wright identifies two kinds of middle-class locations: (1) class locations that are neither exploiting or exploited (such as self-employed producers) belong to the old middle class, (2) class locations that are exploiting on one dimension but exploited on another (such as highly skilled wage earners) belong to the new middle class.

minimal exploited coalition

A concept used in the game theoretic analysis of exploitation. A minimal exploited coalition is an exploited coalition that is no longer exploited if it loses any single member.

minimal exploiting coalition

A concept used in the game theoretic analysis of exploitation. A minimal exploiting coalition is an exploiting coalition that is no longer exploiting if it loses any single member.

monopoly capitalism

A stage of capitalist development characterized by the existence of large corporations and the reduction of price competition in many lines of production. Typically a small number of large corporations dominate production in important industries and are able to establish monopoly prices, that is, prices that maximize their profits.

Nash equilibrium

The fundamental equilibrium concept used in game theory. A Nash equilibrium is a set of strategies for players in a game such that each player's strategy is an optimal response to the strategies of the other players. Every finite game has at least one Nash equilibrium.

neoclassical economics

The dominant school of modern economic thought. It emphasizes the optimal allocation of scarce economic resources to given wants and is often associated with marginalist economic analysis. Neoclassical economics can be contrasted with classical economics, which stressed the sources of wealth and the distribution of income between the various classes of society.

nomenklatura capitalism

A disparaging name for the kind of capitalism emerging in former Communist countries.

organizational exploitation

Exploitation based upon unequal control of organizational assets. *Organizational exploitation* is Wright's reformulation of Roemer's *status exploitation.*

Pareto optimal

A concept named after the Italian economist Vilfredo Pareto and referring to the welfare of a group of people. An outcome is Pareto optimal if no other possible outcome is unambiguously better for all members of the group.

participatory economics

A democratic form of socialism suggested by Albert and Hahnel. Participatory economics is based upon democratic organization of work and highly decentralized economic planning.

periodization

The division of history into distinct periods. Analytical Marxists periodize history in different ways.

petty bourgeoisie

A class location found in simple commodity production whose incumbents neither buy nor sell labor power and own the means of production they use. Small independent farmers are an example of the petty bourgeoisie.

postliberal democracy

An interpretation of democracy proposed by Bowles and Gintis, stressing workplace democracy and community empowerment rather than expansion of the state.

Primacy Thesis

A hypothesis in Cohen's interpretation of historical materialism stating that the development of the productive forces explains the nature of the productive relations.

Prisoner's Dilemma

A simple game that poses a sharp dilemma between selfish and cooperative behavior. The Prisoner's Dilemma interaction has been studied extensively by game theorists. The story on which the interaction is based involves separate interrogation of two prisoners, each of whom is tempted to squeal on the other.

private ownership core

The core of the withdrawal game for the SE2 subsistence economy. Allocations of rewards contained in the private ownership core are such that no viable coalition must work more than is socially necessary.

productive force

An instrument, raw material, human capacity (e.g., strength, skill, knowledge), or anything else that can be used for purposes of economic production.

productive relations

Relations of power over productive forces and over people who control productive forces.

profit squeeze crisis

A capitalist economic crisis that occurs because workers consume so much of the economic product that capitalists have insufficient incentive to accumulate.

proletarianization

An increase in the relative number of working-class positions within a capitalist society. *Deproletarianization* is just the reverse of proletarianization.

proletariat

A term used for the working class in a capitalist society or some fragment of this class. Most commonly, the proletariat is the set of class positions in a capitalist society (and/or the incumbents of these positions) owning no productive assets other than their own labor power and hence compelled to sell their labor power to earn a living. In Wright's class taxonomy, the proletariat consists of those class locations that own no means of production, have no organizational assets, and have no skill/credential assets.

rational choice theory

A theory of individual choice that assumes people are rational actors, and hypothesizes that the choices they make will optimize the outcomes important to them. Game theory is a kind of rational choice theory.

rationality

The ability to select means suitable for the ends one seeks.

realization crisis

A capitalist economic crisis that happens when the volume of production exceeds existing demand and inventories of unsold goods accumulate.

relations of production

The way effective ownership rights over producers and productive forces are distributed. Relations of production are often identified with the economic structure of society.

reproducible solution

A concept of price equilibrium introduced by Roemer. A reproducible solution is a set of market prices that (a) enables each person in the economy to survive, (b) enables society to reproduce its production stocks, (c) requires no more production inputs than society has available, and (d) balances labor power bought and sold.

reswitching

A paradox in the concept of capital first discussed by Sraffa. *Reswitching* refers to strange shifts in the value of capital that can arise when capital consists of a heterogeneous assortment of goods.

revolution

A rapid change from one economic structure to another.

SE1

A subsistence economy modeled by Roemer. It is described as simple commodity production with *communal ownership* of production inputs.

SE2

A subsistence economy modeled by Roemer. It is described as simple commodity production with *private ownership* of production inputs.

SE3

A subsistence economy modeled by Roemer. It is described as commodity production with *private ownership* of stocks and a *labor market*.

skills/credential exploitation

Exploitation based upon unequal distribution of skills and credentials. Skills/credential exploitation is Wright's reformulation of Roemer's socialist exploitation.

social democracy

A political movement that tries to move towards socialism by gradual reform of capitalist society. Social democracy eschews revolution. Instead it uses legal political means to extend bourgeois democracy from the political to the social and economic sphere. Hence the name *social democracy.*

socialism

A form of society characterized by the abolition of capitalist property and domination by the direct producers. Under socialism, income is no longer derived from the ownership of property but is allocated according to the amount and quality of work done. Socialism is sometimes understood to be a transitional phase leading towards a completely classless society.

socialist exploitation

The kind of exploitation that exists in a socialist society. Analytical Marxists think socialist exploitation happens due to the unequal distribution of the kinds of productive property permitted in a socialist society. Specifically, socialist exploitation reflects the unequal distribution of productive skills between people.

socially necessary labor time

The amount of labor time required to produce a commodity and to reproduce the inputs used in producing it—in other words, the amount of labor time required to produce the commodity as a *net* product. Socially necessary labor time is the amount of labor time embodied in a commodity.

social properties

A term used by Cohen to designate rights and powers that some people have with respect to others. *Social properties* are often contrasted with *material properties.*

social relations definition of embodied labor

A definition of the labor embodied in a good used by Roemer. This definition makes the Class Exploitation Correspondence Principle true for a cone technology. It defines the labor embodied in a good as the minimum amount of direct labor needed to produce the good as a net product, *considering only maximum profit production processes.*

SSE

Socialist subsistence economy. A variation of subsistence economy SE1 used by Roemer to study socialist exploitation.

Stackelberg equilibrium

An equilibrium concept for a game in which one player moves first. A Stackelberg equilibrium for a two-person game is an optimal pair of strategies given that one player chooses her strategy first, while the second player selects her strategy with full knowledge of what strategy the first player has chosen.

state

The institution whose incumbents are authorized to make and enforce law and to exercise whatever collective violence is considered proper in that society.

state autonomy

A situation that exists if state policy is determined by forces internal to the state.

state socialism

A form of society characterized by abolition of capitalist property relations and domination by the state. The state bureaucracy determines the nature of economic production and distribution plus many aspects of social and political life. Because the direct producers do not dominate a state socialist society, it cannot be considered a real form of socialism.

status exploitation

Economic inequality based upon possession of organizational or bureaucratic position. Wright calls this *organizational exploitation.*

strategic conception of the state

A conception that tries to avoid the twin dangers of determinism and voluntarism by interpreting the state as an institutional terrain upon which strategic political interactions take place.

strongly neutral person

A concept from the game theoretic analysis of exploitation. A player in a withdrawal game is strongly neutral if she is neither vulnerable nor culpable, that is if she does not belong to any minimal exploited or minimal exploiting coalitions.

structural dependence

The hypothesis that any government in a capitalist society must respect the interests of the capitalist class because this class can throw the economy into crisis by curtailing investment.

subsistence economy

An economy that produces only enough for the people who work to reproduce themselves and nothing more. A subsistence economy produces no surplus and does not accumulate.

superstructure

The noneconomic institutions of society. The term *superstructure* is often used in contrast to *base* (the economic structure of society). Sometimes *superstructure* designates only those noneconomic institutions whose nature is explained by the economic structure of society.

Superstructure Thesis

A hypothesis in Cohen's interpretation of historical materialism stating that the nature of the economic structure explains the noneconomic institutions contained in the superstructure.

surplus labor

An important concept in classical Marxist theory, meaning labor over and above what is needed to reproduce the laborer plus the tools and materials used up in the process. Classical Marxism regarded appropriation of surplus labor as the source of capitalist exploitation.

surplus production

Production beyond what is needed to reproduce the laboring class; production of economic surplus.

surplus value

The value produced by surplus labor.

technology
The method by which human labor power is used to transform nature.

unequal exchange
A pattern of trade between nations by which economic surplus is systematically transferred from one country to another. Emmanuel proposed a theory of imperialism based upon unequal exchange.

use value
A concept of classical Marxism indicating a natural relationship between things and people. The use value of an object is its utility, its value in actual use. *Use value* is often contrasted with *exchange value.*

value
The abstract property of a commodity by virtue of which it can be exchanged on a market. Although value appears to be a characteristic of a physical commodity, it is really a social relationship between people emerging from the fact that social labor must be expended on the production of the commodity. The concept of value is sometimes associated with exchange value as defined by the labor theory of value.

Von Neumann technology
A model of production named after the famous mathematician and founder of game theory John von Neumann. A von Neumann technology allows fixed capital and production of several different goods with the same process. Von Neumann technology is sometimes contrasted with the simpler Leontief technology.

vulnerable person
A concept from the game theoretic analysis of exploitation. A person is vulnerable if she belongs to any minimal exploited coalition. A vulnerable person is contrasted with a culpable person.

withdrawal game
A game used by Roemer as a model for analyzing exploitation. A withdrawal game takes place in a context of economic production. Coalitions of producers can withdraw from the larger economy, taking certain resources with them, and set up production on their own. The rules governing withdrawal determine the nature of the game and the kind of exploitation being analyzed. Roemer considers feudal, capitalist, and socialist withdrawal games.

A BRIEF ANNOTATED
BIBLIOGRAPHY OF
ANALYTICAL MARXISM

The works mentioned in this annotated bibliography have been specially important to the development of Analytical Marxism. Most of them are discussed more fully in the text of this book. The reader should beware that this is not a comprehensive bibliography and that the selection is somewhat idiosyncratic.

Michael Albert and Robin Hahnel, *The Political Economy of Participatory Economics* (1991).

> Albert and Hahnel propose a form of libertarian socialism (called participatory economics) based upon public ownership, decentralized economic planning, and democratic councils of workers and consumers. Perhaps their most original and controversial idea is the use of balanced job complexes combining manual and conceptual labor. Albert and Hahnel construct a mathematical model derived from their own version of welfare economics to defend the feasibility of participatory economics. They claim it will perform better than either market or centrally planned economies.

Alan Carling, *Social Division* (1991).

> This book combines the ideas of Cohen and Roemer to study various types of social division. It uses simple but ingenious rational choice models to theorize social class divisions, gender divisions, and ethnic divisions. While appreciating the ubiquity of rational choice processes in human interaction, Carling also recognizes their limitations for achieving a satisfactory understanding of social division.

341

G. A. Cohen, *Karl Marx's Theory of History: A Defence* (1978).

One of the founding documents of Analytical Marxism. Cohen uses the methods of modern analytical philosophy to defend a traditional conception of historical materialism that treats history as the growth of human productive power. He supports the legitimacy of functional explanation, which he regards as indispensable to Marxist theory. Economic structures are explained through their contribution to the growth of productive power. The text is remarkable for the dexterity of its distinctions and the clarity of its exposition.

G. A. Cohen, *History, Labour, and Freedom: Themes from Marx* (1988).

A series of lucid essays in which Cohen revises and elaborates his technological interpretation of historical materialism. The last third of the book explains the restrictions on freedom emanating from capitalist economic structure.

Jon Elster, *Making Sense of Marx* (1985).

A sophisticated and comprehensive critique of classical Marxist social theory advocating the principle of methodological individualism and the use of rational choice explanations. Elster finds Marx guilty of teleological thinking and theoretical inconsistency. He finds serious fault with virtually every part of classical Marxist theory and advocates the use of game theory to build a more defensible kind of Marxism.

Michał Kalecki, *Selected Essays on the Dynamics of the Capitalist Economy: 1933-1970* (1971).

Important essays on the capitalist business cycle by the great Polish Marxist who independently discovered Keynesian economic theory. The essays provide numerous insights about how capitalism works and show a remarkable ability to integrate Marxist and Keynesian concepts. They make sparing but effective use of mathematical reasoning and also succeed in drawing important political inferences.

Oskar Lange, "On the Economic Theory of Socialism" (1936-1937).

A pioneering theoretical defense of the possibility of market socialism. Lange uses general equilibrium theory to formulate principles that could guide the actions of socialist planners. He is among the first to suggest that neoclassical economics can make an important contribution to Marxist theory.

Stephen A. Marglin, *Growth, Distribution, and Prices* (1984).

A comparison of the neoclassical, neo-Keynesian, and neo-Marxian approaches to analyzing income distribution and economic growth under capitalism. Marglin formulates a simple but indeterminate production model he regards as the common core of all three approaches. He examines the contrasting ways in which these three approaches complete the indeterminate production model. The final chapters present a mathematical synthesis of Marxist and Keynesian ideas on growth and distribution.

David Miller, *Market, State and Community: Theoretical Foundations of Market Socialism* (1989).

The author develops a political theory of democratic socialism by defending public ownership of capital against libertarians on the right, and the use of markets against state socialists on the left. He proposes a pluralistic system in which goods and services are produced for a market within a distributive framework established by the state. Miller's market socialism can be seen as a radical synthesis of libertarianism and traditional socialism.

Richard W. Miller, *Analyzing Marx: Morality, Power and History* (1984).

Miller, like Cohen, uses analytical philosophy to interpret Marx but arrives at very different conclusions. Marx is not a technological determinist; political conflicts are of central importance in his interpretation of history. Marx rejects morality as a suitable basis for political action mainly because social conflict often makes it impossible to specify any moral course of action.

Michio Morishima, *Marx's Economics: A Dual Theory of Value and Growth* (1973).

Linear algebra is used to investigate Marxist economic theory, including the labor theory of value, the theory of exploitation, the transformation problem, and extended reproduction. The mathematical equivalence of positive profit and exploitation (sometimes called the Fundamental Marxian Theorem) is established. Morishima treats Marx as a cofounder of general equilibrium theory (along with Walras) and also appreciates his invaluable contributions to dynamic economic theory. To fulfill its theoretical potential, however, Marxian economics must abandon the labor theory of value.

Adam Przeworski, *Capitalism and Social Democracy* (1985).

A bracing collection of essays exploring the historical and theoretical foundations of working-class politics under capitalism. The book is replete with challenging interpretations and memorable phrases. According to Przeworski, socialist revolution is impossible in advanced capitalist society, and social democracy is really a means of improving capitalism without transforming its basic nature. This defines the basic dilemma of working-class politics in the modern era.

Adam Przeworski, *Democracy and the Market: Political and Economic Reforms in Eastern Europe and Latin America* (1991).

A mixture of historical analysis and simple game theory is used to study the transition to democracy in Eastern Europe and Latin America. The overarching question is whether the young democracies in these regions will be stable or will give way to new dictatorships. Although geography and previous history differentiate Eastern Europe and Latin America, economic realities and social relations suggest that similar political forces may be at work in these two regions.

John E. Roemer, *Analytical Foundations of Marxian Economic Theory* (1981).

Mathematically sophisticated general equilibrium models are used to study such classical Marxist economic problems as the relation between technical change and the rate of profit, the transformation of values into prices, and the nature of capitalist economic crises. Roemer uses a microfoundations approach that derives aggregate phenomena from postulations about how individuals act. Among many interesting results is one asserting that competitively viable technical changes will cause the equilibrium rate of profit to rise.

John E. Roemer, *A General Theory of Exploitation and Class* (1982).

Perhaps the most brilliant work in the entire literature of Analytical Marxism. Roemer proposes a new interpretation of exploitation based upon differential ownership of means of production rather than what happens at the point of production. Using this concept, he investigates models of exploitation in subsistence economies, accumulating capitalist economies, and state socialist economies. The book is peppered with surprising and theoretically important results. The theoretical centerpiece is rigorous derivation of the Class Exploitation Correspondence Principle, specifying a precise relationship between class position and exploitation status.

John E. Roemer, *Free to Lose: An Introduction to Marxist Economic Philosophy* (1988).

A largely successful effort by Roemer to present his analysis of exploitation and class in nontechnical language. The book contains many illuminating theoretical examples plus careful discussions of historical materialism and the political consequences of public ownership.

G. E. M. de Sainte Croix, *The Class Struggle in the Ancient Greek World: From the Archaic Age to the Arab Conquests* (1981).

The historical work closest in spirit to Analytical Marxism. This erudite book starts with a discerning discussion of Marxist concepts of class and exploitation. The ancient Greek world is analyzed as a social formation founded upon slavery, and the class struggles emanating from the slave-master relationship are used to explain its distinctive patterns of evolution. The author provides a penetrating explanation of why the Roman Empire collapsed.

Piero Sraffa, *Production of Commodities by Means of Commodities: Prelude to a Critique of Economic Theory* (1960).

A pathbreaking critique of marginalist economic theory. This brief book (which makes its arguments using only simple linear models of production) shows that theoretical barriers exist to measuring the quantity of capital, and also establishes that the most profitable method of production can switch in ways quite inconsistent with marginalist theory.

Ian Steedman, *Marx After Sraffa* (1977).

The concepts and methods developed by Piero Sraffa are used to critique Marxist economic theory. The result is a sweeping indictment of classical Marxist value theory, which is said to obstruct development of a coherent materialist theory of capitalism.

Allen W. Wood, *Karl Marx* (1981).

A lucid attempt to reconstruct the philosophy of Karl Marx, focusing on alienation, theory of history, materialism, and the dialectical method. The Marxist concept of justice is interpreted to mean correspondence with the prevailing mode of production.

Erik Olin Wright, *Class, Crisis and the State* (1978).

> A stimulating collection of essays on unresolved problems in
> Marxist social theory published before Wright identified himself
> as an Analytical Marxist. The essays demonstrate the author's
> facility for lucid exposition, logical analysis, and conceptual inno-
> vation. Among other things, the essays illuminate Marxist con-
> cepts of determination and explicate the important notion of
> contradictory class locations.

Erik Olin Wright, *Classes* (1985).

> The mature (but not the last) exposition of Wright's ideas on social
> class. After critiquing his former views, Wright develops a general
> framework for analyzing class based upon Roemer's theory of
> exploitation. He shows how this framework clarifies a number of
> theoretical issues, including the role of class structure in historical
> transitions and the position of women in the class structure. The
> second half of the book uses the theoretical framework as a basis
> for empirical comparisons between United States and Swedish
> class structure.

REFERENCES

Abraham, David. 1986. *The Collapse of the Weimar Republic: Political Economy and Crisis,* 2nd ed. New York: Holmes & Meier.

Abraham, Ralph H., and Christopher D. Shaw. 1992. *Dynamics: The Geometry of Behavior,* 2nd ed. Redwood City, CA: Addison-Wesley.

Albert, Michael, and Robin Hahnel. 1991a. *Looking Forward: Participatory Economics for the Twenty First Century.* Boston: South End.

————. 1991b. *The Political Economy of Participatory Economics.* Princeton, NJ: Princeton University Press.

Amariglio, Jack, Antonio Callari, and Stephen Cullenberg. 1989. "Analytical Marxism: A Critical Overview." *Review of Social Economy* 47(4):415-32.

American Social History Project. 1992. *Who Built America? Working People and the Nation's Economy, Politics, Culture and Society From the Gilded Age to the Present.* New York: Pantheon.

Ashton, B., et al. 1984. "Famine in China, 1958-1961." *Population and Development Review* 10(4):613-45.

Aston, T. H., and C. H. E. Philpin, eds. 1985. *The Brenner Debate: Agrarian Class Structure and Economic Development in Pre-industrial Europe.* Cambridge, UK: Cambridge University Press.

Baran, Paul A., and Paul M. Sweezy. 1966. *Monopoly Capital: An Essay on the American Economic and Social Order.* New York: Monthly Review Press.

Bardhan, Pranab. 1991. "Risktaking, Capital Markets, and Market Socialism." Working Paper No. 91-154. Berkeley: University of California, Department of Economics.

Bardhan, Pranab, and John E. Roemer. 1992. "Market Socialism: A Case for Rejuvenation." *Journal of Economic Perspectives* 6(3):101-16.

Bardhan, Pranab, and John E. Roemer, eds. 1993. *Market Socialism: The Current Debate.* New York: Oxford University Press.

Basalla, George. 1988. *The Evolution of Technology.* Cambridge, UK: Cambridge University Press.

Başar, Tamer, and Geert Jan Olsder. 1982. *Dynamic Noncooperative Game Theory.* New York: Academic Press.

Binyan, Lin. 1992. "The Future of China." *New Left Review* 194(July/August):5-16.

347

Bowles, Samuel, and Herbert Gintis. 1986. *Democracy and Capitalism: Property, Community, and the Contradictions of Modern Thought.* New York: Basic Books.

———. 1990. "Contested Exchange: New Microfoundations for the Political Economy of Capitalism." *Politics and Society* 18(2):165-222.

Braverman, Harry. 1974. *Labor and Monopoly Capital: The Degradation of Work in the Twentieth Century.* New York: Monthly Review Press.

Brenner, Robert. 1977. "The Origins of Capitalist Development: A Critique of Neo-Smithian Marxism." *New Left Review* 104:25-92.

———. 1985a. "Agrarian Class Structure and Economic Development in Pre-industrial Europe." Pp. 10-63 in *The Brenner Debate*, edited by T. H. Aston and C. H. E. Philpin. Cambridge, UK: Cambridge University Press.

———. 1985b. "The Agrarian Roots of European Capitalism." Pp. 213-327 in *The Brenner Debate*, edited by T. H. Aston and C. H. E. Philpin. Cambridge, UK: Cambridge University Press.

———. 1986. "The Social Basis of Economic Development." Pp. 23-53 in *Analytical Marxism*, edited by John Roemer. Cambridge, UK: Cambridge University Press.

Burawoy, Michael. 1989. "The Limits of Wright's Analytical Marxism and an Alternative." Pp. 78-99 in *The Debate on Classes*, by Erik Olin Wright, U. Becker, et al. London: Verso.

Burawoy, Michael, and Pavel Krotov. 1992. "The Soviet Transition From Socialism to Capitalism: Worker Control and Economic Bargaining in the Wood Industry." *American Sociological Review* 57(1):16-38.

———. 1993. "The Economic Basis of Russia's Political Crisis." *New Left Review* 198 (March/April):49-70.

Callinicos, Alex, ed. 1989. *Marxist Theory.* Oxford, U.K: Oxford University Press.

———. 1990. "The Limits of 'Political Marxism.'" *New Left Review* 184 (November/December):110-15.

Carens, Joseph H. 1981. *Equality, Moral Incentives, and the Market: An Essay in Utopian Politico-economic Theory.* Chicago: University of Chicago Press.

Carling, Alan. 1986. "Rational Choice Marxism." *New Left Review* 160 (November/December):24-62.

———. 1990. "In Defence of Rational Choice: A Reply to Ellen Meiksins Wood." *New Left Review* 184 (November/December):97-109.

———. 1991. *Social Division.* London: Verso.

———. 1993. "Analytical Marxism and Historical Materialism: The Debate on Social Evolution." *Science and Society* 57(1):31-65.

Cohen, G. A. 1978. *Karl Marx's Theory of History: A Defence.* Princeton: Princeton University Press.

———. 1988. *History, Labour, and Freedom: Themes From Marx.* Oxford, UK: Oxford University Press.

———. 1991. "The Future of a Disillusion." *New Left Review* 190 (November/December):5-20.

Cohen, Joshua. 1982. "Review of *Karl Marx's Theory of History: A Defence* by G. A. Cohen." *Journal of Philosophy* 79:253-73.

Cohen, Joshua, and Joel Rogers. 1983. *On Democracy: Toward a Transformation of American Society.* Middlesex, UK: Penguin.

Cohen, Mark N. 1977. *The Food Crisis in Prehistory*. New Haven, CT: Yale University Press.

Cullenberg, Stephen. 1991. "The Rhetoric of Marxian Microfoundations." *Review of Radical Political Economics* 23(1 & 2):187-94.

Dallin, Alexander. 1992. "Causes of the Collapse of the USSR." *Post-Soviet Affairs* 8(4):279-302.

Dalton, George. 1974. "How Exactly Are Peasants Exploited?" *American Anthropologist* 74:553-61.

de Sainte Croix, G. E. M. 1981. *The Class Struggle in the Ancient Greek World: From the Archaic Age to the Arab Conquests*. Ithaca, NY: Cornell University Press.

Devine, James, and Gary Dymski. 1991. "Roemer's 'General' Theory of Exploitation Is a Special Case: The Limits of Walrasian Marxism." *Economics and Philosophy* 7:235-75.

———. 1992. "Walrasian Marxism Once Again: A Reply to John Roemer." *Economics and Philosophy* 8:157-62.

Domhoff, G. William. 1983. *Who Rules America Now?* Englewood Cliffs, NJ: Prentice Hall.

Ellman, Michael, and Vladimir Kontorovich. 1992. Overview. Pp. 1-39 in *The Disintegration of the Soviet Economic System,* edited by Michael Ellman and Vladimir Kontorovich. London: Routledge.

Elster, Jon. 1978. *Logic and Society*. New York: John Wiley.

———. 1982. "Marxism, Functionalism, and Game Theory: The Case for Methodological Individualism." *Theory and Society* 11:453-82.

———. 1985. *Making Sense of Marx*. Cambridge, UK: Cambridge University Press.

———. 1986. "Further Thoughts on Marxism, Functionalism and Game Theory." Pp. 202-20 in *Analytical Marxism*, edited by John Roemer. Cambridge, UK: Cambridge University Press.

———. 1988. "Marx, Revolution and Rational Choice." Pp. 206-28 in *Rationality and Revolution*, edited by Michael Taylor. Cambridge, UK: Cambridge University Press.

Elster, Jon, and Karl Ove Moene. 1989. Introduction. Pp. 1-35 in *Alternatives to Capitalism,* edited by Jon Elster and Karl Ove Moene. Cambridge, UK: Cambridge University Press.

Emmanuel, Arghiri. 1972. *Unequal Exchange: A Study of the Imperialism of Trade*. New York: Monthly Review Press.

Esping-Anderson, Gosta, and Kees van Kersbergen. 1992. "Contemporary Research on Social Democracy." Pp. 187-208 in *Annual Review of Sociology*, edited by Judith Blake and John Hagan. Palo Alto, CA: Annual Reviews Inc.

Feffer, John. 1992. *Shock Waves: Eastern Europe After the Revolutions*. Boston: South End.

Finifter, Ada W., and Ellen Mickiewicz. 1992. "Redefining the Political System of the USSR: Mass Support and Political Change." *American Political Science Review* 86(4):857-74.

Foster, John Bellamy. 1986. *The Theory of Monopoly Capitalism: An Elaboration of Marxian Political Economy*. New York: Monthly Review Press.

Fudenberg, Drew, and Jean Tirole. 1991. *Game Theory*. Cambridge: MIT Press.

Geras, Norman. 1985. "The Controversy About Marx and Justice." *New Left Review* 150 (March-April):47-85.

Gibson, Bill. 1980. "Unequal Exchange: Theoretical Issues and Empirical Findings." *Review of Radical Political Economics* 12(3):15-35.

Giddens, Anthony. 1981. *A Contemporary Critique of Historical Materialism.* Berkeley: University of California Press.

———. 1985. *The Nation State and Violence.* Berkeley: University of California Press.

Goldfield, Michael. 1987. *The Decline of Organized Labor in the United States.* Chicago: University of Chicago Press.

Goldthorpe, John H., Catriona Llewellyn, and Clive Payne. 1987. *Social Mobility and Class Structure in Modern Britain.* Oxford, UK: Clarendon.

Goldthorpe, John H., and Gordon Marshall. 1992. "The Promising Future of Class Analysis: A Response to Recent Critiques." *Sociology* 26(3):381-400.

Gordon, David. 1990. *Resurrecting Marx: The Analytical Marxists on Freedom, Exploitation, and Justice.* New Brunswick, NJ: Transaction Books.

Hahnel, Robin, and Michael Albert. 1990. *Quiet Revolution in Welfare Economics.* Princeton, NJ: Princeton University Press.

Hale, Jack K., and Hüceyin Koçak. 1991. *Dynamics and Bifurcations.* New York: Springer.

Harcourt, G. C. 1972. *Some Cambridge Controversies in the Theory of Capital.* Cambridge, UK: Cambridge University Press.

Hayek, Friedrich A. 1940. "Socialist Calculations: The Competitive 'Solution.'" *Economica* 7:125-49.

Hinton, William. 1991. "The Chinese Revolution: Was It Necessary? Was It Successful? Is It Going On?" *Monthly Review* 43(6):1-15.

Hirsch, Morris W., and Stephen Smale. 1974. *Differential Equations, Dynamical Systems, and Linear Algebra.* New York: Academic Press.

Hollis, Martin. 1987. *The Cunning of Reason.* Cambridge, UK: Cambridge University Press.

Kalecki, Michał. 1971. *Selected Essays on the Dynamics of the Capitalist Economy: 1933-1970.* Cambridge, UK: Cambridge University Press.

Kieve, Ronald A. 1986. "From Necessary Illusion to Rational Choice? A Critique of Neo-Marxist Rational Choice Theory." *Theory and Society* 15:557-82.

Kimeldorf, Howard. 1988. *Reds or Rackets? The Making of Radical and Conservative Unions on the Waterfront.* Berkeley: University of California Press.

Kornai, Jànos. 1992. *The Socialist System: The Political Economy of Communism.* Princeton, NJ: Princeton University Press.

Kotz, David. 1992. "The Direction of Soviet Economic Reform: From Socialist Reform to Capitalist Transition." *Monthly Review* 44(4):14-34.

Lancaster, Kelvin. 1973. "The Dynamic Inefficiency of Capitalism." *Journal of Political Economy* 81:1092-1109.

Lange, Oskar. 1936-1937. "On the Economic Theory of Socialism." *Review of Economic Studies* 4:53-71, 123-42.

Lange, Oskar, and Fred M. Taylor. 1938. *On the Economic Theory of Socialism.* Edited by Benjamin E. Lippincott. Minneapolis: University of Minnesota Press.

Lebowitz, Michael A. 1988. "Is 'Analytical Marxism' Marxism?" *Science and Society* 52(2):191-214.

Lenski, Gerhard E. 1966. *Power and Privilege: A Theory of Social Stratification*. New York: McGraw-Hill.

Lerner, Abba P. 1936. "A Note on Socialist Economics." *Review of Economic Studies* 4:72-76.

Levine, Andrew. 1988. *Arguing for Socialism*. London: Verso.

Levine, Andrew, Elliott Sober, and Erik Olin Wright. 1987. "Marxism and Methodological Individualism." *New Left Review* 162 (March/April):67-84.

Levine, Andrew, and Erik Olin Wright. 1980. "Rationality and Class Struggle." *New Left Review* 123 (September/October):47-68.

Luce, R. Duncan, and Howard Raiffa. 1957. *Games and Decisions: Introduction and Critical Survey*. New York: John Wiley.

Marglin, Stephen A. 1984. *Growth, Distribution, and Prices*. Cambridge, MA: Harvard University Press.

Marshall, Gordon, David Rose, Howard Newby, and Carolyn Vogler. 1988. *Social Class in Modern Britain*. London: Hutchinson Education.

Marx, Karl. [1859] 1987. "A Contribution to the Critique of Political Economy." Pp. 257-417 in *Karl Marx, Frederick Engels: Collected Works*, vol. 29, *Marx: 1857-1861*. New York: International Publishers.

———. [1867] 1977. *Capital: A Critique of Political Economy*. Vol. 1. Translated by Ben Fowkes. New York: Vintage.

———. [1884] 1981. *Capital: A Critique of Political Economy*. Vol. 2. Translated by David Fernbach. New York: Vintage.

———. [1891] 1989. "Critique of the Gotha Programme." Pp. 75-99 in *Karl Marx, Frederick Engels: Collected Works*, vol. 24, *Marx and Engels: 1874-1883*. New York: International Publishers.

———. [1894] 1981. *Capital: A Critique of Political Economy*. Vol. 3. Translated by David Fernbach. New York: Vintage.

———. 1973. *Grundrisse: Foundations of the Critique of Political Economy*. Translated by Martin Nicolaus. New York: Vintage.

Marx, Karl, and Frederick Engels. [1845-1847] 1976. "The German Ideology." Pp. 19-539 in *Karl Marx, Frederick Engels: Collected Works*, vol. 5, *Marx and Engels: 1845-1847*. New York: International Publishers.

Marx, Karl, and Frederick Engels. [1848] 1976. "Manifesto of the Communist Party." Pp. 477-519 in *Karl Marx, Frederick Engels: Collected Works*, vol. 6, *Marx and Engels: 1848*. New York: International Publishers.

Mayer, Thomas F. 1989. "In Defense of Analytical Marxism." *Science and Society* 53(4):416-41.

Mayer, Thomas F., and Tracy L. Mott. 1990. "Effective Demand and the Structural Dependence of the State." Pp. 53-71 in *Changes in the State: Causes and Consequences*, edited by Edward S. Greenberg and Thomas F. Mayer. Newbury Park, CA: Sage.

McRae, Susan. 1986. *Cross-Class Families: A Study of Wives' Occupational Superiority*. Oxford, UK: Clarendon.

Meek, Ronald L. 1956. *Studies in the Labor Theory of Value*. New York: Monthly Review Press.

Mehlmann, Alexander. 1988. *Applied Differential Games*. New York: Plenum.

Miliband, Ralph. 1969. *The State in Capitalist Society*. New York: Basic Books.

Miller, David. 1989. *Market, State and Community: Theoretical Foundations of Market Socialism*. Oxford, UK: Clarendon.

———. 1991. "The Relevance of Socialism." *Economy and Society* 20(4):350-62.

Miller, Richard W. 1984. *Analyzing Marx: Morality, Power and History*. Princeton, NJ: Princeton University Press.

Moene, Karl Ove. 1989. "Strong Unions or Worker Control?" Pp. 83-97 in *Alternatives to Capitalism*, edited by Jon Elster and Karl Ove Moene. Cambridge, UK: Cambridge University Press.

Morishima, Michio. 1973. *Marx's Economics: A Dual Theory of Value and Growth*. Cambridge, UK: Cambridge University Press.

Myerson, Roger B. 1991. *Game Theory: Analysis of Conflict*. Cambridge, MA: Harvard University Press.

Navarro, Vincente. 1993. "Has Socialism Failed? An Analysis of Health Indicators Under Capitalism and Socialism." *Science and Society* 57(1):6-30.

Neumann, John von. 1945. "A Model of General Economic Equilibrium." *Review of Economic Studies* 13:1-9.

Nove, Alec. 1983. *The Economics of Feasible Socialism*. London: George Allen & Unwin.

———. 1990. "Planned Economy." Pp. 186-97 in *The New Palgrave: Problems of the Planned Economy*, edited by John Eatwell, Murray Milgate, and Peter Newman. New York: Norton.

Offe, Claus. 1985. *Disorganized Capitalism*. Cambridge: MIT Press.

Okishio, Nobuo. 1961. "Technical Changes and the Rate of Profit." *Kobe University Economic Review* 7:85-99.

Ortuño-Ortin, Ignacio, John E. Roemer, and Joaquim Silvestre. forthcoming. "Investment Planning in Market Socialism." In *The Microfoundations of Political Economy: Problems of Participation, Democracy, and Efficiency*, edited by Samuel Bowles and Herbert Gintis. Cambridge, UK: Cambridge University Press.

Ott, Edward. 1993. *Chaos in Dynamical Systems*. Cambridge, UK: Cambridge University Press.

Paige, Jeffrey M. 1975. *Agrarian Revolution: Social Movements and Export Agriculture in the Underdeveloped World*. New York: Free Press.

Perko, Lawrence. 1991. *Differential Equations and Dynamical Systems*. New York: Springer.

Popkin, Samuel L. 1979. *The Rational Peasant*. Berkeley: University of California Press.

———. 1988. "Political Entrepreneurs and Peasant Movements in Vietnam." Pp. 9-62 in *Rationality and Revolution*, edited by Michael Taylor. Cambridge, UK: Cambridge University Press.

Poulantzas, Nicos. 1973. *Political Power and Social Classes*. London: New Left Books and Sheed & Ward.

———. 1975. *Classes in Contemporary Capitalism*. London: New Left Books.

Przeworski, Adam, 1985a. *Capitalism and Social Democracy*. Cambridge, UK: Cambridge University Press.

———. 1985b. "Marxism and Rational Choice." *Politics and Society* 14(4):379-409.

———. 1986. "Some Problems in the Study of the Transition to Democracy." Pp. 47-63 in *Transition From Authoritarian Rule*, edited by Guillermo O'Donnell, Philippe C. Schmitter, and Laurence Whitehead. Baltimore: Johns Hopkins University Press.

———. 1990. *The State and the Economy Under Capitalism*. Chur, Switzerland: Harwood Academic Publishers.

———. 1991a. "Can We Feed Everyone? The Irrationality of Capitalism and the Infeasibility of Socialism." *Politics and Society* 19(1):1-38.

———. 1991b. *Democracy and the Market: Political and Economic Reforms in Eastern Europe and Latin America*. Cambridge, UK: Cambridge University Press.

Przeworski, Adam, and John Sprague. 1986. *Paper Stones: A History of Electoral Socialism*. Chicago: University of Chicago Press.

Przeworski, Adam, and Michael Wallerstein. 1982. "The Structure of Class Conflicts Under Democratic Capitalism." *American Political Science Review* 76:215-38.

———. 1988. "Structural Dependence of the State on Capital." *American Political Science Review* 82:11-31.

Rapoport, Anatol. 1970. *N-Person Game Theory: Concepts and Applications*. Ann Arbor: University of Michigan Press.

Robinson, Joan. [1942] 1966. *An Essay on Marxian Economics*, 2nd ed. London: Macmillan.

Roemer, John E. 1981. *Analytical Foundations of Marxian Economic Theory*. Cambridge, UK: Cambridge University Press.

———. 1982a. *A General Theory of Exploitation and Class*. Cambridge, MA: Harvard University Press.

———. 1982b. "New Directions in the Marxian Theory of Exploitation and Class." *Politics and Society* 11(3):253-87.

———. 1982c. "Property Relations Versus Surplus Value in Marxian Exploitation." *Philosophy and Public Affairs* 11(4):281-313.

———. 1983. "Unequal Exchange, Labor Migration and International Capital Flows: A Theoretical Synthesis." Pp. 34-62 in *Marxism, Central Planning and the Soviet Economy: Economic Essays in Honor of Alexander Erlich*, edited by P. Desai. Cambridge: MIT Press.

———. 1985. "Rationalizing Revolutionary Ideology." *Econometrica* 53 (January): 84-108.

———, ed. 1986a. *Analytical Marxism*. Cambridge, UK: Cambridge University Press.

———. 1986b. *Value, Exploitation and Class*. Chur, Switzerland: Harwood Academic Publishers.

———. 1988a. *Free to Lose: An Introduction to Marxist Economic Philosophy*. Cambridge, MA: Harvard University Press.

———. 1988b. "Rationalizing Revolutionary Ideology: A Tale of Lenin and the Tsar." Pp. 229-44 in *Rationality and Revolution*, edited by Michael Taylor. Cambridge, UK: Cambridge University Press.

———. 1991. "Market Socialism: A Blueprint, How Such an Economy Might Work." *Dissent* (Fall):562-75.

———. 1992a. "Can There Be Socialism After Communism?" *Politics and Society* 20(3):261-76.

———. 1992b. "The Morality and Efficiency of Market Socialism." *Ethics* 102 (April):448-64.

———. 1992c. "What Walrasian Marxism Can and Cannot Do." *Economics and Philosophy* 8:149-56.

———. 1994. *A Future for Socialism*. Cambridge, MA: Harvard University Press.

Rose, David, and Gordon Marshall. 1989. "Constructing the (W)right Classes." Pp. 243-65 in *The Debate on Classes,* by Erik Olin Wright, U. Becker, et al. London: Verso.

Ruccio, David F. 1988. "The Merchant of Venice, or Marxism in the Mathematical Mode." *Rethinking Marxism* 1(4):36-68.

Sahlins, Marshal. 1972. *Stone Age Economics*. Chicago: Aldine.

Sanderson, Stephen K. 1988. *Macrosociology: An Introduction to Human Societies*. New York: Harper & Row.

Schweickart, David. 1991. "The Politics and Morality of Unequal Exchange: Emmanuel and Roemer, Analysis and Synthesis." *Economics and Philosophy* 7(1):13-36.

Sen, Amartya. 1993. "The Economics of Life and Death." *Scientific American* 268(5):40-47.

Shapley, Lloyd. 1971. "Cores of Convex Games." *International Journal of Game Theory* 1:11-26.

Shaw, Bernard. [1928] 1972. *The Intelligent Woman's Guide to Socialism, Capitalism, Sovietism, and Fascism*. New York: Vintage.

Shubik, Martin. 1982. *Game Theory in the Social Sciences: Concepts and Solutions*. Cambridge: MIT Press.

Simis, Konstantin. 1982. *USSR: The Corrupt Society*. New York: Simon & Schuster.

Skocpol, Theda. 1979. *States and Social Revolutions: A Comparative Analysis of France, Russia, and China*. Cambridge, UK: Cambridge University Press.

Sraffa, Piero. 1960. *Production of Commodities by Means of Commodities: Prelude to a Critique of Economic Theory*. Cambridge, UK: Cambridge University Press.

Steedman, Ian. 1977. *Marx After Sraffa*. London: New Left Books.

Steindl, Josef. [1952] 1976. *Maturity and Stagnation in American Capitalism*. New York: Monthly Review Press.

Stiglitz, Joseph E. 1987. "Principal and Agent." In *The New Palgrave: A Dictionary of Economics,* edited by J. Eatwell, M. Milgate, and P. Newman. New York: Norton.

Sweezy, Paul M. 1942. *The Theory of Capitalist Development: Principles of Marxian Political Economy*. New York: Monthly Review Press.

Taylor, Michael. 1976. *Anarchy and Cooperation*. London: John Wiley.

———. 1987. *The Possibility of Cooperation*. Cambridge, UK: Cambridge University Press.

———, ed. 1988a. *Rationality and Revolution*. Cambridge, UK: Cambridge University Press.

———. 1988b. "Rationality and Revolutionary Collective Action." Pp. 63-97 in *Rationality and Revolution,* edited by Michael Taylor. Cambridge, UK: Cambridge University Press.

Thom, René. 1975. *Structural Stability and Morphogenesis: An Outline of a General Theory of Models*. Reading, MA: W. A. Benjamin.

Thompson, E. P. 1963. *The Making of the English Working Class*. New York: Vintage.

Tong, James. 1988. "Rational Outlaws: Rebels and Bandits in the Ming Dynasty, 1368-1644." Pp. 98-128 in *Rationality and Revolution*, edited by Michael Taylor. Cambridge, UK: Cambridge University Press.

Turner, Henry Ashby, Jr. 1985. *German Big Business and the Rise of Hitler.* New York: Oxford University Press.

van der Veen, Robert J., and Philippe Van Parijs. 1987. "A Capitalist Road to Communism." *Theory and Society* 15:635-55.

Van Parijs, Philippe. 1981. *Evolutionary Explanation in the Social Sciences: An Emerging Paradigm.* Totowa, NJ: Rowan & Littlefield.

———. 1989. "A Revolution in Class Theory." Pp. 23-41 in *The Debate on Classes*, by Erik Olin Wright, U. Becker, et al. London: Verso.

———, ed. 1992a. *Arguing for Basic Income.* London: Verso.

———. 1992b. "Basic Income Capitalism." *Ethics* 102(April):465-484.

Volin, L. 1970. *A Century of Russian Agriculture.* Cambridge, MA: Harvard University Press.

Walras, Leon. [1926] 1954. *Elements of Pure Economics or the Theory of Social Wealth.* Translated by William Jaffe. Homewood, IL: Richard D. Irwin.

Ward, Benjamin. 1958. "The Firm in Illyria: Market Syndicalism." *American Economic Review* 48:566-89.

Weldes, Jutta. 1989. "Marxism and Methodological Individualism." *Theory and Society* 18:353-86.

Wood, Allen W. 1981. *Karl Marx.* London: Routledge & Kegan Paul.

Wood, Ellen Meiksins. 1989. "Rational Choice Marxism: Is the Game Worth the Candle?" *New Left Review* 177 (September-October):41-88.

———. 1990. "Explaining Everything or Nothing?" *New Left Review* 184 (November/December):116-128.

Wright, Erik Olin. 1978. *Class, Crisis and the State.* London: New Left Books.

———. 1979. *Class Structure and Income Determination.* New York: Academic Press.

———. 1983. "Capitalism's Futures." *Socialist Review* 68 (March-April):77-126.

———. 1985. *Classes.* London: Verso.

———. 1987. "Why Something Like Socialism Is Necessary for the Transition to Something Like Communism." *Theory and Society* 15(5):657-72.

———. 1989a. "The Comparative Project on Class Structure and Class Consciousness: An Overview." *Acta Sociologica* 32(1):3-22.

———. 1989b. "What Is Analytical Marxism?" *Socialist Review* 19(4):35-56.

———. 1989c. "Women in the Class Structure." *Politics and Society* 17(1):35-66.

Wright, Erik Olin, U. Becker, et al. 1989. *The Debate on Classes.* London: Verso.

Wright, Erik Olin, and Donmoon Cho. 1992. "State Employment, Class Location, and Ideological Orientation: A Comparative Analysis of the United States and Sweden." *Politics and Society* 20(2):167-96.

Wright, Erik Olin, Cynthia Costello, David Hachen, and Joey Sprague. 1982. "The American Class Structure." *American Sociological Review* 47 (December): 709-26.

Wright, Erik Olin, Carolyn Howe, and Donmoon Cho. 1989. "Class Structure and Class Formation: A Comparative Analysis of the United States and Sweden." Pp. 185-217 in *Cross-National Research in Sociology*, edited by Melvin L. Kohn. Newbury Park, CA: Sage.

Wright, Erik Olin, Andrew Levine, and Elliott Sober. 1992. *Reconstructing Marxism: Essays on Explanation and the Theory of History.* London: Verso.

Wright, Erik Olin, and Bill Martin. 1987. "The Transformation of American Class Structure, 1960-1980." *American Journal of Sociology* 93(1):1-29.

Wright, Erik Olin, and Kwang-Yeong Shin. 1988. "Temporality and Class Analysis: A Comparative Study of the Effects of Class Trajectory and Class Structure on Class Consciousness in Sweden and the United States." *Sociological Theory* 6 (Spring):58-84.

Wright, Erik Olin, and Joachim Singelmann. 1982. "Proletarianization in the American Class Structure." *American Journal of Sociology (Supplement)* 88:S176-S209 (*Marxist Inquiries*, edited by Michael Burawoy, and Theda Skocpol).

Wuthnow, Robert. 1980. "The World-Economy and the Institutionalization of Science in Seventeenth Century Europe." In *Studies of the Modern World-System*, edited by Albert Bergesen. New York: Academic Press.

NAME INDEX

SUBJECT INDEX

ABOUT THE AUTHOR

Tom Mayer works in the Department of Sociology and the Institute of Behavioral Science at the University of Colorado in Boulder. He received a doctoral degree from Stanford University in 1966 and taught sociology at the University of Michigan before coming to Boulder. He studies political economy, social conflict, and mathematical sociology and is now working on a method of analyzing class dynamics. He has participated actively in movements for social change from the 1960s onward.